James E. Clark
Wichita State University

Janet L. Wolcutt
Wichita State University

Study Guide

Microeconomics

Fifth Edition
Boyes/Melvin

Houghton Mifflin Company   Boston   New York

Sponsoring Editor: Ann West
Assistant Editor: Jennifer DiDomenico
Senior Manufacturing Coordinator: Marie Barnes
Marketing Manager: Barbara LeBuhn

Printed in the U.S.A.

ISBN: 0-618-12797-6

123456789-VG-05 04 03 02 01

Contents

Correlation Chart

Boyes and Melvin, *Microeconomics*, Fifth Edition
Boyes and Melvin, *Economics*, Fifth Edition

Chapter Title	Chapter Number in *Microeconomics*	Chapter Number in *Economics*
Introduction to the Price System		
Economics: The World Around You	1	1
Appendix: Working with Graphs	1A	1A
Choice, Opportunity Costs, and Specialization	2	2
Markets, Demand and Supply, and the Price System	3	3
The Market System and the Private Sector	4	4
The Public Sector	5	5
Product Market Basics		
Elasticity: Demand and Supply	6	20
Consumer Choice	7	21
Appendix: Indifference Analysis	7A	21A
Supply: The Costs of Doing Business	8	22
Product Markets		
Profit Maximization	9	23
Perfect Competition	10	24
Monopoly	11	25
Monopolistic Competition and Oligopoly	12	26
The New Economy	13	27
Government Policy Toward Business	14	28
Resource Markets		
Resource Markets	15	29
The Labor Market	16	30
The Capital Market	17	31
The Land Market: Natural Resources and Environmental Policy	18	32
Current Issues Involving the Public Sector and the Market Economy		
Aging, Social Security, and Health Care	19	33
Income Distribution, Poverty, and Government Policy	20	34
Issues in International Trade and Finance		
World Trade Equilibrium	21	35
International Trade Restrictions	22	36
Exchange-Rate Systems and Practices	23	37

Using the Study Guide

What's in the Study Guide

All Study Guide chapters are organized the same way; each includes the following:

- *Fundamental Questions* are repeated from the text chapter and are briefly answered. The questions and their answers give you an overview of the chapter's main points.
- *Key Terms* from the chapter are listed to remind you of new vocabulary presented in the chapter.
- A *Quick-Check Quiz* focuses on vocabulary and key concepts from the chapter. These multiple-choice questions allow you to see whether you understand the material and are ready to move on or you need to review some of the text before continuing.
- *Practice Questions and Problems* provide in-depth coverage of important ideas from the chapter and give you the opportunity to apply concepts and work out problems.
- The *Thinking About and Applying* section covers one or more topics in greater depth and will help you learn to apply economics to real-world situations. This section will also show you how various economic concepts are related to one another and, as a result, will help you to think economically.
- *Homework Problems* may be assigned by your instructor and can be carefully removed from the Study Guide and handed in if requested. Answers to the Homework Problems are included in the Instructor's Resource Manual.
- The *Answers* section may be the most important part of the Study Guide. Answers to all questions and problems are provided with explanations of how to arrive at the correct answer. In many cases, explanations are given for what you did wrong if you arrived at certain wrong answers.
- *Sample Tests* appear at the end of each Study Guide part and provide students with a number of questions resembling test bank questions. Taking the Sample Tests will help you determine whether you're really prepared for exams.

How to Study Economics

No one ever said that economics is an easy subject, and many students tell us it is the most challenging subject they have studied. Despite the challenge, most students manage to learn a great deal of economics, and we're sure you can too. But doing well in economics requires a commitment from you to *keep up* your studying and to *study properly.*

Keeping up: Although there may be subjects that can be learned reasonably well by cramming the night before an exam, economics is *not* one of them. Learning economics is like building a house: first you need to lay a solid foundation, and then you must carefully build the walls. To master economics you must first learn the early concepts, vocabulary, and ideas; if you do not, the later ones will not make any sense.

Studying properly: Listening in class, reading the text, and going through the Study Guide are not enough to really learn economics—you must also organize your studying. The textbook and the Study Guide have been designed to help you organize your thinking and your studying. Used together, they will help you learn.

We recommend following these steps for each chapter:

1. Skim the text chapter before your instructor discusses it in class to get a general idea of what the chapter covers.
   a. Read through the Fundamental Questions and the Preview to get a sense of what is to come.
   b. Skim through the chapter, looking only at the section headings and the section Recaps.
   c. Read the chapter Summary. By this point, you should have a good idea of what topics the chapter covers.

2. Read the text chapter and Study Guide one section at a time. Both the text and the Study Guide break down each chapter into several sections so that you will not need to juggle too many new ideas at once.
   a. Read through one section of the text chapter. Pay attention to the marginal notes containing definitions of Key Terms, highlights of important concepts, and Fundamental Questions.
   b. Study the section Recap. If parts of the Recap are not clear to you, review those parts of the section.
   c. In the Study Guide, read the answers to the Fundamental Questions covered in the section you are studying.
   d. Take the Quick-Check Quiz for the section. Write your answers on a separate sheet of paper so that you can use the quiz again later. If you missed any questions, review the applicable section in the text.
   e. Work through the Practice Questions and Problems for the section, writing your answers in the spaces provided. Check your answers, and then review what you missed. Read through the explanations in the Answers section, even if you answered the question or problem correctly.
   f. If there are ideas that are not clear or problems you do not understand, talk to your instructor. Economics instructors are interested in helping their students.

3. Review the chapter as a whole. Although each section should initially be studied alone, you will need to put the pieces together.
   a. Read through the chapter again, paying special attention to the Fundamental Questions, the section Recaps, the Economic Insight boxes, and the chapter Summary. If you like to outline chapters on paper, now is the time to do so. The section headings and subheadings provide an ideal framework for outlining the text.
   b. In the Study Guide, read through the Fundamental Questions and their answers.
   c. Review the list of Key Terms. Write down the definition of each one at this point, and check your definitions against the marginal notes or the glossary. Study any terms you missed.
   d. Work through the Exercises at the end of the text chapter.
   e. Read through the Economically Speaking section in the text to see how the real world contains examples of economic thinking.
   f. Work through the Thinking About and Applying section of the Study Guide.
   g. Complete the Homework section of the Study Guide and hand it in if your instructor requests it; otherwise, save it for exam review.

4. Ideally, studying for exams should be a repetition of steps 1, 2, and 3. However, economists recognize the existence of opportunity costs, and you have many other things to do with your time in addition to studying economics. If you cannot study for an exam as thoroughly as you should, you can use some techniques to help refresh your memory. These techniques assume that you *did* study the materials at least once (there is no magic way to learn economics without doing some serious studying).
   a. Review the Fundamental Questions, the section Recaps, the Key Terms lists, and the chapter Summaries in the text.
   b. Read again the Fundamental Questions and their answers in the Study Guide.
   c. Take the Quick-Check Quiz again, writing your answers in the Study Guide this time. Questions that you miss will direct you to the areas you need to study most.

d. Take a Sample Test, found at the end of each part in the Study Guide. These questions are likely to closely resemble the questions you'll see on your exam. They cover one part's worth of chapters in one test, because you are likely to be tested this way. Check your answers against the answer key; review the appropriate sections of the text if you answer any of the questions incorrectly.

If you follow these suggestions, you are sure to meet with success in your study of economics.

Use the Text as a System

The text presents all the key concepts of economics. In addition it explains how people use these concepts—in business, in government, and in ordinary households. In both the world of theory and the real world of application, knowing the relationships of ideas is crucial. No one can move about in either world without knowing the pathways that relationships form. The features of the text provide these pathways; taking advantage of them will help your studying immensely. The *Fundamental Questions* point to main issues and help you categorize details, examples, and theories accordingly. Colors in the *graphs* help you classify curves and see relationships to data in the *tables*. The *Recaps* reinforce overarching ideas; they orient you before you go on to the next big section. The *system of referencing* sections and headings by number will help you group concepts and also keep track of what level of ideas you are working with. If you use these features of the text, the text can be more than an authoritative source of information—it can be a system for comprehension.

Take More than One View

As you work through the chapters of this book, you will examine in close-up each particular concept. Yet, to understand the material and to get a feel for how economists think, you need to have a second point of view too—an overview. Keeping yourself "up above it" at the same time you are "down in it" will help you remember what you are reading much better and also help you understand and use the concepts you learn more easily. Taking more than one view of your subject has another benefit; it is an ingredient of good critical thinking.

J.E.C.
J.L.W.

ECONOMICS: THE WORLD AROUND YOU

FUNDAMENTAL QUESTIONS

1. What is economics?

   Economics is the study of how people choose to allocate scarce **resources** to satisfy their unlimited wants. There are several words in this definition that should be emphasized. First, people allocate *scarce* resources. If there was enough of a resource to go around so that everyone could have as much as he or she wanted, there would be no need to allocate.

   The definition states that people have *unlimited wants.* Notice that it says *wants,* not *needs.* People *act* on the basis of their wants, not necessarily on the basis of their needs. (Otherwise they would not buy strawberry sundaes.) If each of us made a list right now of the top ten things we would like to have and our fairy godmother popped out of the air and gave us what we wanted, most of us immediately would find that there are ten *more* things we'd like to have. Because resources are scarce and wants are unlimited, economics studies the best way to allocate resources so that none are wasted.

2. What is the economic way of thinking?

   The economic way of thinking focuses on **positive,** as opposed to **normative, analysis,** and applies the five-step **scientific method:** (1) recognize the problem, (2) cut away unnecessary detail by making **assumptions,** (3) develop a **model** or story, (4) make predictions, and (5) test the model.

Key Terms

scarcity
economic good
free good
economic bad
resources
factors of production
inputs
land

labor
capital
rational self-interest
positive analysis
normative analysis
scientific method
theory
model

assumptions
ceteris paribus
test
fallacy of composition
association as causation
microeconomics
macroeconomics

Quick-Check Quiz

Section 1: The Definition of Economics

1. Which of the following is *not* an economic good?
   a. wine
   b. bicycles
   c. refrigerators
   d. air pollution
   e. education

2. Which of the following is *not* one of the three categories of resources?
   a. land
   b. automobiles
   c. capital
   d. labor
   e. None of the above are categories for resources.

3. The payment for capital is called
   a. rent.
   b. wages.
   c. salaries.
   d. interest.
   e. profit.

4. If an item is scarce,
   a. it is not an economic good.
   b. at a zero price the amount of the item that people want is less than the amount that is available.
   c. there is not enough of the item to satisfy everyone who wants it.
   d. there is enough to satisfy wants even at a zero price.
   e. it must be a resource as opposed to an input.

5. Which of the following is a free good?
   a. clean air
   b. water from a river
   c. education
   d. golf lessons
   e. None of the above is a free good.

6. The payment for land is called
   a. wages and salaries.
   b. rent.
   c. interest.
   d. profit.
   e. financial capital.

7. Rational self-interest
   a. dictates that individuals with the same information will make identical choices.
   b. means that people are completely selfish.
   c. explains why people give money to charitable organizations.
   d. explains why all drivers wear seat belts.
   e. means that people choose options that they think will give them the smallest amount of satisfaction.

Section 2: The Economic Approach

1. Analysis that does not impose the value judgments of one individual on the decision of others is called _____ analysis.
   a. positive
   b. normative
   c. economic
   d. noneconomic
   e. the scientific method of

2. Which of the following is *not* one of the five steps in the scientific method?
   a. Recognize the problem.
   b. Make assumptions in order to cut away unnecessary detail.
   c. Develop a model of the problem.
   d. Test the hypothesis.
   e. Make a value judgment based on the results of the hypothesis test.

3. If an individual decides to save more, he or she can save more. Therefore, if society as a whole decides to save more, it will be able to save more. This reasoning is faulty and as such is an example of
   a. *ceteris paribus.*
   b. the fallacy of composition.
   c. the interpretation of association as causation.
   d. the scientific method.
   e. none of the above—this reasoning is not faulty.

4. Tim has noticed that every time he washes his car in the morning, it rains that afternoon. Because he believes he can cause it to rain by washing his car, he has decided to sell his services to farmers in drought-stricken areas. This reasoning is mistaken and as such is an example of
   a. *ceteris paribus.*
   b. the fallacy of composition.
   c. the mistaken interpretation of association as causation.
   d. the scientific method.
   e. none of the above—Tim's reasoning is not faulty.

5. Which of the following is a normative statement?
   a. Lower interest rates encourage people to borrow.
   b. Higher prices for cigarettes discourage people from buying cigarettes.
   c. If the price of eggs fell, people probably would buy more eggs.
   d. There should be a higher tax on cigarettes, alcohol, and other "sin" items to discourage people from buying them.
   e. A higher interest rate encourages people to save more.

6. Microeconomics includes the study of
   a. how an individual firm decides the price of its product.
   b. inflation in the United States.
   c. how much output will be produced in the U.S. economy.
   d. how many workers will be unemployed in the U.S. economy.
   e. how the U.S. banking system works.

Practice Questions and Problems

Section 1: The Definition of Economics

1. _____ exists when less of something is available than people want at a zero price.

2. Any good that is scarce is a(n) _____ good.

3. If there is enough of a good available at a zero price to satisfy wants, the good is called a(n) _____ good.

4. A good that people will pay to have less of is called an economic _____ .

5. People use scarce resources to satisfy their _____ wants.

6. _____ means that people make the choices that they think will give them the greatest amount of satisfaction.

7. List the three categories of resources and the payments associated with each.

   _____

   _____

   _____

8. _____ includes all natural resources, such as minerals, timber, and water, as well as the land itself.

9. _____ refers to the physical and intellectual services of people.

10. _____ is a manufactured or created product used solely to produce goods and services.

11. _____ capital refers to the money value of capital as represented by stocks and bonds.

12. Resources also are called _____ or _____ .
13. _____ are nonphysical products.
14. Economists believe human beings are _____ , not selfish.
15. What is economics?

_____

_____

_____

_____

Section 2: The Economic Approach

1. Analysis that does not impose the value judgments of one individual on the decisions of others is called _____ analysis.
2. _____ analysis involves imposing value judgments on the decisions of others.
3. Economists generally agree on the _____ aspects of economics.
4. List the five steps in the scientific method.

_____

_____

_____

_____

_____

5. The role of models and _____ is to reduce the complexity of a problem.
6. _____ means "other things being equal."
7. A theory, or _____ , is a simplification that is used to explain an event.
8. _____ is the study of economics at the level of the individual economic entity.
9. The _____ is the error of attributing what applies to one to the case of many.
10. The mistaken interpretation of _____ occurs when unrelated or coincidental events that occur at about the same time are believed to have a cause-and-effect relationship.
11. The outcome of positive analysis _____ as society's norms change.
12. The study of the economy as a whole is called _____ .

Thinking About and Applying Economics: The World Around You

I.   The Relationship Between Speed Limits and Highway Deaths

In twenty-two of the thirty-eight states that chose to raise the speed limit on rural highways, highway deaths jumped 46 percent between May and July 1986. Former Transportation Committee Chairman James Howard attributed the increase in deaths to the higher speed limit. Can you think of any other reasons that highway deaths might have increased? If states that did not increase rural speed limits experienced a similar increase in highway deaths, what common mistake might Chairman Howard have made?

_____

_____

_____

_____

II.   Scarce Parking in Wichita?

The following is an excerpt from the *Wichita Eagle:*

> It's become part of Wichita lore. Folks in these parts are nutty about parking.
>
> They want it free. They want it at the front door of wherever they're going. They refuse to look for a parking space anywhere for more than eight or 10 seconds. And they think the downtown Wichita parking situation is horrible.
>
> The fact is, there's plenty of parking in the city's core. About 20,000 people work downtown. There are almost 19,000 parking spaces. That nearly 1-to-1 ratio is better than other cities in the region such as Oklahoma City, and it's just as good as Topeka. And the average distance a person has to walk is about a block. That's better than similar-sized cities.

The editorial laments that people don't go downtown for activities because they think they'll have trouble parking and comments on a new report by the Metropolitan Area Planning Commission.

Relying on the information in the editorial, discuss whether parking spaces can be considered a scarce resource in downtown Wichita.

_____

_____

_____

_____

III. Resource and Income Flows

Complete the figure below.

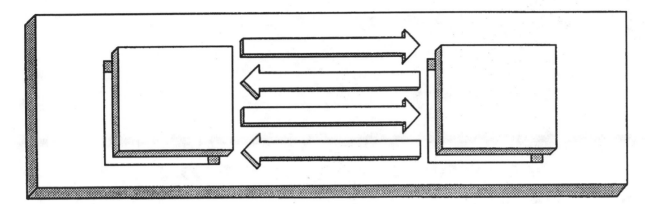

Chapter 1   Homework Problem

Name _____

A recent edition of the *Wall Street Journal* reported that some states were subsidizing Amtrak passenger trains so that state residents would have railroad transportation available.

The state of Oregon, however, had just decided to stop subsidizing a train between Eugene and Portland, Oregon, even though that meant the train would stop running. State Senator Greg Walden explained the decision this way: "Subsidizing rail passengers isn't as high a priority as kids' education and keeping criminals behind bars."

Using the concepts you learned in Chapter 1, explain the economic logic underlying Senator Walden's comments.

If your instructor assigns this problem, write your answer above, then tear out this page and hand it in.

Answers

Quick-Check Quiz

Section 1: The Definition of Economics

1. d; 2. b; 3. d; 4. c; 5. e; 6. b; 7. c
If you missed any of these questions, you should go back and review Section 1 in Chapter 1.

Section 2: The Economic Approach

1. a; 2. e; 3. b; 4. c; 5. d; 6. a
If you missed any of these questions, you should go back and review Section 2 in Chapter 1.

Practice Questions and Problems

Section 1: The Definition of Economics

1. Scarcity
2. economic
3. free
4. bad
5. unlimited
6. Rational self-interest
7. land; rent
   labor; wages
   capital; interest
8. Land
9. Labor
10. Capital
11. Financial
12. factors of production; inputs
13. Services
14. self-interested
15. Economics is the study of how people choose to use their scarce resources to attempt to satisfy their unlimited wants.

Section 2: The Economic Approach

1. positive
2. Normative
3. positive
4. Recognize the problem.
   Make assumptions in order to cut away unnecessary detail.
   Develop a model of the problem.
   Make predictions.
   Test the model.
5. assumptions
6. *Ceteris paribus*
7. model

8. Microeconomics
9. fallacy of composition
10. association as causation
11. does not vary
12. macroeconomics

Thinking About and Applying Economics: The World Around You

I. The Relationship Between Speed Limits and Highway Deaths

Other factors that might have increased highway deaths include the following:

1. Has there been an increase in population? It seems reasonable to expect more accidents as congestion increases.
2. Are Americans buying more smaller cars? If so, auto deaths would be expected to increase because smaller cars provide less protection in a crash.
3. Has there been an increase in the number of people drinking (or otherwise impaired) and driving? If so, we would expect an increase in the number of traffic fatalities no matter what the speed limit was.

Perhaps you can think of other factors that might account for the increase in traffic fatalities that Howard attributed to the higher speed limit. If Howard had wrongly attributed the higher death toll to the higher speed limit, he would have been mistaking association for causation.

II. Scarce Parking in Wichita?

If there is not enough of an item to satisfy everyone who wants it at a zero price, then an item is scarce. If people want parking at the front door of wherever they are going and have to walk, on average, about a block, parking is scarce.

III. Resource and Income Flows

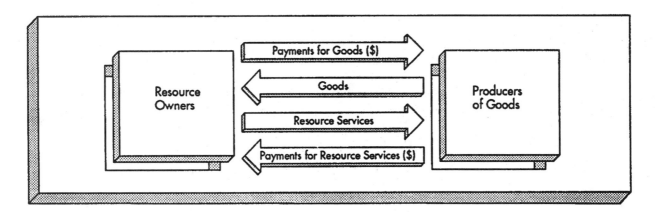

WORKING WITH GRAPHS

Summary

Most people are visually oriented: they are better able to understand things that they can "picture." The pictures that economists use to explain concepts are called *graphs*.

There are three commonly used types of graphs: the line graph, the bar graph, and the pie graph. The pie graph (or chart) is used to show the relative magnitude of the parts that make up a whole. Line graphs and bar graphs are used to show the relationship between two variables. One of the variables, the **independent variable,** has values that do not depend on the values of other variables. The values of **dependent variables** do depend on the values of other variables.

When two variables move in the same direction together, their relationship is called a **direct,** or **positive, relationship,** and the **slope** of the line or curve relating the two variables will be positive. When two variables move together but in opposite directions, their relationship is an **inverse,** or **negative, relationship,** and the slope of the line or curve relating the two variables will be negative. A curve **shifts** when, for each combination of variables measured on the horizontal and vertical axes, one of the variables changes by a certain amount while the other variable remains the same. Shifts occur when variables other than those on the axes are allowed to change.

The slope of a line is the ratio of the rise to the run. The slope of a straight line is the same at all points on the line. The slope of a curve that is not a straight line changes at every point on the curve. We can find the maximum or minimum point on a curve by finding where the slope of the curve is equal to zero. Where a slope goes from positive to zero to negative, a maximum occurs. Where a slope goes from negative to zero to positive, a minimum occurs.

Key Terms

independent variable
dependent variable
direct relationship

positive relationship
inverse relationship
negative relationship

slope

Practice Questions and Problems

1. The owner of a business that sells home heating oil has noticed that the amount of heating oil sold increases as the temperature outside decreases. Heating oil is the _____ (dependent, independent) variable. The relationship between the two variables is _____ (direct,

inverse), and the slope of the line will be _____ (positive, negative). Use the graph below to show the nature of the relationship between home heating oil sales and outside temperature. Be sure to label your axes.

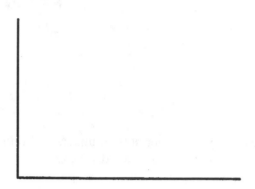

2. The slope of a straight-line curve is the same at all points. True or false?

3. The table below shows the relationship between the price of milk and the quantity of milk that dairy farmers are willing to offer for sale. This relationship is _____ (direct, inverse). The slope of the line will be _____ (positive, negative). Plot the curves on the graph below.

Price of Milk	Quantity of Milk Offered for Sale
$ .50	0
.75	2
1.00	4
1.25	6
1.50	8

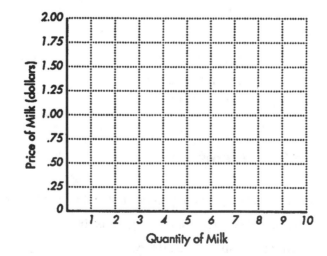

4. Consider the relationship between household spending (consumption) and national income on the graph below and answer the following questions.

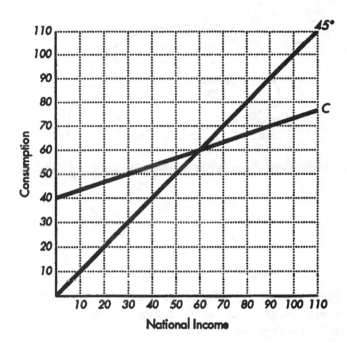

a. The relationship between consumption and income is _____ (direct, inverse).

b. What is the slope of the line? _____

    The intercept? _____

c. What is the equation for this line? _____

d. At what point does consumption equal income? _____

5. The graph below shows the percentages of income that the King family spends, pays in taxes, and saves. What kind of graph is this? _____

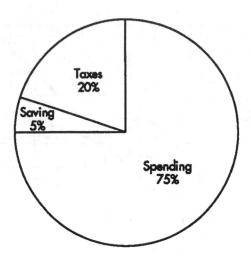

6. The table below shows the relationship between the quantity of airplanes built at a production plant in Wichita and the average cost per airplane. Make up a set of figures that shows that a minimum average cost occurs at 40,000 airplanes.

Quantity of Airplanes	Average Cost per Airplane
10,000	_____
20,000	_____
30,000	_____
40,000	_____
50,000	_____
60,000	_____
70,000	_____
80,000	_____

7. The demand for Mardi's Tacos in Hammondville is given by the equation $P = \$2.00 - .02Q$, where P is the price of tacos in dollars and Q is the quantity demanded of tacos. Plot the demand for Mardi's Tacos on the graph below.

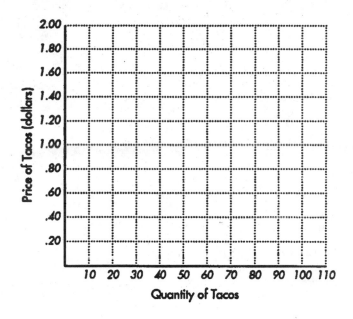

The relationship between price and quantity demanded is _____ (direct, inverse).

8. The supply for tacos in Hammondville is given by the equation $P = \$.40 + .005Q$, where P is the price of tacos in dollars and Q is the quantity supplied of tacos. Plot the supply of tacos on the graph below. Label the supply S.

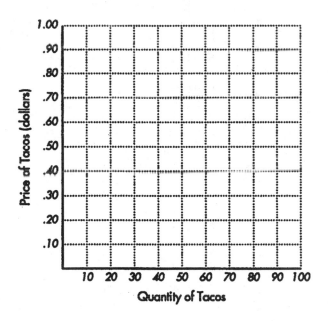

The relationship between price and quantity supplied is _____ (direct, inverse).

9. Several taco sellers in Hammondville have closed down, changing the equation for the supply of tacos to $P = \$.60 + .005Q$. Plot the new supply on the graph above and label the line S_1.

At each price, sellers will produce a _____ (larger, smaller) quantity than before.

Answers

1. dependent; inverse; negative

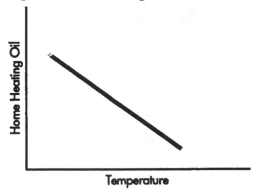

2. true
3. direct; positive

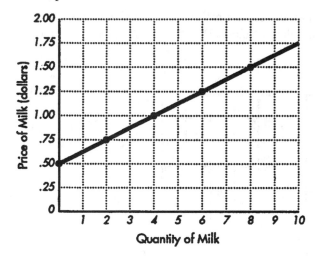

4. a. direct
   b. $\frac{1}{3}$; 40
   c. $C = 40 + \frac{1}{3}Y$
   d. 60
5. pie chart

6. There are many possible solutions. The numbers need to decrease until you reach the quantity 40,000 and increase thereafter. Here is one possible solution:

Quantity of Airplanes	Average Cost per Airplane
10,000	$40
20,000	30
30,000	20
40,000	10
50,000	20
60,000	30
70,000	40
80,000	50

7. inverse

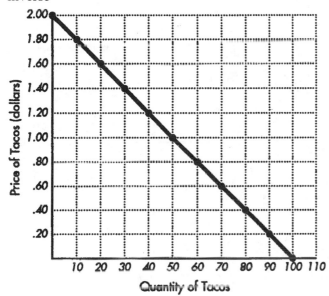

8. direct

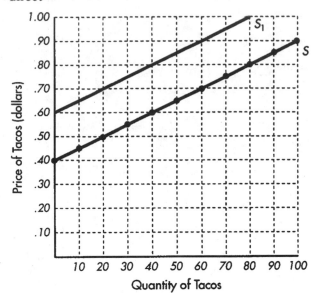

9. smaller

CHOICE, OPPORTUNITY COSTS, AND SPECIALIZATION

FUNDAMENTAL QUESTIONS

1. What are opportunity costs? Are they part of the economic way of thinking?

    The **opportunity cost** of something is what you need to give up in order to get it. For example, if you would prefer to be sleeping now instead of studying economics, the opportunity cost of studying is the sleep you could be enjoying. Opportunity costs are a key element in the way economists look at the world.

2. What is a production possibilities curve?

    A **production possibilities curve** shows all the combinations of output that could be produced with a given set of resources, assuming that the resources are fully and efficiently used.

3. How are specialization and opportunity costs related?

    Resources tend to be specialized—that is, better at producing one kind of good or service than another. For example, suppose that Vickeryland can produce either guns or butter. If Vickeryland throws all its resources into producing guns, some resources will not be good at producing guns. If some cows are switched over from making guns to making butter, they will probably be much better at making butter than at making guns. Vickeryland will gain a lot of butter and lose very few guns. But as more and more butter is produced, eventually some resources that were very good at making guns will have to be switched into making butter. If these resources are very good at making guns and not so good at making butter, Vickeryland will give up lots of guns and gain very little butter. When you give up an increasing number of guns to get each additional unit of butter, the opportunity cost of each additional unit of butter increases. If resources were equally adaptable among uses, the opportunity cost of each additional unit of butter would remain constant. The **marginal opportunity cost** would be constant.

4. Why does specialization occur?

    It pays to specialize whenever opportunity costs are *different*. Two parties can specialize and then trade, which makes both parties better off. Even if one person or nation does something more efficiently than another in the production of a good or service, it does not mean that that person or nation should produce that good or service. Specialization occurs as a result of **comparative,** not absolute, **advantage.** Specialization according to comparative advantage minimizes opportunity costs.

5. What are the benefits of trade?

If both parties specialize according to comparative advantage, trading enables them to acquire more of the goods and services they want.

Key Terms

opportunity costs
tradeoff
marginal
marginal cost

marginal benefit
production possibilities curve
  (PPC)
marginal opportunity cost

comparative advantage

Quick-Check Quiz

Section 1: Opportunity Costs

1. Janine is an accountant who makes $30,000 a year. Robert is a college student who makes $8,000 a year. All other things being equal, who is more likely to stand in a long line to get a concert ticket?
   a. Janine, because her opportunity cost is lower
   b. Janine, because her opportunity cost is higher
   c. Robert, because his opportunity cost is lower
   d. Robert, because his opportunity cost is higher
   e. Janine, because she is better able to afford the cost of the ticket

2. Which of the following statements is *false*?
   a. At points inside the production possibilities curve, resources are not being fully or efficiently used.
   b. Points outside the production possibilities curve represent combinations that are not attainable with the current level of resources.
   c. If an individual is producing a combination on his or her production possibilities curve, in order to get more of one good, he or she must give up some of the other.
   d. As a nation obtains more resources, its production possibilities curve shifts outward.
   e. The "guns or butter" decision is a rare example of a costless choice.

3. At point *A* on a production possibilities curve, there are 50 tons of corn and 60 tons of wheat. At point *B* on the same curve, there are 40 tons of corn and 80 tons of wheat. If the farmer is currently at point *A,* the opportunity cost of moving to point *B* is
   a. 10 tons of corn.
   b. 20 tons of wheat.
   c. 1 ton of corn.
   d. 2 tons of wheat.
   e. 40 tons of corn.

4. President Johnson thought it was possible to spend more resources in Vietnam without giving up consumer goods at home. President Johnson must have believed that the
   a. American economy was operating at top efficiency.
   b. American economy was operating at a point inside its production possibilities curve.
   c. American economy was operating at a point on its production possibilities curve.
   d. American economy was operating at a point outside its production possibilities curve.
   e. production possibilities curve would shift in as the war progressed.

Use the table below to answer questions 5 through 8.

Combination	Clothing	Food
A	0	110
B	10	105
C	20	95
D	30	80
E	40	60
F	50	35
G	60	0

5. If the economy currently is producing at point B, the opportunity cost of 10 additional units of clothing is
   a. 25 units of food.
   b. 5 units of food.
   c. 10 units of food.
   d. 35 units of food.
   e. 3.5 units of food.

6. If the economy currently is producing at point F, the opportunity cost of 10 additional units of clothing is
   a. 25 units of food.
   b. 5 units of food.
   c. 10 units of food.
   d. 35 units of food.
   c. 3.5 units of food.

7. A combination of 20 units of clothing and 80 units of food is
   a. unattainable.
   b. inefficient.
   c. possible by giving up 15 units of food.
   d. possible if the economy obtains more resources.
   e. possible if an improvement in technology shifts the production possibilities curve inward.

8. A combination of 50 units of clothing and 70 units of food
   a. is inefficient.
   b. is obtainable by giving up 35 units of food.
   c. does not fully utilize resources.
   d. is unattainable.
   e. is possible if an improvement in technology shifts the production possibilities curve inward.

Section 2. Specialization and Trade

Use the table below to answer questions 1 through 4.

Combination	Alpha		Beta	
	Beef	Microchips	Beef	Microchips
A	0	200	0	300
B	25	150	25	225
C	50	100	50	150
D	75	50	75	75
E	100	0	100	0

1. The opportunity cost of a microchip in Alpha is _____ unit(s) of beef, and the opportunity cost of a microchip in Beta is _____ unit(s) of beef. The opportunity cost of a unit of beef is _____ unit(s) of microchips in Alpha and _____ unit(s) of microchips in Beta.
   a. $\frac{1}{3}$; $\frac{1}{2}$; 3; 2
   b. 2; 3; $\frac{1}{2}$; $\frac{1}{3}$
   c. $\frac{1}{2}$; $\frac{1}{3}$; 2; 3
   d. 3; 2; $\frac{1}{3}$; $\frac{1}{2}$
   e. $\frac{1}{2}$; 3; $\frac{1}{3}$; 2

2. Alpha has a comparative advantage in _____, and Beta has a comparative advantage in _____. Alpha should produce _____, and Beta should produce _____.
   a. beef; microchips; beef; microchips
   b. beef; microchips; microchips; beef
   c. microchips; beef; microchips; beef
   d. microchips; beef; beef; microchips
   e. There is no basis for specialization and trade between these two countries because Beta can produce just as much beef and more microchips than Alpha.

3. Which of the following statements is true?
   a. Alpha can produce more beef than Beta.
   b. Alpha can produce more microchips than Beta.
   c. Beta can produce more beef than Alpha.
   d. Beta can produce more microchips than Alpha.
   e. Alpha can produce both more beef and more microchips than Beta.

4. Which of the following statements is true?
   a. Individuals, firms, and nations specialize in the production of the good or service that has the highest opportunity cost.
   b. An individual, firm, or nation first must be able to produce more of a good or service before it can have a comparative advantage in the production of that good or service.
   c. Comparative advantage exists whenever one person, firm, or nation engaging in an activity incurs the same costs as some other individual, firm, or nation.
   d. An individual, firm, or nation specializes according to comparative advantage.
   e. An individual, firm, or nation should trade with parties that have the same opportunity costs for the goods and services produced.

Practice Questions and Problems

Section 1: Opportunity Costs

1. _____ are forgone opportunities or forgone benefits.

2. People purchase items and participate in activities that _____ (maximize, minimize) opportunity costs.

3. The opportunity cost of an activity is the _____-valued alternative that must be forgone.

4. A(n) _____ is a graph that illustrates the tradeoffs facing a society.

5. A point that lies _____ the production possibilities curve indicates that resources are not being fully or efficiently used.

6. Points outside the production possibilities curve represent combinations of goods and services that are _____.

7. A new semiconductor chip is designed that can deliver more computing power for less cost. As a result, the production possibilities curve will shift _____.

8. A society that prohibits certain groups of people from working (for example, women, children, and African Americans) is producing at a point _____ its production possibilities curve.

9. It is possible to produce more of one good without giving up units of another good if a society is producing _____ its production possibilities curve.

10. It is not possible to produce more of one good without giving up units of another good if a society is producing _____ its production possibilities curve.

11. Opportunity cost is a(n) _____ (objective, subjective) concept.

12. Use the graph below to answer the following questions.

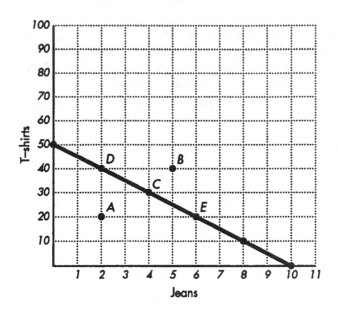

a. Point *A* represents a combination of T-shirts and jeans that is _____ .

b. Point *B* represents a combination of T-shirts and jeans that is _____ .

13. Mardi and Martin paid $20 each to see a new foreign film. Halfway through the film, Mardi got disgusted and wanted to leave. Martin insisted that they stay because they had paid $40 to see the film and he wanted to get his money's worth out of it. Can you offer them some economic insight to help them resolve the argument?

_____

_____

_____

_____

14. Roger Southby was almost finished with his accounting degree when he discovered the wonderful world of marketing. Roger would like to switch majors but does not want to waste the years of schooling he already has. What can you tell Roger to help him make his decision?

_____

_____

_____

_____

Section 2: Specialization and Trade

1. The _____ is the amount of one good or service that must be given up to obtain one additional unit of another good or service.

2. It is in your best interest to specialize where your opportunity costs are _____ (highest, constant, lowest).

3. A nation has a comparative advantage in those activities in which it has _____ (the highest, constant, the lowest) opportunity costs.

4. People specialize according to their _____ advantage.

5. If a country specializes in the production of goods and services in which it has a comparative advantage, it can trade with other countries and enjoy a combination of goods and services that lies _____ its production possibilities curve.

6. Use the table below to answer the following questions.

	Robinson Crusoe		Man Friday	
Combination	Coconuts	Fish	Coconuts	Fish
A	5	0	10	0
B	4	1	8	1
C	3	2	6	2
D	2	3	4	3
E	1	4	2	4
F	0	5	0	5

a. The marginal opportunity costs for Robinson Crusoe and Friday are _____ (increasing, constant, decreasing).

b. The marginal opportunity cost of a coconut is _____ fish for Robinson Crusoe and _____ fish for Friday.

c. The marginal opportunity cost of a fish is _____ coconut(s) for Robinson Crusoe and _____ coconut(s) for Friday.

d. Robinson Crusoe has a comparative advantage in _____, and Friday has a comparative advantage in _____.

e. Robinson Crusoe should specialize in producing _____, and Friday should specialize in producing _____.

f. Plot Robinson Crusoe's and Friday's production possibilities curves on the graphs below.

Friday's Production Possibilities Curve

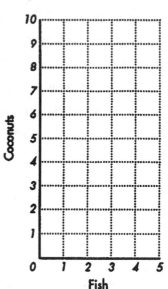

Robinson Crusoe's Production Possibilities Curve

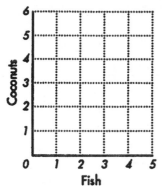

g. Without specialization, Robinson Crusoe would choose to produce 4 coconuts and 1 fish. Without specialization, Friday would choose to produce 4 coconuts and 3 fish.

Suppose they specialize according to comparative advantage and agree to trade in a ratio of 3 coconuts for 2 fish. Friday keeps 4 coconuts and trades _____ coconut(s) for _____ fish. Robinson Crusoe keeps 1 fish and trades _____ fish for _____ coconut(s).

With specialization and trade, Robinson Crusoe now has _____ coconut(s) and _____ fish. Label this point *R* on Crusoe's graph. Friday now has _____ coconuts and _____ fish. Label this point *S* on Friday's graph. Notice that both *R* and *S* are outside the original production possibilities curves, so specialization and trade enable both parties to have more fish and coconuts than they had before.

Robinson Crusoe's gain from trade is(are)_____; Friday's gain from trade is(are)_____.

7. Use the graph below to answer the following questions.

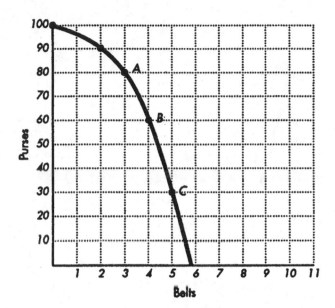

a. If an individual currently is producing the combination of purses and belts at point A, the marginal opportunity cost of 1 belt is _____ purse(s).

b. If an individual currently is producing the combination of purses and belts at point B, the marginal opportunity cost of an additional belt is _____ purse(s).

c. The marginal opportunity cost is _____ (increasing, constant, decreasing).

d. If an individual currently is producing the combination of purses and belts at point B, the marginal opportunity cost of an additional purse is approximately _____ belt(s).

e. If an individual currently is producing the combination of purses and belts at point A, the marginal opportunity cost of an additional purse is approximately _____ belt(s).

8. Use the graph below to answer the following questions.

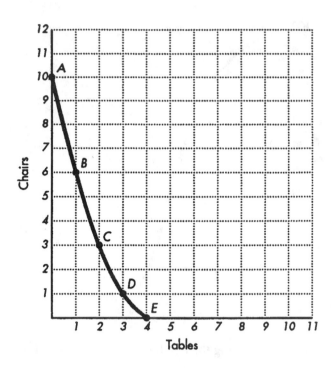

a. If an individual currently is producing the combination of chairs and tables at point *A,* the marginal opportunity cost of an additional table is _____ chair(s).

b. If an individual currently is producing the combination of chairs and tables at point *B,* the marginal opportunity cost of an additional table is _____ chair(s).

c. The marginal opportunity cost is _____ (increasing, constant, decreasing).

d. If an individual currently is producing the combination of chairs and tables at point *C,* the marginal opportunity cost of an additional chair is approximately _____ table(s).

e. If an individual currently is producing the combination of chairs and tables at point *B,* the marginal opportunity cost of an additional chair is approximately _____ table(s).

9. A straight-line production possibilities curve illustrates _____ (increasing, constant, decreasing) marginal opportunity costs.

10. A bowed-out production possibilities curve illustrates _____ (increasing, constant, decreasing) marginal opportunity costs.

11. A bowed-in production possibilities curve illustrates _____ (increasing, constant, decreasing) marginal opportunity costs.

12. Because resources tend to be specialized, the production possibilities curve is likely to be _____ (bowed in, bowed out, a straight line), indicating that marginal opportunity costs are _____ (increasing, decreasing, constant).

Thinking About and Applying Choice, Opportunity Costs, and Specialization

I. Opportunity Costs

Marc and Shelly Colby are a couple in their thirties with two children. Marc owns his own company and makes $150,000 a year, and Shelly has been responsible for raising their children. Now that the children are in school all day, Shelly is considering going back to school to finish her degree. She estimates that tuition will cost about $3,000. Marc likes carpentry and is thinking about going to a special school for a year to learn more about it. He estimates that the school will cost about $1,500. After they discuss it, they decide that Shelly should go back to school but that it costs too much for Marc to go to carpentry school. Explain.

_____

_____

_____

_____

II. More on Opportunity Costs

Mr. Safi and Mr. Nohr are neighbors. Mr. Safi makes $200 an hour as a consultant, while Mr. Nohr makes $10 an hour as an aerobics instructor. The men are complaining that the grass on their lawns has grown so fast due to recent rainy weather that it is hard to keep their lawns looking nice. Mr. Safi comments that he hires a neighbor's child to cut his grass "because it is too expensive for me to cut it myself." Explain Mr. Safi's comment.

_____

_____

_____

_____

Chapter 2 Homework Problems

Name _____

1. If you spent all evening next Friday studying economics, what would be your opportunity cost?

2. What do economists call a graph showing the different combinations of two products that a society can produce with given resources and technology?

3. Bob and Bill are woodcarvers. In a week of work, Bob can carve *either* one bird *or* two bookends. In a week of work, Bill can carve *either* two birds *or* six bookends.

   a. What is Bob's opportunity cost of making one bird?

   b. What is Bill's opportunity cost of making one bird?

   c. Does Bob or Bill have a comparative advantage in making birds? Why?

4. Bill is thinking about asking Bob to work with him in a woodcarving partnership. Since Bill can make more birds in a week than Bob can, and Bill can also make more bookends in a week than Bob can, why would Bill want to work with Bob?

5. The Longs and the Shorts are neighbors. Both husbands work full-time during the day, and both families have two small children. Mrs. Long stays at home during the day to care for her children, but Mrs. Short works full-time during the day and sends her children to day care. The Short family has a higher income, primarily because Mrs. Short works outside the home.

   a. There are two grocery stores near the Longs and the Shorts. One is a "no-frills" store that claims to have the lowest prices in town. The aisles are not marked, and specific items are hard to find. The other is a "superstore." Its prices are higher, but it is easy to find specific items, and the same store also offers dry cleaning, banking, photo developing, a pharmacy, and postal services. Which family is more likely to shop at the "no-frills" store? Use your economic reasoning to explain your answer.

   b. One family clips cents-off coupons from newspapers and magazines, watches for sales, and buys whatever brand is least expensive. The other family does not clip coupons and usually buys its favorite brands, whether on sale or not. Which family clips coupons and buys sale items? Explain why.

   c. Which family is more likely to buy milk and other small items at convenience stores? Why?

If your instructor assigns these problems, write your answers above, then tear out this page and hand it in.

Answers

Quick-Check Quiz

Section 1: Opportunity Costs

1. c; 2. e; 3. a; 4. b; 5. c; 6. d; 7. b; 8. d
If you missed any of these questions, you should go back and review Section 1 in Chapter 2.

Section 2: Specialization and Trade

1. c; 2. a; 3. d; 4. d
If you missed any of these questions, you should go back and review Section 2 in Chapter 2.

Practice Questions and Problems

Section 1: Opportunity Costs

1. Opportunity costs
2. minimize
3. highest
4. production possibilities curve (PPC)
5. inside
6. unattainable
7. outward
8. inside
9. inside
10. on
11. subjective
12. a. inefficient (does not fully utilize all resources)
    b. unattainable
13. Whether they stay or leave, they cannot get their $40 back. It is a *sunk cost* and should not enter the decision-making process. The relevant costs are the opportunity costs of staying versus the opportunity costs of leaving.
14. The years of schooling Roger already has are a *sunk cost*—he cannot get them back whether he continues as an accounting major or switches to marketing. These costs should have no effect on his decision to change majors because he cannot change what already has happened. The relevant costs are the opportunity costs of continuing his accounting major versus the opportunity costs of switching to marketing.

Section 2: Specialization and Trade

1. marginal opportunity cost
2. lowest
3. the lowest
4. comparative
5. outside
6. a. constant
   b. 1; $\frac{1}{2}$

c. 1; 2
d. fish; coconuts
e. fish; coconuts
f.

Robinson Crusoe's Production Possibilities Curve

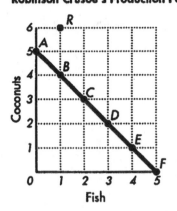

Friday's Production Possibilities Curve

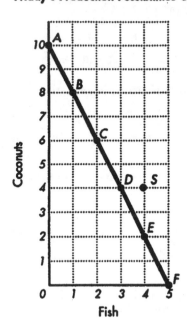

g. 6; 4; 4; 6; 6; 1; 4; 4; 2 coconuts; 1 fish

7. a. 20
   b. 30 (To get an additional belt, we must move from *B* to *C*. At *B*, we had 60 purses and 4 belts. At *C*, we have 30 purses and 5 belts. We gave up 30 purses for 1 belt.)
   c. increasing
   d. 0.05 (We must move toward point *A* to get additional purses. Moving from *B* to *A*, we give up 1 belt for 20 purses. For 1 purse, we give up approximately $\frac{1}{20}$ or 0.05 belt.)
   e. 0.1 (We must move up the curve to get additional purses. At point *A* we have 80 purses and 3 belts. Moving up the curve, we have 90 purses and 2 belts. We gave up 1 belt for 10 purses. For 1 purse, we give up approximately $\frac{1}{10}$ or 0.1 belt. Notice that as we make more purses, the opportunity cost in terms of belts increases.)

8. a. 4
   b. 3 (To get more tables, we must move from *B* to *C*. At *B*, we had 6 chairs and 1 table. At *C*, we have 3 chairs and 2 tables. We gave up 3 chairs for 1 table.)
   c. decreasing
   d. $\frac{1}{3}$ (To get more chairs, we must move toward point *B*. At point *C* we had 2 tables and 3 chairs. At point *B* we have 1 table and 6 chairs. We gave up 1 table for 3 chairs. To get 1 chair, we give up approximately $\frac{1}{3}$ table.)
   e. $\frac{1}{4}$ (To get more chairs, we must move toward point *A*. At point *B* we had 1 table and 6 chairs. At point *A* we have no tables and 10 chairs. We gave up 1 table for 4 chairs. To get 1 chair, we give up approximately $\frac{1}{4}$ table.)

9. constant
10. increasing

11. decreasing
12. bowed out; increasing

Thinking About and Applying Choice, Opportunity Costs, and Specialization

I. Opportunity Costs

Tuition isn't the only cost. If Marc has to give up $150,000 a year to go to carpentry school for a year, he and Shelly may feel that the benefits from carpentry school are not worth $150,000. Carpentry school costs too much. Because Shelly is not working outside the home, her major cost is the leisure time she will have now that their children are in school. She may feel that the benefits of having her degree are worth giving up her leisure time.

II. More on Opportunity Costs

The opportunity cost for Mr. Safi to cut his grass is $200 an hour—what he would make in his next best use. It is better for him to spend his hour consulting and pay the neighbor's child to cut the grass (unless the neighbor's child charges $200 an hour!).

MARKETS, DEMAND AND SUPPLY, AND THE PRICE SYSTEM

FUNDAMENTAL QUESTIONS

1. What is a market?

   A **market** is a place or service that allows buyers and sellers to exchange goods and services. A market may be a specific place or the exchange of a particular good or service at many different locations. Market transactions may involve the use of money or **barter.** In all markets, goods and services are exchanged and prices are determined.

2. What is demand?

   Demand is the quantity of a good or service that consumers are willing and able to buy at every possible price during a specific period of time, all other things being equal. People often confuse demand with quantity demanded. Demand refers to a list of prices and corresponding quantities. **Quantity demanded** is the amount of a good or service that people are willing and able to buy at *one* particular price. It is correct to say, "If the price of a hair dryer is $15, the *quantity demanded* is 20." It is not correct to say "If the price of a hair dryer is $15, the *demand* is 20."

   The **law of demand** states that as the price of a good decreases, people buy more (and vice versa). That's why stores have sales to get rid of merchandise they can't sell: they know that if they lower the price, people will buy more.

   When economists construct a **demand schedule,** they hold everything except the price of the good constant and determine the quantity consumers will buy at all the possible prices. However, things other than price affect how much of a good or service people are willing to buy. These other **determinants of demand** are income, tastes, prices of related goods or services, consumers' expectations, and number of buyers. When a good or service is sold in more than one country, the exchange rate is also a determinant of demand. When one of these determinants of demand changes, the whole demand schedule changes.

   Economists take seriously the adage "A picture is worth a thousand words," so they draw pictures of demand schedules. These pictures are called **demand curves.** Price is put on the vertical axis and quantity on the horizontal axis. Demand curves slope down from left to right. When one of the determinants of demand changes, the demand curve shifts to the left or the right. Increases in demand shift the curve to the right, and decreases in demand shift the curve to the left. A change in the price of a good or service does not shift the demand curve but instead is represented by a movement from one point to another along the same curve.

3. What is supply?

Supply is the quantity of a good or service that producers are willing and able to offer at each possible price during a specific period of time, all other things being equal. People often confuse supply with quantity supplied. Supply refers to a list of prices and corresponding quantities. **Quantity supplied** is the amount of a good or service offered for sale at *one* particular price. It is correct to say, "If the price of a hair dryer is $15, the *quantity supplied* will be 10." It is not correct to say, "If the price of a hair dryer is $15, the *supply* is 10."

The **law of supply** states that as the price of a good increases, producers will offer more for sale (and vice versa). That's why people offer a seller a higher price for the product when there is a shortage: they know the higher price will entice the producer to produce more.

When economists construct a **supply schedule,** they hold everything except the price of the good constant and determine the quantity producers will offer for sale at all the possible prices. However, things other than price affect how much of a good or service producers are willing to supply. These other **determinants of supply** are prices of resources, technology and **productivity,** expectations of producers, number of producers, and prices of related goods or services. When one of these determinants of supply changes, the whole supply schedule changes.

A picture of a supply schedule is called a **supply curve.** Again price goes on the vertical axis and quantity on the horizontal axis. Supply curves slope up from left to right. When one of the five determinants of supply changes, the supply curve shifts to the left or the right. Increases in supply shift the curve to the right; decreases in supply shift the curve to the left. A change in the price of a good or service does not shift the supply curve but instead is represented by a movement from one point to another along the same curve.

4. How is price determined by demand and supply?

The price of a good or service changes until the equilibrium price is reached. **Equilibrium** is the point at which the quantity demanded equals the quantity supplied at a particular price. At prices above the equilibrium price, the quantity supplied is greater than the quantity demanded, so a **surplus** develops. Sellers must lower their prices to get rid of the goods and services that accumulate. At prices below the equilibrium price, the quantity demanded is greater than the quantity supplied, and a **shortage** develops. Sellers see the goods and services quickly disappear and realize they could have asked a higher price. The price goes up until the shortage disappears. The price continues to adjust until the quantity demanded and the quantity supplied are equal.

5. What causes price to change?

Price may change when demand, supply, or both change. A change in demand causes price to change in the same direction: an increase in demand causes price to increase. A change in supply causes price to change in the opposite direction: an increase in supply causes price to decrease. If demand and supply both change, the direction of the change in price depends on the relative size of the changes in demand and supply. For example, if demand and supply both increase but the demand change is larger, price will increase: it will act as if the only change had been a change in demand. If demand and supply both increase but the supply change is larger, price will decrease: it will act as if the only change had been a change in supply.

6. What happens when price is not allowed to change with market forces?

When price is not allowed to change, the market can't reach equilibrium. If a price ceiling is set that is below the market equilibrium price, a shortage will exist and will stay in existence as long as the ceiling price is maintained. Similarly, if a price floor is set that is above the equilibrium price, a surplus will exist.

Key Terms

market
barter
double coincidence of wants
transaction costs
relative price
demand
quantity demanded
law of demand
determinants of demand

demand schedule
demand curve
substitute goods
complementary goods
exchange rate
supply
quantity supplied
law of supply
determinants of supply

supply schedule
supply curve
productivity
equilibrium
disequilibrium
surplus
shortage
price floor
price ceiling

Quick-Check Quiz

Section 1: Markets

1. A double coincidence of wants exists when
   a. A and B want the same good or service.
   b. A has what B wants.
   c. A has what B wants and B has what A wants.
   d. A has what B and C want.
   e. A has what C wants and B has what A wants.

2. Which of the following allocation schemes provides incentives for quantities of scarce goods to increase?
   a. first-come, first-served
   b. government scheme
   c. market system
   d. random allocation
   e. allocation of the good by members of the clergy on the basis of perceived need

3. In Mongoverna this year, apples cost $.50 each and oranges cost $.35 each. Suppose that next year, inflation runs rampant in Mongoverna. The price of apples increases to $1 each, and the price of oranges increases to $.70 each. Which of the following statements is true?
   a. The relative price of an apple has not changed.
   b. The relative price of an orange has changed.
   c. The absolute price of an apple has not changed.
   d. The absolute price of an orange has not changed.
   e. Both c and d are correct.

4. Which of the following statements is true?
   a. The transaction costs of finding a double coincidence of wants in order to barter are usually quite low.
   b. Money reduces transaction costs.
   c. People base economic decisions only on transaction costs.
   d. If all money prices doubled, relative prices would change.
   e. A double coincidence of wants is necessary to conduct money transactions.

5. If the price of a T-shirt is $12 and the price of a pair of designer jeans is $66, the relative price of a pair of designer jeans is
   a. $5\frac{1}{2}$ T-shirts.
   b. $\frac{2}{11}$ T-shirt.
   c. $5\frac{1}{2}$ jeans.
   d. $\frac{2}{11}$ jean.
   e. $66.

Section 2: Demand

1. Which of the following would *not* cause a decrease in the demand for bananas?
   a. Reports surface that imported bananas are infected with a deadly virus.
   b. Consumers' incomes drop.
   c. The price of bananas rises.
   d. A deadly virus kills monkeys in zoos across the United States.
   e. Consumers expect the price of bananas to decrease in the future.

2. Which of the following is a determinant of demand?
   a. the number of sellers
   b. the exchange rate
   c. producers' expectations
   d. an increase in productivity
   e. a change in technology

3. Which of the following is *not* a determinant of demand?
   a. income
   b. tastes
   c. prices of resources
   d. prices of complements
   e. consumers' expectations about future prices

4. A pair of Reebok shoes costs $50 in the United States and £30 in the United Kingdom. Which of the following statements is true?
   a. $1 is equivalent to £.60.
   b. $1 is equivalent to £1.67.
   c. £1 is equivalent to $.60.
   d. Reebok shoes are more expensive in the United States.
   e. Reebok shoes are more expensive in the United Kingdom.

5. A decrease in quantity demanded could be caused by a(n)
   a. decrease in consumers' incomes.
   b. decrease in the price of a substitute good.
   c. increase in the price of a complementary good.
   d. decrease in the price of the good.
   e. increase in the price of the good.

6. A recent Wichita State University study analyzed the effects of anticipated 6,000-plus layoffs at Boeing, a major Wichita employer. As a result of the anticipated layoffs,
   a. the demand for goods and services in Wichita will increase.
   b. the demand for goods and services in Wichita will decrease.
   c. the demand for Boeing airplanes will decrease.
   d. the demand for goods and services in Wichita will shift to the right.
   e. a and d are both correct.

7. The law of demand states that as the price of a good
   a. rises, the quantity demanded falls, *ceteris paribus*.
   b. rises, the quantity supplied falls, *ceteris paribus*.
   c. rises, the quantity demanded rises, *ceteris paribus*.
   d. rises, the quantity supplied rises, *ceteris paribus*.
   e. falls, the quantity demanded falls, *ceteris paribus*.

8. Which of the following would cause an increase in the demand for eggs?
   a. The price of eggs drops.
   b. The price of bacon rises.
   c. A government report indicates that eating eggs three times a week increases the chances of having a heart attack.
   d. A decrease in the cost of chicken feed makes eggs less costly to produce.
   e. None of the above would increase the demand for eggs.

9. If the price of barley, an ingredient in beer, increases,
   a. the demand for beer will increase.
   b. the demand for beer will not change.
   c. the demand for beer will decrease.
   d. the quantity of beer demanded will increase.
   e. a and d are both correct.

10. A freeze in Peru causes the price of coffee to skyrocket. Which of the following will happen?
    a. The demand for coffee will increase, and the demand for tea will increase.
    b. The demand for coffee will increase, and the quantity demanded of tea will increase.
    c. The quantity demanded of coffee will increase, and the demand for tea will increase.
    d. The quantity demanded of coffee will increase, and the quantity demanded of tea will increase.
    e. The quantity demanded of coffee will decrease, and the demand for tea will increase.

Section 3: Supply

1. According to the law of supply, as the price of a good or service
   a. rises, the quantity supplied decreases, *ceteris paribus*.
   b. rises, the quantity supplied increases, *ceteris paribus*.
   c. rises, the quantity demanded increases, *ceteris paribus*.
   d. rises, the quantity demanded decreases, *ceteris paribus*.
   e. falls, the quantity supplied increases, *ceteris paribus*.

2. Which of the following is *not* a determinant of supply?
   a. prices of resources
   b. technology and productivity
   c. prices of complements
   d. producers' expectations
   e. the number of producers

3. Japanese producers of a type of microchip offered such low prices that U.S. producers of the chip were driven out of business. As the number of producers decreased,
   a. the market supply of microchips increased—that is, the supply curve shifted to the right.
   b. the market supply of microchips increased—that is, the supply curve shifted to the left.
   c. the market supply of microchips decreased—that is, the supply curve shifted to the right.
   d. the market supply of microchips decreased—that is, the supply curve shifted to the left.
   e. there was no change in the supply of microchips (this event is represented by a movement from one point to another on the same supply curve).

4. Electronics firms can produce more than one type of good. Suppose that electronics firms are producing both military radios and microchips. A war breaks out, and the price of military radios skyrockets. The electronics firms throw more resources into making military radios and fewer resources into making microchips. Which of the statements below is true?
   a. The supply of microchips has decreased, and the quantity supplied of military radios has increased.
   b. The supply of microchips has decreased, and the supply of military radios has increased.
   c. The quantity supplied of microchips has decreased, and the supply of military radios has decreased.
   d. The quantity supplied of microchips has decreased, and the quantity supplied of military radios has decreased.
   e. There has been no change in the supply of microchips or in the supply of military radios.

5. Suppose that a change in technology makes car phones cheaper to produce. Which of the following will happen?
   a. The supply curve will shift to the left.
   b. The supply curve will shift to the right.
   c. The supply of car phones will increase.
   d. The supply of car phones will decrease.
   e. Both b and c are correct.

6. Which of the following is a determinant of supply?
   a. income
   b. tastes
   c. number of buyers
   d. the exchange rate
   e. the prices of resources

7. Suppose that automakers expect car prices to be lower in the future. What will happen now?
   a. Supply will increase.
   b. Supply will decrease.
   c. Supply will not change.
   d. Demand will increase.
   e. Demand will decrease.

8. Which of the following would *not* cause an increase in the supply of milk?
   a. an increase in the number of dairy farmers
   b. a change in technology that reduces the cost of milking cows
   c. a decrease in the price of cheese
   d. a decrease in the price of milk
   e. a decrease in the price of cow feed

9. Which of the following would *not* change the supply of beef?
   a. The U.S. government decides to give a subsidy to beef producers.
   b. An epidemic of cow flu renders many cattle unfit for slaughter.
   c. The price of fish increases
   d. A new hormone makes cows fatter and they require less feed.
   e. Beef producers expect lower beef prices next year.

Section 4: Equilibrium: Putting Demand and Supply Together

1. If demand increases and supply does not change,
   a. equilibrium price and quantity increase.
   b. equilibrium price and quantity decrease.
   c. equilibrium price increases and equilibrium quantity decreases.
   d. equilibrium price decreases and equilibrium quantity increases.
   e. the demand curve shifts to the left.

2. If supply decreases and demand does not change,
   a. equilibrium price and quantity increase.
   b. equilibrium price and quantity decrease.
   c. equilibrium price increases and equilibrium quantity decreases.
   d. equilibrium price decreases and equilibrium quantity increases.
   e. the supply curve shifts to the right.

3. Prices above the equilibrium price cause a(n)
   a. shortage to develop and drive prices up.
   b. shortage to develop and drive prices down.
   c. surplus to develop and drive prices up.
   d. surplus to develop and drive prices down.
   e. increase in supply.

4. Prices below the equilibrium price cause a(n)
   a. shortage to develop and drive prices up.
   b. shortage to develop and drive prices down.
   c. surplus to develop and drive prices up.
   d. surplus to develop and drive prices down.
   e. increase in demand.

5. Utility regulators in some states are considering forcing operators of coal-fired generators to be responsible for cleaning up air and water pollution resulting from the generators. Utilities in these states currently do not pay the costs of cleanup. If this law goes into effect,
   a. demand for electricity will increase, and price and quantity will increase.
   b. demand for electricity will decrease, and price and quantity will decrease.
   c. the supply of electricity will decrease, and price and quantity will decrease.
   d. the supply of electricity will increase, price will decrease, and quantity will decrease.
   e. the supply of electricity will decrease, price will increase, and quantity will decrease.

6. Medical research from South Africa indicates that vitamin A may be useful in treating measles. If the research can be substantiated, the
   a. supply of vitamin A will increase, causing equilibrium price and quantity to increase.
   b. supply of vitamin A will increase, causing equilibrium price to fall and quantity to increase.
   c. demand for vitamin A will increase, causing equilibrium price and quantity to increase.
   d. demand for vitamin A will increase, causing equilibrium price to rise and quantity to fall.
   e. supply of vitamin A will increase, causing equilibrium price to rise and quantity to fall.

7. Since 1900, changes in technology have greatly reduced the costs of growing wheat. The population also has increased. If you know that the changes in technology had a greater effect than the increase in population, then since 1900 the
   a. price of wheat has increased and the quantity of wheat has decreased.
   b. price and quantity of wheat have increased.
   c. price and quantity of wheat have decreased.
   d. price of wheat has decreased and the quantity of wheat has increased.
   e. quantity of wheat has increased, and you haven't got the faintest idea what happened to the price.

8. Which of the following statements is *false*?
   a. Disequilibrium may persist in some markets because it is too costly to change prices rapidly.
   b. A ceiling price set higher than the equilibrium price will cause a shortage.
   c. Prices set by governments can be lower than equilibrium prices.
   d. Part of the cost of a restaurant meal is the opportunity cost of the time spent waiting for a table.
   e. All of the above are true.

Use the table below to answer questions 9 through 12.

Price	Quantity Demanded	Quantity Supplied
$0	24	0
1	20	2
2	16	4
3	12	6
4	8	8
5	4	10
6	0	12

9. The equilibrium price is
   a. $1.
   b. $2.
   c. $3.
   d. $4.
   e. $5.

10. The equilibrium quantity is
    a. 2.
    b. 4.
    c. 6.
    d. 8.
    e. 10.

11. If the price is $2, a _____ of _____ units will develop, causing the price to _____.
    a. shortage; 12; increase
    b. shortage; 12; decrease
    c. surplus; 12; increase
    d. surplus; 12; decrease
    e surplus; 19; decrease

12. If the price is $5, a _____ of _____ units will develop, causing the price to _____.
    a. shortage; 6; increase
    b. shortage; 6; decrease
    c. surplus; 6; increase
    d surplus; 6; decrease
    e. shortage; 12; increase

Use the graph below to answer questions 13 through 16.

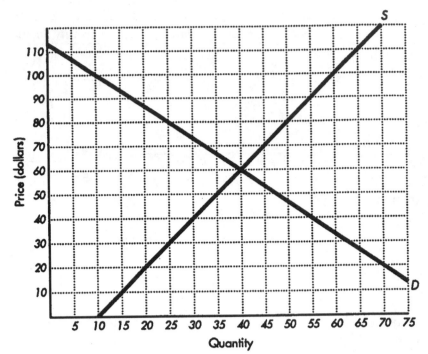

13. The equilibrium price is
    a. $20.
    b. $40.
    c. $60.
    d. $80.
    e. $100.

14. The equilibrium quantity is
    a. 25.
    b. 30.
    c. 35.
    d. 40.
    e. 45.

15. A price of $80 would cause a _____ of _____ units to develop, driving the price _____.
    a. shortage; 6; up
    b. shortage; 25; up
    c. surplus; 6; down
    d. surplus; 25; down
    e. surplus; 25; up

16. A price of $20 would result in a _____ of _____ units, driving the price _____.
    a. shortage; 10; up
    b. shortage; 50; up
    c. surplus; 10; down
    d. surplus; 50; down
    e. shortage; 50; down

Use the graph below to answer questions 17 through 20. The original supply curve is S_1, and the original demand curve is D_1.

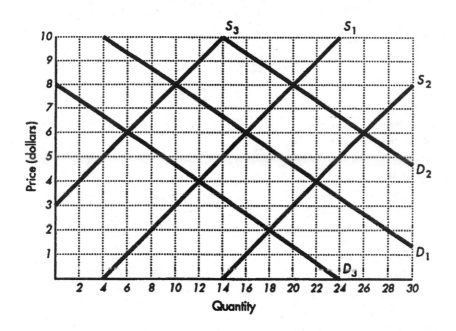

17. The original equilibrium price is _____, and the original equilibrium quantity is _____ units.
    a. $6; 6
    b. $4; 12
    c. $8; 20
    d. $6; 16
    e. $8; 20

18. An increase in the price of a resource causes _____ to shift to _____. The new equilibrium price is _____, and the new equilibrium quantity is _____ units.
    a. demand; D_2; $8; 20
    b. demand; D_3; $4; 12
    c. supply; S_2; $4; 22
    d. supply; S_3; $8; 10
    e. supply; S_3; $10; 14

19. Begin at the original equilibrium position at the intersection of D_1 and S_1. Now a decrease in the price of a complementary good causes _____ to shift to _____. The new equilibrium price is _____, and the new equilibrium quantity is _____ units.
    a. demand; D_2; $8; 20
    b. demand; D_3; $4; 12
    c. supply; S_2; $4; 22
    d. supply; S_3; $8; 10
    e. supply; S_3; $10; 14

20. Begin at the original equilibrium position at the intersection of D_1 and S_1. An increase in income occurs at the same time as a change in technology decreases the costs of production. The new equilibrium price will be _____, and the new equilibrium quantity will be _____ units.
    a. $6; 26
    b. $4; 22
    c. $8; 20
    d. $10; 14
    e. $6; 8

21. An increase in demand
    a. shifts the demand curve to the left.
    b. causes an increase in equilibrium price.
    c. causes a decrease in equilibrium price.
    d. causes a decrease in equilibrium quantity.
    e. does not affect equilibrium quantity.

22. When demand decreases,
    a. price and quantity increase.
    b. price and quantity decrease.
    c. price increases and quantity decreases.
    d. price decreases and quantity increases.
    e. supply decreases.

23. When supply decreases,
    a. the supply curve shifts to the right.
    b. equilibrium price and equilibrium quantity both increase.
    c. equilibrium price and equilibrium quantity both decrease.
    d. equilibrium price decreases and equilibrium quantity increases.
    e. equilibrium price increases and equilibrium quantity decreases.

Practice Questions and Problems

Section 1: Markets

1. A(n) _____ is a place or service that enables buyers and sellers to exchange goods and services.

2. The exchange of goods and services directly, without money, is called _____.

3. In a barter economy, trade cannot occur unless there is a(n) _____ of wants.

4. _____ prices are a measure of opportunity costs.

5. _____ occurs when an auto mechanic tunes up an accountant's car in exchange for the accountant's doing the mechanic's income taxes.

6. The costs involved in making a barter exchange are called _____ costs.

7. The price established when an exchange occurs is called the _____ price.

8. If all prices double, relative prices _____ (do, do not) change.

Section 2: Demand

1. _____ refers to the quantities of a well-defined commodity that consumers are willing and able to buy at every possible price during a given time period, *ceteris paribus*.

2. According to the law of demand, if you _____ your price, people will buy more, *ceteris paribus*.

3. List six determinants of demand.

   _____

   _____

   _____

   _____

   _____

   _____

4. Demand curves slope down because of the _____ relationship between price and _____.

5. Suppose that an increase in the price of Nohr Cola causes you to switch to Sooby Cola. You therefore buy less Nohr Cola. Sooby Cola is a(n) _____ for Nohr Cola.

6. The higher people's _____, the more goods they can purchase at any price.

7. A(n) _____ is a graph of a demand schedule.

8. _____ goods can be used in place of each other; these goods would not be consumed at the same time.

9. Goods that are used together are called _____ goods.

10. Dot, Diane, and Mardi are college students who share an apartment. Dot loves strawberries and buys them whenever they are available. Diane is a fair-weather strawberry eater: she only buys them if she thinks she is getting a good price. Mardi eats strawberries for their vitamin C content but isn't crazy about them. The table on the following page shows the individual demand schedules for Dot, Diane, and Mardi. Suppose that these three are the only consumers in the local market for strawberries. Add their individual demands to get the market demand schedule.

Price per Quart	Quantity			Market
	Dot	Diane	Mardi	
$0	6.00	4.00	2.00	_____
1	5.00	3.50	1.50	_____
2	4.00	3.00	1.00	_____
3	3.25	2.00	0.75	_____
4	2.00	1.50	0.50	_____
5	1.25	0.50	0.25	_____
6	0	0	0	_____

Plot the market demand for strawberries on the graph below.

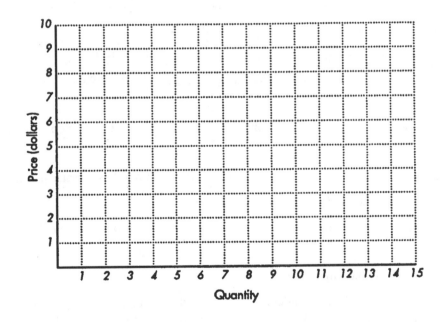

11. Suppose that the price of strawberries increases from $2 to $3 per quart. The increase in price would cause a decrease in the _____ (demand, quantity demanded) of strawberries. Show the effect of this change in the price of strawberries on the graph above.

12. Suppose that Dot reads in the paper that eating strawberries increases the health of females. As a group, Dot and her friends decide to buy twice as many strawberries as they did before at any price. Plot the new market demand curve in the graph above, and label it D_2. This change in tastes has caused a(n) _____ (increase, decrease) in _____ (demand, quantity demanded).

13. An increase in income _____ (increases, decreases) the _____ (demand, quantity demanded) for haircuts.

14. Many Americans have decreased their consumption of beef and switched to chicken in the belief that eating chicken instead of beef lowers cholesterol. This change in tastes has _____ (increased, decreased) the _____ (demand, quantity demanded) for beef and _____ (increased, decreased) the _____ (demand, quantity demanded) for chicken.

15. In the graph below, the price of good X increased, causing the demand for good Y to change from D_1 to D_2. The demand for good Y _____ (increased, decreased). X and Y are _____ (substitutes, complements).

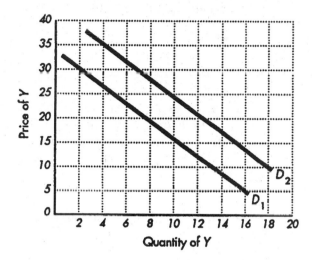

16. Mr. and Mrs. Gertsen are retiring next year and expect that their future income will be less than it is now. If D_1 is their current demand for bacon, show the effect of this expectation on the graph below. Label your new curve D_2. Demand for bacon has _____ (increased, decreased).

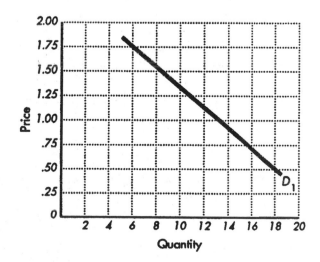

17. In the year 2000, one out of every five Americans will be over 65 years old. The demand for health-care facilities for the elderly will _____ (increase, not change, decrease).

18. A crisis in the Middle East causes people to expect the price of gasoline to increase in the future. The demand for gasoline today will _____ (increase, not change, decrease).

19. If the price of Pepsi increases, the demand for Coke and other substitutes will _____.

Section 3: Supply

1. _____ is the amount of a good or service that producers are willing and able to offer for sale at each possible price during a period of time, *ceteris paribus*.

2. According to the law of supply, as price _____, quantity supplied decreases.

3. A table or list of the prices and corresponding quantity supplied of a well-defined good or service is called a(n) _____.

4. A(n) _____ is a graph of a supply schedule.

5. Market supply curves have _____ slopes.

6. There are only two strawberry producers in the little town where Dot, Diane, and Mardi live. Their individual supply schedules are shown below. Add the individual supplies to get market supply, and then plot market supply (curve S_1) on the graph on the following page.

	Quantity Supplied		
Price per Quart	Farmer Dave	Farmer Ruth	Market
$0	2	2	_____
1	3	3	_____
2	4	4	_____
3	5	5	_____
4	6	6	_____
5	7	7	_____
6	8	8	_____

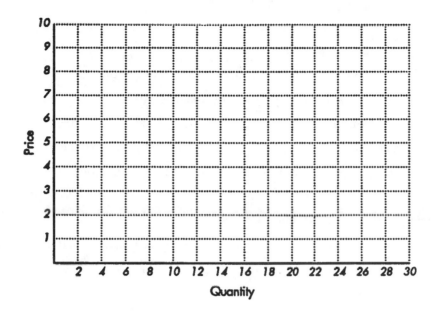

7. List the five determinants of supply.

_____

_____

_____

_____

_____

8. Suppose that a crisis in the Middle East cuts off the supply of oil from Saudi Arabia. If S_1 is the original market supply of oil, draw another supply curve, S_2, on the graph to show the effect of Saudi Arabia's departure from the market. The _____ (quantity supplied, supply) has _____ (increased, decreased)

9. If the price of tomato sauce increases, the _____ (supply, quantity supplied) of pizza will _____ (increase, decrease).

10. _____ is the quantity of output produced per unit of resource.

11. A new process for producing microchips is discovered that will decrease the cost of production by 10 percent. The supply of microchips will _____ (increase, decrease, not change), which means the supply curve will _____ (shift to the right, shift to the left, not change).

12. A paper manufacturer can produce notebook paper or wedding invitations. If the price of wedding invitations skyrockets, we can expect the supply of _____ (notebook paper, wedding invitations) to _____ (increase, decrease).

13. A real-estate developer who specializes in two-bedroom homes believes that the incomes of young couples will decline in the future. We can expect the supply of this realtor's two-bedroom homes to _____ (increase, decrease).

14. Changes in quantity supplied are caused by changes in the _____ of the good.

Section 4: Equilibrium: Putting Demand and Supply Together

1. The point at which the quantity demanded equals the quantity supplied at a particular price is known as the point of _____.

2. Whenever the price is greater than the equilibrium price, a(n) _____ arises.

3. A(n) _____ arises when the quantity demanded is greater than the quantity supplied at a particular price.

4. Shortages lead to _____ (increases, decreases) in price and quantity supplied and _____ (increases, decreases) in quantity demanded.

5. Surpluses lead to _____ (increases, decreases) in price and quantity supplied and _____ (increases, decreases) in quantity demanded.

6. The only goods that are not scarce are _____ goods.

7. As long as supply does not change, a change in equilibrium price and quantity is in the _____ (same, opposite) direction as a change in demand.

8. Balloon manufacturers are nervous about a children's movement that may affect their product. The children are lobbying state legislatures to ban launchings of more than ten balloons at a time, citing the danger that balloons can pose to wildlife. If the children are successful, we can expect the _____ (demand for, supply of) balloons to _____ (increase, decrease), causing the equilibrium price to _____ and the equilibrium quantity to _____.

9. If design changes in the construction of milk cartons cause the cost of production to decrease, we can expect the _____ (demand for, supply of) cartons to _____ (increase, decrease), the equilibrium price to _____, and the equilibrium quantity to _____.

10. A decrease in supply leads to a(n) _____ in price and a(n) _____ in quantity.

11. Remember Dot, Diane, and Mardi and the strawberry farmers Dave and Ruth? The local market for strawberries (before Dot read about the effects of strawberries on women's health) is reproduced in the graph below. The original demand is D_1 and the original supply S. The equilibrium price is _____, and the equilibrium quantity is _____.

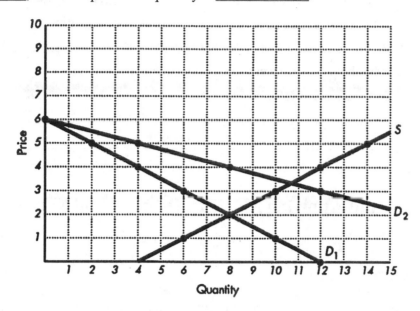

After Dot read the article on strawberries and health, the market demand curve shifted to D_2. The new equilibrium price is _____, and the new equilibrium quantity is _____. There was also a change in _____ (supply, quantity supplied).

12. _____ occurs when the quantity demanded and the quantity supplied are not equal.

13. The graph below shows the market for corn. The equilibrium price is _____, and the equilibrium quantity is _____.

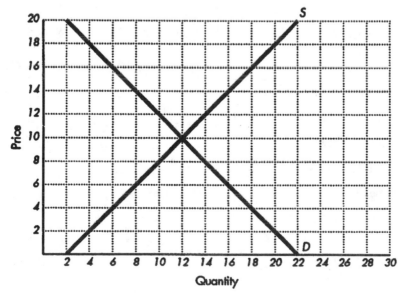

If the price of corn is $14, the quantity demanded will be _____, and the quantity supplied will be _____. A(n) _____ of _____ units will develop, causing the price and quantity supplied to _____ and the quantity demanded to _____.

If the price is $4, the quantity demanded will be _____, and the quantity supplied will be _____. A(n) _____ of _____ units will develop, causing the price and quantity supplied to _____ and the quantity demanded to _____.

14. List three reasons why there can be excess supply or demand in a market.

_____

_____

_____

Thinking About and Applying Markets, Demand and Supply, and the Price System

I. Changes in Demand

Indicate whether there is an increase or decrease in demand, an increase or decrease in quantity demanded, or no effect on demand. The market of interest is in italic.

1. *TV sets*. The number of producers of TV sets decreases.   _____

2. *Radios*. The price of radios goes up.   _____

3. *Cassette recorders*. The price of cassette recorders falls.   _____

4. *Coffee*. The price of tea falls.   _____

II. Changes in Supply

Indicate whether the supply curve would shift to the left or right in the following situations. If there is no effect, say so.

	Right	Left	No Effect
1. The number of producers of the product decreases.	_____	_____	_____
2. Consumers expect higher prices in the future.	_____	_____	_____
3. The price of the product goes up.	_____	_____	_____
4. The cost of an input decreases.	_____	_____	_____
5. Consumers' incomes fall.	_____	_____	_____
6. A change in technology reduces the costs of producing the product.	_____	_____	_____
7. A tariff is placed on the product.	_____	_____	_____

	Right	Left	No Effect
8. The price of a substitute in production increases.	_____	_____	_____
9. A tax on the product is increased.	_____	_____	_____
10. The price of the product falls.	_____	_____	_____

III. Distinguishing Changes in Demand from Changes in Supply

It is important that you be able to distinguish between factors that affect demand and factors that affect supply. Place a *D* next to items that are determinants of demand and an *S* next to items that affect supply.

_____ 1. producers' expectations

_____ 2. income

_____ 3. exchange rates

_____ 4. changes in technology

_____ 5. prices of substitutes in production

_____ 6. prices of related goods

_____ 7. number of sellers

_____ 8. tastes

_____ 9. prices of complements

_____ 10. consumers' expectations

_____ 11. number of buyers

_____ 12. changes in productivity

_____ 13. prices of resources

_____ 14. prices of substitutes in consumption

IV. The Market for Battery-Operated Dancing Flowers

For each event below, indicate whether it affects the demand or supply of battery-operated dancing flowers and the direction (increase or decrease) of the change. Also indicate what will happen to equilibrium price and quantity. Remember, the determinants of demand are income, tastes, prices of related goods or services, consumers' expectations, number of buyers, and exchange rates. The determinants of supply are prices of resources, changes in technology or productivity, producers' expectations, number of producers, and prices of related goods or services (goods that are substitutes in production).

1. There is a change in tastes toward battery-operated dancing gorillas.

2. The price of plastic falls.

3. A technological breakthrough makes it cheaper to produce plastic flowers.

4. Consumers' incomes rise.

5. The price of battery-operated dancing gorillas rises.

6. The price of plastic flowers skyrockets.

7. A fire destroys a major production facility for dancing flowers.

8. Consumers expect lower prices for dancing flowers in the future.

	Demand	Supply	Price	Quantity
1.	_____	_____	_____	_____
2.	_____	_____	_____	_____
3.	_____	_____	_____	_____
4.	_____	_____	_____	_____
5.	_____	_____	_____	_____
6.	_____	_____	_____	_____
7.	_____	_____	_____	_____
8.	_____	_____	_____	_____

V. Drinking and Cancer

The *Wichita Eagle* reported the results of a study that suggest that the anticancer benefit of eating lots of fruits and vegetables is lost if you wash them down with more than two drinks of alcohol.

As a result of this study, the _____ (demand, supply) for alcoholic drinks will _____ (increase, not change, decrease). The equilibrium price will _____ (increase, not change, decrease), and the equilibrium quantity will _____ (increase, not change, decrease).

Assume the market for alcoholic drinks was in equilibrium before the study, as shown below. Illustrate the effects of the research linking the loss of anticancer benefits with alcohol. Be sure your graph matches your answers above.

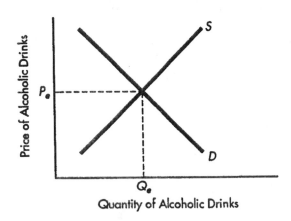

VI. Simultaneous Shifts in Demand and Supply: A Shortcut Approach

What do you do if events occur that shift both demand and supply at the same time? If you know the relative magnitudes of the shifts in demand and supply, you can predict both the equilibrium price and the equilibrium quantity. If you do not know the relative magnitudes of the shifts, you will be able to predict either equilibrium price or equilibrium quantity, but not both. Let's look at a quick way to do this.

Suppose demand and supply both increase. Look at what happens to price and quantity when you consider *only* an increase in demand:

	$D\uparrow$
Price	$\uparrow$
Quantity	$\uparrow$

Now add what happens to price and quantity when you consider *only* an increase in supply:

	$D\uparrow$	$S\uparrow$
Price	$\uparrow$	$\downarrow$
Quantity	$\uparrow$	$\uparrow$

When you look at the changes *together*, it's easy to see that the quantity increases but that the effect on price is uncertain. If the demand change is larger than the supply change, price increases. If the supply change is larger than the demand change, price decreases.

Let's try it again. Suppose demand increases and supply decreases. First look at what happens to price and quantity when you consider *only* an increase in demand:

	$D\uparrow$
Price	$\uparrow$
Quantity	$\uparrow$

Now add what happens to price and quantity when you consider *only* a decrease in supply:

	$D\uparrow$	$S\downarrow$
Price	$\uparrow$	$\uparrow$
Quantity	$\uparrow$	$\downarrow$

When you look at the changes together, can you see that the price increases but that the effect on quantity is uncertain? If the demand change is larger than the supply change, quantity increases. If the supply change is larger than the demand change, quantity decreases.

1. In the chart below, indicate a decrease in demand coupled with an increase in supply, then predict in what direction price and quantity will change.

	D	S
Price		
Quantity		

   P _____ , Q _____

2. Now try a decrease in demand coupled with a decrease in supply, then predict in what direction price and quantity will change.

	D	S
Price		
Quantity		

   P _____ , Q _____

Now let's try some more concrete examples.

3. We are analyzing the market for home computers. We foresee three main events coming up that will affect this market:

   a. Consumers' incomes are likely to increase.

   b. There will be an increase in the number of buyers as more schoolchildren become familiar with home computers in the classroom.

   c. We expect improvements in technology that will decrease the costs of production.

Use the chart below to determine what will happen to the equilibrium price and equilibrium quantity of home computers.

	D	S
Price		
Quantity		

   P _____ , Q _____

4. Suppose the cost of turkey food increases at the same time the price of chicken increases. What will happen to the market for turkey? Defend your answer with this chart.

	D	S
Price		
Quantity		

   P _____ , Q _____

VII. Wooden Bats Versus Metal Bats

The supply of wooden bats is shown as S_w on the graph below. It has a steeper slope than the supply of metal bats, S_m, reflecting the fact that it is easier to produce additional metal bats than additional wooden bats.

1. Assume D_m is the demand for metal bats. Suppose baseball purists are willing to pay more for a "sweet crack" sound than for a dull metallic "ping" when they connect with a fastball. Draw a demand curve for wooden bats and label it D_w.

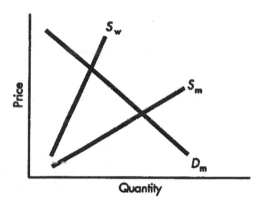

2. What are the consequences for the relative prices of wooden and metal bats?

_____

_____

_____

_____

VIII. For the Algebraically Inclined

1. The Market Demand for Commodity X
   The market for commodity X has three consumers: Gene, Darren, and Todd. The schedules below show each consumer's demand for commodity X.

Gene		Darren		Todd	
P	*Q*	*P*	*Q*	*P*	*Q*
$6	0	$6	0	$6	0
5	2	5	1	5	3
4	4	4	2	4	6
3	6	3	4	3	8
2	8	2	6	2	10
1	10	1	8	1	12

a. Derive and plot the market demand for X on the graph below. Label the curve D_1. The market supply curve is $Q = 3P + 18$. Plot market supply (curve S) on the graph.

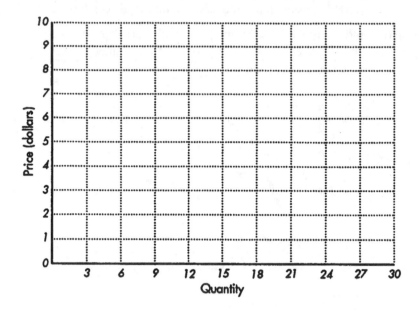

b. The equilibrium price is _____. The equilibrium quantity is _____ units.

2. The Market Demand for Commodity Y
   The market for commodity Y has three consumers: Andreas, Katinka, and Sophia. The schedules below show each consumer's demand for commodity Y.

Andreas		Katinka		Sophia	
P	Q	P	Q	P	Q
$10	0	$10	0	$10	0
9	2	9	2	9	0
8	4	8	3	8	1
7	6	7	4	7	2
6	8	6	5	6	3
5	10	5	6	5	4
4	12	4	7	4	5
3	14	3	8	3	6
2	16	2	9	2	7
1	18	1	10	1	8
0	20	0	11	0	9

a. Derive and plot the market demand curve for Y on the graph below. Label the curve D_1. The market supply curve is $Q = 2P - 2$. Plot market supply (curve S) on the graph.

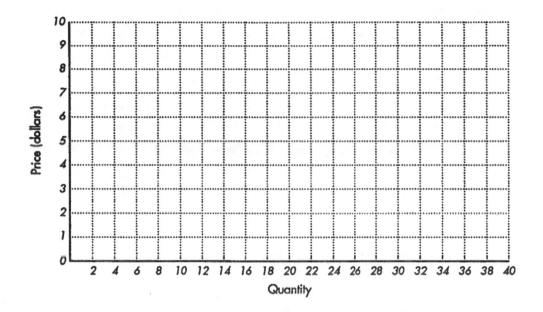

b. The equilibrium price is _____. The equilibrium quantity is _____ units.

c. Now suppose the price of Z increases, shifting market demand to $Q = 34 - 4P$. Plot and label the new curve D_2.

d. The new equilibrium price is _____. The new equilibrium quantity is _____.

e. Z and Y are _____ (complements, substitutes).

3. Market Equilibrium

a. The equation for demand is $Q = -20P + 110$. Plot demand (curve D) on the graph below. The equation for supply is $Q = 20P - 10$. Plot supply (curve S).

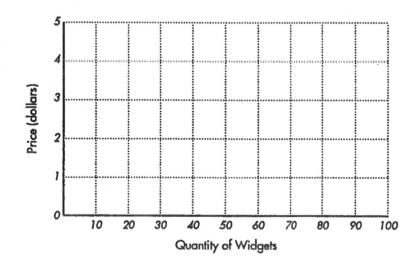

b. The equilibrium price is _____. The equilibrium quantity is _____ units.

c. A price ceiling of $2 will cause _____ (a shortage, a surplus, no change in equilibrium).

d. A price floor of $4 will cause _____ (a shortage, a surplus, no change in equilibrium).

e. A price ceiling of $4 will cause _____ (a shortage, a surplus, no change in equilibrium).

f. A price floor of $2 will cause _____ (a shortage, a surplus, no change in equilibrium).

4. Surpluses and Shortages

a. The market supply equation is $Q = P - 4$. Plot market supply on the graph below. Label it S. The market demand equation is $Q = 12 - P$. Plot market demand. Label it D_1.

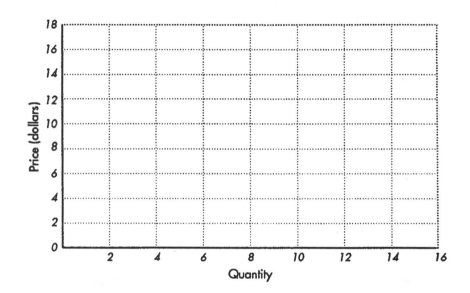

b. The equilibrium price is _____. The equilibrium quantity is _____ units.

c. If the price was $10, a _____ (surplus, shortage) of _____ units would develop, driving the price _____ (up, down).

d. If the price was $6, a _____ (surplus, shortage) of _____ units would develop, driving the price _____ (up, down).

e. Now suppose consumers' incomes increase, shifting market demand to $Q = 16 - P$. Plot the new demand curve. Label it D_2.

f. The new equilibrium price is _____, and the new equilibrium quantity is _____ units.

Chapter 3   Homework Problems

Name _____

1. State the law of demand and the law of supply.

2. List the six determinants of demand.

3. Explain the difference between a change in demand and a change in quantity demanded.

4. List the five determinants of supply.

5. Recently, the *Wall Street Journal* ran a story entitled "Man's New Best Friend: The Scaly Iguana." According to the article, iguanas have become very popular pets in some parts of the United States, with sales rising from 28,000 per year in 1986 to over 500,000 per year now. The movie *Jurassic Park* is cited as a reason for the new popularity of iguanas.

   a. Assuming that the supply of iguanas hasn't changed since 1986, sketch a graph showing what happened in the market for iguanas that explains the increase in sales.

   b. Of the six demand determinants, which one best explains the change in the market for iguanas?

   c. As iguanas became more popular, what do you think happened to the price of iguanas?

If your instructor assigns these problems, write your answers above, then tear out this page and hand it in.

Answers

Quick-Check Quiz

Section 1: Markets

1. c; 2. c; 3. a; 4. b; 5. a
   If you missed any of these questions, you should go back and review Section 1 in Chapter 3.

Section 2: Demand

1. c (A change in the price of a good causes movement along the curve—a change in quantity demanded—not a change in demand.); 2. b; 3. c; 4. a; 5. e (Items a, b, and c are determinants of demand and cause the demand curve to shift. Item d causes an *increase* in quantity demanded.); 6. b; 7. a; 8. e (Item a causes an increase in quantity demanded. Items b and c cause decreases in demand. Item d affects the *supply* of eggs.); 9. b; 10. e (The demand for coffee tells us the quantity demanded when the price changes, so it does not shift when price changes: you move from one price to another on the same curve. Coffee and tea are substitutes in consumption. When the price of coffee rises, people buy less coffee and substitute tea. They buy more tea at every price, so the demand for tea increases.)
   If you missed any of these questions, you should go back and review Section 2 in Chapter 3.

Section 3: Supply

1. b; 2. c; 3. d; 4. a (The supply of military radios tells us the quantity of military radios supplied when the price of radios changes. Supply doesn't change when the price changes: you simply move from one price to another on the same curve. Because microchips and military radios are substitutes in production, when the price of military radios increases, the supply of microchips decreases.); 5. e; 6. c; 7. a; 8. d (A change in the price of a good causes a change in quantity supplied, not a change in supply. Cheese and milk are substitutes in production, so if the price of cheese decreases, the supply of milk increases.); 9. c
   If you missed any of these questions, you should go back and review Section 3 in Chapter 3.

Section 4: Equilibrium: Putting Demand and Supply Together

1. a; 2. c; 3. d; 4. a; 5. e; 6. c; 7. d (Item e would be correct if you did not know that the supply change was greater than the demand change.); 8. b; 9. d; 10. d; 11. a; 12. d; 13. c; 14. d; 15. d; 16. b; 17. d; 18. d; 19. a; 20. a; 21. b; 22. b; 23. e
   If you missed any of these questions, you should go back and review Section 4 in Chapter 3.

Practice Questions and Problems

Section 1: Markets

1. market
2. barter
3. double coincidence
4. Relative
5. Barter
6. transaction

7. relative
8. do not

Section 2: Demand

1. Demand
2. lower
3. income
   tastes
   prices of related goods or services
   consumers' expectations
   number of buyers
   the exchange rate
4. inverse; quantity
5. substitute good
6. income
7. demand curve
8. Substitute
9. complementary
10. _____

Price per Quart	Market
$0	12
1	10
2	8
3	6
4	4
5	2
6	0

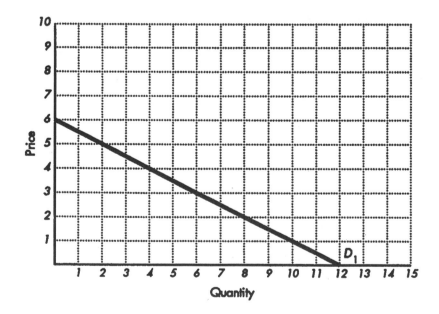

11. quantity demanded

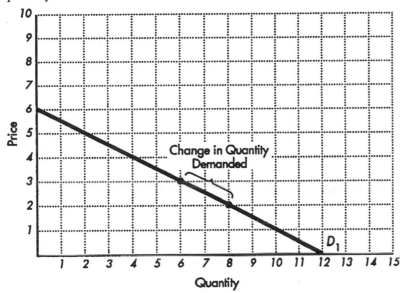

12. increase; demand

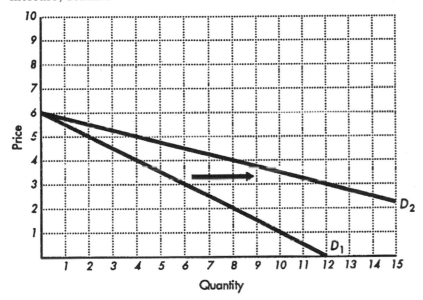

13. increases; demand
14. decreased; demand; increased; demand
15. increased; substitutes
16. decreased

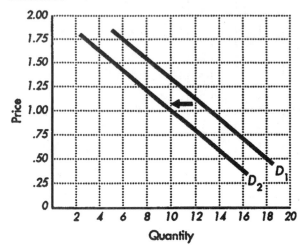

17. increase
18. increase
19. increase

Section 3: Supply

1. Supply
2. decreases
3. supply schedule
4. supply curve
5. positive
6. _____

Price per Quart	Market
$0	4
1	6
2	8
3	10
4	12
5	14
6	16

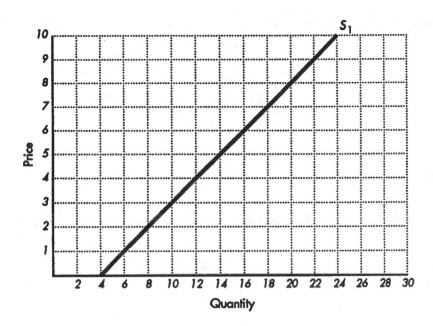

7. prices of resources
   technology and productivity
   expectations of producers
   number of producers
   prices of related goods or services
8. supply; dccrcascd

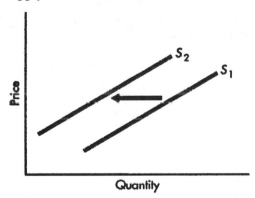

9. supply; decrease
10. Productivity
11. increase; shift to the right
12. notebook paper; decrease
13. increase (The real-estate developer will try to offer as many homes for sale *now,* before incomes drop and the prices of houses drop.)
14. price

Section 4: Equilibrium: Putting Demand and Supply Together

1. equilibrium
2. surplus
3. shortage
4. increases; decreases
5. decreases; increases
6. free
7. same
8. demand for; decrease; decrease; decrease
9. supply of; increase; decrease; increase
10. increase; decrease
11. $2; 8; 3⅓; 10⅔ (The last two values are eyeballed from the graph.); quantity supplied
12. Disequilibrium
13. $10; 12; 8; 16; surplus; 8; decrease; increase; 18; 6; shortage; 12; increase; decrease
14. Government intervention affects prices (price ceilings or floors).
    Price changes can be slow.
    Buyers and sellers may not want price changes.

Thinking About and Applying Markets, Demand and Supply, and the Price System

I. Changes in Demand

1. No effect on demand. The decrease in supply causes the price to increase, which ultimately will decrease the quantity demanded.
2. No effect on demand. This movement along the demand curve decreases the quantity demanded.
3. No effect on demand. This movement along the demand curve increases the quantity demanded.
4. The demand for coffee decreases (because some people will switch to tea). The quantity demanded decreases.

II. Changes in Supply

1. Left
2. No effect (Consumers' expectations affect demand.)
3. No effect (This is a movement along the supply curve.)
4. Right
5. No effect (This affects demand.)
6. Right
7. Left (A tariff increases producers' costs.)
8. Left (Producers move out of this product and produce the substitute instead.)
9. Left (Taxes increase producers' costs.)
10. No effect (This is a movement along the curve.)

III. Distinguishing Changes in Demand from Changes in Supply

1. S
2. D
3. D
4. S
5. S

6. D, S
7. S
8. D
9. D
10. D
11. D
12. S
13. S
14. D

IV. The Market for Battery-Operated Dancing Flowers

	Demand	Supply	Price	Quantity
1.	decrease	no change	decrease	decrease
2.	no change	increase	decrease	increase
3.	no change	increase	decrease	increase
4.	increase	no change	increase	increase
5.	increase	no change	increase	increase
6.	no change	decrease	increase	decrease
7.	no change	decrease	increase	decrease
8.	decrease	no change	decrease	decrease

V. Drinking and Cancer

demand; decrease; decrease; decrease

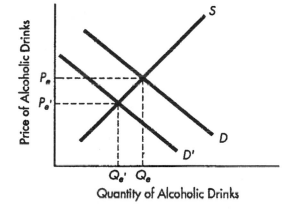

VI. *Simultaneous Shifts in Demand and Supply: A Shortcut Approach*

1.

	D↓	S↑
Price	↓	↓
Quantity	↓	↑

Price will surely decrease, but the effect on quantity is uncertain. If the demand change is larger than the supply change, quantity will decrease. If the supply change is larger than the demand change, quantity will increase.

2.

	D↓	S↓
Price	↓	↑
Quantity	↓	↓

Quantity will surely decrease, but the effect on price is uncertain. If the demand change is larger than the supply change, price will decrease. If the supply change is larger than the demand change, price will increase.

3. An increase in consumers' incomes is one of the six determinants of demand, so this factor will cause demand to increase. Likewise, an increase in the number of buyers will increase demand. Improvements in technology are one of the five determinants of supply. Because these improvements lower costs, supply will increase. We therefore are looking at an increase in demand coupled with an increase in supply. Our chart looks like this:

	D↑	S↑
Price	↑	↓
Quantity	↑	↑

The quantity of home computers will surely increase, but whether the price rises or falls depends on whether the demand shifts outweigh the supply shift. If the shifts in demand overwhelm the shift in supply, prices will increase. If the supply change is larger than the demand change, prices will decrease.

4.

	D↑	S↓
Price	↑	↑
Quantity	↑	↓

Turkey food is an input for turkey, so if the cost of turkey food increases, the supply of turkey will decrease. Chicken and turkey are substitutes. If the price of chicken increases, consumers will switch to turkey, and the demand for turkey will increase. The price of turkey will surely increase, but whether the quantity increases or decreases depends on which shift (supply or demand) is greater.

VII. Wooden Bats Versus Metal Bats

1.

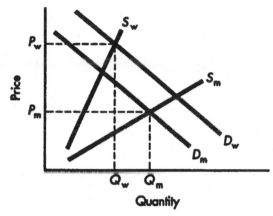

2. If baseball purists prefer wooden bats to metal bats, the demand for wooden bats (D_w) will be to the right of the demand for metal bats (D_m). The price of wooden bats will be higher than the price of metal bats.

VIII. For the Algebraically Inclined

1. The Market Demand for Commodity X
   a. _____

Market Demand	
P	Q
$6	0
5	6
4	12
3	18
2	24
1	30

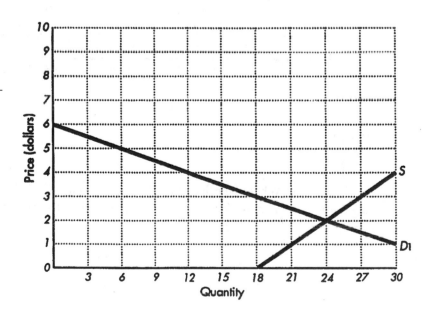

b. $2; 24

2. The Market Demand for Commodity Y

a. _____

Market Demand	
P	Q
$10	0
9	4
8	8
7	12
6	16
5	20
4	24
3	28
2	32
1	36
0	40

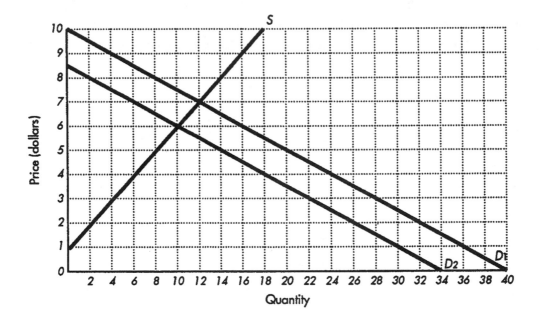

b. $7; 12
c. See graph.
d. $6; 10
e. complements (When the price of Z increases, consumers buy less of Z. Because the demand for Y decreased when less of Z was bought, Y and Z are complements.)

3. Market Equilibrium
   a.

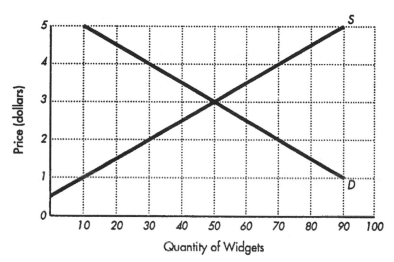

   b. $3; 50
   c. a shortage (of 40 units)
   d. a surplus (of 40 units)
   e. no change in equilibrium
   f. no change in equilibrium

4. Surpluses and Shortages
   a.

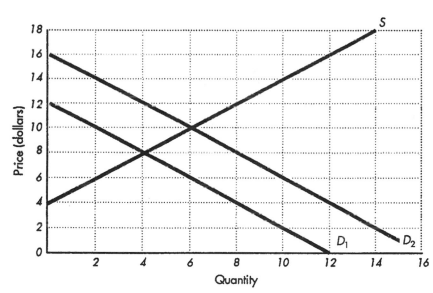

   b. $8; 4
   c. surplus; 4; down
   d. shortage; 4; up
   e. See a.
   f. $10; 6

THE MARKET SYSTEM AND THE PRIVATE SECTOR

FUNDAMENTAL QUESTIONS

1. In a market system, who decides what goods and services are produced and how they are produced, and who obtains the goods and services that are produced?

   In a market system, consumers decide what goods and services are produced by means of their purchases. If consumers want more of a good or service and are willing to pay for it, demand increases and the price of the good or service increases. Higher profits then attract new producers to the industry. If consumers want less of an item, demand decreases and the price of the item decreases. Resources are then attracted away from the industry.

   The search for profits dictates how goods and services are produced. Firms must use the least-cost combination of resources or be driven out of business.

   Income and prices determine who gets what. Income is determined by ownership of resources: those who own highly valued resources get more income. Output then is allocated to whoever is willing to pay the price.

2. What is a household, and what is household income and spending?

   A **household** consists of one or more persons who occupy a unit of housing. Household spending is called **consumption** and is the largest component of total spending in the economy.

3. What is a business firm, and what is business spending?

   A **business firm** is a business organization controlled by a single management. Business firms can be organized as **sole proprietorships, partnerships,** or **corporations.** Business spending by firms is called **investment** and consists of expenditures of capital goods that are used in producing goods and services.

4. How does the international sector affect the economy?

   The nations of the world can be divided into two categories: industrial countries and developing countries. The economies of industrial nations are highly interdependent. As business conditions change in one country, business firms shift resources among countries so that economic conditions in one country spread to other countries.

   The international trade of the United States occurs primarily with the industrial countries, especially Canada and Japan. **Exports** are products the United States sells to foreign countries. **Imports** are products it buys from other countries.

5. How do the three private sectors—households, businesses, and the international sector—interact in the economy?

Households own the **factors of production** and sell them to firms in return for income. Business firms combine the factors of production into goods and services and sell them to households and the international sector in exchange for revenue. The international sector buys and sells goods and services to business firms. The **circular flow diagram** illustrates these relationships.

Key Terms

consumer sovereignty	sole proprietorship	exports
private sector	partnership	trade surplus
public sector	corporation	trade deficit
household	multinational business	net exports
consumption	investment	financial intermediaries
business firm	imports	circular flow diagram

Quick-Check Quiz

Section 1: The Market System

1. In a market system, _____ decide what is produced.
   a. producers
   b. consumers
   c. politicians
   d. government authorities
   e. central planning boards

2. Many fitness educators are advocating step exercise as a way to improve cardiovascular fitness. Special boxes are used by participants, who step up and down, from side to side, and so on. If these boxes catch on, the _____ them will _____ , their price will _____ , and _____ boxes will be produced.
   a. demand for; increase; increase; more
   b. supply of; increase; increase; more
   c. supply of; increase; decrease; more
   d. demand for; increase; decrease; more
   e. supply of; increase; decrease; fewer

3. Assume that land costs $1 per unit, labor costs $3 per unit, and capital costs $2 per unit. All of the following combinations of resources produce 35 units of good X. How should good X be produced?
   a. 3 units of land, 4 units of labor, and 2 units of capital
   b. 2 units of land, 1 unit of labor, and 2 units of capital
   c. 5 units of land, 1 unit of labor, and 2 units of capital
   d. 1 unit of land, 2 units of labor, and 3 units of capital
   e. 2 units of land, 2 units of labor, and 3 units of capital

Section 2: Households

1. Householders _____ years old make up the largest number of households.
   a. 15 to 24
   b. 25 to 34
   c. 35 to 44
   d. 45 to 54
   e. 55 to 64

2. Householders _____ years old have the largest median annual income.
   a. 15 to 24
   b. 25 to 34
   c. 35 to 44
   d. 45 to 54
   e. 55 to 64

3. The largest percentage of households consist of _____ person(s).
   a. one
   b. two
   c. three
   d. four
   e. five

4. Household spending, or consumption, is the _____ component of total spending in the economy.
   a. largest
   b. second largest
   c. third largest
   d. fourth largest
   e. smallest

Section 3: Business Firms

1. In _____ the owner of the business is responsible for all the debts incurred by the business and may have to pay those debts from his or her personal wealth.
   a. sole proprietorships
   b. partnerships
   c. corporations
   d. sole proprietorships and partnerships
   e. sole proprietorships, partnerships, and corporations

2. _____ are the most common form of business organization, but _____ account for the largest share of total revenues.
   a. Sole proprietorships; partnerships
   b. Sole proprietorships; corporations
   c. Partnerships; corporations
   d. Corporations; sole proprietorships
   e. Partnerships; sole proprietorships

3. *Investment* as used in the text is
   a. a financial transaction, like buying bonds or stock.
   b. business spending on capital goods.
   c. equal to about one half of household spending.
   d. a relatively stable form of spending.
   e. All of the above describe *investment.*

Section 4: The International Sector

1. The United States tends to import primary products such as agricultural produce and minerals from _____ countries.
   a. low-income
   b. medium-income
   c. high-income
   d. industrial
   e. developing

2. About one-third of U.S. imports and more than a third of U.S. exports came from trade between the United States and
   a. the United Kingdom and Germany.
   b. eastern Europe.
   c. Canada and Japan.
   d. oil exporters.
   e. developing countries.

3. A trade surplus occurs when
   a. net exports are positive.
   b. net exports are negative.
   c. a country buys more from other countries than it sells to other countries.
   d. imports exceed exports.
   e. industrial countries sell to developing countries.

4. Low-income countries are concentrated heavily in
   a. Central America.
   b. South America.
   c. North America.
   d. Africa and Asia.
   e. western Europe.

5. Which of the following statements is false?
   a. Imports are products that a country buys from another country.
   b. Exports are products that a country sells to another country.
   c. Net exports equal exports minus imports.
   d. Net exports equal imports minus exports.
   e. A trade surplus is the same as positive net exports.

Section 5: Linking the Sectors

1. Which of the following statements is false?
   a. Households sell the factors of production in exchange for money payments.
   b. Firms buy the factors of production from households.
   c. The value of output must equal the value of income.
   d. The value of input must equal the value of household income.
   e. Money that is saved by households reenters the economy in the form of investment spending.

2. _____ own the factors of production.
   a. Corporations
   b. Partnerships
   c. The international sector
   d. State and local governments
   e. Households

Practice Questions and Problems

Section 1: The Market System

1. The _____ system is an economic system in which supply and demand determine what goods and services are produced and the prices at which they are sold.

2. To clarify the operation of the national economy, economists usually group individual buyers and sellers into three sectors: _____ , _____ , and _____ .

3. _____ is the authority of consumers to determine, by means of their purchases, what is produced.

4. Resources tend to flow from _____-valued uses to _____-valued uses as firms seek to make a profit.

5. When consumers' tastes change in favor of a good, _____ (demand, supply) _____ (increases, decreases) and the _____ (higher, lower) price attracts new firms to the production of that good.

6. When consumers' tastes change away from a good, _____ (demand, supply) _____ (increases, decreases) and the _____ (higher, lower) price causes firms to reduce production of that good.

7. In a market system, _____ dictate what is produced by means of their purchases of goods and services.

Section 2: Households

1. A(n) _____ consists of one or more persons who occupy a unit of housing.

2. Household spending is called _____ .

3. Householders between _____ and _____ years old have the largest median incomes.

4. A household is most likely to consist of _____ persons.

Section 3: Business Firms

1. A(n) _____ is a business organization controlled by a single management.

2. A(n) _____ is a business owned by one person.

3. A(n) _____ is a business owned by two or more individuals who share both the profits of the business and the responsibility for the firm's losses.

4. A(n) _____ is a legal entity owned by shareholders whose liability for the firm's losses is limited to the value of the stock they own.

5. A(n) _____ business is a firm that owns and operates producing units in foreign countries.

6. In the United States, the most common form of business organization is the _____ .

7. _____ is the expenditure by business firms for capital goods.

8. _____ account for the largest percentage of business revenue.

Section 4: The International Sector

1. The _____ is an international organization that makes loans to developing countries.

2. Low-income economies are heavily concentrated in _____ and _____ .

3. Products that a country buys from another country are called _____ .

4. Products that a country sells to another country are called _____ .

5. The United States trades the most with two countries, _____ and _____ .

6. A trade _____ exists when exports exceed imports.

7. A trade _____ exists when imports exceed exports.

8. _____ equal exports minus imports.

9. _____ net exports signal a trade surplus; _____ net exports signal a trade deficit.

Section 5: Linking the Sectors

1. List the three factors of production.

   _____

   _____

   _____

2. _____ own the factors of production.

3. The _____ is a model showing the flow of output and income from one sector of the economy to another.

Thinking About and Applying the Market System and the Private Sector

I. The Demand for Services in the Travel Industry

Consider the economic incentives for travel firms to add services. These services add costs to the expenses of the firm but may also increase demand. If the demand shift is greater than the supply shift, it pays the firm to add the service. If the supply shift is greater than the demand shift, it does not pay the firm to add the service.

1. The graph below represents the demand for hotel rooms without daily delivery of newspapers. Plot new demand and supply curves (D_2 and S_2) that show the effects of providing daily newspapers. Construct your curves to make it profitable for hotels to provide the newspapers.

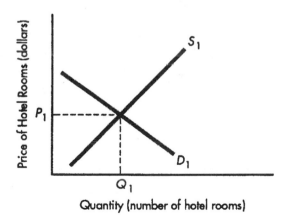

2. What happens to the price of hotel rooms?

   _____

   _____

II. The Circular Flow Diagram

Use the diagram below to see if you understand how the three sectors of the economy are linked together. In the blanks below, fill in the appropriate labels. Money flows are represented by broken lines. Flows of physical goods and services are represented by solid lines.

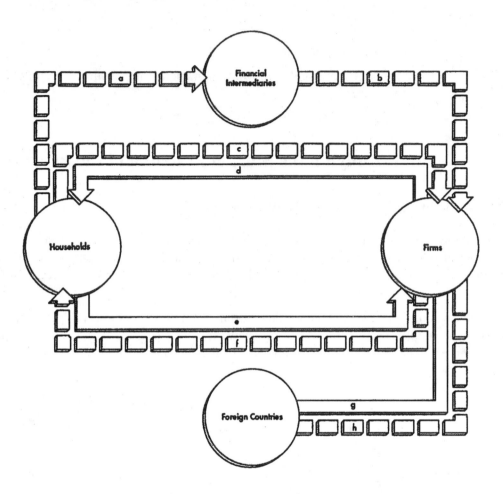

a. _____   e. _____

b. _____   f. _____

c. _____   g. _____

d. _____   h. _____

Chapter 4   Homework Problems

Name _____

1. In a market economy, who owns the factors of production, and who pays for their use?

2. How do economists define the term *household?*

3. What two countries are the largest trading partners of the United States?

4. In the 1970s, parrots were very popular pets in the United States. In the 1990s, iguanas became very popular.
    a. What would you predict happened to the prices and quantities of iguanas and parrots sold between the 1970s and 1990s?

    b. What economic principle describes *why* markets react to changes in people's tastes for pets?

5. Suppose you were an English merchant in the 1600s, trying to start a business shipping cargoes of raw materials to England from the newly established English colonies around the world and shipping finished goods back from England to the colonies. The business will be risky; many cargo ships sink due to storms or navigation hazards.

   You need to raise money from many investors to start the business. Think about the differences between partnerships and corporations and explain why setting up the business as a corporation would make it much easier to attract investors to your business.

If your instructor assigns these problems, write your answers above, then tear out this page and hand it in.

Answers

Quick-Check Quiz

Section 1: The Market System

1. b; 2. a; 3. b
If you missed any of these questions, you should go back and review Section 1 in Chapter 4.

Section 2: Households

1. c; 2. d; 3. b; 4. a
If you missed any of these questions, you should go back and review Section 2 in Chapter 4.

Section 3: Business Firms

1. d; 2. b; 3. b
If you missed any of these questions, you should go back and review Section 3 in Chapter 4.

Section 4: The International Sector

1. e; 2. c; 3. a; 4. d; 5. d
If you missed any of these questions, you should go back and review Section 4 in Chapter 4.

Section 5: Linking the Sectors

1. d; 2. e
If you missed either of these questions, you should go back and review Section 5 in Chapter 4.

Practice Questions and Problems

Section 1: The Market System

1. market
2. households; business firms; the international sector
3. Consumer sovereignty
4. lower, higher
5. demand; increases; higher
6. demand; decreases; lower
7. consumers

Section 2: Households

1. household
2. consumption
3. 45; 54
4. two

Section 3: Business Firms

1. business firm
2. sole proprietorship
3. partnership
4. corporation
5. multinational
6. sole proprietorship
7. Investment
8. Corporations

Section 4: The International Sector

1. World Bank
2. Africa; Asia
3. imports
4. exports
5. Canada; Japan
6. surplus
7. deficit
8. Net exports
9. Positive; negative

Section 5: Linking the Sectors

1. land
   labor
   capital
2. Households
3. circular flow diagram

Thinking About and Applying the Market System and the Private Sector

I. The Demand for Services in the Travel Industry

1. If your graph is correct, the demand shift (to the right) is greater than the supply shift (to the left). If the new equilibrium price and quantity are greater than the original equilibrium price and quantity, you've plotted the curves correctly.

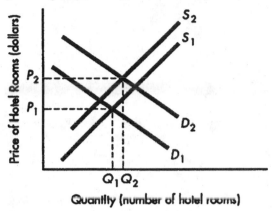

2. The price of hotel rooms increases.

II. The Circular Flow Diagram

a. saving
b. investment
c. payments for goods and services
d. goods and services
e. resource services
f. payments for resource services
g. net exports
h. payments for net exports

THE PUBLIC SECTOR

FUNDAMENTAL QUESTIONS

1. How does the government interact with the other sectors of the economy?

   Households sell resources to the government—which uses those resources to produce government services—in return for income. Business firms sell the goods and services they produce to the government for revenue. Taxes are the income the government receives from households and firms. In reality, the government may interact directly with foreign consumers and businesses, but most government activity with the international sector occurs when the government uses business firms as intermediaries.

2. What is the economic role of government?

   One outcome of the market system is **economic efficiency**—that is, no one can be made better off without making someone else worse off. However, economic efficiency can be limited by **market imperfections, externalities, public goods, monopolies,** and **business cycles.** The economic role of government is to reduce economic inefficiencies by controlling these factors.

3. Why is the public sector such a large part of a market economy?

   There are two explanations for the role of government in the market economy. One view suggests that government intervenes in the economy only to correct market failures. Another argument suggests that government actions result from the rent-seeking behaviors of the individuals who make up the government. That is, voters and politicians use the power of government to transfer benefits to themselves from others.

4. What does the government do?

   The economic role of government can be divided into two categories: microeconomic policy and macroeconomic policy. Microeconomic policy deals with providing public goods, correcting externalities, and promoting competition. Macroeconomic policy is divided into two categories: fiscal policy and monetary policy. **Monetary policy** is directed toward control of money and credit, and **fiscal policy** is directed toward government spending and taxation.

5. How do the sizes of public sectors in various countries compare?

   The United States and Canada are representative of market systems which rely on the decisions of individuals and in which the public sector is relatively small. Nations like Cuba rely on a planning board or central committee and have large public sectors. The economics of France, the United Kingdom, Germany, Japan, and Sweden lie in between.

Key Terms

economic efficiency	free ride	Federal Reserve
technical efficiency	monopoly	fiscal policy
market imperfection	business cycles	transfer payments
externalities	rent seeking	budget surplus
public goods	public choice	budget deficit
private property right	monetary policy	centrally planned economy

Quick-Check Quiz

Section 1: The Circular Flow

1. The text assumes that the government sector does not interact directly with
   a. households.
   b. business firms.
   c. foreign countries.
   d. foreign countries and business firms.
   e. households and the international sector.

2. Which of the following statements is *false*?
   a. The government employs the factors of production to produce government services.
   b. Money flows from the government to households.
   c. The value of private production equals the value of household income.
   d. The total value of output in the economy equals the total income received.
   e. In a sense, the household sector purchases goods and services from the government.

Section 2: The Role of Government in the Market System

1. *Economic efficiency* refers to
   a. the combination of inputs that results in the lowest cost.
   b. a situation in which no one can be made better off without making someone else worse off.
   c. the role of central planning boards in determining what goods and services should be produced.
   d. the role of government in providing public goods.
   e. the role of government in imposing taxes on those goods and services that produce negative externalities.

2. Which of the following is an example of a market externality problem?
   a. Lana hates her new haircut.
   b. Stan's new car turns out to be a clunker.
   c. Jan's neighbor blasts her out of bed with his new stereo at 4:00 A.M.
   d. Dan's new sweater falls apart the first time he washes it.
   e. Tim buys expensive basketball shoes that hurt his feet.

3. Which of the following does *not* involve negative externalities?
   a. cigarette smoke in a crowded restaurant
   b. acid rain
   c. Amazon rain forests, which help neutralize the effects of air pollution
   d. a blaring stereo
   e. the use of a highway by an additional vehicle

4. A lighthouse is an example of a
   a. negative externality.
   b. positive externality.
   c. public good.
   d. commonly owned good.
   e. private property right.

5. If negative externalities are involved in the production or consumption of a good, _____ of the good is produced or consumed. The government should _____ to encourage producers to produce _____ of the good.
   a. too little; grant subsidies; more
   b. too little; impose taxes; less
   c. too much; impose taxes; more
   d. too much; impose taxes; less
   e. too much; grant subsidies; less

6. Which of the following statements is *false*?
   a. It is not possible to exclude people from the benefits of public goods.
   b. Education is an example of a good with positive externalities.
   c. People have an incentive to try for a free ride when goods are public goods.
   d. If a good has positive externalities, too little of the good is produced.
   e. The price system ensures that the appropriate amount of public goods is produced.

7. The market system does *not* work efficiently when
   a. the market price reflects the full costs and benefits of producing and consuming a particular good or service.
   b. the least-cost combinations of resources are used.
   c. the benefits derived from consuming a particular good or service are available only to the consumer who buys the good or service.
   d. private property rights exist.
   e. market imperfections exist.

8. Public choice economists believe that
   a. people who do not like a market outcome use the government to change the outcome.
   b. the government intervenes only to correct market inefficiencies.
   c. rent-seeking activities increase economic efficiency.
   d. resources devoted to enacting the transfer of benefits are productive.
   e. redistributing income increases economic efficiency.

9. Which of the following is *not* a public good?
   a. police protection
   b. national defense
   c. streetlights
   d. cable television
   e. education

Section 3: Overview of the United States Government

1. Combined government spending on goods and services is larger than _____ but smaller than _____ .
   a. consumption; net exports
   b. consumption; investment
   c. net exports; investment
   d. investment; net exports
   e. investment; consumption

2. A budget deficit
   a. exists when federal revenues exceed federal spending.
   b. last occurred in the United States in 1969.
   c. occurs when federal spending exceeds federal revenues.
   d. has no effect on consumption and investment.
   e. has no effect on economic relationships with other countries.

3. Which of the following is *not* a microeconomic function of government?
   a. provision of public goods
   b. control of money and credit
   c. correction of externalities
   d. promotion of competition
   e. minimizing the free-rider problem

4. Which of the following is a macroeconomic function of government?
   a. redistribution of income
   b. promotion of competition
   c. determining the level of government spending and taxation
   d. provision of public goods
   e. correction of externalities

5. The _____ is (are) responsible for fiscal policy, and the _____ is (are) responsible for monetary policy.
   a. Federal Reserve; Congress
   b. Federal Reserve; Congress and the president
   c. Congress; Federal Reserve
   d. Congress and the president; Federal Reserve
   e. Congress; Federal Reserve and the president

Section 4: Government in Other Economies

1. Which of the following has an economy that is primarily centrally planned?
    a. United Kingdom
    b. Japan
    c. Cuba
    d. Germany
    e. Canada

2. In _____ , government spending (as a percentage of total output) was lower than that of Japan in 1997.
    a. the United States
    b. Sweden
    c. France
    d. Germany

Practice Questions and Problems

Section 1: The Circular Flow

1. Government in the United States exists at the _____ , _____ , and _____ levels.

2. The household sector obtains government goods and services primarily by _____ .

3. The _____ illustrates how the main sectors of the economy fit together.

Section 2: The Role of Government in the Market System

1. _____ efficiency is the combination of inputs that results in the lowest cost.

2. _____ efficiency is the point at which no one in society can be made better off without making someone else worse off.

3. A small company continues to use an old mimeograph machine even though a new personal copier would cut the company's copying costs by 50 percent. This is an example of _____ inefficiency.

4. An African American repeatedly is passed over for promotion because of race. This is an example of _____ inefficiency.

5. Situations in which the least-cost combination of resources is not used or in which a resource is not used where it has its highest value are called _____ .

6. _____ are the costs or benefits of a market activity borne by someone who is not a party to the market transaction.

7. When negative externalities exist, the market price _____ (overstates, understates) the full cost of the activity.

8. _____ are goods whose consumption benefits more than the person who purchased the good.

9. The limitation of ownership to an individual is called a(n)_____ .

10. A producer or consumer who enjoys the benefits of a good without having to pay for it is getting a(n) _____ .

11. Common ownership of a resource results in _____ (overutilization, underutilization).

12. Market imperfections may result from _____ or inaccurate information.

13. Once streetlights exist, people who have not paid for them cannot be excluded from their benefits. Streetlights are _____ goods.

14. A situation in which there is only one producer of a good is called a(n)_____ .

15. Fluctuations in the economy are called _____ .

16. The use of resources to transfer income from one sector of the economy to another is called _____ .

17. Monopolies may produce _____ (more, less) of a good in order to be able to charge a higher price.

18. _____ theory says that the government may be brought into the market system whenever someone or some group can benefit, even if efficiency is not served.

Section 3: Overview of the United States Government

1. List three microeconomic functions of government.

   _____

   _____

   _____

2. The macroeconomic functions of government are _____ and _____ policies.

3. The _____ is the central bank of the United States.

4. Monetary policy is directed toward control of _____ and _____ .

5. Fiscal policy is directed toward _____ and _____ .

6. Monetary policy is the responsibility of the _____ .

7. Fiscal policy is the responsibility of the _____ .

8. The _____ usually initiates major policy changes.

9. If federal government spending is less than tax revenue, a budget _____ exists.

10. If federal government spending is greater than tax revenue, a budget _____ exists.

Section 4: Government in Other Economies

1. A(n) _____ is an economy in which the government determines what goods and services are produced and the prices at which they are sold.

2. Match the country with the description of its economy.

   France   United Kingdom
   Cuba   Germany
   Japan   Sweden

   a. a capitalist economy in which the government plays an important role
      through its influence on industrial families   _____

   b. a market economy in the production of goods and services in which the gov-
      ernment accounts for nearly 45 percent of total purchases   _____

   c. a country in which the public sector owns few businesses but intervenes a
      great deal to foster social programs   _____

   d. a country whose economy is primarily centrally planned   _____

   e. a European country in which public-sector spending was about 40 percent
      of total output   _____

   f. a market economy in which a national economic plan has been used to in-
      fluence resource allocation   _____

3. A market economy relies on _____ and _____ to solve economic problems. In a centrally planned economy, the _____ decides what is produced, how it is produced, and who gets what.

Thinking About and Applying the Public Sector

I.   The Circular Flow Diagram

Use the diagram below to see if you understand how the four sectors of the economy are linked together. In the blanks below, fill in the appropriate labels. Money flows are represented by broken lines. Flows of physical goods and services are represented by solid lines.

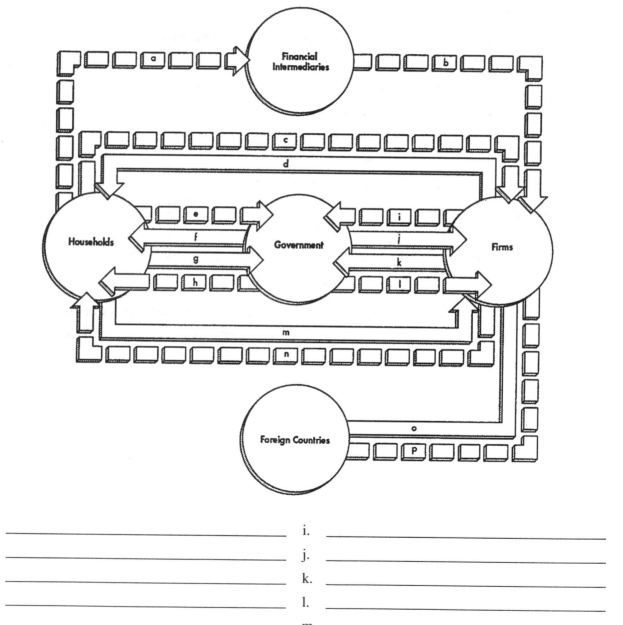

a. _____   i. _____

b. _____   j. _____

c. _____   k. _____

d. _____   l. _____

e. _____   m. _____

f. _____   n. _____

g. _____   o. _____

h. _____   p. _____

II. Government Response to Externalities

1. The graph below shows the demand and supply of an industry's product. This industry currently spews pollution into the air but bears no costs for its actions. If the industry is made responsible for the cleanup, show the effect on the market for this firm's product.

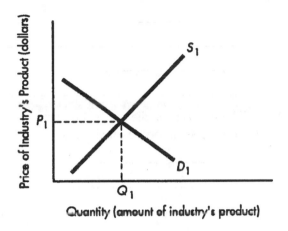

2. How could the government make this cost internal to the firm? What would this do to the price of the firm's output?

_____

_____

_____

_____

III. Justifying the Nutrition Labeling and Education Act

The Nutrition Labeling and Education Act requires food manufacturers to disclose what is in their products in a uniform manner. The idea of the act is to allow consumers to compare the nutritional values of dissimilar products.

Consider the role of the public sector as explained in the text, and provide the economic rationale for the Nutrition Labeling and Education Act.

_____

_____

_____

_____

IV. Extending Regulation

A few years ago, the *Wall Street Journal* ran the following headline: "Clinton's Team Moves to Extend Regulation in Variety of Industries." Consider the role of the public sector as explained in the text, and provide the economic rationale for the following actions:

1. "Major airlines have been put on notice that the government is scrutinizing their pricing practices."

    _____

    _____

    _____

    _____

2. "Strict quality-control rules will be imposed on the seafood industry, and more inspectors will be sent into meat and poultry plants to curb a rise in food-borne illness."

    _____

    _____

    _____

    _____

3. "The prescription-drug industry may get slapped with price controls."

    _____

    _____

    _____

    _____

Chapter 5   Homework Problems

Name _____

1. What is included in the U.S. government's microeconomic policy?

2. What is included in macroeconomic fiscal policy? In the United States, who makes decisions regarding fiscal policy?

3. What is included in macroeconomic monetary policy? In the United States, who makes decisions regarding monetary policy?

4. Last year, the government of an island nation spent $100,000 to build a lighthouse on a dangerous rock 10 miles from the nation's main harbor. Before the lighthouse was built, an average of 25 ships a year ran onto the rock, causing the loss of several millions of dollars every year. During the year the lighthouse has been in operation, no ships have run onto the rock. Why didn't a private company build the lighthouse before, since the benefits are so much more than the costs?

5. The "Economic Insight" box in this chapter describes the problem of overfishing of halibut around Alaska, and how the U.S. government created ownership rights to fish caught in that area as a way to limit the number of fish caught.

   In a market economy, resources that nobody owns, like fish in the ocean or clean air, tend to become overused. Think about the way that halibut fishing permits created ownership rights and an economically efficient market, and describe how a market for air pollution permits could be an economically efficient way to limit the amount of pollution.

If your instructor assigns these problems, write your answers above, then tear out this page and hand it in.

Answers

Quick-Check Quiz

Section 1: The Circular Flow

1. c; 2. c
If you missed either of these questions, you should go back and review Section 1 in Chapter 5.

Section 2: The Role of Government in the Market System

1. b; 2. c; 3. c; 4. c; 5. d; 6. e; 7. e; 8. a; 9. d
If you missed any of these questions, you should go back and review Section 2 in Chapter 5.

Section 3: Overview of the United States Government

1. e; 2. c; 3. b; 4. c; 5. d
If you missed any of these questions, you should go back and review Section 3 in Chapter 5.

Section 4: Government in Other Economies

1. c; 2. a
If you missed either of these questions, you should go back and review Section 4 in Chapter 5.

Practice Questions and Problems

Section 1: The Circular Flow

1. federal; state; local
2. paying taxcs
3. circular flow diagram

Section 2: The Role of Government in the Market System

1. Technical
2. Economic
3. technical
4. economic
5. market imperfections
6. Externalities
7. understates
8. Goods with positive externalities, or public goods,
9. private property right
10. free ride
11. overutilization
12. incomplete
13. public
14. monopoly
15. business cycles

16. rent seeking
17. less
18. Public choice

Section 3: Overview of the United States Government

1. provision of public goods
   correction of externalities
   promotion of competition
2. fiscal; monetary
3. Federal Reserve
4. money; credit
5. government spending; taxation
6. Federal Reserve
7. Congress and the president
8. president
9. surplus
10. deficit

Section 4: Government in Other Economies

1. centrally planned economy
2. a. Japan
   b. Sweden
   c. Germany
   d. Cuba
   e. United Kingdom
   f. France
3. individual actions; prices; government

Thinking About and Applying the Public Sector

I. The Circular Flow Diagram

a. saving
b. investment
c. payments for goods and services
d. goods and services
e. taxes
f. government services
g. resource services
h. payments for resource services
i. taxes
j. government services
k. goods and services
l. payments for goods and services
m. resource services
n. payments for resource services

o. net exports
p. payments for net exports

II. Government Response to Externalities

1. If the industry is forced to pay for the cleanup, costs will rise, shifting the supply curve to the left (curve S_2). The price of the firm's output will rise, and the quantity produced will fall.

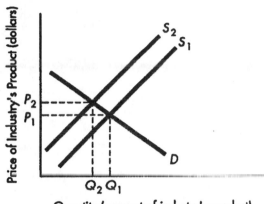

2. The government could achieve this effect by imposing a tax on the industry or by setting quotas on its output. The price would increase.

III. Justifying the Nutrition Labeling and Education Act

When information is not perfect, market imperfections can result. This means that least-cost combinations of resources may not be used or that resources may not be used where they have the highest value. The Nutrition Labeling and Education Act is an attempt to give consumers accurate and complete information.

IV. Extending Regulation

1. The government plans to do this to promote competition, which in turn should encourage technical and economic efficiency.
2. Because consumers lack complete information regarding the safety of seafood, meat, and poultry products, firms do not bear the full cost of improper practices.
3. The government is considering price controls to promote competition. Also, lower drug costs have positive externalities.

Sample Test
Chapters 1–5
(*Economics* Chapters 1–5)

1. A good economic model is one that
   a. relies on assumptions that mirror reality.
   b. incorporates knowledge agreed on by all economists.
   c. is limited to predictive statements.
   d. explains or predicts well.
   e. describes reality as closely as possible.

2. One of the key assumptions in economics is that
   a. people make choices that maximize their own self-interest.
   b. resources are limited only because income is distributed unequally.
   c. people focus on those activities in which their opportunity costs are highest.
   d. individual wants are homogeneous.
   e. the government dictates individual consumer behavior.

3. "The United States government must ensure that jobs are provided for the entire labor force." This is an example of a
   a. "what is" statement.
   b. fallacy of composition.
   c. positive statement.
   d. normative statement.
   e. *ceteris paribus* statement.

4. In economics, individuals must make choices because resources
   a. and wants are unlimited.
   b. are scarce and wants are unlimited.
   c. are unlimited and wants are limited.
   d. are unlimited and wants are uniform.
   e. are scarce and wants are limited.

5. A bowed-out production possibilities curve shows
   a. that the marginal opportunity costs of producing a good are constant.
   b. that the incremental costs of a first good are constant as we produce successively larger increments of a second good.
   c. the increasing difficulty or cost of moving resources from one activity to another.
   d. that it is possible to produce more of both goods with available resources.
   e. that the incremental costs of a first good fall as we produce successively larger increments of a second good.

Use the figure below to answer questions 6 and 7.

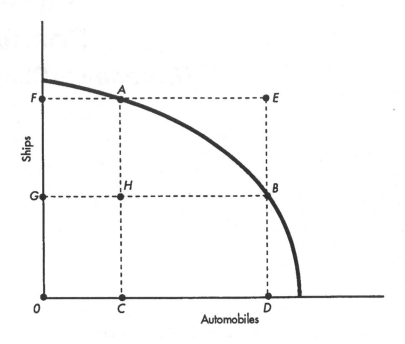

6. The combination of 0–C automobiles and 0–F ships
   a. implies that economic resources are not fully employed.
   b. is not attainable given society's available pool of resources.
   c. suggests that opportunity costs are constant.
   d. is a more efficient output combination than the one at point B.
   e. is one maximum output that can be produced under full employment of available resources.

7. Which of the following statements about point E is true?
   a. It represents a combination of automobiles and ships that underutilizes resources.
   b. It requires an outward shift of the current production possibilities curve to be attainable.
   c. It requires an inward shift of the current production possibilities curve to be attainable.
   d. It represents the maximum amount of automobiles and ships that can be produced with available resources.
   e. It implies that 0–D automobiles can be produced only if 0–F ships are forgone.

Suppose that Mike can produce either 10 surfboards or 2 bicycles per day. Tim, on the other hand, can produce either 12 surfboards or 3 bicycles per day. Use this information to answer questions 8 and 9.

8. The opportunity cost of producing one surfboard is
   a. $\frac{1}{5}$ bicycle for Mike and $\frac{1}{4}$ bicycle for Tim.
   b. $\frac{1}{4}$ bicycle for Mike and $\frac{1}{5}$ bicycle for Tim.
   c. 5 bicycles for Mike and 4 bicycles for Tim.
   d. $\frac{1}{5}$ bicycle for Mike and 4 bicycles for Tim.
   e. 5 bicycles for Mike and $\frac{1}{4}$ bicycle for Tim.

9. From the information above we can conclude that
    a. Mike has a comparative advantage in producing bicycles.
    b. Tim and Mike incur the same opportunity cost in producing surfboards.
    c. Tim has a comparative advantage in producing bicycles.
    d. Mike has a comparative advantage in producing both surfboards and bicycles.
    e. Tim incurs a lower opportunity cost in producing surfboards than does Mike.

10. When we specialize in production activities in which we are most efficient and trade for those goods
    and services in which other individuals are more efficient, we are applying the principle of
    a. declining opportunity costs.
    b. comparative advantage.
    c. market externalities.
    d. consumer sovereignty.
    e. unlimited wants.

11. A barter system
    a. involves the exchange of goods for money.
    b. exists only when there is no trade.
    c. has fewer transaction costs than does a monetary system.
    d. is an ancient trading system that was eliminated in the Middle Ages.
    e. relies on a double coincidence of wants.

12. The term *price* in the context of individual trade always refers to the
    a. money, or absolute, price of a good.
    b. relative price of a good.
    c. average price of all goods and services in the economy.
    d. transaction costs associated with finding a double coincidence of wants.
    e. value of a good in terms of gold.

13. Changes along the demand curve for a good are changes in
    a. demand caused by changes in the price of the good.
    b. the quantity demanded caused by changes in income.
    c. the quantity demanded caused by changes in the price of the good.
    d. the quantity supplied caused by changes in the price of the good.
    e. demand caused by changes in the price of a complement.

14. The market demand curve can be derived by
    a. adding all individual demand curves horizontally.
    b. adding all individual demand curves vertically.
    c. subtracting all individual demand curves from all individual supply curves.
    d. subtracting all individual demand curves vertically.
    e. picking the midpoint of all individual demand curves.

15. Assume that the market for good Y is initially in equilibrium. If everything else is held constant, an increase in demand for good Y will result in a(n)
    a. decrease in the equilibrium price for good Y.
    b. decrease in the equilibrium quantity demanded of good Y.
    c. increase in the equilibrium quantity of good Y.
    d. decrease in the price of complementary goods.
    e. increase in the supply of good Y.

Use the figure below to answer questions 16 and 17.

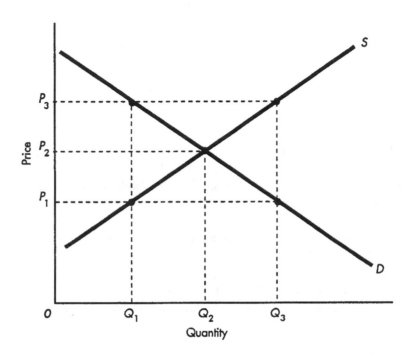

16. An increase in price from P_2 to P_3 would result in a
    a. surplus of $Q_3 - Q_1$ units.
    b. surplus of $Q_1 - 0$ units.
    c. shortage of $Q_3 - Q_1$ units.
    d. shortage of $Q_2 - 0$ units.
    e. surplus of $Q_3 - 0$ units.

17. If price is currently at P_1, over time it will
    a. increase to P_3 because firms will raise prices until they earn a profit.
    b. increase to P_2 because the shortage will put upward pressure on price.
    c. stay at P_1 unless the government imposes a price ceiling.
    d. drop to zero because the shortage will put downward pressure on price.
    e. result in a surplus equal to $Q_3 - Q_1$ units.

18. A leftward shift of the demand curve for a good would most likely be caused by
    a. a reduction in resource costs.
    b. technological improvements.
    c. a decrease in the number of producers.
    d. optimistic profit expectations.
    e. a decrease in the price of a substitute good.

19. Consumer sovereignty refers to the idea that
    a. consumers determine where goods and services are produced.
    b. consumers determine what goods and services are produced.
    c. business firms dictate for whom goods and services are produced.
    d. government dictates the production and sale of certain goods and services.
    e. consumers determine how to deal with inflation.

20. In the circular flow diagram,
    a. the value of national output always exceeds national income.
    b. business firms supply factors of production in exchange for the goods and services provided by households.
    c. financial services are supplied only to business firms.
    d. negative net exports imply a net inflow of foreign goods and services into the home country.
    e. business revenues constitute payment for resource services provided by households.

21. Which of the following is *not* a factor of production?
    a. a risk-taking, innovative architect who starts her own business
    b. $1,000,000 of financial capital provided to PolyGram Record Company
    c. a robot used to speed up production of computer microchips
    d. the acquisition of 50 acres of farmland to be used for cultivating wheat
    e. the entrance of 1,500 people with new Ph.D.s in economics into the labor force

22. Externalities are the
    a. costs of the factors of production.
    b. costs associated with public goods.
    c. efficiency losses associated with a monopoly.
    d. costs or benefits of a transaction that are borne by someone not directly involved in the transaction.
    e. social costs associated with business cycles.

23. What is a key problem associated with public goods?
    a. Public goods can be produced in unlimited quantities.
    b. Public goods are subject to external costs.
    c. It is difficult to exclude individuals from free consumption of public goods.
    d. Frequent government intervention in production processes causes an underallocation of public goods.
    e. Public goods are deemed "economic bads" and so require tax subsidies to be consumed by individuals.

24. Public choice theory
    a. seeks to understand the dynamics of an economic system in which market participants have perfect information.
    b. argues that government intervention in the marketplace tends to benefit small special-interest groups at the expense of a majority of the population.
    c. supports a strong role for government in the economy, to minimize the harmful social effects of market imperfections.
    d. claims that free-riding is not really a problem associated with public goods.
    e. seeks to make monetary and fiscal policies subject to the public's approval.

25. Which of the following is *not* one of the economic responsibilities of government?
    a. manipulating the nation's money supply
    b. promoting fair business practices
    c. subsidizing goods that provide external benefits to society
    d. minimizing the social costs associated with business cycles
    e. providing resources to businesses

Answers to Sample Test

1. d (Chapter 1, Section 2.b; *Economics* Chapter 1)
2. a (Chapter 1, Section 1.c; *Economics* Chapter 1)
3. d (Chapter 1, Section 2.a; *Economics* Chapter 1)
4. b (Chapter 1, Section 1.b; *Economics* Chapter 1)
5. c (Chapter 2, Section 2.a; *Economics* Chapter 2)
6. e (Chapter 2, Section 1.c; *Economics* Chapter 2)
7. b (Chapter 2, Section 1.c; *Economics* Chapter 2)
8. a (Chapter 2, Section 2.b; *Economics* Chapter 2)
9. c (Chapter 2, Section 2.c; *Economics* Chapter 2)
10. b (Chapter 2, Section 2.c; *Economics* Chapter 2)
11. e (Chapter 3, Section 1.b; *Economics* Chapter 3)
12. b (Chapter 3, Section 1.c; *Economics* Chapter 3)
13. c (Chapter 3, Section 2.e; *Economics* Chapter 3)
14. a (Chapter 3, Section 2.d; *Economics* Chapter 3)
15. c (Chapter 3, Section 4.b; *Economics* Chapter 3)
16. a (Chapter 3, Section 4.a; *Economics* Chapter 3)
17. b (Chapter 3, Section 4.a; *Economics* Chapter 3)
18. e (Chapter 3, Section 2.e; *Economics* Chapter 3)
19. b (Chapter 4, Section 1.a; *Economics* Chapter 4)
20. d (Chapter 4, Section 5.b; *Economics* Chapter 4)
21. b (Chapter 4, Section 1.b; *Economics* Chapter 4)
22. d (Chapter 5, Section 2.c; *Economics* Chapter 5)
23. c (Chapter 5, Section 2.d; *Economics* Chapter 5)
24. b (Chapter 5, Section 2.g; *Economics* Chapter 5)
25. e (Chapter 5, Section 3; *Economics* Chapter 5)

ELASTICITY: DEMAND AND SUPPLY

FUNDAMENTAL QUESTIONS

1. How do we measure how much consumers alter their purchases in response to a price change?

   When your favorite clothing store has a sale on jeans, do you go out and buy some? When the bookstore raised the price of required textbooks, did you buy fewer textbooks? We know from our study of demand that people usually respond to prices and price changes by changing the quantity they buy, but how big is the response? Most people respond more to changes in the price of jeans than they do to changes in the price of required textbooks. Is there any way to measure how much more?

   Elasticity gives us a way to measure how people react to price changes or to changes in other variables. Specifically, the **price elasticity of demand** measures how much consumers respond to changes in price by changing the quantity demanded, *ceteris paribus*. Price elasticity of demand is calculated using this formula:

   $$e_d = \frac{|\text{ percentage change in quantity demanded }|}{|\text{ percentage change in price }|}$$

   The absolute value signs in the formula ensure that the price elasticity of demand is always a positive number.

   For most products, the price elasticity of demand is different at different prices. If Pepsi® usually cost \$.05 a can, you would pay much less attention to a sale on Pepsi than you would if Pepsi cost \$5 a can. If we follow along a straight-line demand curve, we find that demand is *elastic* at high prices (e_d more than 1), *inelastic* at low prices (e_d less than 1), and *unit-elastic* (e_d equal to 1) in the middle.

2. Why are measures of elasticity important?

   Buyers respond to price changes by changing the quantity they want to buy. Elasticity measurements give economists a way to compare consumers' responses to price changes for different products.

3. How does a business determine whether to increase or decrease the price of the product it sells in order to increase revenues?

    When your favorite store has a sale on jeans, it sells more jeans but takes in less money per pair. Did it gain or lose revenue from the sale? That depends on the price elasticity of demand for the jeans. If the demand for the jeans is elastic, the percentage change in quantity is bigger than the percentage change in price, so a sale on jeans increases **total revenue.** But if the demand for jeans is inelastic, the percentage change in price is bigger than the percentage change in quantity, so a sale on jeans would decrease total revenue. When demand is inelastic, increasing the price increases total revenue.

4. Why might senior citizens or children receive price discounts relative to the rest of the population?

    Senior citizens and children receive discounts because they usually have more elastic demands than the rest of the population. If children's demand for movies is elastic, giving them a discount lowers the price they pay and increases the theater's total revenue. The rest of us aren't as responsive to the price of movies, so the theater doesn't gain by giving us a discount. Whenever different groups of customers have different price elasticities of demand, firms can increase their total revenue by using **price discrimination.**

5. What determines whether consumers alter their purchases a little or a lot in response to a price change?

    Three factors help determine how elastic the demand for a particular product is. First, the greater the number of close *substitutes,* the more elastic the demand. If the price of Kellogg's Corn Flakes goes up, you can find lots of other things to eat. If the price of required economics textbooks goes up, you can't just buy a cheaper anthropology text instead—not if you expect to pass economics.

    Second, the greater the proportion of a household's budget a good constitutes, the more elastic the demand. For example, the demand for salt is very inelastic. We only spend pennies a week on salt, so we don't respond much to price changes. For most of us, though, a trip to Europe or the Far East would take a large chunk of our incomes, so we're much more sensitive to the price of foreign travel.

    Third, the longer the period under consideration, the more elastic the demand. When the price of gasoline went up sharply in the 1970s, people didn't reduce their purchases very much at first; the demand was very inelastic. The response to the higher prices took a while to show up because it took people time to change their driving habits, to buy more fuel-efficient cars, and so on. Over longer periods of time, the demand for gasoline became more elastic.

6. How do we measure how much income changes, changes in the prices of related goods or changes in advertising expenditures affect consumer purchases?

    The **income elasticity of demand,** the percentage change in demand divided by the percentage change in income, measures how much changes in income affect consumer purchases. The **cross-price elasticity of demand,** the percentage change in demand of one good divided by the percentage change in the price of a related good, measures how much changes in the price of related goods affect consumer purchases. The advertising elasticity of demand, the percentage change in demand divided by the percentage change in advertising expenditures, measures how much changes in advertising expenditures affect consumer purchases.

7. How do we measure how much producers respond to a price change?

   We do this in the same basic way we measure whether consumers respond to a price change: we calculate the **price elasticity of supply.** The price elasticity of supply is the percentage change in the quantity supplied divided by the percentage change in price. The price elasticity of supply depends primarily on the length of time producers have to vary their output in response to changes in price.

Key Terms

price elasticity of demand	total revenue (TR)	inferior goods
perfectly elastic demand curve	price discrimination	price elasticity of supply
perfectly inelastic demand curve	cross-price elasticity of demand	short run
	income elasticity of demand	long run
arc elasticity	normal goods	tax incidence

Quick-Check Quiz

Section 1: The Price Elasticity of Demand

1. The price elasticity of demand is a measure of the degree to which
   a. consumers alter the prices they pay for a product in response to changes in the quantities they buy of that product.
   b. sellers alter the quantities of a product they offer for sale in response to changes in the price of that product.
   c. consumers alter the quantities of a product they purchase in response to changes in their family income.
   d. consumers alter the quantities of a product they purchase in response to changes in the price of that product.
   e. sellers alter the quantities of a product they offer for sale in response to changes in the incomes of buyers.

2. Mathematically, the price elasticity of demand is a
   a. ratio.
   b. graph.
   c. sum.
   d. straight line.
   e. curved line.

3. Which of the following is the equation for price elasticity of demand?

a. $e_d = \dfrac{|\text{change in quantity demanded}|}{|\text{change in price}|}$

b. $e_d = \dfrac{|\text{change in price}|}{|\text{change in quantity demanded}|}$

c. $e_d = \dfrac{|\text{percentage change in quantity demanded}|}{|\text{percentage change in price}|}$

d. $e_d = \dfrac{|\text{percentage change in price}|}{|\text{percentage change in quantity demanded}|}$

e. $e_d = \dfrac{|\text{change in price}|}{|\text{percentage change in quantity demanded}|}$

4. When the price elasticity of demand is greater than 1, demand is
   a. elastic.
   b. unit-elastic.
   c. inelastic.
   d. nonelastic.
   e. perfectly inelastic.

5. When the price elasticity of demand is less than 1, demand is
   a. elastic.
   b. unit-elastic.
   c. inelastic.
   d. nonelastic.
   e. perfectly elastic.

6. When the price elasticity of demand is equal to 1, demand is
   a. elastic.
   b. unit-elastic.
   c. inelastic.
   d. nonelastic.
   e. perfectly inelastic.

Section 2: The Use of Price Elasticity of Demand

1. The total expenditures made on a product by a group of buyers is found by multiplying
   a. price times elasticity.
   b. price times quantity bought.
   c. elasticity times quantity bought.
   d. quantity bought divided by price.
   e. elasticity divided by price.

Price times quantity is also the way to calculate
a. total revenue.
b. the foreign exchange rate.
c. the price elasticity of demand.
d. price discrimination.
e. the price elasticity of supply.

When elasticity is greater than 1, total revenue increases if price
a. decreases.
b. increases.
c. holds constant.

When elasticity is less than 1, total revenue increases if price
a. decreases.
b. increases.
c. holds constant.

Charging different customers different prices for the same product is called
a. foreign exchange exploitation.
b. labor exploitation.
c. perfect elasticity.
d. price discrimination.
e. pure price competition.

A business knows that it has two sets of customers, one of which has a much more elastic demand than the other. If the business uses price discrimination, which set of customers should receive a lower price?
a. Both sets should receive the same price.
b. Both sets should receive a higher price.
c. It doesn't matter to the business which gets a lower price.
d. The set with the more elastic demand should receive a lower price.
e. The set with the less elastic demand should receive a lower price.

Compared with people addicted to narcotics, potential narcotics users have a price elasticity of demand for narcotics that is
a. the same as addicts' demand because it is based on the same factors.
b. the same as addicts' demand but based on different factors.
c. less elastic than addicts' demand.
d. more elastic than addicts' demand.
e. more perfectly elastic than addicts' demand.

tion 3: Determinants of the Price Elasticity of Demand

One factor price elasticity of demand depends on is
a. how elastic the budgets of consumers are.
b. the total revenues taken in by sellers of a particular product.
c. how readily consumers can switch their purchases from one product to another.
d. the amount of taxes paid by consumers.
e. the number of consumers in the market.

2. The price elasticity of demand for a product is largest when there
   a. are no good substitutes for the product.
   b. is only one good substitute for the product.
   c. are two or three good substitutes for the product.
   d. are many good substitutes for the product.

3. The price elasticity of demand for a product is largest when the
   a. product constitutes a large portion of the consumer's budget.
   b. product constitutes a small portion of the consumer's budget.
   c. time period under consideration is very short.

4. The price elasticity of demand for a product is largest when the
   a. time period under consideration is long.
   b. time period under consideration is very short.
   c. product constitutes a small portion of the consumer's budget.

Section 4: Other Demand Elasticities

1. The percentage change in quantity demanded of one product divided by the percentage change in the price of a related product is called the
   a. cross-price elasticity of demand.
   b. price elasticity of demand.
   c. income elasticity of demand.
   d. straight-line demand curve.
   e. price elasticity of supply.

2. Two goods that have a positive cross-price elasticity of demand are called
   a. substitutes.
   b. complements.
   c. luxuries.
   d. necessities.
   e. supply-oriented goods.

3. Two goods that have a negative cross-price elasticity of demand are called
   a. substitutes.
   b. complements.
   c. luxuries.
   d. necessities.
   e. demand-oriented goods.

4. The percentage change in demand divided by the percentage change in income is called the
   a. cross-price elasticity of demand.
   b. price elasticity of demand.
   c. income elasticity of demand.
   d. straight-line demand curve.
   e. price elasticity of supply.

5. Luxuries have a larger income elasticity of demand than do
   a. necessities.
   b. substitutes.
   c. complements.
   d. independents.

Section 5: Supply Elasticities

1. Which of the following is the equation for price elasticity of supply?

   a. $e_s = \dfrac{\text{change in quantity supplied}}{\text{change in price}}$

   b. $e_s = \dfrac{\text{change in price}}{\text{change in quantity supplied}}$

   c. $e_s = \dfrac{\text{percentage change in quantity supplied}}{\text{percentage change in price}}$

   d. $e_s = \dfrac{\text{percentage change in price}}{\text{percentage change in quantity supplied}}$

   e. $e_s = \dfrac{\text{change in price}}{\text{percentage change in quantity supplied}}$

2. The price elasticity of supply depends in large part on
   a. the length of time producers have to vary their output in response to price changes.
   b. how willing consumers are to buy additional units of output at the current price.
   c. the number of buyers in the market.
   d. the price elasticity of demand.
   e. whether a good is a complement or a substitute.

3. Which of the following statements is correct?
   a. The short run is less than two weeks; the long run is more than two weeks.
   b. The short run is less than two months; the long run is more than two months.
   c. The short run is less than two years; the long run is more than two years.
   d. The short run is just short enough that the quantities of all resources cannot be varied; the long run is just long enough that the quantities of all resources can be varied.
   e. The short run is just short enough that the quantities of all resources can be varied; the long run is just long enough that the quantities of all resources cannot be varied.

4. Tax incidence refers to
   a. who pays a tax.
   b. the level of government that imposes a tax.
   c. the form of business organization that must pay a tax.
   d. the amount of revenue generated by a tax.
   e. whether government agencies must pay a tax.

Practice Questions and Problems

Section 1: The Price Elasticity of Demand

1. Elasticity is a way to measure the _____ of consumers or producers to a(n) _____ in some variable.

2. The price elasticity of demand measures the degree to which consumers alter their _____ in response to a(n) _____ change, *ceteris paribus*.

3. The equation used to calculate the price elasticity of demand is

$$e_d = \frac{\text{| percentage change in _____ |}}{\text{| percentage change in _____ |}}$$

4. If e_d is less than 1, demand is _____ .

5. If e_d is greater than 1, demand is _____ .

6. If e_d is equal to 1, demand is _____ .

7. A(n) _____ demand curve shows that consumers can purchase any quantity they want at the prevailing price.

8. A(n) _____ demand curve shows no change in quantity demanded as the price changes.

9. As you move down a straight-line demand curve, the price elasticity of demand _____ (increases, decreases).

10. If a 5 percent change in the price of movies causes a 10 percent change in the number of movie tickets sold, e_d equals _____ and demand is _____ (elastic, inelastic, unit-elastic).

11. If a 6 percent change in the price of coffee causes a 3 percent change in the quantity of coffee bought, e_d equals _____ and demand is _____ (elastic, inelastic, unit-elastic).

12. If a 2 percent change in the price of wine causes a 2 percent change in the number of bottles of wine bought, e_d equals _____ and demand is _____ (elastic, inelastic, unit-elastic).

13. If a 5 percent change in the price of heroin causes no change in the amount of heroin bought, e_d equals _____ and demand is _____ (perfectly elastic, perfectly inelastic).

14. Below is a hypothetical demand for box seats at a baseball game. Fill in the blanks to calculate the elasticities for the different price ranges. Refer to Section 1.d, "Average or Arc Elasticity," in Chapter 6 (*Economics,* Chapter 20) if you need help.

Quantity Demanded	Change in Quantity Demanded	Price	Change in Price	Average Quantity $[(Q_1+Q_2)/2]$	Average Price $[(P_1+P_2)/2]$	Percent Change in Q	Percent Change in P	Elasticity
400		$100						
	____		____	____	____	____	____	____
500		90						
	____		____	____	____	____	____	____
600		80						
	____		____	____	____	____	____	____
700		70						
	____		____	____	____	____	____	____
800		60						

15. Suppose that a movie theater knows that it will sell 450 tickets per day if it charges $4.50 per ticket; if the ticket price goes up to $5.50, the theater will only sell 350 tickets per day. What is the theater's price elasticity of demand for this price range?
   a. 1.00
   b. 1.57
   c. 0.80
   d. 1.25
   e. 1.22

16. Suppose that an airline knows that it will have 90 passengers per day on a particular route if it charges $200 per ticket; if the fare goes down to $180, the airline will sell 110 tickets per day. What is the airline's price elasticity of demand for this price range?
   a. 1.90
   b. 0.53
   c. 2.22
   d. 1.64
   e. 2.00

Section 2: The Use of Price Elasticity of Demand

1. Total revenue is found by multiplying _____ by _____ .

2. a. Demand is elastic. The percentage change in _____ (quantity, price) is larger than the percentage change in _____ (quantity, price).

   b. When price decreases, quantity increases and total revenue _____ (increases, decreases).

3. a. Demand is inelastic. The percentage change in _____ (quantity, price) is larger than the percentage change in _____ (quantity, price).

   b. When price decreases, quantity increases and total revenue _____ (increases, decreases).

4. Complete the table below.

Demand Elasticity	Price Change	Effect on Total Revenue (Increase, Decrease, Unchanged)
Elastic	Increase	_____
Elastic	Decrease	_____
Inelastic	Increase	_____
Inelastic	Decrease	_____
Unit-elastic	Increase	_____
Unit-elastic	Decrease	_____

For questions 5 through 7, suppose that you are the president of Wonderful Widget Works, Inc. Widgets are a hypothetical product that you produce in many different colors.

5. Your marketing manager tells you that you can increase total revenue for blue widgets if you lower their price from $2.00 to $1.80. You know that the demand for blue widgets in this price range is
   a. elastic.
   b. inelastic.
   c. unit-elastic.

6. Next, your marketing manager tells you that if you lower the price of red widgets from $1.20 to $1.00 you will decrease total revenue for red widgets. You know that the demand for red widgets in this price range is
   a. elastic.
   b. inelastic.
   c. unit-elastic.

7. Your marketing manager admits that he can't figure out what's happening with orange widgets. When he lowers the price from $1.60 to $1.40, total revenue stays the same. Because you understand elasticity, you know that the demand for orange widgets in this price range is
   a. elastic.
   b. inelastic.
   c. unit-elastic.

8. Suppose you are the city manager of a small midwestern city. Your city-owned bus system is losing money, and you have to find a way to take in more revenue. Your staff recommends raising bus fares, but bus riders argue that reducing bus fares to attract new riders would increase revenue. You conclude that
   a. your staff thinks that the demand for bus service is elastic, whereas the bus riders think that demand is inelastic.
   b. your staff thinks that the demand for bus service is inelastic, whereas the bus riders think that demand is elastic.
   c. both your staff and the bus riders think that the demand for bus service is elastic.
   d. both your staff and the bus riders think that the demand for bus service is inelastic.
   e. both your staff and the bus riders think that the demand for bus service is unit-elastic.

9. Airlines know from experience that vacation travelers have an elastic demand for air travel, whereas business travelers have an inelastic demand for air travel. If an airline wants to increase its total revenue, it should
   a. decrease fares for both business and vacation travelers.
   b. increase fares for both business and vacation travelers.
   c. increase fares for business travelers and decrease fares for vacation travelers.
   d. decrease fares for business travelers and increase fares for vacation travelers.
   e. leave fares the same for both groups.

For questions 10 through 13, assume you are the owner of the only movie theater in a small town. From past experience, you have calculated that the price elasticity of demand for movie tickets varies with the age of the customer. At your current prices, senior citizens have a demand elasticity of 2.0, younger adults have a demand elasticity of 1.0, and teenagers have a demand elasticity of 0.5. You want to adjust your prices to increase your total revenue.

10. Should you change the ticket price for senior citizens to increase your revenues?
    a. No. You should leave the price where it is.
    b. Yes. You should increase the price for senior citizens.
    c. Yes. You should decrease the price for senior citizens.

11. Should you change the ticket price for younger adults to increase your revenues?
    a. No. You should leave the price where it is.
    b. Yes. You should increase the price for younger adults.
    c. Yes. You should decrease the price for younger adults.

12. Should you change the ticket price for teenagers to increase your revenues?
    a. No. You should leave the price where it is.
    b. Yes. You should increase the price for teenagers.
    c. Yes. You should decrease the price for teenagers.

13. Suppose you decided (correctly) to lower the ticket price for senior citizens. To get the most revenue from this set of customers, how far should you lower the ticket price?
    a. You should let the senior citizens in for free.
    b. You should charge only a very low price.
    c. You should keep cutting the price as long as each price cut increases ticket sales.
    d. You should keep cutting the price as long as demand is still elastic.

Section 3: Determinants of the Price Elasticity of Demand

1. List the three determinants of the price elasticity of demand.

   _____

   _____

   _____

2. A product with _____ (many, few) good substitutes would have a more elastic demand than a product with _____ (many, few) good substitutes.

3. The demand for new cars is likely to be _____ (more, less) elastic than the demand for new Chevrolet cars.

4. The demand for paperback novels is likely to be _____ (more, less) elastic than the demand for required college textbooks.

5. A product that takes a _____ (large, small) portion of a consumer's budget has a more elastic demand than a product that takes a _____ (large, small) portion.

6. The demand for European vacations is likely to be _____ (more, less) elastic than the demand for videocassette tapes.

7. When consumers have a _____ (long, short) time to react to price changes, demand is more elastic than when consumers have a _____ (long, short) period of time to react.

8. The price elasticity of demand for gasoline in the short run is substantially lower than the price elasticity of demand for gasoline in the long run. Explain why the elasticity values are different.

   _____

   _____

   _____

   _____

Section 4: Other Demand Elasticities

1. The _____ elasticity of demand measures how consumers adjust their purchases of a product when the price of a related product changes.

2. The _____ elasticity of demand measures how much demand for a product changes when consumers' incomes change.

3. If the cross-price elasticity of demand is positive, the two goods are _____ ; if the cross-price elasticity of demand is negative, the two goods are _____ .

4. _____ (Luxuries, Necessities) have a higher income elasticity of demand than do _____ (luxuries, necessities).

5. When the price of Kellogg's Corn Flakes increases 5 percent, the quantity demanded of Post Corn Flakes increases 20 percent. The cross-price elasticity of Post Corn Flakes with respect to Kellogg's Corn Flakes is _____ . These two products are _____ .

6. When the price of milk increases 4 percent, the quantity demanded of corn flakes decreases 2 percent. The cross-price elasticity of corn flakes with respect to the price of milk is _____ . These two products are _____ .

7. The income elasticity of demand is the percentage change in _____ divided by the percentage change in _____ . Economists classify goods whose income elasticity of demand is positive as _____ goods, and goods whose income elasticity of demand is negative as _____ goods.

8. Suppose that the demand for Mercedes-Benz automobiles goes up 15 percent when people's incomes go up 10 percent. The income elasticity of demand for Mercedes-Benz autos is _____ ; these autos are _____ (normal, inferior) goods.

9. Suppose that the demand for ten-year-old used cars goes down 10 percent when people's incomes go up 10 percent. The income elasticity of demand for these old used cars is _____ ; they are _____ (normal, inferior) goods.

10. The _____ elasticity of demand measures how consumers adjust their purchases of a product when the amount of advertising expenditures changes.

Section 5: Supply Elasticities

1. The price elasticity of supply is the percentage change in _____ divided by the percentage change in _____ . The price elasticity of supply depends primarily on the _____ producers have to vary their output in response to price changes.

2. a. Sketch a perfectly inelastic supply curve on graph a, a typical short-run supply curve on graph b, and a typical long-run supply curve on graph c. For prices P_1 and P_2, mark the quantities supplied on the graphs.

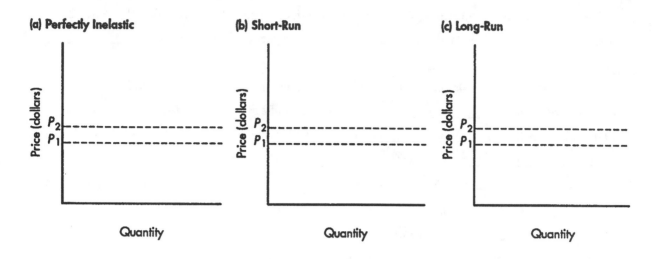

(a) Perfectly Inelastic   **(b) Short-Run**   **(c) Long-Run**

b. The smallest change occurred on graph _____ ; this is the _____ (most, least) elastic supply curve.

c. The largest change occurred on graph _____ ; this is the _____ (most, least) elastic supply curve.

3. Other things being equal, when demand is elastic and supply is inelastic, the incidence of a tax will fall more on _____ (consumers, businesses) and less on _____ (consumers, businesses).

4. Other things being equal, when demand is inelastic and supply is elastic, the incidence of a tax will fall more on _____ (consumers, businesses) and less on _____ (consumers, businesses).

Thinking About and Applying Elasticity: Demand and Supply

I. Elasticity and Bruce Springsteen

Great news! Bruce Springsteen is going to give a concert at the local convention center. The table below gives the demand for concert tickets.

Price per Ticket	Quantity Sold	Total Expenditure	Elasticity
$100	0	_____	
			_____
90	2,500	_____	
			_____
80	5,000	_____	
			_____
70	7,500	_____	
			_____
60	10,000	_____	
			_____
50	12,500	_____	
			_____
40	15,000	_____	
			_____
30	17,500	_____	
			_____
20	20,000	_____	
			_____
10	22,500	_____	
			_____
0	25,000	_____	

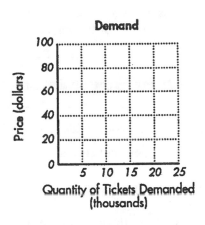

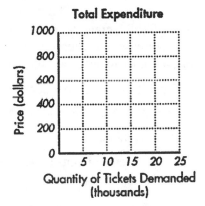

1. Calculate the total expenditure ($P \times Q$) at each ticket price and the demand elasticity for each of the price changes listed, and insert the amounts in the table. Then, draw the demand curve and the total expenditure curve on the appropriate graphs, and mark the segments of the demand curve that are elastic, inelastic, and unit-elastic.

2. The convention center has asked you to organize the concert. Under the agreement, you can keep all the profits for yourself. Renting the convention center will cost you $5,000, you must pay Bruce Springsteen $100,000 for the concert, and you have $35,000 in miscellaneous expenses. The convention center seats 22,500 customers.

    a. Your total costs are _____ .

    b. The price you should charge per ticket to get the maximum profit (total revenue minus all costs) is _____ .

    c. At this price, you will sell _____ tickets.

    d. Your profit would be _____ .

3. Would your ticket price be any different if you had to pay Bruce $200,000? Explain your answer.

_____

_____

_____

_____

4. Assuming you have to pay Bruce $100,000, is there anything you could do to increase your total revenues and profits even more?

_____

_____

_____

5. Suppose you decide to sell 2,500 seats at each of the prices listed between $90 and $10, with the

   seats getting better as the price goes up. If you sell all the seats, you will take in _____ .

II. Taxing Tobacco

According to the law of demand, taxes that increase the price of a product are expected (*ceteris paribus*) to reduce consumption of the product. In 1988, California increased its cigarette tax by $.25 a pack; by the middle of 1989, cigarette purchases in California had declined by 10 percent. For simplicity, assume that all of this decrease was caused by the price of cigarettes increasing $.25 as a result of the tax increase. Use this information to answer the following questions.

1. Cigarettes cost $1 per pack before the tax increase, and $1.25 after. The demand elasticity for

   cigarettes over this price range is _____ . Demand for this product is _____

   (elastic, inelastic).

2. Use the determinants of demand elasticity discussed in Section 3 of the chapter to explain why you would expect the demand for cigarettes to be inelastic.

   _____

   _____

3. One billion (1,000,000,000) packs of cigarettes were sold in California before the tax increase. After

   the tax went into effect, _____ packs were sold, and the state earned _____ in tax

   revenue.

4. What do you think will happen if California raises the tax on cigarettes by $.25 *every year* from now until the year 2000? Will California's tax revenue from the cigarette tax keep increasing the whole time?

   _____

   _____

   _____

III. Price Discrimination in Airline Fares

Recently, the *Wall Street Journal* published an article about one airline's 35 percent fare cuts for summer travel. The article described several restrictions:

Travel must begin on or after May 27 and be completed by September 15.
The nonrefundable tickets require 14-day advance purchase.
Travelers must stay at their destination over a Saturday night.

   People taking a plane trip for a vacation usually can plan their trip far in advance and don't mind spending a weekend at their vacation destination. Business travelers, on the other hand, frequently have to travel without much advance notice and want to be back home on weekends.

1. The main customers for the discounted tickets will be _____ (business, vacation) travelers.

2. Does the airline think the demand for airline tickets for vacation travel is elastic, inelastic, or

   unit-elastic? Explain your answer.

   _____

   _____

   _____

3. On the basis of the restrictions it sets and the effects of those restrictions on business and vacation

   travelers, the airline must think that _____ (business, vacation) travelers have a higher

   price elasticity of demand.

Chapter 6 (*Economics* Chapter 20)   Homework Problems

Name _____

1. Write the formula for the price elasticity of demand.

2. When demand is elastic, increasing the price _____ (increases, decreases) total revenue.

    When demand is inelastic, increasing the price _____ (increases, decreases) total revenue.

3. What three factors determine how elastic the demand for a product is?

4. Your friend Randy Cheapskate attended a Brice Wintersteen concert in another city. Randy was absolutely amazed that the concert hadn't sold out. "Those promoters sure were dumb! If they had any business sense at all, they would have charged less for the tickets, and more people would have come," says Randy. "They could have sold out."

    Were the promoters dumb, or could there be a sound business reason for setting the price of the tickets so high that they would not sell out? (*Hint:* The "Elasticity and Bruce Springsteen" problem in the Thinking About and Applying Elasticity section may give you some clues.)

5. Auld Lang Syne University is the only four-year college in a five-hundred-square-mile area. The university estimates its price elasticity of demand to be .85. Officials at ALSU are concerned about a recent proposal to eliminate some forms of federal aid to its students. For most of ALSU's students, the proposals would have the effect of raising their tuition by 2 percent.

   a. The price elasticity of demand for an education at this university is _____ (elastic, unit-elastic, inelastic). Why do you think education at this university is characterized by this type of elasticity?

   b. If the proposal to eliminate some forms of federal aid to ALSU's students goes into effect, the university can expect the number of students to _____ (increase, not change, decrease) by _____ percent.

   c. If the proposal went into effect, ALSU's revenues would _____ (increase, decrease, not change). If ASLU needs more revenue to offset increasing costs, it should _____ (increase, not change, decrease) its tuition if the proposal goes into effect.

   d. How would your answers to b and c change if ALSU's demand were elastic?

If your instructor assigns these problems, write your answers above, then tear out this page and hand it in.

Answers

Quick-Check Quiz

Section 1: The Price Elasticity of Demand

1. d; 2. a; 3. c; 4. a; 5. c; 6. b

If you missed any of these questions, you should go back and review Section 1 in Chapter 6 (*Economics,* Chapter 20).

Section 2: The Use of Price Elasticity of Demand

1. b; 2. a; 3. a; 4. b; 5. d; 6. d; 7. d

If you missed any of these questions, you should go back and review Section 2 in Chapter 6 (*Economics,* Chapter 20).

Section 3: Determinants of the Price Elasticity of Demand

1. c; 2. d; 3. a, 4. a

If you missed any of these questions, you should go back and review Section 3 in Chapter 6 (*Economics,* Chapter 20).

Section 4: Other Demand Elasticities

1. a; 2. a; 3. b; 4. c; 5. a

If you missed any of these questions, you should go back and review Section 4 in Chapter 6 (*Economics,* Chapter 20).

Section 5: Supply Elasticities

1. c; 2. a; 3. d; 4. a

If you missed any of these questions, you should go back and review Section 5 in Chapter 6 (*Economics,* Chapter 20).

Practice Questions and Problems

Section 1: The Price Elasticity of Demand

1. responsiveness; change
2. purchases; price
3. quantity demanded; price
4. inelastic
5. elastic
6. unit-elastic
7. perfectly elastic
8. perfectly inelastic
9. decreases

10. 2; elastic (Remember the equation for the price elasticity of demand:

$$e_d = \frac{|\text{percentage change in quantity demanded}|}{|\text{percentage change in price}|}$$

The change in quantity demanded is 10 percent, and the change in price is 5 percent, so $e_d = 10/5 = 2$. This is more than 1, so demand must be elastic.)

11. 0.5; inelastic (Refer to the equation for the price elasticity of demand above. In this problem, the change in quantity demanded is 3 percent, and the change in price is 6 percent, so $e_d = 3/6 = 0.5$. This is less than 1, so demand must be inelastic.)

12. 1; unit-elastic (Refer to the equation for the price elasticity of demand above. In this problem, the change in quantity demanded is 2 percent, and the change in price is 2 percent, so $e_d = 2/2 = 1$. Therefore, demand must be unit-elastic.)

13. 0; perfectly inelastic (Refer to the equation for the price elasticity of demand above. In this problem, the percentage change in quantity demanded is 0 percent, and the change in price is 5 percent, so $e_d = 0/5 = 0$. Therefore, demand must be perfectly inelastic.)

14.

Quantity Demanded	Change in Quantity Demanded	Price	Change in Price	Average Quantity $[(Q_1+Q_2)/2]$	Average Price $[(P_1+P_2)/2]$	Percent Change in Q	Percent Change in P	Elasticity
400		$100						
	100		$10	450	$95	.2222	.1053	2.11
500		90						
	100		10	550	85	.1818	.1176	1.55
600		80						
	100		10	650	75	.1538	.1333	1.15
700		70						
	100		10	750	65	.1333	.1538	0.87
800		60						

15. d (If you don't know how to do this problem, use the same process you went through in question 14 above. If you chose answer a, b, or e, you didn't remember to use the *average* quantity and *average* price. Reread Section 1.d in Chapter 6 [*Economics,* Chapter 20]; and then try it again. If you chose answer c, you had the equation upside down: the percentage change in *quantity* is on top, and the percentage change in *price* is on the bottom. Reread Section 1.d in Chapter 6 [*Economics,* Chapter 20], and then try it again.)

16. a (If you don't know how to do this problem, use the same process you went through in question 14 above. If you chose answer b, you had the equation upside down: the percentage change in *quantity* is on top, and the percentage change in *price* is on the bottom. Reread Section 1.d in Chapter 6 [*Economics,* Chapter 20], and then try it again. If you chose answer c, d, or e, you didn't remember to use the *average* quantity and *average* price. Reread Section 1.d in Chapter 6 [*Economics,* Chapter 20], and then try it again.)

Section 2: The Use of Price Elasticity of Demand

1. price; quantity sold
2. a. quantity; price
   b. increases

3. a. price; quantity
    b. decreases

4.

Demand Elasticity	Price Change	Effect on Total Revenue (Increase, Decrease, Unchanged)
Elastic	Increase	Decrease
Elastic	Decrease	Increase
Inelastic	Increase	Increase
Inelastic	Decrease	Decrease
Unit-elastic	Increase	Unchanged
Unit-elastic	Decrease	Unchanged

5. a (Decreasing the price increases total revenue. Because price and revenue move in opposite directions, the quantity change must be larger than the price change, so demand must be elastic.)
6. b (Decreasing the price decreases total revenue. Because price and revenue move in the same direction, the price change must be larger than the quantity change, so demand must be inelastic.)
7. c (If total revenue is unchanged, the percentage change in quantity must be the same size as the percentage change in price, so the price elasticity of demand must be 1, or unit-elastic.)
8. b (Your staff thinks that increasing the price will increase total revenue; this will happen only if demand is inelastic. The bus riders think that decreasing the price will increase total revenue; this will happen only if demand is elastic.)
9. c (When demand is elastic [vacationers], reducing the price increases total revenue. When demand is inelastic [business travelers], increasing the price increases total revenue.)
10. c (Senior citizens have an elastic demand [$e_d = 2.0$, which is greater than 1], so decreasing the price increases total revenue.)
11. a (With unit-elastic demand, total revenue is as high as possible.)
12. b (Teenagers have an inelastic demand [$e_d = 0.5$, which is less than 1], so increasing the price increases total revenue.)
13. d (As price decreases, demand usually becomes less elastic. As long as the senior citizens' demand is still elastic, decreases in price will increase total revenue. When demand becomes unit-elastic, you have reached the maximum total revenue and shouldn't reduce price any further. [See Figure 2 in the text for further help.] Answer a can't be correct. If tickets are free, total revenue from senior citizens will be zero. Answer b isn't likely to be correct. If the ticket price is very low, demand is probably inelastic, and you should raise the price some to increase total revenue. Answer c isn't correct. Even when prices are very low, a further cut usually increases sales. But because demand is usually inelastic at low prices, further price cuts would reduce total revenue.)

Section 3: Determinants of the Price Elasticity of Demand

1. existence of substitutes
    importance of the product in the consumer's total budget
    the time period under consideration
2. many; few
3. less (For most people, there are many good substitutes for Chevrolets: Fords, Plymouths, Toyotas, Volkswagens, and so on. The demand for a particular brand of a product is usually more elastic than the demand for the product itself.)
4. more (There are few, if any, good substitutes for required texts, but many other forms of literature, and entertainment in general, are available as substitutes for paperback novels.)
5. large; small

6. more (Videocassettes are relatively inexpensive; for most of us, a European vacation would take a large share of our budgets.)
7. long; short
8. It is difficult to change gasoline consumption in a short period of time. The number of miles you drive depends on where you live relative to where you must go to attend class, work, and shop, and the miles per gallon depend on your car's efficiency. None of these factors is easy to change quickly. Over a longer period, you can take gasoline prices into account when deciding where to live and work and what kind of car to buy.

Section 4: Other Demand Elasticities

1. cross-price
2. income
3. substitutes; complements
4. Luxuries; necessities
5. +4; substitutes (Cross-price elasticity is the percentage change in the quantity demanded of one good divided by the percentage change in the price of another good. The quantity demanded of Post Corn Flakes increases 20 percent when the price of Kellogg's Corn Flakes increases by 5 percent, so the cross-price elasticity is +20%/+5% = +4. Because Post's quantity increases when Kellogg's price increases, the two goods are substitutes: people will switch from Kellogg's to Post's when the price of Kellogg's goes up.)
6. –0.5; complements (The cross-price elasticity is –2%/+4% = –0.5. Milk and corn flakes are complements [most people put milk on their corn flakes], so an increase in the price of milk makes corn flakes with milk more expensive, reducing the amount of corn flakes bought.)
7. demand; income; normal; inferior
8. +1.5; normal (The income elasticity of demand is +15%/+10% = +1.5. Because demand increases when income increases, the income elasticity of demand is positive [greater than zero], so Mercedes-Benz autos are normal goods.)
9. –1; inferior (The income elasticity of demand is –10%/+10% = –1. Because demand decreases when income increases, the income elasticity of demand is negative [less than zero], so ten-year-old used cars are inferior goods. If you could afford it, wouldn't you buy a Mercedes rather than an old used car? The higher your income, the more likely you are to buy a Mercedes and the less likely you are to buy an old used car.)
10. advertising

Section 5: Supply Elasticities

1. quantity supplied; price; length of time
2. a.

(a) Perfectly Inelastic

(b) Short-Run

(c) Long-Run

    b. a; least

    c. c; most

3. businesses; consumers
4. consumers; businesses

Thinking About and Applying Elasticity: Demand and Supply

I. *Elasticity and Bruce Springsteen*

1. If you had problems with the graphs or the calculations, refer to Section 1.d, "Average or Arc Elasticity," in Chapter 6 (*Economics,* Chapter 20).

Price per Ticket	Quantity Sold	Total Expenditure	Elasticity
$100	0	$ 0	
			18.99
90	2,500	225,000	
			5.67
80	5,000	400,000	
			3.00
70	7,500	525,000	
			1.86
60	10,000	600,000	
			1.22
50	12,500	625,000	
			0.82
40	15,000	600,000	
			0.54
30	17,500	525,000	
			0.33
20	20,000	400,000	
			0.18
10	22,500	225,000	
			0.05
0	25,000	0	

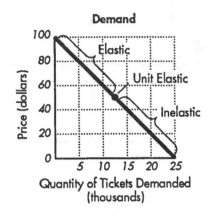

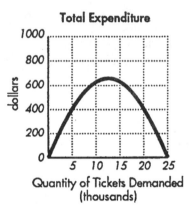

2. a. $150,000 ($10,000 for donation, $5,000 for rent, $100,000 for Bruce, $35,000 for miscellaneous expenses)
    b. $50 (None of the costs will change with the number of tickets sold, so your problem is simple: you want to set the ticket price where it will give you the maximum total revenue. Of course, you could find that price by looking at the total expenditure figures; you also could find it by looking at the elasticities. If demand is elastic [as it is for all prices above $50], you know that lowering the price will increase total revenue. If demand is inelastic [as it is for all prices below $50], you know that raising the price will increase total revenue. At the price where demand is unit-elastic, total revenue is at its maximum.)
    c. 12,500
    d. $475,000 ($625,000 revenue minus $150,000 costs)
3. No. Whatever your costs, $50 is still the price that gives you the maximum revenue and profit. Your profit, of course, would be lower (only $375,000) if you had to pay Bruce $200,000 rather than $100,000.

4. You could try price discrimination. If you raise the price of the seats closest to the stage, the people willing to pay $90 might buy them at those prices; if you set a low price for seats farther away, people who wouldn't pay $50 for a seat might come if the price was, say, $30.

5. $1,125,000.

Each set of 2,500 seats will be a separate set of consumers, and each set of consumers will have its own separate price. The calculation looks like this:

Price per Seat	Quantity Sold at That Price	Revenue from Those Seats
$90	2,500	$ 225,000
80	2,500	200,000
70	2,500	175,000
60	2,500	150,000
50	2,500	125,000
40	2,500	100,000
30	2,500	75,000
20	2,500	50,000
10	2,500	25,000
	Total revenue =	$1,125,000

Whenever market conditions allow price discrimination to be used, you can increase total revenue by discriminating.

II. Taxing Tobacco

1. 0.45 (If cigarette prices increased from $1 to $1.25 per pack, this would be about a 22 percent increase relative to the average price. Because the quantity demanded decreased only 10 percent when the price increased 22 percent, the price elasticity of demand for cigarettes is $10\%/22\% = 0.45$. Remember that this calculation isn't exactly accurate. The 10 percent decrease in quantity probably was determined relative to the starting quantity rather than the average quantity.); inelastic (Because the price elasticity of demand is less than 1, demand is inelastic.)

2. To people who smoke cigarettes, there are few, if any, good substitutes; many cigarette smokers consider cigarettes a necessity.

3. 900,000,000 (a 10 percent decrease from 1 billion); $225,000,000 (900,000,000 packs × $.25)

4. Each tax increase will be reflected in an increase in the price paid by buyers. As the price paid increases, demand usually becomes more elastic. At high enough prices (and taxes) demand will become elastic; further tax increases beyond that point will decrease sales enough that tax revenues eventually will begin to fall.

III. Price Discrimination in Airline Fares

1. vacation (Vacation travelers don't mind the restrictions of 14-day advance purchase and a Saturday stayover, but many business travelers do.)

2. elastic (The airline reduced the price for vacation travelers, so it must think demand is elastic, that a price cut would increase revenues.)

3. vacation (If the airline thought that business travelers had a higher price elasticity of demand, it would have cut the price of their tickets.)

CONSUMER CHOICE

FUNDAMENTAL QUESTIONS

1. How do consumers allocate their limited incomes among the billions of goods and services that exist?

   When you walk into a mall, you don't just go into the first store and spend all your money on the first thing you see. You shop around and buy the things that give you the most value for your money. You probably don't think about it in these terms, but what you're doing is maximizing your utility by following the **equimarginal principle:** allocating your limited dollars among goods and services in such a way that the marginal utilities per dollar of expenditure on the last unit of each good purchased will be as nearly equal as possible.

   This really is just common sense. If 7UP® has a marginal utility of 20 per $1 and Pepsi® has a marginal utility of 10 per $1, 7UP is a better buy. If you were buying Pepsi now, you'd get more utility by switching to 7UP. The only time you can't get more utility by switching products is when the marginal utilities per dollar are the same.

2. Why does the demand curve slope down?

   The **income effect** and the **substitution effect** explain why the demand curve slopes down, that is, why people want to buy more of a product when its price goes down, and less when the price goes up.

   For example, Jan really likes strawberries: last week, when the price was $4 a pint, she bought five pints, spending a total of $20 on strawberries last week. This week, the price of strawberries dropped to $2 a pint, Jan could still buy five pints. But now the five pints cost her only $10 instead of $20—she has an extra $10 to spend this week, even if she buys exactly the same things she bought last week. Jan will probably spend some of that extra $10 on strawberries. This is the **income effect.**

   If Jan gets 40 units of utility from the last pint of strawberries (the fifth pint) she bought last week when the price was $4, her *MU* per $1 for strawberries was 10 (40 units divided by the $4 price). When the price dropped to $2 a pint, her *MU* per $1 went up to 20 units per dollar, making strawberries a relatively better buy this week than last week. According to the **equimarginal principle,** Jan will buy more strawberries, since their *MU* per $1 went up, and less of some other product whose *MU* per $1 stayed the same. This is the **substitutuion effect.**

3. What is consumer surplus?

   Buyers frequently get more value from buying a product than the amount they have to pay for the product; the difference is called **consumer surplus.** For example, Jonathan thinks that seeing the new *Star Wars* movie is worth $12 to him—he will pay to see the movie as long as the price isn't

145

more than $12. If the price is actually $7, Jonathan gets something he values at $12 for a price of only $7. Jonathan got $5 of consumer surplus: the difference between the $12 value and the $7 price.

Key Terms

utility
diminishing marginal utility
marginal utility

disutility
total utility
equimarginal principle

consumer equilibrium
consumer surplus

Quick-Check Quiz

Section 1: Decisions

1. When economists use the term *utility,* they are talking about
   a. the usefulness of a good in everyday life (shovels have utility, but diamond rings don't).
   b. a measure of the satisfaction received from owning or consuming goods and services.
   c. a business that sells electricity or natural gas.
   d. the satisfaction received from a good minus the price of the good.
   e. the satisfaction received from a good plus the price of the good.

2. Total utility measures the
   a. total satisfaction derived from consuming a good or service divided by the price of the good or service.
   b. extra utility derived from consuming one more unit of a good or service.
   c. total satisfaction derived from consuming a quantity of a good or service.
   d. extra utility derived from consuming one more unit of a good or service divided by the price of the good or service.
   e. total satisfaction derived from consuming a good or service multiplied by the price of the good or service.

3. Marginal utility measures the
   a. total satisfaction derived from consuming a good or service divided by the price of the good or service.
   b. extra utility derived from consuming one more unit of a good or service.
   c. total satisfaction derived from consuming a quantity of a good or service.
   d. extra utility derived from consuming one more unit of a good or service divided by the price of the good or service.
   e. total satisfaction derived from consuming a good or service multiplied by the price of the good or service.

4. As a consumer eats additional pieces of pie today, total utility
   a. always keeps increasing.
   b. always keeps decreasing.
   c. keeps increasing until dissatisfaction sets in.
   d. keeps decreasing until dissatisfaction sets in.
   e. decreases until just before dissatisfaction sets in and then increases.

5. When marginal utility is zero, total utility is
   a. increasing.
   b. decreasing.
   c. at its maximum.
   d. at its minimum.
   e. zero.

6. According to the principle of diminishing marginal utility,
   a. total utility declines with each additional unit of a good or service that the consumer obtains.
   b. marginal utility declines with each additional unit of a good or service that the consumer obtains.
   c. total utility always grows with each additional unit of a good or service that the consumer obtains.
   d. marginal utility always grows with each additional unit of a good or service that the consumer obtains.
   e. marginal utility always remains constant.

Section 2: Utility and Choice

1. To decide which of two goods is the better buy, a consumer should compare the products'
   a. marginal utilities.
   b. total utilities.
   c. marginal utilities per dollar.
   d. total utilities per dollar.
   e. disutility.

2. Jennifer is trying to decide whether to buy a croissant or a bran muffin for tomorrow's breakfast. The croissant costs $2 and has a marginal utility of 30. The muffin costs $1 and has a marginal utility of 20. Which should she buy?
   a. the croissant because it has a higher marginal utility
   b. the croissant because it has a lower marginal utility per dollar
   c. the muffin because it costs less
   d. the muffin because it has a higher marginal utility per dollar
   e. It doesn't matter because the croissant and the muffin have the same value to her.

3. Consumer equilibrium occurs when
   a. consumers have lots of money to spend.
   b. the marginal utilities per dollar obtained from the last unit of all products consumed are the same.
   c. consumers buy all goods that have a positive marginal utility.
   d. consumers buy all goods that have a positive total utility.
   e. consumers buy all goods that do not give disutility.

4. When consumers are in equilibrium,
   a. they do not reallocate income.
   b. they should buy more of all products.
   c. they should buy more of some products and less of other products.
   d. the total utility obtained from all products consumed is the same.
   e. they should buy less of all products.

Section 3: The Demand Curve Again

1. The relation between the price of a product and the quantity demanded is
   a. inverse.
   b. direct.
   c. reverse.
   d. complex.
   e. positive.

2. When the price of strawberries increases, the
   a. marginal utility of strawberries decreases.
   b. marginal utility of strawberries increases.
   c. marginal utility per dollar of strawberries decreases.
   d. marginal utility per dollar of strawberries increases.
   e. total utility of strawberries increases.

3. When a good becomes less expensive, it yields more satisfaction per dollar, so consumers buy more of it and less of other goods. This is called the _____ effect of a price change.
   a. substitution
   b. income
   c. replacement
   d. augmentation
   e. disbursement

4. When a good becomes less expensive, consumers' real incomes increase and consumers purchase more of all goods. This is called the _____ effect of a price change.
   a. substitution
   b. income
   c. replacement
   d. augmentation
   e. disbursement

5. Consumer surplus is
   a. marginal utility divided by the price of a good.
   b. the difference between what a consumer is willing to pay and the market price of a good.
   c. a consumer's unspent income.
   d. a consumer's total spending on a good.
   e. the difference between the total utility and the marginal utility of a good.

6. The market demand curve is obtained by _____ individual demand curves.
   a. summing
   b. multiplying
   c. dividing
   d. subtracting
   e. finding the ratios of

7. Which of the following is *not* held constant in determining the market demand for a good?
   a. individual consumers' incomes
   b. the number of consumers
   c. the prices of other goods
   d. the time period under consideration
   e. All of the above are held constant in determining the market demand for a good.

Practice Questions and Problems

Section 1: Decisions

1. _____ (Total, Marginal) utility is the overall satisfaction that a consumer obtains from consuming a quantity of some good or service, whereas _____ (total, marginal) utility is the extra utility derived from consuming one more unit of a good or service.

2. According to the principle of _____ , marginal utility declines with each additional unit of a good or service.

3. Total utility increases until _____ sets in.

4. The total utility of a good is at its maximum when marginal utility is _____ .

5. Josephine gets 30 utils of satisfaction from eating three slices of cake in a day, and she gets 35 utils of satisfaction from eating four slices. Her marginal utility for the fourth slice of cake is _____ utils.

6. Napoleon gets 20 utils of satisfaction from eating three slices of bread in a day, and he gets four additional utils of satisfaction from eating a fourth slice. His total utility for four slices of bread is _____ utils.

The table below shows Napoleon's total utility from eating slices of bread. Use the table to answer questions 7 through 9.

Slices of Bread per Day	Total Utility	Marginal Utility
1	4	_____
2	14	_____
3	20	_____
4	24	_____
5	24	_____
6	21	_____

7. Fill in the blanks in the table with Napoleon's marginal utility from eating slices of bread.

8. Plot Napoleon's total and marginal utility from slices of bread on the graphs below.

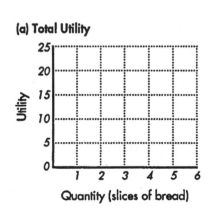

(a) Total Utility

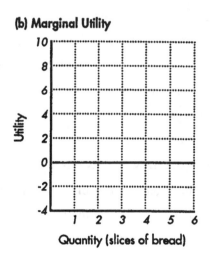

(b) Marginal Utility

9. Explain how the principle of diminishing marginal utility applies to Napoleon's consumption of bread in a day.

_____

_____

_____

_____

_____

The table below shows Josephine's total and marginal utility from eating slices of cake. Use the table to answer questions 10 through 14.

Slices of Cake per Day	Marginal Utility	Total Utility
1	20	20
2	25	45
3	18	63
4	_____	75
5	7	_____
6	3	85
7	0	85
8	−4	81

10. Use your knowledge of the relationship between total and marginal utility to fill in the blanks in the table.

11. With the _____ slice of cake, Josephine encounters diminishing marginal utility.

12. Josephine gets disutility from the _____ slice of cake.

13. If Josephine could get all the cake she wanted for free, the largest number of slices of cake she would choose to eat in a day is _____ .

14. Can you think of any circumstances in which Josephine would voluntarily choose to eat eight slices of cake in a day?

_____

_____

_____

Section 2: Utility and Choice

1. Stephanie is sitting in the cafeteria after lunch thinking about having some more cake for dessert. Cake costs $.25 a slice. To maximize her total utility, Stephanie should keep on buying more cake as long as her marginal utility from another slice of cake is greater than
   a. zero.
   b. or equal to zero.
   c. the marginal utility of anything else she could buy.
   d. the marginal utility of anything else she could buy for $.25.

STOP HERE! If you didn't choose answer d, go back and review Section 2 of the chapter before you go on.

2. The equimarginal principle says, "In order to maximize utility, consumers must allocate their limited incomes among goods and services in such a way that the _____ per _____ of

expenditure on the _____ unit of each good _____ will be as nearly _____ as possible."

3. The point at which the marginal utilities per dollar of expenditure on the last unit of each good purchased are equal is called _____ .

4. Consumers are in equilibrium when they have no _____ to _____ their limited budget or income.

5. For recreation, George likes to go to the video arcade and play: Golden Eye, Mortal Kombat, and Tomb Raider. Write the equation George should try to follow to make sure he gets the most utility from the money he spends on these video games _____ .

6. The table below gives George's marginal utilities for Golden Eye, Mortal Kombat, and Tomb Raider. Calculate the *MU/P* for each game, using the prices given.

Golden Eye (*P* = $.50)			Mortal Kombat (*P* = $2)			Tomb Raider (*P* = $1)		
Games per Day	*MU*	*MU/P*	Games per Day	*MU*	*MU/P*	Games per Day	*MU*	*MU/P*
1	55	_____	1	270	_____	1	120	_____
2	50	_____	2	240	_____	2	110	_____
3	47	_____	3	220	_____	3	100	_____
4	45	_____	4	200	_____	4	90	_____
5	40	_____	5	180	_____	5	72	_____
6	37	_____	6	160	_____	6	63	_____
7	34	_____	7	120	_____	7	54	_____
8	31	_____	8	80	_____	8	45	_____

7. One afternoon, George strolls into the video arcade with $5 in his pocket that he wants to spend on video games. To get the most utility for his money, George should play _____ first.

8. After he has played the first game of Mortal Kombat, George has _____ left.

9. After the first game of Mortal Kombat, George should play _____ and then _____ .

10. Can George play any more games? Explain your answer.

_____

_____

11. When George used up his $5, he had played two games of Mortal Kombat and one game of Tomb Raider. The *MU/P* for the second game of Mortal Kombat is _____ . The *MU/P* for the first game of Tomb Raider is _____ .

12. Because the *MU/P* is the same for both games, George must have attained _____ .

13. Suppose that some other afternoon George has $12 to spend in the arcade. Use the method shown in Table 2 in your text to fill in the table on page 154 and to determine which combination of games gives George the most utility for his $12.

14. When she studies, Ashley likes to munch on either corn chips or potato chips. Last month she bought 24 bags of corn chips and 20 bags of potato chips. For the amounts she bought last month, her current *MU* for corn chips would be 40 and her current *MU* for potato chips would be 50. If corn chips cost $1 per bag and potato chips cost $2 per bag, would Ashley be at consumer equilibrium if she purchased the same amounts this month as she did last month? Explain your answer.

_____

_____

15. a. To move toward consumer equilibrium while keeping her total spending on corn chips and potato chips the same, Ashley should buy _____ (fewer, more) corn chips and _____ (fewer, more) potato chips.

    b. Why?

_____

_____

Section 3: The Demand Curve Again

1. The demand curve shows that there is a(n) _____ (direct, inverse) relationship between the _____ of a product and the _____ .

2. The two economic principles that explain the inverse relationship between the price of a product and the quantity demanded are the principle of _____ and the _____ principle.

3. A change in the price of a product affects consumers in two ways: these are called the _____ effect and the _____ effect.

4. Sam usually buys lots of videotapes every month. If the price of videotapes drops this month, videotapes will give him _____ (more, less) satisfaction per dollar than before, so that relative to other goods he buys, he will buy _____ (more, fewer) videotapes than before and _____ (more, less) of some other things. This is known as the _____ effect of a price change.

5. When the price of videotapes drops this month, Sam can buy the same number of videotapes and everything else he bought last month with _____ (more, less, the same amount of) money than he spent last month. This change in his buying possibilities is known as the _____ effect of a price change.

6. The difference between what a consumer is willing and able to pay and the market price of a good is known as _____ .

Steps	Choices	Decision	Remaining Budget

7. Remember Ashley, who likes to munch corn chips or potato chips while she studies? (If you don't remember, review questions 14 and 15 in Section 2 above.) She's been studying consumer choice in her economics class and thinking about her spending choices. This month, she bought 28 bags of corn chips and 18 bags of potato chips. For the amounts she bought this month, her *MU* for corn chips was 30 and her *MU* for potato chips was 60. If corn chips cost $1 per bag and potato chips cost $2 per bag, is Ashley at consumer equilibrium now? Explain your answer.

   _____

   _____

8. This month Ashley is spending _____ on corn chips and potato chips.

9. When Ashley goes to the grocery store to buy next month's batch of chips, she finds that there's a sale on potato chips—they're only $1 a bag.

   a. With the sale, Ashley would spend _____ if she bought the same amounts of corn chips and potato chips as in question 7.

   b. If Ashley keeps spending $64 per month on chips, she can buy _____ (more, fewer) chips than before. This is an example of the _____ effect of a price change.

   c. If Ashley keeps buying 28 bags of corn chips and 18 bags of potato chips after the price of potato chips drops, is she still in consumer equilibrium? _____ Explain your answer.

   _____

   _____

   d. To move toward a new consumer equilibrium, should she buy more or fewer bags of potato chips? _____ Explain your answer.

   _____

   _____

   e. This change is an example of the _____ effect of a price change.

10. The table below gives Jim's demand for videotape rentals each week.

Price per Rental	Number of Rentals Each Week
$5	1
4	2
3	3
2	4
1	5

   a. If the only video store in town charges $3 per rental, Jim will rent _____ tapes each week.

   b. Jim will spend _____ on videotape rentals.

   c. Jim's consumer surplus will be _____ .

11. Suppose the video store raises its prices to $4 per rental but offers a special "three rentals for $11" bargain package rate. Jm _____ (would, would not) be willing to rent three tapes at the bargain rate. His consumer surplus now is _____ .

12. If you owned the video store and wanted people like Jim to rent three tapes a week, would you take in more money charging $3 per rental or charging the "three rentals for $11" package rate? Explain your answer.

    _____

    _____

13. On page 157 are the demand curves for Jill and Jack for Perrier bottled water. Plot their individual demand curves on the graphs; then calculate and plot their market demand curve.

| Price | Quantities Demanded by | | |
per Bottle	Jill	Jack	Market
$3.00	1	0	_____
2.50	2	0	_____
2.00	4	2	_____
1.50	6	4	_____
1.00	10	7	_____
.50	20	12	_____

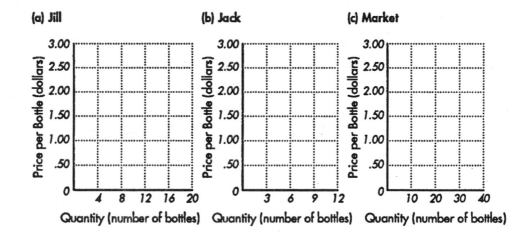

(a) Jill   (b) Jack   (c) Market

Thinking About and Applying Consumer Choice

I. The Demand for Video Games

1. Remember George, the guy in Section 2 who spends his afternoons at the video arcade? The table below repeats George's marginal utilities for Golden Eye, Mortal Kombat, and Tomb Raider. Calculate the *MU/P* for each game using the prices given.

Golden Eye (P = $.50)			Mortal Kombat (P = $2)			Tomb Raider (various prices)					
Games per Day	MU	MU/P	Games per Day	MU	MU/P	Games per Day	MU	MU/P (P = $2)	MU/P (P = $1.50)	MU/P (P = $1)	MU/P (P = $.50)
1	55	_____	1	270	_____	1	120	_____	_____	_____	_____
2	50	_____	2	240	_____	2	110	_____	_____	_____	_____
3	47	_____	3	220	_____	3	100	_____	_____	_____	_____
4	45	_____	4	200	_____	4	90	_____	_____	_____	_____
5	40	_____	5	180	_____	5	72	_____	_____	_____	_____
6	37	_____	6	160	_____	6	63	_____	_____	_____	_____
7	34	_____	7	120	_____	7	54	_____	_____	_____	_____
8	31	_____	8	80	_____	8	45	_____	_____	_____	_____

2. Before we do anything with these numbers, let's look at some of the patterns and relationships in the Tomb Raider section of the table.

a. As the price of Tomb Raider games decreases from $2 to $.50, the added satisfaction (marginal utility) George gets from any game of Tomb Raider _____ (does, does not) change.

b. As the price decreases, how does the added satisfaction *per dollar (MU/P)* change?

_____

c. The mathematical term for the relationship between the added satisfaction per dollar *(MU/P)* and the price is _____ .

d. If the price is cut in half (say, from $2 to $1, or from $1 to $.50), what happens to the *MU/P*?

_____

_____

3. One evening George strolls into the video arcade with $16 to spend on video games. Using the prices of Golden Eye and Mortal Kombat given, figure out the number of games of Golden Eye, Mortal Kombat, and Tomb Raider George should play to reach consumer equilibrium for each of the prices for Tomb Raider.

Price of Tomb Raider	Games of Golden Eye	Games of Mortal Kombat	Games of Tomb Raider
$2.00	_____	_____	_____
1.50	_____	_____	_____
1.00	_____	_____	_____
.50	_____	_____	_____

4. Draw George's demand curve for Tomb Raider on the graph.

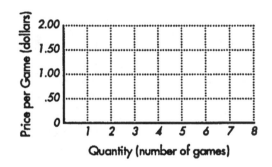

5. Use the income and substitution effects to explain why George plays more games of Tomb Raider when the price of Tomb Raider goes down.

_____

_____

_____

6. Use the income and substitution effects to explain why George plays fewer games of Golden Eye and Mortal Kombat when the price of Tomb Raider goes down.

_____

_____

_____

II. Imports and Consumer Choices

Some people make the argument that U.S. consumers should "Buy American." One effect of that idea is that Congress sometimes decides to restrict imports. Let's look at what would happen to our friend George if Congress tried to discourage George from playing Tomb Raider.

1. Go back and look at your answers to question 3 on page 158. Calculate the total utility George gets from his $16 when the price of Tomb Raider is $1, and then calculate his total utility when the price of Tomb Raider is $.50. (*Hint:* Add up the *MU*s of the games he buys at each price. Don't add up the *MU/P* figures!)

   a. The total utility when Tomb Raider costs $1 per game is _____ units.

   b. The total utility when Tomb Raider costs $.50 per game is _____ units.

   c. In terms of total utility, George is better off when the price of Tomb Raider is _____

      ($1, $.50).

2. Let's suppose that George plays Tomb Raider on an imported machine with a price of $.50 per game; the Golden Eye and Mortal Kombat machines are American. Now suppose Congress decides to encourage George to play American video games by putting a tax of $.50 a game on Tomb Raider. This means that George must pay $1 per game to play Tomb Raider. What effect does this tax have on George?

   _____

   _____

III. Fried Chicken and Consumer Surplus

"Smilin' Sam's Home-Style Fried Chicken" restaurant make the best fried chicken in town—nobody makes it better. From experience and market research, Smilin' Sam knows that his average customer's demand looks like this:

Price per Piece of Fried Chicken	Quantity Demanded by Average Customer
$4.00	0
3.50	1
3.00	2
2.50	3
2.00	4
1.50	5
1.00	6
.00	6

1. Graph the demand curve for Sam's average customer.

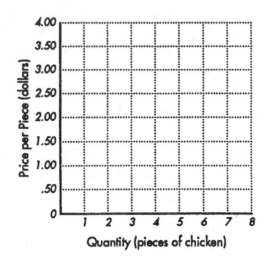

2. For the last year or so, Sam has been charging $2 per piece for his chicken. At this price the average

   customer buys _____ pieces of chicken and has a consumer surplus of _____ .

3. The average customer spends _____ on chicken at Sam's. If it costs Sam only $.50 to

   prepare a piece of chicken, Sam gets _____ in profit from the average customer. (As you'll

   find out in a few chapters, both costs and profits are really much more complicated than this, but we

   are keeping things simple for now.)

4. Sam and his wife have just decided that they really want a matched pair of Rolls-Royce limousines,
   but Sam has to find a way to make more money from the restaurant before they can buy them. Re-
   membering what he learned in his economics classes, Sam decides to raise his regular price to $3 per
   piece and offer a "four pieces for $10" special. Will Sam's average customer still buy four pieces of
   chicken? Explain your answer.

   _____

   _____

   _____

5. After the change from $2 per piece to the "four pieces for $10" special, Sam's average customer will

   have a consumer surplus of _____ . Compared with the situation in question 2, the surplus

   has dropped _____ . This means that at the special price, Sam will take in an additional

   _____ .

6. Sam is thinking about offering on "all you can eat" special. What is the most money Sam's average
   customer would be willing to spend for this special? Explain your answer.

   _____

   _____

7. If Sam offers an "all you can eat for $13" special, explain why he would make more profit than he did on the "four pieces for $10" special.

_____

_____

_____

_____

8. Most of his customers eat all their fried chicken at the restaurant now, but Sam lets people order more than they can eat for dinner and take the leftovers home to eat later. Explain why Sam needs to change this policy if he starts offering "all you can eat" specials.

_____

_____

_____

_____

Chapter 7 (*Economics* Chapter 21)   Homework Problems

Name _____

1. What is marginal utility? What happens to marginal utility as additional units of a good or service are consumed.

2. What is consumer surplus?

3. Write the formula that summarizes consumer equilibrium, or utility maximization.

4. Karla is a big fan of Bruce Springsteen. Use the income and substitution effects to explain why Karla buys more Springsteen CDs when the price of Springsteen CDs goes down.

5. Many people want to promote a better-quality environment, even if that means paying more for other goods and services. Surveys show that our willingness to pay more to protect the environment increased substantially between 1981 and 1990.

    Let's take a closer look at the idea of how we make tradeoffs between environmental quality and other things we want. Suppose that we lump together all the goods and services we want (except environmental quality) and call this lump "other things." We get utility from these other things, and we get utility from environmental quality; both of these are subject to the law of diminishing marginal utility. The table below has hypothetical marginal utilities for "other things" and for environmental quality in 1981 and 1990. We assume that units of "other things" and units of environmental quality both cost $5,000 each.

"Other Things" (P = $5,000)			Environmental Quality (P = $5,000)					
Units	MU	MU/P	Units	MU (1981)	MU/P (1981)	MU (1990)	MU/P (1990)
1	50,000	_____	1	30,000	_____	40,000	_____
2	45,000	_____	2	26,000	_____	35,000	_____
3	40,000	_____	3	22,000	_____	30,000	_____
4	35,000	_____	4	18,000	_____	26,000	_____
5	30,000	_____	5	15,000	_____	23,000	_____
6	25,000	_____	6	12,000	_____	21,000	_____

a. i. In the table, calculate the *MU/P* for "other things" and for environmental quality in 1981.

   ii. If this consumer has $30,000 to spend, her equilibrium consumption of "other things" is

   _____ units, and her equilibrium consumption of environmental quality is

   _____ units.

b. Surveys show that people in the United States think that the environment is in worse shape now than in the past. If so, people probably got more satisfaction (marginal utility) from additional units of environmental quality in 1990 than they did in 1981, as shown in the table.

   i. Calculate the *MU/P* for environmental quality in 1990.

   ii. Assuming the same $30,000 spending as in 1981, the consumer's 1990 consumer equilibrium is

   _____ units of "other things" and _____ units of environmental quality.

c. What can you conclude about how people's willingness to spend money on environmental

   improvements is affected by increases in the utility to them of a better environment?

   _____

   _____

   _____

   _____

This analysis applies to other cases where changes in tastes occur. If our tastes change so that we get more utility from potato chips, the marginal utility per dollar spent on potato chips will increase, leading us to increase our demand and buy more potato chips. On the other hand, if our tastes change so that we get less utility from videotape rentals, the marginal utility per dollar spent on videos will decrease, leading us to decrease our demand and rent fewer videos.

If your instructor assigns these problems, write your answers above, then tear out this page and hand it in.

Answers

Quick-Check Quiz

Section 1: Decisions

1. b; 2. c; 3. b; 4. c; 5. c; 6. b
If you missed any of these questions, you should go back and review Section 1 in Chapter 7 (*Economics,* Chapter 21).

Section 2: Utility and Choice

1. c; 2. d; 3. b; 4. a
If you missed any of these questions, you should go back and review Section 2 in Chapter 7 (*Economics,* Chapter 21).

Section 3: The Demand Curve Again

1. a; 2. c; 3. a; 4. b; 5. b; 6. a; 7. e
If you missed any of these questions, you should go back and review Section 3 in Chapter 7 (*Economics,* Chapter 21).

Practice Questions and Problems

Section 1: Decisions

1. Total; marginal
2. diminishing marginal utility
3. disutility
4. zero (Look at Figure 1 in the text for help.)
5. 5 (Total utility increases by 5 utils [from 30 to 35] after eating the fourth slice of cake.)
6. 24 (Eating three slices gives him 20 utils; he gets an additional 4 utils from the fourth slice, so his total utility for four slices is 20 + 4 = 24.)
7.

Slices of Bread per Day	Total Utility	Marginal Utility	Calculation
(0)	(0)	—	
1	4	4	Increased from 0 to 4; 4 − 0 = 4
2	14	10	Increased from 4 to 14; 14 − 4 = 10
3	20	6	Increased from 14 to 20; 20 − 14 = 6
4	24	4	Increased from 20 to 24; 24 − 20 = 4
5	24	0	Unchanged at 24; 24 − 24 = 0
6	21	−3	Decreased from 24 to 21; 21 − 24 = −3

8.

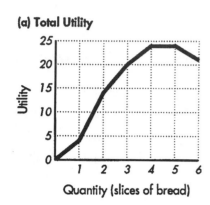

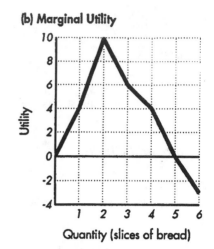

9. As Napoleon eats more and more bread, his marginal utility starts to fall. The third slice has a smaller *MU* (6) than the second slice (10); the fourth slice is even smaller (4); and the fifth slice adds no utility at all.

10. The marginal utility of the fourth slice of cake is the total utility of four slices (75) minus the total utility of three slices (63): 75 – 63 = 12. The total utility of five slices is the total utility of four slices (75) plus the marginal utility of the fifth slice (7): 75 + 7 = 82.

11. third (The second slice of cake's *MU* [25] is more than the first slice's *MU* [20], so marginal utility isn't diminishing yet. The third slice's *MU* [18] is lower than the second slice's, so marginal utility starts diminishing with the third slice. The eighth slice of cake is where *total* utility starts to diminish; this is where marginal utility becomes negative. *Marginal* utility can be diminishing while total utility is still increasing, as long as marginal utility is more than zero. Look at slices 3 through 6: marginal utility is getting smaller, while total utility is increasing.)

12. eighth (The marginal utility of the eighth slice is negative: Josephine has less satisfaction after eating it than before. In other words, she is worse off.)

13. 6 or 7 (She doesn't get any satisfaction from the seventh slice, but she isn't any worse off either: it doesn't matter to her whether she has the seventh slice or not. She definitely wouldn't eat the eighth slice. She has more utility from seven slices because the *MU* of the eighth slice is negative.)

14. Someone would have to pay her enough money for eating the eighth slice of cake that the money (or what she could buy with it) would compensate for the loss of 4 units of satisfaction.

Section 2: Utility and Choice

1. d (One of the key ideas in consumer choice is that people have only a limited amount of money to spend, so they look at the value of any purchase *relative to* other possible purchases—that is, they compare the marginal utility per dollar of different purchases and buy those goods and services with the highest *MU* per dollar.)

2. marginal utility; dollar; last; purchased; equal

3. consumer equilibrium

4. incentive; reallocate

5. $$\frac{MU_{\text{Golden Eye}}}{P_{\text{Golden Eye}}} = \frac{MU_{\text{Mortal Kombat}}}{P_{\text{Mortal Kombat}}} = \frac{MU_{\text{Tomb Raider}}}{P_{\text{Tomb Raider}}}$$

6.

Golden Eye (P = $.50)			Mortal Kombat (P = $2)			Tomb Raider (P = $1)		
Games per Day	*MU*	*MU/P*	Games per Day	*MU*	*MU/P*	Games per Day	*MU*	*MU/P*
1	55	110	1	270	135	1	120	120
2	50	100	2	240	120	2	110	110
3	47	94	3	220	110	3	100	100
4	45	90	4	200	100	4	90	90
5	40	80	5	180	90	5	72	72
6	37	74	6	160	80	6	63	63
7	34	68	7	120	60	7	54	54
8	31	62	8	80	40	8	45	45

7. Mortal Kombat
8. $3
9. second game of Mortal Kombat; first game of Tomb Raider (Because they have the same *MU/P*, doesn't matter which George plays first.)
10. No. He's used all his money.
11. 120; 120
12. consumer equilibrium

13.

Steps	Choices			Decision	Remaining Budget
1st purchase	1st Golden Eye: 1st Mortal Kombat: 1st Tomb Raider:	$MU/P = 110$ $MU/P = 135$ $MU/P = 120$		Mortal Kombat	$12 − $2 = $10
2nd purchase	1st Golden Eye: 2nd Mortal Kombat: 1st Tomb Raider:	$MU/P = 110$ $MU/P = 120$ $MU/P = 120$		Mortal Kombat	$10 − $2 = $8
3rd purchase	1st Golden Eye: 3rd Mortal Kombat: 1st Tomb Raider:	$MU/P = 110$ $MU/P = 110$ $MU/P = 120$		Tomb Raider	$8 − $1 = $7
4th purchase	1st Golden Eye: 3rd Mortal Kombat: 2nd Tomb Raider:	$MU/P = 110$ $MU/P = 110$ $MU/P = 110$		Golden Eye	$7 − $.50 = $6.50
5th purchase	2nd Golden Eye: 3rd Mortal Kombat: 2nd Tomb Raider:	$MU/P = 100$ $MU/P = 110$ $MU/P = 110$		Mortal Kombat	$6.50 − $2 = $4.50
6th purchase	2nd Golden Eye: 4th Mortal Kombat: 2nd Tomb Raider:	$MU/P = 100$ $MU/P = 100$ $MU/P = 110$		Tomb Raider	$4.50 − $1 = $3.50
7th purchase	2nd Golden Eye: 4th Mortal Kombat: 3rd Tomb Raider:	$MU/P = 100$ $MU/P = 100$ $MU/P = 100$		Golden Eye	$3.50 − $.50 = $3
8th purchase	3rd Golden Eye: 4th Mortal Kombat: 3rd Tomb Raider:	$MU/P = 94$ $MU/P = 100$ $MU/P = 100$		Mortal Kombat	$3 − $2 = $1
9th purchase	3rd Golden Eye: 5th Mortal Kombat: 3rd Tomb Raider:	$MU/P = 94$ $MU/P = 90$ $MU/P = 100$		Tomb Raider	$1 − $1 = 0

14. No. The equimarginal principle says that the *MU/P* has to be equal, or almost equal, for Ashley to be at consumer equilibrium. Her *MU/P* for corn chips is 40/$1 = 40, and her *MU/P* for potato chips is 50/$2 = 25. Because 40 isn't equal to 25 (it's not even close), Ashley should reallocate her income.

15. a. more; fewer

b. At the amounts she bought last month, corn chips have a higher *MU/P* (40) than potato chips have (only 25). If Ashley spent $1 *less* on potato chips, she would have to give up 25 utils, but if she now spent $1 *more* on corn chips, she would get 40 utils from the additional corn chips. She would end up with 15 more utils of satisfaction for the same number of dollars. Whenever the *MU/P* for one product is higher than the *MU/P* for a different product, you can gain by spending less on the product with the lower *MU/P* and more on the product with the higher *MU/P*.

Section 3: The Demand Curve Again

1. inverse; price; quantity demanded (If you aren't sure you understand about inverse and direct relationships, review the Appendix to Chapter 1, "Working with Graphs.")

2. diminishing marginal utility; equimarginal

3. substitution; income
4. more; more; less; substitution (If the price of videotapes decreases, the marginal utility of videotapes won't change, so the *MU/P* of videotapes must be higher than before; *per dollar spent* on videotapes, Sam now gets more utility. Videotapes are now a better buy than before, so Sam will reallocate some of his income, buying more videotapes and less of something else.)
5. less; income
6. consumer surplus
7. Yes. Her *MU/P*s for corn chips and potato chips are now equal: 30/$1 = 60/$2 = 30.
8. $64 ($28 for 28 bags of corn chips at $1 per bag and $36 for 18 bags of potato chips at $2)
9. a. $46 ($28 for the corn chips and $18 for the potato chips, now that they are both $1 per bag.)
   b. more; income
   c. No. The *MU/P* for corn chips is still 30/$1 = 30, but the *MU/P* for potato chips has increased to 60/$1 = 60. She still gets the same utility from potato chips, but she doesn't have to give up as many dollars to get it.
   d. More. Potato chips are a better buy since the price went down: Ashley gets more utils per dollar from potato chips than from corn chips. When Ashley starts buying more potato chips, the principle of diminishing marginal utility says that the *MU* of potato chips will fall. Eventually, the *MU* of potato chips will decrease enough so that the *MU/P* of potato chips will be equal to the *MU/P* of corn chips. At that point, Ashley will have reached consumer equilibrium again.
   e. substitution
10. a. three
    b. $9 ($3 each on 3 rentals: $3 × 3 = $9)
    c. $3 (His consumer surplus on the first rental is $2 [the $5 Jim would be willing to pay minus the $3 he actually paid], and his consumer surplus on the second rental is $1 [the $4 he would be willing to pay minus $3], so his total consumer surplus is $2 + $1 = $3.)
11. would; $1 (The value of the first, second, and third rental to Jim is $12 — $5 for the first, $4 for the second, and $3 for the third. Because he gets $12 worth of value from the $11 rental of three tapes, he would be willing to rent the tapes.)
12. "Three rentals for $11" package rate. You take in more money using the package rate for providing the same service. What you have really done is found a way to put some of the consumer surplus Jim got at the $3 per rental price into your bank account.
13.

Price per Bottle	Quantities Demanded by		
	Jill	**Jack**	**Market**
$3.00	1	0	1
2.50	2	0	2
2.00	4	2	6
1.50	6	4	10
1.00	10	7	17
.50	20	12	32

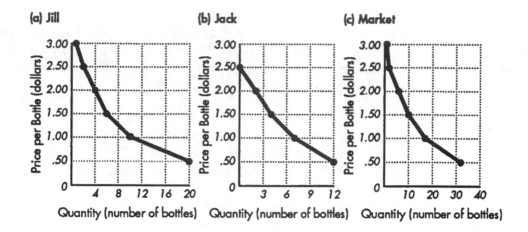

(a) Jill

(b) Jack

(c) Market

Thinking About and Applying Consumer Choice

I. The Demand for Video Games

1.

Golden Eye (P = $.50)			Mortal Kombat (P = $2)			Tomb Raider (various prices)					
Games per Day	*MU*	*MU/P*	Games per Day	*MU*	*MU/P*	Games per Day	*MU*	*MU/P* (P = $2)	*MU/P* (P = $1.50)	*MU/P* (P = $1)	*MU/P* (P = $.50)
1	55	110	1	270	135	1	120	60	80	120	240
2	50	100	2	240	120	2	110	55	73.3	110	220
3	47	94	3	220	110	3	100	50	66.7	100	200
4	45	90	4	200	100	4	90	45	60	90	180
5	40	80	5	180	90	5	72	36	48	72	144
6	37	74	6	160	80	6	63	31.5	42	63	126
7	34	68	7	120	60	7	54	27	36	54	108
8	31	62	8	80	40	8	45	22.5	30	45	90

2. a. does not
   b. Because the *MU* isn't changed by a change in price, the *MU/P* increases when the price decreases and the *MU/P* decreases when the price increases.
   c. inverse (Review the Appendix to Chapter 1 if you didn't get this right.)
   d. When the price is cut in half (divided by 2), the *MU/P* doubles (multiplied by 2). If the price was multiplied by 3, the *MU/P* would be divided by 3. The price and the *MU/P* are inversely proportional.

3.

Price of Tomb Raider	Games of Golden Eye	Games of Mortal Kombat	Games of Tomb Raider
$2.00	8	6	0
1.50	5	6	1
1.00	4	5	4
.50	4	5	8

4.

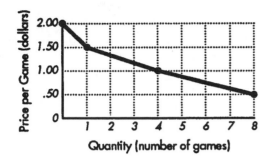

5. Income effect: When the price of Tomb Raider decreases, George can buy the same number of games of Tomb Raider (and other games) for less money. He has some money left that he can spend on more games of Tomb Raider.

   Substitution effect: When the price of Tomb Raider decreases, the *MU/P* increases, and Tomb Raider becomes a better buy than other games. George will reallocate his income to buy more games of Tomb Raider.

6. Income effect: When the price of Tomb Raider decreases, George can buy the same number of games of Golden Eye, Mortal Kombat, and Tomb Raider for less money—he has some money left that he can spend on more games of Golden Eye and Mortal Kombat. Because he ended up buying fewer games of Golden Eye and Mortal Kombat, the income effect didn't have much effect in this case.

   Substitution effect: When the price of Tomb Raider decreases, its *MU/P* increases, and Tomb Raider becomes a better buy than Golden Eye and Mortal Kombat. George will reallocate his income to buy more games of Tomb Raider and fewer games of Golden Eye and Mortal Kombat.

II. *Imports and Consumer Choices*

1. a. 1,727 (197 units for the four games of Golden Eye [55 + 50 + 47 + 45], plus 1,110 for the five games of Mortal Kombat [270 + 240 + 220 + 200 + 180], plus 420 for the four games of Tomb Raider [120 + 110 + 100 + 90])

   b. 1,961 (197 units for the four games of Golden Eye [55 + 50 + 47 + 45], plus 1,110 for the five games of Mortal Kombat [270 + 240 + 220 + 200 + 180], plus 654 for the eight games of Tomb Raider [120 + 110 + 100 + 90 + 72 + 63 + 54 + 45])

   c. George gets more utility when the price is $.50. This shouldn't surprise you—when the price of something is lower, you can buy more.

2. George reduces his purchases of Tomb Raider from eight games to four games, losing 234 units of utility. In this case, George doesn't end up buying any more games of either Golden Eye or Mortal Kombat, so the tax doesn't increase the demand for those games.

III. *Fried Chicken and Consumer Surplus*

1.

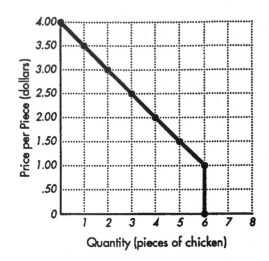

2. four; $3 (At $2 per piece, Sam's customer gets a consumer surplus of $1.50 on the first piece [$3.50 – $2.00], plus $1.00 on the second piece [$3.00 – $2.00], plus $.50 on the third piece [$2.50 – $2.00], for a total consumer surplus of $1.50 + $1.00 + $.50 = $3.00.)

3. $8; $6 (Sam's income per customer is $8 [$2 per piece times four pieces], and his costs are $2 [$.50 per piece times four pieces], giving him a profit [income minus costs] of $6.)

4. Yes. The four pieces of chicken are worth $11 to Sam's customers ($3.50 + $3.00 + $2.50 + $2.00), so they would be willing to pay $10 for four pieces.

5. $1 (The customer would be willing to pay $11 [$3.50 + $3.00 + $2.50 + $2.00], for the four pieces of chicken, but only has to pay $10, leaving a consumer surplus of $1.); $2 (In question 2, the consumer surplus was $3, so it dropped by $2. In fact, it dropped from the consumer into Sam's wallet); $2

6. $13.50 (The maximum amount is the sum of the prices the customer is willing to pay for each of the six pieces the customer is willing to buy: $3.50 + $3.00 + $2.50 + $2.00 + $1.50 + $1.00 = $13.50.)

7. Sam's average customer would eat six pieces of chicken instead of four and would pay $13 instead of $10. Sam takes in an additional $3 in income and only has an additional $1 in costs (2 more pieces times $.50 cost per piece), so Sam ends up with an additional $2 in profit. Remember the discussion of Disneyland's pricing in the text? Disneyland's pricing system is about the same as Sam's "all you can eat for $13" special.

8. The principle of diminishing marginal utility explains why Sam's average customers won't eat more than six pieces of fried chicken for a meal: after six pieces, they're completely full of chicken, and their marginal utility from more has diminished so much that it is negative. After they've had time to digest the chicken and get hungry again, they'll be happy to eat more of Sam's delicious chicken. If Sam lets his customers take home chicken to eat later, the principle of diminishing marginal utility won't apply in the same way. There's still a limit to how much free fried chicken someone would eat in a year, but it's a lot more than 6 pieces.

INDIFFERENCE ANALYSIS

Summary

Indifference analysis is an alternative, graphical way of looking at how consumers make choices and reach consumer equilibrium. Instead of looking at tables of marginal utilities, we look at **indifference curves,** each of which represents all combinations of two goods that give a consumer equal satisfaction. Because the consumer gets the same utility from any combination on the curve, the consumer is **indifferent** (doesn't care) about which combination is chosen. There are different indifference curves for different amounts of satisfaction. The complete set of all indifference curves is called the **indifference map.**

Instead of calculating the marginal utility per dollar (*MU/P*) to find consumer equilibrium, indifference analysis uses a **budget line** that is derived from the prices of the two goods and the amount of income the consumer has to spend on those goods. Together, the budget line and the indifference map determine consumer equilibrium. The consumer gets the most satisfaction from the available income at the point where an indifference curve just touches, or is tangent to, the budget line.

Key Terms

indifferent	indifference map
indifference curve	budget line

Practice Questions and Problems

1. Indifference curves show all combinations of _____ goods that give the consumer the same level of _____ .

2. An indifference _____ is a complete set of indifference curves. It fills up the _____ quadrant of a graph.

3. The budget line shows the combinations of two goods that a consumer is _____ .

4. Referring to the budget line and indifference curves, where does consumer equilibrium occur?

   _____

   _____

5. At point _____ on the indifference map below, the consumer has the most utility; at point _____ , the least utility.

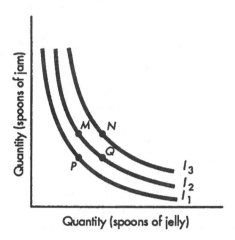

6. Let's use our friend George (Remember George? He plays video games at the arcade.) to explore indifference analysis. This time, we'll make George's problem simpler. The Mortal Kombat game is broken, so he only wants to play Golden Eye or Tomb Raider. Let's suppose that George has $6 to spend on video games and that both Golden Eye and Tomb Raider each cost $2 today.

a. If George spends all his money on Golden Eye, he can play _____ games today.

b. If George spends all his money on Tomb Raider he can play _____ games today.

c. You just figured out the two endpoints on George's budget line. Plot the two endpoints on the graph below. Label the one with only games of Golden Eye as point *A* and the one with only games of Tomb Raider as point *B*. Connect points *A* and *B* with a straight line (use a ruler or straightedge). This is George's budget line.

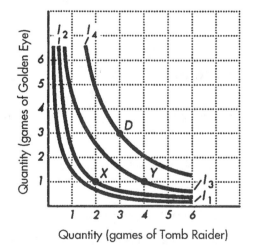

d. A combination of _____ game(s) of Golden Eye and _____ game(s) of Tomb Raider gives George the highest utility for his $6. Mark this combination on the graph as point *C*.

e. Why doesn't George choose the combination shown at point *D*?

_____

_____

_____

7. Suppose the price of Tomb Raider is only $1 per game instead of $2 per game.

a. Draw George's new budget line on the graph below.

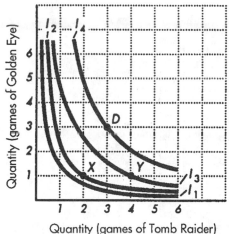

b. Now a combination of _____ game(s) of Golden Eye and _____ game(s) of Tomb Raider give George the highest utility for his $6.

8. You just figured out two points on George's demand curve for Tomb Raider. Plot these two points on the graph below.

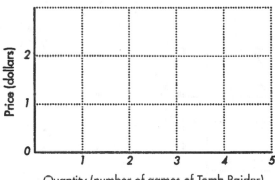

Answers

1. two; total utility
2. map; positive
3. able to buy
4. at the point where an indifference curve is just touching the budget line
5. *N; P*
6. a. Three (George has $6 to spend. If Golden Eye costs $2 per game, he can only buy $6/$2 = 3 games.)
   b. Three
   c.

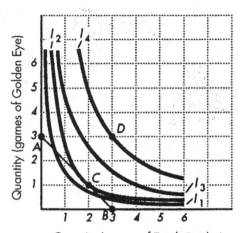

   d. one; two (This is the point where George's budget line is just touching an indifference curve.)
   e. At $2 per game for Golden Eye and Tomb Raider, it would cost George $12 to play three games of Golden Eye and three games of Tomb Raider; he has only $6 to spend. Before he can reach point *D*, he has to get more money or the prices of Golden Eye and Tomb Raider have to come down.
7. a.

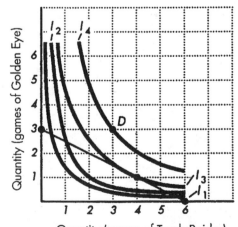

b. one; four

8.

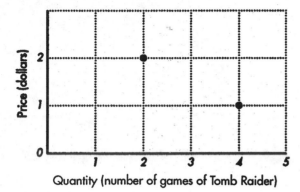

Quantity (number of games of Tomb Raider)

SUPPLY: THE COSTS OF DOING BUSINESS

FUNDAMENTAL QUESTIONS

1. What is the law of diminishing marginal returns?

    The **law of diminishing marginal returns** is a description of the relationship between the amount of resources used in production and the amount of output produced when the amount of some resources cannot be changed (the short run). For example, the law describes how many hamburgers Joe's Gourmet Burger Stand can produce with different numbers of workers when the size of the hamburger grill stays the same.

    Starting with only one worker, as Joe adds more workers, the total number of hamburgers that can be produced (the **total physical product,** or **TPP**) goes up, as each worker adds more output (the **marginal physical product,** or **MPP**) to the total. With only one worker, total output (TPP) is pretty low: Joe's has a big grill, and one worker can't flip burgers fast enough to use all of it. As Joe adds more workers, for a while both total output (TPP) and the output added by each additional worker (MPP) increase because the additional workers make more efficient use of the grill. Eventually, though, there are so many workers that the area around the grill gets crowded and workers start to get in one another's way. At this point, the MPP starts going down. Each additional worker adds smaller numbers of hamburgers to the total product. Even though adding one more worker still increases TPP, the MPP declines.

    The law of diminishing marginal returns says that all short-run production processes in the world work the same way Joe's Gourmet Burger Stand does: as you add more and more workers (variable resources) to use the grill (a fixed resource), eventually the workers' MPP starts to get smaller. More formally, the law of diminishing returns states that when successive equal amounts of a variable resource are combined with a fixed amount of another resource, there is a point beyond which the extra or marginal product that can be attributed to each additional unit of the variable resource declines.

2. What is the relationship between costs and output in the short run?

    Average- and marginal-cost curves are usually U-shaped: they start out at relatively high values, decrease for a while as output increases, reach a minimum, and eventually begin increasing as output continues to increase. Short-run average-cost curves are U-shaped because of the law of diminishing marginal returns. In the case of Joe's Gourmet Burger Stand, the size of the hamburger grill is fixed. If Joe produces only a few hamburgers, Joe's workers can't make efficient use of the grill: it's too big for just a few people to use all of it. These one or two workers have to spend much of their time running from one end of the grill to another to flip all the burgers, not to mention having to run around putting lettuce, tomato, and all of Joe's special ingredients on the burgers.

Hiring more people lets Joe increase the number of hamburgers produced at a lower cost per burger. Some people can stand in one place at the grill flipping burgers while others work at putting the burgers together; in this way, both sets of workers work more efficiently, lowering the costs. As Joe keeps increasing the number of workers so he can produce more burgers, eventually the workers start to get in one another's way, fighting to use the grill or trying to find a place to put together more burgers. Some of their time is spent waiting to use the fixed resource, which reduces their efficiency and increases the costs per burger.

3. What is the relationship between costs and output in the long run?

In the short run, Joe can't do anything to increase the size of his grill to let his many workers be more efficient. Although he could buy a larger grill in the long run, his cost curves still could be U-shaped because of **economies of scale** and **diseconomies of scale.** Small businesses often are less efficient and have higher average costs than larger businesses. Some businesses get so big that they can't be managed efficiently, and their average costs are higher than those of businesses that aren't quite so large.

Key Terms

total physical product (*TPP*)
law of diminishing marginal
    returns
average physical product (*APP*)
marginal physical product
    (*MPP*)
average total costs (*ATC*)
marginal costs (*MC*)

total fixed costs (*TFC*)
total variable costs (*TVC*)
total costs (*TC*)
average fixed costs (*AFC*)
average variable costs (*AVC*)
short-run average total cost
    (*SRATC*)

long-run average total cost
    (*LRATC*)
scale
economies of scale
diseconomies of scale
constant returns to scale
minimum efficient scale (*MES*)

Quick-Check Quiz

Section 1: Firms and Production

1. The term economists use to refer to all types of businesses is
    a. *sole proprietorship.*
    b. *partnership.*
    c. *firm.*
    d. *corporation.*
    e. *entrepreneurship.*

2. The total physical product (*TPP*) is the
    a. maximum output that can be produced when successive units of a variable resource are added to fixed amounts of other resources.
    b. additional quantity that is produced when one additional unit of a resource is used in combination with the same quantities of all other resources.
    c. least-cost combination of resources that can produce a specified level of output.
    d. output per unit of resource.
    e. value of the output that can be produced from a combination of resources.

3. The marginal physical product (*MPP*) is the
    a. maximum output that can be produced when successive units of a variable resource are added to fixed amounts of other resources.
    b. additional quantity that is produced when one additional unit of a resource is used in combination with the same quantities of all other resources.
    c. least-cost combination of resources that can produce a specified level of output.
    d. output per unit of resource.
    e. value of the output that can be produced from a combination of inputs.

4. The average physical product (*APP*) is the
    a. maximum output that can be produced when successive units of a variable resource are added to fixed amounts of other resources.
    b. additional quantity that is produced when one additional unit of a resource is used in combination with the same quantities of all other resources.
    c. least-cost combination of resources that can produce a specified level of output.
    d. output per unit of resource.
    e. value of the output that can be produced from a combination of resources.

5. The law of diminishing returns says that when successive equal amounts of
    a. a fixed resource are combined with a given amount of a variable resource, the *MPP* of the fixed resource eventually will decline.
    b. a variable resource are combined with a fixed amount of another resource, the *MPP* of the variable resource eventually will decline.
    c. a good are consumed, the marginal utility of the good eventually will decline.
    d. a good are consumed, the *MPP* of the good eventually will decline.
    e. all resources are increased, eventually the units costs will begin to increase.

Section 2: From Production to Costs

1. Which pair of curves are mirror images of each other?
    a. marginal cost and average total cost
    b. marginal cost and marginal product
    c. average cost and marginal product
    d. total product and average product
    e. average product and total cost

2. Short-run cost curves are U-shaped because of
    a. economies and diseconomies of scales.
    b. the law of diminishing marginal utility.
    c. the law of diminishing marginal returns.
    d. taxes.
    e. constant returns to scale.

3. Which of these statements about marginal and average curves is true?
   a. When the marginal curve is above the average curve, the average curve is falling.
   b. When the marginal curve is equal to the average curve, the marginal curve is neither rising nor falling.
   c. When the marginal curve is below the average curve, the average curve is rising.
   d. When the average curve is below the marginal curve, the average curve is falling.
   e. When the marginal curve is above the average curve, the average curve is rising.

Section 3: Cost Schedules and Cost Curves

1. Total costs are the sum of
   a. average fixed and average variable costs.
   b. total fixed and total variable costs.
   c. total variable and marginal costs.
   d. average variable and marginal costs.
   e. total fixed and average marginal costs.

2. Fixed costs
   a. increase in proportion to output.
   b. are the sum of marginal and variable costs.
   c. fall as production falls.
   d. are the additional costs of producing one more unit of output.
   e. are costs that must be paid regardless of how much the firm produces.

3. The average-fixed-cost curve
   a. always decreases as output increases.
   b. always increases as output increases.
   c. first decreases, then reaches a minimum, and then increases as output increases.
   d. first increases, then reaches a maximum, and then decreases as output increases.
   e. is always a horizontal line.

4. The average-variable-cost curve
   a. always decreases as output increases.
   b. always increases as output increases.
   c. first decreases and then increases as output increases.
   d. first increases and then decreases as output increases.
   e. is always a horizontal line.

5. Average costs—average total, average fixed, and average variable—are derived by dividing the corresponding _____ costs by _____ .
   a. total; change in output
   b. change in total; change in output
   c. change in total; quantity of output
   d. marginal; quantity of output
   e. total; quantity of output

6. Which of the following statements is false?
   a. $ATC = AFC + AVC$
   b. MC crosses ATC at the low point on the ATC curve.
   c. MC crosses AVC at the low point on the AVC curve.
   d. ATC crosses AVC at the low point on the MC curve.
   e. $TC = TFC + TVC$

Section 4: The Long Run

1. The long-run average-total-cost curve is the
   a. lowest-cost combination of resources with which each level of output is produced when all resources are variable.
   b. lowest-cost combination of resources with which each level of output is produced when all resources are fixed.
   c. output level at which the cost per unit of output is the lowest.
   d. average of the explicit-cost curves.
   e. sum of the short-run average-cost curves.

2. Economies of scale exist
   a. when unit costs decrease as the quantity of production increases and all resources are variable.
   b. at the minimum point on the long-run average-cost curve.
   c. when unit costs increase as the quantity of production increases and all resources are variable.
   d. at the output level at which the cost per unit is the lowest.
   e. when unit costs remain constant as the quantity of production increases and all resources are variable.

3. Diseconomies of scale exist
   a. when unit costs decrease as the quantity of production increases and all resources are variable.
   b. at the minimum point on the long-run average-cost curve.
   c. when unit costs increase as the quantity of production increases and all resources are variable.
   d. at the output level at which the cost per unit is the lowest.
   e. when unit costs remain constant as the quantity of production increases and all resources are variable.

4. Constant returns to scale exist
   a. when unit costs decrease as the quantity of production increases and all resources are variable.
   b. at the minimum point on the long-run average-cost curve.
   c. when unit costs increase as the quantity of production increases and all resources are variable.
   d. at the output level at which the cost per unit is the lowest.
   e. when unit costs remain constant as the quantity of production increases and all resources are variable.

5. The minimum efficient scale is
   a. when unit costs decrease as the quantity of production increases and all resources are variable.
   b. the minimum point on the long-run average-cost curve.
   c. when unit costs increase as the quantity of production increases and all resources are variable.
   d. the output level at which the cost per unit is the lowest.
   e. both b and d above.

Practice Questions and Problems

Section 1: Firms and Production

1. Economists use the word _____ to refer to any of these three types of businesses: _____ , _____ , and _____ .

2. Fill in the blanks with the terms that match the definitions below.

   a. _____ : the additional quantity that is produced when one additional unit of a resource is used in combination with the same quantities of all other resources

   b. _____ : the maximum output that can be produced when successive units of a variable resource are added to fixed amounts of other resources

   c. _____ : the output per unit of resource

3. The _____ is a period just short enough that the quantity of at least one resource cannot be altered.

4. The law of diminishing marginal returns applies
   a. only in the immediate period.
   b. only in the short run.
   c. only in the long run.
   d. in both the short run and the long run, but not in the immediate period.
   e. in the immediate period, in the short run, and in the long run.

5. The table below gives the number of hamburgers produced per hour at Joe's Gourmet Burger Stand with different numbers of workers.

   a. Find the *TPP, MPP,* and *APP* at each number of workers. Then plot the *TPP* curve on graph a, and the *MPP* and *APP* curves on graph b.

Number of Workers	Number of Burgers	*TPP*	*MPP*	*APP*
1	5	_____	_____	_____
2	23	_____	_____	_____
3	50	_____	_____	_____
4	80	_____	_____	_____
5	100	_____	_____	_____
6	110	_____	_____	_____
7	110	_____	_____	_____
8	100	_____	_____	_____

(a) TPP

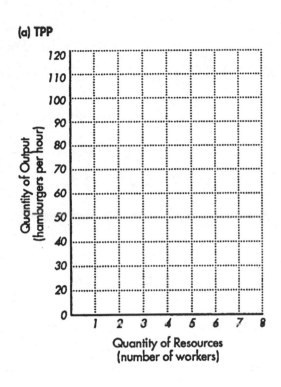

Quantity of Output (hamburgers per hour)

Quantity of Resources
(number of workers)

(b) MPP, APP

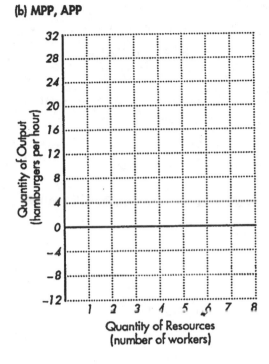

Quantity of Output (hamburgers per hour)

Quantity of Resources
(number of workers)

b. When *APP* equals *MPP*, *APP* is at its _____ value.

c. When *MPP* equals zero, *TPP* is at its _____ value.

6. Use the law of diminishing returns to explain why you can't grow enough wheat in a small flower pot to feed the entire world.

_____

_____

_____

_____

Section 2: From Production to Costs

1. Average total cost is the cost per unit of _____ .

2. Marginal cost is the _____ divided by the _____ .

3. Every firm will face a _____-shaped cost curve in the short run because of

___ _____ .

4. When a marginal curve is _____ an average curve, the average curve must be rising.

Section 3: Cost Schedules and Cost Curves

1. Total costs include both _____ and _____ costs.

2. *ATC* = _____ .

3. *MC* = _____ .

4. When the marginal value is below the average, the average _____ (falls, rises, stays the same). When the marginal value is above the average, the average _____ (falls, rises, stays the same).

5. The table below gives the short-run total costs of Joe's Gourmet Burger Stand for different amounts of output per minute.

Burgers	TC	TFC	TVC	AFC	AVC	ATC	MC
0	$ 5.50	$_____	$_____				
1	9.00	_____	_____	$_____	$_____	$_____	$_____
2	10.00	_____	_____	_____	_____	_____	_____
3	10.50	_____	_____	_____	_____	_____	_____
4	11.50	_____	_____	_____	_____	_____	_____
5	13.00	_____	_____	_____	_____	_____	_____
6	15.00	_____	_____	_____	_____	_____	_____
7	17.50	_____	_____	_____	_____	_____	_____
8	20.50	_____	_____	_____	_____	_____	_____
9	24.00	_____	_____	_____	_____	_____	_____
10	28.00	_____	_____	_____	_____	_____	_____

(a) Total Costs

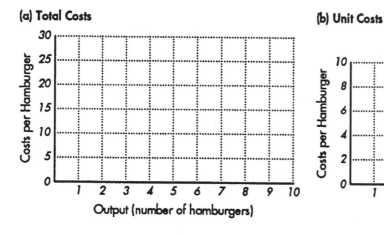

(b) Unit Costs

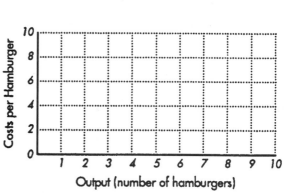

a. Joe's total fixed cost is _____ .

b. Fill in the columns in the table. Then plot the *TC, TFC,* and *TVC* curves on graph a and the *ATC, AVC, AFC,* and *MC* curves on graph b.

6. a. The *MC* curve crosses the *AVC* curve at _____ units.

   b. The *MC* curve crosses the *ATC* curve at _____ units.

7. Explain why the following curves are shaped the way they are.

   a. *AFC*

   _____

   _____

   _____

   _____

   b. *MC*

   _____

   _____

   _____

   _____

   c. *AVC*

   _____

   _____

   _____

   _____

   d. *ATC*

   _____

   _____

   _____

   _____

Section 4: The Long Run

1. Economies of scale result when increases in output lead to _____ in unit costs when all resources are _____ .

2. Diseconomies of scale result when increases in output lead to _____ in unit costs when all resources are _____ .

3. Constant returns to scale result when increases in output lead to _____ in unit costs when all resources are _____ .

4. The table below contains the short-run average total costs (*SRATC*) of Joe's Gourmet Burger Stand for four different sizes of stands.

Number of Burgers	Size #1 SRATC	Size #2 SRATC	Size #3 SRATC	Size #4 SRATC	LRATC
1	$3.45	$4.40	$6.00	$14.00	$_____
2	3.20	3.70	4.70	9.50	_____
3	3.00	3.20	4.10	6.90	_____
4	3.20	2.80	3.65	5.70	_____
5	3.50	2.50	3.30	5.10	_____
6	3.90	2.75	3.00	4.65	_____
7	4.40	3.00	2.75	4.30	_____
8	5.00	3.50	2.50	4.00	_____
9	5.70	4.00	3.00	3.50	_____
10	6.50	4.75	3.50	3.25	_____
11	8.00	5.75	4.00	3.50	_____
12	9.90	7.25	4.50	4.20	_____

a. Graph the four *SRATC* curves on the graph below.

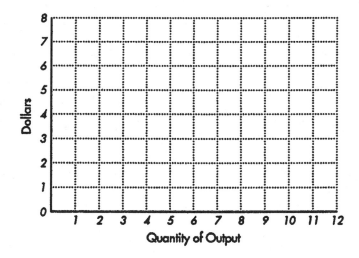

b. If we assume that these are the only possible sizes for Joe's stand, fill in the table for the long-run average-total-cost (*LRATC*) curve for Joe's Gourmet Burger and graph the *LRATC* curve. (*Hint*: If Joe wants to get the most profit for a particular level of output, what size stand should he choose for that output level?)

5. The graph below shows the long-run average-total-cost curve for Joe's Gourmet Burger Stand, taking into account *all* possible sizes for the burger stand. On the graph, which range of output levels shows

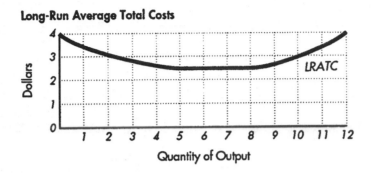

a. economies of scale? _____

b. constant returns to scale? _____

c. diseconomies of scale? _____

d. the minimum efficient scale is _____ burgers.

6. Give some reasons that might explain why Joe's Gourmet Burger Stand shows economies of scale at small levels of output.

_____

_____

_____

_____

7. Give some reasons that might explain why Joe's Gourmet Burger Stand shows diseconomies of scale at large levels of output.

_____

_____

_____

_____

Thinking About and Applying Supply: The Costs of Doing Business

I. The Relationship Between Product and Cost Curves

In Section 1 of the chapter, we looked at product curves: *TPP, MPP,* and *APP.* In Sections 2 and 3, we looked at cost curves: *ATC, AFC, AVC,* and *MC,* among others. The cost curves can be derived from the product curves if we know the prices of the resources used because the product curves tell us how many resources are needed to produce different amounts of output. The table below shows basically the same product curves for Joe's Gourmet Burger Stand that you calculated previously; also given are the wage Joe pays his workers and his fixed costs (to keep things simple, we've left out all other costs).

Wage = $10 per worker
Total fixed cost (TFC) = $500

Number of Workers	Number of Burgers	TPP	MPP	MC	APP	AVC	AFC	ATC
1	5	5	5	$2.00	5.00	$2.00	$100.00	$102.00
2	23	23	18	.56	11.50	.87	21.74	22.61
3	50	50	27	_____	16.67	_____	_____	_____
4	80	80	30	_____	20.00	_____	_____	_____
5	100	100	20	_____	20.00	_____	_____	_____
6	110	110	10	_____	18.33	_____	_____	_____
7	111	111	1	_____	15.86	_____	_____	_____

Let's look at the relationship between the product and cost curves. The *MPP* curve shows how many more burgers one more worker can produce: the marginal costs of each of those burgers are the added costs paid to the additional worker (the wage of $10) divided by the number of burgers that person produced. For example, hiring the first worker costs Joe an additional $10, and the worker produces 5 more burgers, so each of those 5 burgers adds $2 ($10/5 burgers) to Joe's costs. The second worker produces an additional 18 burgers for an additional cost of $10, so each of those burgers adds $.56 ($10/18) to Joe's costs.

The *AVC* curve is derived from the *APP* curve in a similar way. *APP* shows the average number of burgers produced per worker. Because we're assuming that labor is the only variable resource, the average variable cost is the labor cost per burger: the cost of an average worker (the wage) divided by the number of burgers produced by the average worker (*APP*). When Joe is hiring two workers, total output is 23 burgers, or 11.5 burgers per worker on average. Each worker costs Joe $10, so the *AVC* is $.87 per burger ($10/11.5 burgers) when two workers are used.

The *AFC* and *ATC* curves are calculated described as in Section 3: *AFC* = *TFC/Q* (*Q* is the number of burgers), and *ATC* = *AFC* + *AVC*.

1. Fill in the blanks in the table; then graph the product curves on graph a on the next page and the cost curves on graphs b and c. Be careful: graph b has the number of *workers* on the horizontal axis, and graph c has the number of *burgers* on the horizontal axis.

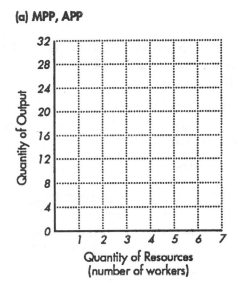

(a) MPP, APP

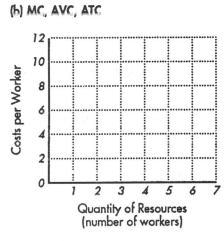

(h) MC, AVC, ATC

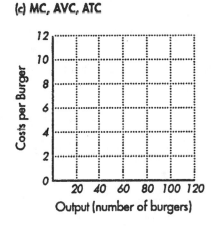

(c) MC, AVC, ATC

2. Looking at graphs a and b, what is the relationship between the maximum *MPP* and the minimum *MC*? Why do the curves have this relationship?

_____

_____

_____

_____

3. On graphs a and b, what is the relationship between the maximum *APP* and the minimum *AVC*? Why do the curves have this relationship?

_____

_____

_____

_____

II. Taxes and Production Costs

In the "Economically Speaking" section in this chapter, we saw that Raytheon Co. had been pressuring Massachusetts officials for tax breaks to reduce its operating costs. Let's look at the effects on Joe's Gourmet Burger Stand of two possible taxes.

1. Suppose that the state government decides to raise money for education by requiring Joe to pay a $.50 per hour tax on each hour that his employees work. What effect (increase, decrease, no effect) would this tax have on Joe's short-run *AFC, AVC, ATC,* and *MC* curves?

   a. *AFC* _____   c. *ATC* _____

   b. *AVC* _____   d. *MC* _____

2. Suppose that Joe's local government decides to raise money to hire more police by requiring Joe to pay a $500 tax every year for a license to operate the burger stand. What effect (increase, decrease, no effect) would this tax have on Joe's short-run *AFC, AVC, ATC,* and *MC* curves?

   a. *AFC* _____   c. *ATC* _____

   b. *AVC* _____   d. *MC* _____

III. The Costs of Driving

The excerpts below are from an article on the hidden costs of driving from a recent edition of the *Wichita Eagle:*

> Every time your odometer registers another mile, you've lost roughly half a dollar. . . . Calculations [are] based on operating costs for gasoline and oil, maintenance and tires, and ownership costs for insurance, license/registration/taxes, depreciation and finance charges.

   The article says that a mid-sized car costs $4,514 per year. Because people drive an average of 10,000 miles per year, that works out to about $.45 per mile.
   On the basis of this information and what you've learned in this chapter about fixed and variable costs, explain why it doesn't really cost you "roughly half a dollar" to drive another mile.

_____

_____

_____

_____

Chapter 8 (*Economics* Chapter 22)   Homework Problems

Name _____

1. What is the law of diminishing marginal returns?

2. What is the relationship between cost curves and their corresponding product curves?

3. Short-run cost curves owe their shape to _____ .
   Long-run cost curves owe their shape to _____ .

4. Write the formulas for *APP, MPP, TC, ATC, MC, AFC,* and *AVC.*

5. On the planet Lightover, Andrew Walkenow rents land on which he grows wheat. The table below shows the number of tons of wheat per year that can be produced with varying amounts of land. The planetary government is trying to encourage colonists, so it will provide everything that Andrew needs, like workers, equipment, seed, etc., for a flat fee of $500 per year. However, Andrew must agree to pay the $500 whether he farms the land or not and must also pay $5 a year for every acre of land that he rents. Fill in the table below. Be careful!

Acres of Land	Tons of Wheat	*MPP*	*TC*	*ATC*	*AVC*	*MC*	*AFC*
0	0	X		X	X	X	X
1	5	5					
2	15	10					
3	20	5					
4	23	3					
5	24	1					

a. Diminishing marginal returns set in with the _____ acre of land.

b. The average variable cost reaches its minimum somewhere between the _____ and _____ acre of land.

c. Why can't we see the spot where *MC* = *AVC* on the table?

If your instructor assigns these problems, write your answers above, then tear out this page and hand it in.

Answers

Quick-Check Quiz

Section 1: Firms and Production

1. c; 2. a; 3. b; 4. d; 5. b
If you missed any of these questions, you should go back and review section 1 in Chapter 8 (*Economics*, Chapter 22).

Section 2: From Production to Costs

1. b; 2. c; 3. e
If you missed any of these questions, you should go back and review Section 2 in Chapter 8 (*Economics*, Chapter 22).

Section 3: Cost Schedules and Cost Curves

1. b; 2. e; 3. a; 4. c; 5. e, 6. d
If you missed any of these questions, you should go back and review Section 3 in Chapter 8 (*Economics*, Chapter 22).

Section 4: The Long Run

1. a; 2. a; 3. c; 4. e; 5. e
If you missed any of these questions, you should go back and review Section 4 in Chapter 8 (*Economics*, Chapter 22).

Practice Questions and Problems

Section 1: Firms and Production

1. firm; sole proprietorships; partnerships; corporations
2. a. *Marginal physical product (MPP)*
   b. *Total physical product (TPP)*
   c. *Average physical product (APP)*
3. short run
4. b
5. a.

Number of Workers	Number of Burgers	TPP	MPP	APP
1	5	5	5	5.00
2	23	23	18	11.50
3	50	50	27	16.67
4	80	80	30	20.00
5	100	100	20	20.00
6	110	110	10	18.33
7	110	110	0	15.71
8	100	100	−10	12.50

TPP is the same as the number of burgers.
MPP is the change in *TPP* from using one more worker.
APP is *TPP* divided by the number of workers.

(a) TPP

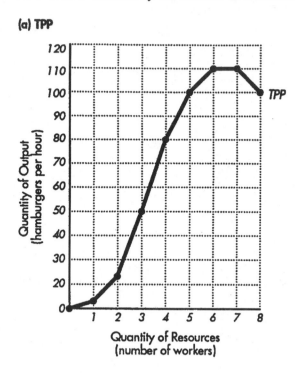

(b) MPP, APP

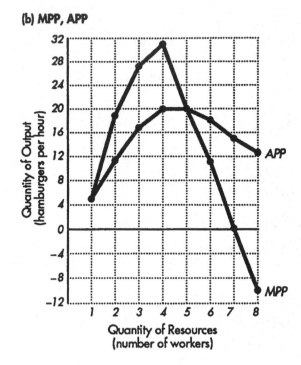

  b. highest
  c. highest

6. As you add more seed, fertilizer, and water (variable resources) to the dirt in the flower pot (the fixed resource), the added output gets smaller and smaller. Eventually the wheat is drowned or burned, and the *TPP* actually declines. The fixed resource, the space in which to grow wheat, limits the quantity of wheat that can be produced.

Section 2: From Production to Costs

1. output
2. change in total cost; change in output
3. U; the law of diminishing marginal returns
4. above

Section 3: Cost Schedules and Cost Curves

1. fixed; variable
2. *TC/Q* (total cost divided by output quantity)
3. change in *TC*/change in *Q*
4. falls; rises

5. a. $5.50 (The total cost of producing zero units of output is the fixed cost.)

b.

Burgers	TC	TFC	TVC	AFC	AVC	ATC	MC
0	$ 5.50	$5.50	$ 0				
1	9.00	5.50	3.50	$5.50	$3.50	$9.00	$3.50
2	10.00	5.50	4.50	2.75	2.25	5.00	1.00
3	10.50	5.50	5.00	1.83	1.67	3.50	.50
4	11.50	5.50	6.00	1.38	1.50	2.88	1.00
5	13.00	5.50	7.50	1.10	1.50	2.60	1.50
6	15.00	5.50	9.50	.92	1.58	2.50	2.00
7	17.50	5.50	12.00	.79	1.71	2.50	2.50
8	20.50	5.50	15.00	.69	1.88	2.56	3.00
9	24.00	5.50	18.50	.61	2.06	2.67	3.50
10	28.00	5.50	22.50	.55	2.25	2.80	4.00

TFC is always $5.50.
$TVC = TC - TFC$
$AFC = TFC/Q$
$AVC = TVC/Q$
$ATC = TC/Q = AFC + AVC$
$MC = $ change in TC/change in Q

(a) Total Costs

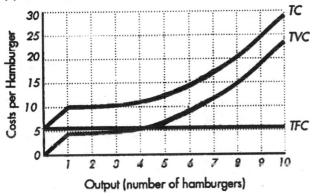

Output (number of hamburgers)

(b) Unit Costs

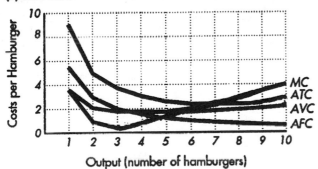

Output (number of hamburgers)

6. a. 5 (the low point on the AVC curve)
    b. 7 (the low point on the ATC curve)

7. a. *AFC* always decreases as *Q* increases because *TFC* is fixed: as *Q* increases, the same amount of costs is spread over more and more units of output.

   b. *MC* is U-shaped because in the short run some resource is fixed in amount. At very low amounts of output, there are not enough variable resources to use the fixed resource efficiently. As output increases, the fixed resource can be used more efficiently, so *MPP* increases and *MC* decreases. As you keep expanding output by adding more variable resources, eventually you are using so many variable resources that they cannot all use the fixed resource efficiently. *MPP* starts to fall, and *MC* increases.

      Look back at question 5 for Section 1. As Joe's Gourmet Burger Stand increased its output from zero, marginal physical product (added output per worker) increased at first. The second worker added more hamburgers (18) to the total than did the first worker (5): having 2 workers let both of them use Joe's grill more efficiently. Each worker is paid the same amount of money per hour, so the marginal cost of the second worker's hamburgers is lower than the marginal cost of the hamburgers produced by the first worker. If the workers are paid $5 each and labor is the only variable resource, the marginal cost of the 5 hamburgers produced by the first worker is $1 each ($5 for the worker divided by the 5 hamburgers produced). The marginal cost of the hamburgers produced by the second worker is only about $.28 ($5/18 burgers) because adding the second worker increased efficiency. As Joe adds more and more workers, the *MPP* eventually starts to decrease (the law of diminishing marginal returns), as each worker gets to use a smaller fraction of the grill. As *MPP* starts going down, *MC* increases.

   c. *AVC* is also U-shaped for similar reasons. At low levels of output, the average output per worker (*APP*) is low because there are not enough workers to use the fixed resources efficiently. As more variable resources are added and output increases, the fixed resource is used more efficiently, *APP* increases, and *AVC* decreases. Eventually there are more than enough variable resources, and output per worker starts to fall, causing *AVC* to increase.

      Looking at Joe's Gourmet Burger Stand again, when Joe is using 2 workers and producing 23 burgers, the average output per worker (*APP*) is 11.5. If each worker costs Joe $5, the labor cost per burger is about $.43 ($5 per worker/11.5 burgers per worker). If Joe hires 4 workers and produces 80 burgers, the *APP* is 20, so the labor cost per burger is only about $.25 ($5/20 burgers). If labor is the only variable resource, the labor cost per burger is the *AVC*.

   d. *ATC* is the sum of *AFC* and *AVC*. At low levels of output, both *AFC* and *AVC* are falling, so *ATC* also must be falling. As output expands, *AFC* keeps going down, but at a slower and slower rate, while *AVC* increases. Eventually the increase in *AVC* becomes larger than the fall in *AFC,* and *ATC* begins to increase.

      If you want further information on the shape of cost curves, review Sections 1.b and 3.b in the text, and the discussion of Fundamental Questions 1 and 3 above. Problem I in the section "Thinking About and Applying the Costs of Doing Business" also deals with the shape of cost curves and the relationship between cost and product curves.

Section 4: The Long Run

1. decreases; variable
2. increases; variable
3. no change; variable

4. a.

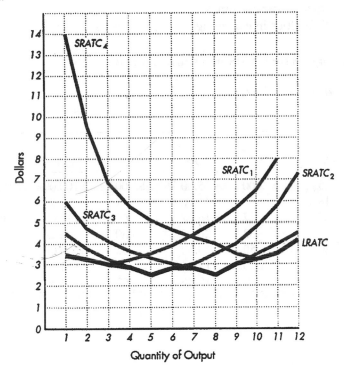

b.

Number of Burgers	Size #1 SRATC	Size #2 SRATC	Size #3 SRATC	Size #4 SRATC	LRATC	Stand Size
1	$3.45	$4.40	$6.00	$14.00	$3.45	#1
2	3.20	3.70	4.70	9.50	3.20	#1
3	3.00	3.20	4.10	6.90	3.00	#1
4	3.20	2.80	3.65	5.70	2.80	#2
5	3.50	2.50	3.30	5.10	2.50	#2
6	3.90	2.75	3.00	4.65	2.75	#2
7	4.40	3.00	2.75	4.30	2.75	#3
8	5.00	3.50	2.50	4.00	2.50	#3
9	5.70	4.00	3.00	3.50	3.00	#3
10	6.50	4.75	3.50	3.25	3.25	#4
11	8.00	5.75	4.00	3.50	3.50	#4
12	9.90	7.25	4.50	4.20	4.20	#4

In the long run, Joe can choose whatever size stand he wants, on the basis of the number of burgers he expects to be able to sell. For each output level from 1 burger through 12 burgers, Joe will choose the stand size with the lowest *SRATC*. The *SRATC* figures for the stands chosen make up the *LRATC* curve (also shown in Figure 8). The stands with the lowest *SRATC* are listed in the table above.

5. a. up to 5 burgers (where *LRATC* is falling)
   b. from 5 to 8 burgers (where *LRATC* is level)
   c. beyond 8 burgers (where *LRATC* is rising)
   d. 5 (the smallest output where *LRATC* is at its minimum value)

6. At small levels of output, there are not enough workers to take advantage of specialization, and small-scale machinery usually is less efficient than larger machines.
7. Diseconomies of scale can result from difficulties in managing large enterprises.

Thinking About and Applying Supply: The Costs of Doing Business

I. The Relationship Between Product and Cost Curves

1. _____

Number of Workers	Number of Burgers	TPP	MPP	MC	APP	AVC	AFC	ATC
1	5	5	5	$ 2.00	5.00	$2.00	$100.00	$102.00
2	23	23	18	.56	11.50	.87	21.74	22.61
3	50	50	27	.37	16.67	.60	10.00	10.60
4	80	80	30	.33	20.00	.50	6.25	6.75
5	100	100	20	.50	20.00	.50	5.00	5.50
6	110	110	10	1.00	18.33	.55	4.55	5.10
7	111	111	1	10.00	15.86	.63	4.50	5.13

(a) MPP, APP

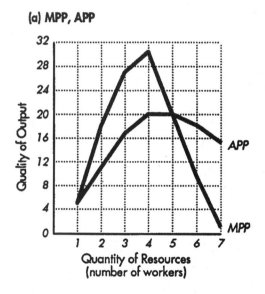

(b) MC, AVC, ATC

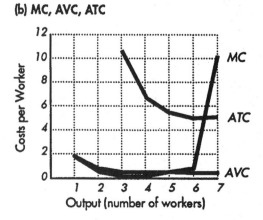

(c) MC, AVC, ATC

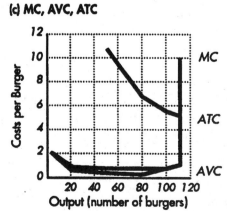

2. When *MPP* is at its highest value, *MC* is at its lowest value. The larger the additional output per worker (*MPP*), the more units of output the cost of that worker can be spread over, so each additional unit of output takes less labor time and cost.
3. When *APP* is at its highest value, *AVC* is at its lowest value. The larger the average output per worker (*APP*), the more units of output the cost of the average worker can be spread over, so each unit of output takes less labor time and cost.

II. *Taxes and Production Costs*

1. a. no effect
   b. increase
   c. increase
   d. increase

   The amount Joe will pay in tax depends on how many hours his employees work, so the tax is a variable cost. It would not affect the *AFC* curves, but it would affect all other short-run cost curves.
2. a. increase
   b. no effect
   c. increase
   d. no effect

   The amount Joe will pay doesn't vary with his output, so it is a fixed cost. The *AFC* curve is affected, and so is the *ATC* curve because average fixed costs are a part of average total costs.

III. *The Costs of Driving*

Many of the costs listed are not variable costs. Insurance, license and registration fees, taxes, finance charges, and most of depreciation are fixed costs: they don't increase when you drive another mile. As stated more accurately later in the article, the marginal cost of driving a mile in a mid-sized car is less than $.10, not $.45.

Sample Test I
Chapters 6–8
(*Economics* Chapters 20–22)

1. If the price elasticity of demand is equal to 2, a 1 percent increase in price will cause the quantity demanded to _____ from 200 units to _____ units.
   a. increase; 202
   b. decrease; 198
   c. increase; 400
   d. increase; 201
   e. decrease; 196

2. Suppose that 200 gallons of gasoline are demanded at a particular price. If the price drops by 1 percent, the quantity demanded of gasoline increases to 200.5 gallons. Which of the following statements is true?
   a. The elasticity of demand is equal to 0.5.
   b. Demand is elastic.
   c. Demand is inelastic.
   d. Demand is unit-elastic.
   e. Demand is perfectly inelastic.

3. Assume that the price elasticity of demand, $e_d = 0.30$. Given a 10 percent increase in price, there will occur a
   a. 30 percent increase in the quantity demanded.
   b. 3 percent decrease in the quantity demanded.
   c. 30 percent decrease in the quantity demanded.
   d. 0.3 percent decrease in the quantity demanded.
   e. 3 percent increase in the quantity demanded.

4. Julie buys one 24-ounce diet soft drink a day regardless of the price. Which of the following is true with respect to Julie's price elasticity of demand for diet soft drinks?
   a. It is equal to 0.
   b. It is equal to 1.
   c. She is very sensitive to price changes.
   d. It is infinitely elastic.
   e. It is unit-elastic.

5. When the fitness center increased its fees by 10 percent, the number of memberships it sold fell by 15 percent. This fitness center is faced with _____ demand.
   a. an inelastic
   b. an elastic
   c. a unit-elastic
   d. an infinitely elastic
   e. a perfectly elastic

6. Suppose that the price of product X increases from $10 to $20, and, in response, quantity demanded falls from 200 to 160. Using the midpoint or arc-elasticity formula, what is the price elasticity of demand?
   a. 0.33
   b. 0.5
   c. 0.67
   d. 2
   e. 3

7. If a popular nightclub has decided to increase beverage prices to pay for a new dance floor, we can conclude that the nightclub owners believe that
   a. the demand for beverages at the nightclub is elastic.
   b. total revenues will fall.
   c. the manager is ineffective.
   d. the absolute value of the coefficient of the elasticity of demand is greater than 1.
   e. the demand for beverages at the nightclub is inelastic.

8. When the cross-price elasticity of demand is a large negative number, this indicates that
   a. the goods are normal goods.
   b. the goods are inferior.
   c. the goods are substitutes.
   d. the goods are complements.
   e. total revenue will increase when the price increases.

9. Last year, Valerie purchased 20 pounds of chicken wings when her income was $20,000. This year, her income was $30,000, and she purchased 25 pounds. Based on this information, which of the following is most likely the case for Valerie?
   a. Her demand for chicken wings is price inelastic.
   b. Her demand for chicken wings is price elastic.
   c. Chicken wings and income are substitutes.
   d. Chicken wings are a normal good.
   e. Chicken wings are an inferior good.

10. What is most important in determining the prices that people are willing to pay for goods and services?
   a. the cost of producing the goods or services
   b. the total utility derived from the goods or services
   c. the marginal utility derived from the goods or services
   d. the availability of the goods or services
   e. the legality of the goods or services

11. Brenda says, "You would have to pay me to listen to an opera." We can assume that, for Brenda, the marginal utility of listening to opera is
    a. positive.
    b. positive, but decreasing.
    c. negative.
    d. constant, but positive.
    e. zero.

12. Total utility must decrease when marginal utility
    a. decreases.
    b. increases at a decreasing rate.
    c. cannot be determined.
    d. becomes negative.
    e. is positive.

13. Mary has $1.50 to spend at the concession stand. A muffin, a banana, and an apple cost $.75 each. If Mary's *MU/P* (ratio of marginal utility to price) of a muffin is 58, *MU/P* of a banana is 67, and *MU/P* of an apple is 49, she will purchase _____ first and _____ second.
    a. an apple; a muffin
    b. a banana; an apple
    c. an apple; a banana
    d. a banana; a muffin
    e. a muffin; a banana

14. Harry is purchasing peanuts and soft drinks at the football game, and he is in equilibrium. The prices of the last units of peanuts and soft drinks are $2 and $1 respectively. It can be concluded that Harry
    a. likes peanuts twice as much as soft drinks.
    b. liked the last unit of peanuts twice as much as the last unit of soft drink.
    c. likes soft drinks twice as much as peanuts.
    d. is purchasing two soft drinks for every bag of peanuts.
    e. is purchasing two bags of peanuts for every soft drink.

15. Assume that a consumer purchases a combination of products A and B and the $MU_A/P_A = 97$ and the $MU_B/P_B = 36$. To maximize utility without spending more dollars, this consumer should reallocate his budget to purchase
    a. more of both A and B.
    b. less of A only if the price of A increases.
    c. less of both A and B.
    d. more of B and less of A.
    e. more of A and less of B.

16. Suppose that Max is willing to pay $3.50 for his first order of tortilla chips and salsa, $2.50 for a second order of chips and salsa, and $1.50 for a third order of chips and salsa. If Max is able to purchase all three orders of chips and salsa for $1.50 each, he can realize a consumer surplus of
    a. $1.00.
    b. $1.50.
    c. $2.50.
    d. $3.00.
    e. $3.50.

Use the following figure to answer questions 17 and 18.

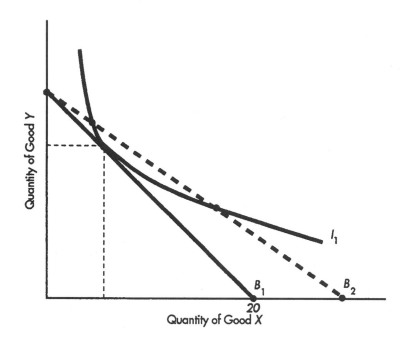

17. If the price of good X is $5 and the price of good Y is $4, what is the maximum quantity of Y that can be purchased?
    a. 25 units
    b. 20 units
    c. 100 units
    d. 4 units
    e. The maximum quantity is impossible to determine from the information given.

18. What could cause a shift from B_1 to B_2?
    a. This consumer's income has increased.
    b. The price of X has increased.
    c. The price of X has decreased.
    d. The price of Y has increased.
    e. The price of Y has decreased.

19. If an increase in the use of a variable resource increases the total product, what can be concluded about marginal physical product?
    a. It increases at an increasing rate.
    b. It increases at a decreasing rate.
    c. It is constant.
    d. It is positive.
    e. It is zero.

20. Assume that one laborer can produce 8 units of output, two laborers 19 units, three laborers 24 units, and four laborers 28 units. Diminishing returns set in when the firm hires the _____ worker.
    a. first
    b. second
    c. third
    d. fourth
    e. Diminishing returns do not set in.

21. Assume that one laborer can produce 8 units of output, two laborers 19 units, three laborers 24 units, and four laborers 28 units. If the cost is $20 per unit of labor and total costs for producing eight units are $360, what are total fixed costs?
    a. $20
    b. $160
    c. $340
    d. $45
    e. Total fixed costs cannot be determined from the information given.

22. If a firm has total revenues of $200,000, the owner's labor in the firm is valued at $30,000, and the firm has explicit costs of $70,000, then
    a. economic profit is $100,000.
    b. accounting profit is $100,000.
    c. economic loss is $30,000.
    d. accounting loss is $30,000.
    e. accounting costs are $100,000.

Use the following figure to answer questions 23 and 24.

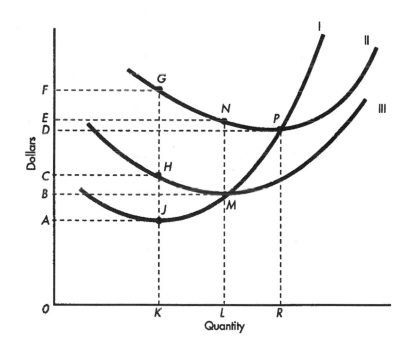

23. At an output of *L,* average variable costs are equal to
    a. 0*B.*
    b. 0*E.*
    c. 0*A.*
    d. 0*D.*
    e. none of these.

24. At an output level of *K,* what are total fixed costs?
    a. 0*AJK*
    b. 0*CHK*
    c. 0*FGK*
    d. *CFGH*
    e. Total fixed costs cannot be determined from the information given.

25. Economies of scale are reflected by
    a. an upward-sloping portion of a long-run *ATC* curve.
    b. a downward-sloping portion of a long-run *ATC* curve.
    c. a downward-sloping portion of a short-run *ATC* curve.
    d. an upward-sloping portion of a short-run *AVC* curve.
    e. a downward-sloping *AFC* curve.

Answers to Sample Test I

1. e (Chapter 6, Section 1.a; *Economics* Chapter 20)
2. c (Chapter 6, Section 1.a; *Economics* Chapter 20)
3. b (Chapter 6, Section 1.a; *Economics* Chapter 20)
4. a (Chapter 6, Section 1.a; *Economics* Chapter 20)
5. b (Chapter 6, Section 1.a; *Economics* Chapter 20)
6. a (Chapter 6, Section 1.d; *Economics* Chapter 20)
7. e (Chapter 6, Section 2.a; *Economics* Chapter 20)
8. d (Chapter 6, Section 4.a; *Economics* Chapter 20)
9. d (Chapter 6, Section 4.b; *Economics* Chapter 20)
10. c (Chapter 7, Section 1.b; *Economics* Chapter 21)
11. c (Chapter 7, Section 1.b; *Economics* Chapter 21)
12. d (Chapter 7, Section 1.b; *Economics* Chapter 21)
13. d (Chapter 7, Section 2.a; *Economics* Chapter 21)

14. b (Chapter 7, Section 2.b; *Economics* Chapter 21)
15. e (Chapter 7, Section 2.b; *Economics* Chapter 21)
16. d (Chapter 7, Section 3.c; *Economics* Chapter 21)
17. a (Chapter 7, Appendix; *Economics* Chapter 21)
18. c (Chapter 7, Appendix; *Economics* Chapter 21)
19. d (Chapter 8, Section 1.b; *Economics* Chapter 22)
20. c (Chapter 8, Section 1.b; *Economics* Chapter 22)
21. c (Chapter 8, Section 3.a; *Economics* Chapter 22)
22. a (Chapter 8, Section 2.b; *Economics* Chapter 22)
23. a (Chapter 8, Section 3.a; *Economics* Chapter 22)
24. d (Chapter 8, Section 3.a; *Economics* Chapter 22)
25. b (Chapter 8, Section 4.a; *Economics* Chapter 22)

Sample Test II
Chapters 6–8
(*Economics* Chapters 20–22)

1. If the price of a product increases by 10 percent and the quantity demanded decreases by 12 percent,
   a. the product has an inelastic demand.
   b. the producer should raise prices further to increase total revenue.
   c. the product has an elastic demand.
   d. total consumption expenditures will be unaffected.
   e. the product has a unit-elastic demand.

2. If gasoline prices suddenly increased by 15 percent and the quantity demanded did not change, then one could conclude that in the short run the demand for gasoline is
   a. perfectly inelastic.
   b. perfectly elastic.
   c. unit-elastic.
   d. very price sensitive.
   e. relatively elastic.

3. A tax attorney recently raised his rates and was surprised to notice declining revenues. What can accurately be concluded?
   a. The demand for the tax attorney's services is elastic.
   b. The demand curve for the tax attorney's services is positively sloped.
   c. The income elasticity of demand for the tax attorney's services is greater than 1.
   d. The cost-price elasticity of demand for the tax attorney's services is greater than 1.
   e. The demand for the tax attorney's services is inelastic.

Use the following table to answer questions 4–6.

		Quantity Purchased		
Income	Personal Computers	Popcorn	Milk
$25,000	1	12	7
$75,000	2	9	9

4. What is the income elasticity of demand for personal computers (using the midpoint or arc-elasticity formula)?
   a. 2/3
   b. –2/3
   c. 3/2
   d. –3/2
   e. approaching zero

5. Popcorn is found to be
   a. a normal good.
   b. a complement for milk.
   c. an inferior good.
   d. very price elastic.
   e. a luxury good.

6. Milk is found to be
   a. a normal good.
   b. a substitute for popcorn.
   c. an inferior good.
   d. very price inelastic.
   e. a luxury good.

7. If the price elasticity of supply is .5, it implies that
   a. a $10 increase in the price increases the quantity supplied by 20 units.
   b. a 10 percent increase in the price increases the quantity supplied by 5 percent.
   c. a 10-unit increase in supply reduces the price by $20.
   d. a 10 percent increase in the quantity supplied increases the price by 20 percent.
   e. total revenue is .5 times total cost.

8. Holding all else constant, which of the following results in a tax incidence falling less on businesses and more on consumers?
   a. a more elastic demand and less elastic supply
   b. a more elastic demand and more elastic supply
   c. a less elastic demand and more elastic supply
   d. a less elastic demand and less elastic supply
   e. a flatter demand curve and steeper supply curve

9. The cross-price elasticity of demand coefficient will be highest when
   a. the two goods are strong substitutes.
   b. the two goods are strong complements.
   c. the two goods are inferior.
   d. the two goods are normal.
   e. the two goods are unrelated.

10. Dominque has $30 that she plans to spend purchasing 6 units of good X (priced at $3 per unit) and 3 units of good Y (priced at $4 per unit). The marginal utility of the sixth unit of X is 24, and the marginal utility of the third unit of Y is 16. To maximize utility, Dominque should
    a. not buy anything.
    b. buy more of X and less of Y.
    c. buy more of Y and less of X.
    d. buy X and Y according to her plan.
    e. do none of the above.

11. If, for a particular consumer, the *MU* of burgers is three times as large as the *MU* of fries, then the consumer will be in equilibrium if
    a. the price of burgers is one-third the price of fries.
    b. the price of burgers is equal to the price of fries.
    c. the price of burgers is three times the price of fries.
    d. the price of burgers is twice the price of fries.
    e. It is impossible to tell from the information given.

12. If Stefanie was willing to pay $25 for a new pair of jeans but found the jeans on sale for $14, then Stefanie
    a. experienced a paradox of value.
    b. did not have consumer sovereignty.
    c. received a consumer surplus of $14.
    d. received a consumer surplus of $11.
    e. decreased her total utility.

13. An increase in an individual's income is reflected by
    a. an outward shift of the budget line.
    b. the budget line's becoming steeper.
    c. the budget line's becoming flatter.
    d. an outward shift of the indifference curve.
    e. an inward shift of the indifference curve.

Use the following figure to answer questions 14 and 15.

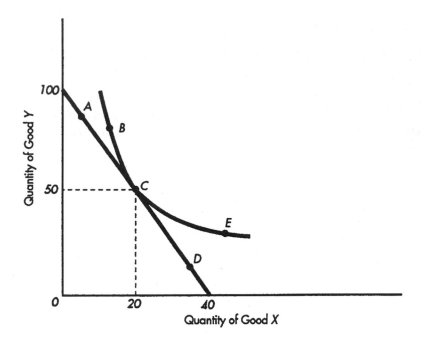

14. At an income level of $100,
    a. the price of X is $2.50 and the price of Y is $1.
    b. the price of X is $1 and the price of Y is $2.50.
    c. the price of X is $20 and the price of Y is $50.
    d. the price of X is $40 and the price of Y is $100.
    e. It is impossible to determine prices from the information given.

15. A consumer prefers which of the following?
    a. *B* to *E*
    b. *C* to *E*
    c. *D* to *B*
    d. *A* to *B*
    e. *E* to *A*

16. Alex is trying to decide whether to buy a cappuccino or an espresso after dinner. The cappuccino costs $3 and yields a marginal utility of 30, whereas the espresso costs $2.50 and yields a marginal utility of 20. Which should he buy?
    a. the cappuccino because it has a higher marginal utility
    b. the cappuccino because it has a lower marginal utility per dollar spent
    c. the espresso because it costs less
    d. the cappuccino because it has a higher marginal utility per dollar spent
    e. It doesn't matter; Alex values them both the same.

Consider the following figure for questions 17–19.

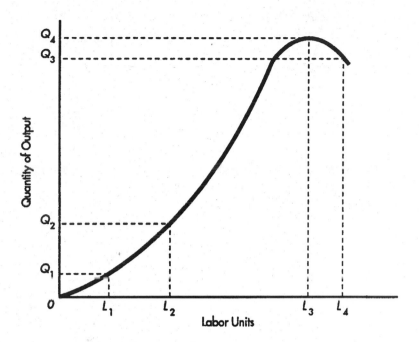

17. Diminishing returns set in for additional labor units beyond
    a. 0.
    b. L_1.
    c. L_2.
    d. L_3.
    c. L_4.

18. Marginal physical product is zero at labor unit level
    a. 0.
    b. L_1.
    c. L_2.
    d. L_3.
    e. L_4.

19. It is always true that no rational firm would employ
    a. less than L_3 labor units.
    b. more than L_3 labor units.
    c. less than L_2 labor units.
    d. more than L_2 labor units.
    e. less than L_4 labor units.

Consider the following table for questions 20–22.

Quantity of Output (units)	Total Cost ($)
0	20
1	30
2	40
3	55
4	75
5	100
6	130

20. The marginal cost for the third unit of output is
   a. $10.
   b. $15.
   c. $20.
   d. $25.
   e. $30.

21. The total variable cost for an output of 5 units is
   a. $100.
   b. $80.
   c. $20.
   d. $16.
   e. Total variable cost cannot be determined from the information given.

22. The average fixed cost for an output of 4 units is
   a. $75.
   b. $20.
   c. $5.
   d. $18.75.
   e. Average fixed cost cannot be determined from the information given.

23. If marginal cost lies below average variable cost, then
   a. marginal cost must be rising.
   b. average variable cost must be rising.
   c. average variable cost must be falling.
   d. average fixed cost must be rising.
   e. marginal cost must be falling.

24. If the cost per unit increases as output rises, the long-run average-total-cost curve displays
   a. economies of scale.
   b. increasing marginal returns.
   c. constant returns to scale.
   d. decreasing average fixed costs.
   e. diseconomies of scale.

25. In the long run,
    a. no resources are fixed.
    b. firms can introduce new technology.
    c. firms can enter or exit the field.
    d. there are no fixed costs.
    e. all of the above are true.

Answers to Sample Test II

1. c (Chapter 6, Section 1.a; *Economics* Chapter 20)
2. a (Chapter 6, Section 1.b; *Economics* Chapter 20)
3. a (Chapter 6, Section 2.a; *Economics* Chapter 20)
4. a (Chapter 6, Section 4.b; *Economics* Chapter 20)
5. c (Chapter 6, Section 4.b; *Economics* Chapter 20)
6. a (Chapter 6, Section 4.b; *Economics* Chapter 20)
7. b (Chapter 6, Section 5.a; *Economics* Chapter 20)
8. c (Chapter 6, Section 5.c; *Economics* Chapter 20)
9. a (Chapter 6, Section 4.a; *Economics* Chapter 20)
10. b (Chapter 7, Section 1.b; *Economics* Chapter 21)
11. c (Chapter 7, Section 2.b; *Economics* Chapter 21)
12. d (Chapter 7, Section 3.c; *Economics* Chapter 21)
13. a (Chapter 7, Appendix; *Economics* Chapter 21)
14. a (Chapter 7, Appendix; *Economics* Chapter 21)
15. e (Chapter 7, Appendix; *Economics* Chapter 21)
16. d (Chapter 7, Section 2.a; *Economics* Chapter 21)
17. c (Chapter 8, Section 1.b; *Economics* Chapter 22)
18. d (Chapter 8, Section 1.b; *Economics* Chapter 22)
19. b (Chapter 8, Section 1.b; *Economics* Chapter 22)
20. b (Chapter 8, Section 3.a; *Economics* Chapter 22)
21. b (Chapter 8, Section 3.a; *Economics* Chapter 22)
22. c (Chapter 8, Section 3.a; *Economics* Chapter 22)
23. c (Chapter 8, Section 3.a; *Economics* Chapter 22)
24. e (Chapter 8, Section 4.a; *Economics* Chapter 22)
25. e (Chapter 8, Section 4.b; *Economics* Chapter 22)

PROFIT MAXIMIZATION

FUNDAMENTAL QUESTIONS

1. What is the role of economic profit in allocating resources?

    Business owners want to get the most profit possible from their resources. This means not only making profits from their current business, but also constantly looking around for other opportunities to increase profits. If you own a fried chicken restaurant, you pay attention to how much profit other types of restaurants are making. Suppose consumers decide they like hamburgers more than fried chicken. Hamburger sellers will then be making more profits than fried chicken sellers. You may decide to close your fried chicken restaurant, and reopen as a hamburger restaurant, to get more profit.

    Your decision to change from selling fried chicken to selling hamburgers has an impact on how resources are used in the economy. There are now more people working in the hamburger industry, and fewer in the fried chicken industry. The demand for hamburger meat will increase, increasing the quantity of hamburger meat produced; there will also be an increase in the amount of other products that go into hamburger, like rolls, ketchup, and so on. On the other hand, production of all the inputs used to make fried chicken will go down.

    These kinds of changes go on all the time in a market economy. If you think about it, when consumers decide they want more hamburgers and less fried chicken, we want the economy to make more hamburgers, and less fried chicken. In a market economy, the mechanism that makes sellers respond to changes in consumers' wants is sellers' pursuit of profits.

2. Why do economists and accountants measure profit differently?

    Accountants measure only the direct costs. Economists measure all opportunity costs in order to help people make better decisions regarding the allocation of their scarce resources.

3. How do firms decide how much to supply?

    The objective here is to choose the amount to supply that maximizes profit. That's easier to say than to do, however. A firm's economic profit at various amounts of output depends on the factors that affect the price elasticities of demand and supply. The fundamental supply rule is to produce and offer for sale the output quantity at which marginal revenue (*MR*) equals marginal cost (*MC*).

4. What is a market structure?

    To economists (and to you as a student of economics), a market structure is a model of the way business firms behave under certain conditions.

A model is a simplification of reality. Few businesses in the real world exactly match one market structure or another, but almost all are close enough to one of the four market-structure models that understanding the models can help us understand the behavior of a real-world business.

Market structure is defined by three characteristics:

- The number of firms that make up the market
- The ease with which new firms can enter the market and begin producing the good or service
- The degree to which the products produced are different

We classify products as either standardized (nondifferentiated) or differentiated. **Standardized products** are perceived by buyers as identical; **differentiated products** are perceived as having characteristics that other sellers' products do not have. The key idea here is people's perceptions. Regardless of whether there are chemical differences among brands of gasoline, if you think all brands of gasoline are the same, then it's a standardized product *to you*. If you think some brands are better than others, then gasoline is a differentiated product *to you*.

5. What are price makers and price takers?

Price makers (price setters, price searchers) are firms that determine the quantity they produce and the price at which they sell their product. Firms in a monopolistic, monopolistically competitive, or oligopolistic market are price makers.

Price takers are business firms that are forced to take the market price for their products: individually, there is nothing they can do to change the market price. Firms in perfectly competitive markets are price takers. If a single firm tries to raise its price even a little bit, buyers immediately will switch to other sellers.

Key Terms

adding value	normal accounting profit	positive economic profit
debt	negative economic profit	(above-normal profit)
equity	zero economic profit (normal	price taker
economic profit	profit)	price maker, price setter, or
accounting profit		price searcher

Quick-Check Quiz

Section 1: Profit Maximization

1. Economists use what term to describe any profit-making organization that combines resources to produce a good or service?
   a. *nonprofit*
   b. *corporation*
   c. *partnership*
   d. *proprietorship*
   e. *firm*

2. Which of the following is *not* one of the general groups of resources?
   a. labor
   b. stocks and bonds
   c. land
   d. capital
   e. All of the above are general groups of resources.

3. The difference between accounting profit and economic profit is that
   a. accountants include the opportunity costs of the owner's capital used in the business and economists don't.
   b. economists include the opportunity costs of the owner's capital used in the business and accountants don't.
   c. accountants include the equity and economists don't.
   d. economists include debt and accountants don't.
   e. economists include only money costs and accountants include the costs of all resources.

4. When a firm creates output that is more valuable than the resources used to create the output, economists say that the firm is
   a. exploiting its workers.
   b. exploiting its stockholders.
   c. adding value.
   d. experiencing negative cash flow.
   e. creating utility.

5. A firm whose total revenue is more than its total costs including all opportunity costs is receiving a
   a. positive economic profit.
   b. negative economic profit.
   c. zero economic profit.
   d. normal profit.
   e. both c and d above.

6. A firm whose total revenue is less than its total costs including all opportunity costs is receiving a
   a. positive economic profit.
   b. negative economic profit.
   c. zero economic profit.
   d. normal profit.
   e. both c and d above.

7. A firm whose total revenue is equal to its total costs including all opportunity costs is receiving a
   a. positive economic profit.
   b. negative economic profit.
   c. zero economic profit.
   d. normal profit.
   e. both c and d above.

Section 2: Marginal Revenue and Marginal Cost

1. According to the supply rule, firms should produce and offer for sale the quantity at which marginal
   a. revenue exceeds marginal cost by the largest amount.
   b. cost exceeds marginal revenue by the largest amount.
   c. revenue equals marginal cost.
   d. revenue is zero.
   e. cost is zero.

2. The curve that shows average revenue is the
   a. demand curve.
   b. supply curve.
   c. marginal-revenue curve.
   d. marginal-cost curve.
   e. curve that shows the difference between marginal revenue and marginal cost.

Section 3: Selling Environments or Market Structure

1. Which of the market characteristics listed below is *not* used to define market structures?
   a. the number of firms in the market
   b. the ease of entry into the market by new firms
   c. the percentage of a firm's income that is paid in taxes
   d. the type of product produced (standardized or differentiated)
   e. the ease with which new firms can begin producing a product

2. Which of the following is *not* one of the market structures defined in the chapter?
   a. perfect competition
   b. monopoly
   c. monopolistic competition
   d. oligopoly
   e. oligopolistic competition

3. In which of the following market structures does only one firm supply the product and entry is not possible?
   a. perfect competition
   b. monopolistic competition
   c. oligopoly
   d. monopoly
   e. None of these market structures matches the definition.

4. In which of the following market structures do a few firms produce either a standardized or differentiated product, with entry possible but not easy?
   a. perfect competition
   b. monopolistic competition
   c. oligopoly
   d. monopoly
   e. None of these market structures matches the definition.

5. In which of the following market structures do very many firms produce a standardized product?
   a. perfect competition
   b. monopolistic competition
   c. oligopoly
   d. monopoly
   e. None of these market structures matches the definition.

6. In which of the following market structures do many firms produce differentiated products?
   a. perfect competition
   b. monopolistic competition
   c. oligopoly
   d. monopoly
   e. None of these market structures matches the definition.

7. In which of the following market structures are firms interdependent?
   a. perfect competition
   b. monopolistic competition
   c. oligopoly
   d. monopoly
   e. Firms in all of the above market structures are interdependent.

8. A natural monopoly is caused by
   a. economies of scale.
   b. government intervention.
   c. anticompetitive practices by large firms.
   d. control over natural resource supplies.
   e. patent laws.

Practice Questions and Problems

Section 1: Profit Maximization

1. In analyzing business behavior, economists usually assume that the firm's objective is to

   _____ .

2. Economists include _____ in calculating profits; accountants don't.

3. Business firms can acquire capital through _____ (taking out loans) and through

   _____ (selling shares of stock).

Use this information to answer questions 4 through 7.

You currently work as a doughnut-hole maker, at a salary of $25,000 a year. You also have $50,000 in the bank earning 10 percent interest per year. You decide to quit your job, invest your $50,000 in buying your own doughnut-hole shop, and spend your time running your own doughnut-hole shop.

4. What are your opportunity costs for a year?
    a. Zero
    b. $5,000
    c. $25,000
    d. $30,000
    e. $75,000

5. If your total revenues for your doughnut are $20,000 per year, you are getting a _____ economic profit.

6. If your total revenues for your doughnut are $40,000 per year, you are getting a _____ economic profit.

7. If your total revenues for your doughnut are $30,000 per year, you are getting a _____ economic profit. This is also called a _____ profit.

Section 2. Marginal Revenue and Marginal Cost

1. Profit is maximized at the output level where _____ = _____ .

2. The Kilroy Manufacturing Company makes and sells a computer game called "Kilroy Was Here." The company knows from experience that it can sell 10 games per day when it charges a price of $50. If it wants to sell 11 games per day, it has to cut the price to $49. The marginal revenue of the eleventh game Kilroy sells per day is _____ .

3. Sally Smith is a world-famous artist who carves exquisite models of birds out of rare, expensive woods. Sally knows that if she carves only 1 bird per month, her customers will pay a high price for it because of its rarity. If she makes more birds per month, people will only be willing to pay lower prices. Moreover, when she carves more birds per month, her hands get very sore and she has to spend more money having them massaged.

a. The table below lists the price Sally can charge for different numbers of birds sold per month and her total costs of making different numbers of birds per month. Calculate Sally's total revenue, marginal revenue, marginal cost, and profit for each output level.

Q	P	TR	TC	MR	MC	Profit
0	—	$ 0	$ 500	—	—	_____
1	$2,000	_____	700	_____	_____	_____
2	1,800	_____	1,100	_____	_____	_____
3	1,600	_____	1,700	_____	_____	_____
4	1,400	_____	2,500	_____	_____	_____
5	1,200	_____	3,500	_____	_____	_____
6	1,000	_____	4,700	_____	_____	_____

b. Sally's profit is at its maximum at an output level of _____ bird(s).

c. Sally's marginal revenue equals her marginal cost at an output level of _____ bird(s).

d. On graph a on the following page, plot Sally's profit at each output level. On graph b, plot Sally's marginal cost and marginal revenue. As you can see, profit is maximized at the output level where $MR = MC$ (4 birds).

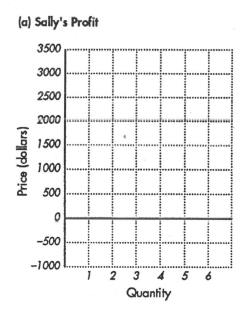

(a) Sally's Profit

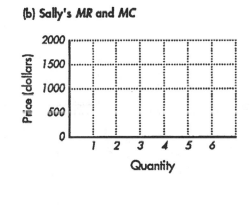

(b) Sally's MR and MC

Section 3: Selling Environments or Market Structure

1. The four market structures are _____ , _____ , _____ , and _____ .

2. Perfect competition is a market structure in which _____ firm(s) is(are) producing a _____ product and entry is _____ .

3. Monopolistic competition is a market structure in which _____ firm(s) is(are) producing a _____ product and entry is _____ .

4. Oligopoly is a market structure in which _____ firm(s) is(are) producing a _____ product and entry is _____ .

5. Monopoly is a market structure in which _____ firm(s) is(are) supplying a product and entry is _____ .

6. Oligopoly is the only market structure in which firms are _____ .

7. When buyers perceive different sellers' products to be identical, we say the products are _____ ; when buyers perceive different sellers' products to be different, we say the products are _____ .

8. Price makers are found in the _____ , _____ , and _____ market structures.

9. On the graph below, sketch the shape of a demand curve for the product sold by a firm that is a price taker.

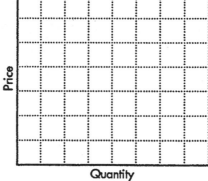

10. Firms that are price takers are found in a(n) _____ market structure.

Thinking About and Applying Profit Maximization

I.   The Market Structures of Aspirin

The next time you're in the grocery store or drug store, walk by the aspirin displays and take a look at the different brands of plain aspirin and their prices. Chances are you'll find several different brands: one or more nationally advertised brands (Bayer, for example), the store's own brand, maybe some aspirin with no brand name at all, and probably some other local or regional brands. If you look in other stores, you'll find many other brands of aspirin. When you read the labels, you'll find that all regular-strength aspirin has the same active ingredient: 325 mg of aspirin (or acetylsalicylic acid, the chemical name for aspirin); extra-strength aspirin has 500 mg of aspirin.

1.   Because there seem to be a large number of firms selling an identical product, aspirin seems to fit

   into the _____ market structure.

2.   If aspirin is sold in a perfectly competitive market, all sellers should charge _____ (the

   same, different) price(s).

3.   When you check the prices, you'll find that they are very different. The prices probably follow a pre-dictable pattern: the national brands are most expensive, followed by other regional and local brands; the store's own brand is least expensive unless there's generic, no-brand aspirin available. Use what you have learned in this chapter to explain how this could come about.

   _____

   _____

   _____

   _____

II.   Profit Maximization and Pollution Reduction

The ideas of profit maximization and of comparing marginal revenue and marginal cost to find the profit-maximizing output level can be useful even for organizations that aren't involved in profit maximization. All organizations need to find the most effective ways of reaching their goals.

   Suppose you are the head of the Environmental Protection Agency (EPA), and you have to decide how much, if any, pollution a particular water treatment plant should be allowed to produce. Right now, the plant produces 4 tons of pollutants per day. The plant is owned by the federal government, so any cleanup costs will be paid for through taxes. Let's assume that the EPA knows what the benefits and cost (in dollars) are from reducing pollution by various amounts. Using the benefits and costs in the table below, find the amount of pollution reduction that gives people the biggest "profit." Profit in this case is the net value people get from pollution reduction: the total benefits minus the total costs.

Pollution Improvement: Tons Reduced per Day	Marginal Benefits	Marginal Costs
1	$10 million	$ 1 million
2	5 million	4 million
3	2 million	10 million
4	1 million	30 million

1. The plant should reduce pollution by _____ tons per day.

2. Explain why you chose this amount.

   _____

   _____

   _____

   _____

   _____

   _____

   _____

Chapter 9 (*Economics* Chapter 23) Homework Problems

Name _____

1. Write the equations for accounting profit and economic profit.

2. Write the rule for determining how much output a firm should produce.

3. Market structure is defined by three characteristics. Name them.

4. Carol Monopolist can sell her product in two separate markets, Asturias and Hammerfell. The marginal cost is constant at $30 in both markets. The price in Asturias is $60 and the marginal revenue is $25 at her current output. In Hammerfell, her price is $50 and the marginal revenue is $30 at her current output. Is Carol maximizing her profits, or do you have some advice to give her?

5. You are the proud owner of Office Slave, a self-service copying center located on the campus of Auld Lang Syne University. You basically have a monopoly on providing this service, as there is no other self-service copier for five hundred square miles. Your supplier charges you $200 per month plus a charge of 1 cent for every copy made. You figure it costs you about 1 cent for ink, paper, a normal profit, etc., for every copy your customers make.

   You have estimated the demand and marginal revenue for your copies to be as shown on the graph below.

   How many copies should you make each month?

   What price will you need to set so that your customers will make this many copies?

   What is your monthly profit?

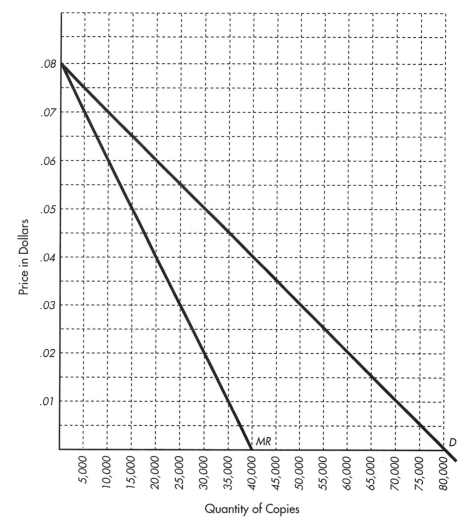

If your instructor assigns these problems, write your answers above, then tear out this page and hand it in.

Answers

Quick-Check Quiz

Section 1: Profit Maximization

1. e; 2. b; 3. b; 4. c; 5. a; 6. b; 7. e

If you missed any of these questions, you should go back and review Section 1 in Chapter 9 (*Economics*, Chapter 23).

Section 2: Marginal Revenue and Marginal Cost

1. c; 2. a

If you missed either of these questions, you should go back and review Section 2 in Chapter 9 (*Economics*, Chapter 23).

Section 3: Selling Environment or Market Structure

1. c; 2. e; 3. d; 4. c; 5. a; 6. b; 7. c; 8. a

If you missed any of these questions, you should go back and review Section 3 in Chapter 9 (*Economics*, Chapter 23).

Practice Questions and Problems

Section 1: Profit Maximization

1. add value
2. opportunity cost of capital
3. debt; equity
4. d (Answer a is wrong: your time and capital have other valuable uses. Answer b is wrong: you didn't count the salary from your current job as an opportunity cost. Answer c is wrong: you didn't count the forgone interest from your capital as an opportunity cost. Answer e is wrong: the opportunity cost of using your capital is the interest forgone, not the whole amount of capital.)
5. negative
6. positive
7. zero; normal

Section 2: Marginal Revenue and Marginal Cost

1. *MR; MC*
2. $39 (At $50, Kilroy's total revenue is $500 [price of $50 times quantity of 10 games]; at $49, total revenue is $539. Marginal revenue is the additional revenue obtained by selling an additional unit of output, or $539 − $500 = $39.)

3. a.

Q	P	TR	TC	MR	MC	Profit
0	—	$ 0	$ 500	—	—	$ −500
1	$2,000	2,000	700	$2,000	$ 200	1,300
2	1,800	3,600	1,100	1,600	400	2,500
3	1,600	4,800	1,700	1,200	600	3,100
4	1,400	5,600	2,500	800	800	3,100
5	1,200	6,000	3,500	400	1,000	2,500
6	1,000	6,000	4,700	0	1,200	1,300

TR = $P \times Q$.

MR is the change in TR from selling 1 more bird per month.

MC is the change in TC from making 1 more bird per month.

Profit = $TR - TC$

b. Both 3 birds and 4 birds give Sally $3,100 profit per month.

c. 4 ($MR = MC = \$800$ at 4 birds per month.)

d.

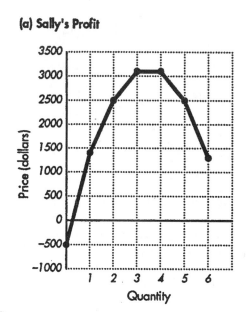

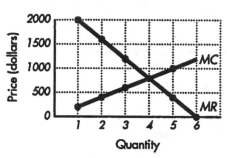

Section 3: Selling Environment or Market Structure

1. perfect competition; monopoly; monopolistic competition; oligopoly
2. very many; standardized (or nondifferentiated); easy
3. many; differentiated; easy
4. few; standardized or differentiated; impeded
5. one; not possible
6. interdependent
7. standardized (or nondifferentiated); differentiated
8. monopoly; monopolistic competition; oligopoly

9.

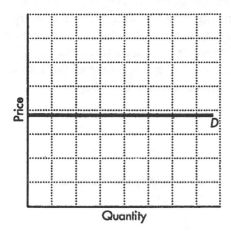

The demand curve for a firm in a perfectly competitive market structure is horizontal.

10. perfect competition

Thinking About and Applying Profit Maximization

I. *The Market Structures of Aspirin*

1. perfect competition
2. same
3. At least some aspirin buyers must perceive aspirin as a differentiated product. If everyone perceived aspirin as a standardized product, no one would pay more for specific brands. Even though all aspirin has the same active ingredient, the packaging can be different: the size and shape of the tablet, how the aspirin is held in the tablet, what the tablet is made of besides aspirin, and so on. Whether these differences are significant enough to justify the price differences can be argued both ways, but it is clear that some buyers behave as though the differences are significant to them.

II. *Profit Maximization and Pollution Reduction*

1. 2
2. For the first 1-ton reduction, people gain $10 million in benefits at a cost of $1 million; the "profit" is $9 million from the first 1-ton reduction.

   The second 1-ton reduction gives us $5 million in benefits at a cost of $4 million; we gain an additional $1 million profit from the second 1-ton reduction. After reducing pollution by 2 tons, we have total benefits of $15 million ($10 million + $5 million), and total costs of $5 million ($1 million + $4 million), for a total net gain or profit of $10 million.

   If we made the third 1-ton reduction, we would gain $2 million in benefits at a cost of $10 million; we'd "lose" $8 million on the third 1-ton reduction. If we reduced pollution by a total of 3 tons, our total benefits would be $17 million ($10 million + $5 million + $2 million), and our total costs would be $15 million ($1 million + $4 million + $10 million), for a total net gain of $2 million. By the criterion specified for this example, we would be better off with only 2 tons of pollution reduction; we would get more value from spending $10 million on other things than on the third 1-ton reduction of pollution.

Although making decisions about pollution reduction is much more complex than this simple example, the problem does illustrate the basic concepts involved, including some of the economic principles we've been studying in the last few chapters. The principle of diminishing marginal utility applies to pollution reduction as well as to other desirable results; the marginal benefits in the example decrease as we continue to reduce pollution. The law of diminishing marginal returns explains why the marginal costs of pollution reduction increase as more pollution is eliminated. We'll look further at the economics of the environment and environmental protection in a later chapter.

PERFECT COMPETITION

FUNDAMENTAL QUESTIONS

1. What is perfect competition?

   Perfect competition is a market structure in which many small firms are producing an identical product, entry and exit are easy, and buyers and sellers have perfect information. Very few, if any, real-world markets fit this definition exactly; agriculture, illegal drugs, the scrap metal market, and video rentals come closest. In fact, they come close enough for the perfectly competitive model to be useful in explaining how they work. Perfect competition also is worth studying because, to the economist's way of thinking, perfectly competitive markets work better than other market structures.

2. What does the demand curve facing the individual firm look like, and why?

   Put yourself in the shoes of an average wheat farmer: you produce and sell a product that is identical to the product sold by thousands of other wheat farmers. The market price for wheat is set by the overall market demand and supply. If you try to charge more than the market price, buyers can find so many other farmers to buy from that they won't be willing to deal with you. All you can do is take the market price or leave it.

   The wheat farmer is typical of an individual firm in perfect competition. The firm's demand curve is a horizontal line at the market price. The firm is a price taker: the only thing it can control is how much it chooses to sell.

3. How does the firm maximize profit in the short run?

   The firm chooses the output level that maximizes its profits. That output level can be found at the point where marginal revenue equals marginal cost.

4. At what point does a firm decide to suspend operations?

   A firm has to be able to pay all its variable costs to remain in operation. It will shut down temporarily if the market price is below its **shutdown price,** the minimum point on the average-variable-cost curve. At this point, the firm loses less money if it shuts down than if it keeps on producing.

5. When will a firm shut down permanently?

   A firm will shut down permanently if it can't cover all of its costs in the long run. If the market price is below the minimum point on the firm's average-total-cost curve and is expected to stay there, the firm will shut down permanently. The firm is not producing enough revenue to pay the opportunity costs of the resources provided by its owner, so the owner could do better by taking his or her resources elsewhere in the economy.

6. What is the breakeven price?

A firm breaks even when economic profits are zero—that is, when the demand curve (the market price) just equals the minimum point on the average-total-cost curve. At the **breakeven price,** the firm is covering all of its costs, including the opportunity costs of resources provided by the owner.

7. What is the firm's supply curve in the short run?

As long as revenue equals or exceeds variable costs, the firm produces at the level where *MR = MC*. The firm's supply curve in the short run is the portion of the marginal-cost curve that lies above the minimum point on the average-variable-cost curve.

8. What is the firm's supply curve in the long run?

In the long run, the firm will shut down permanently if price is below the minimum point on the average-total-cost curve. The firm's long-run supply curve, then, is the portion of the marginal-cost curve that lies above the minimum point on the average-total-cost curve.

9. What are the long-run equilibrium results of a perfectly competitive market?

Long-run equilibrium in a perfectly competitive market is the point at which firms are earning just a normal profit (zero economic profit). This means that firms are producing at the lowest possible cost, that there is no waste. An important element of long-run equilibrium, then, is **economic efficiency**—there is no way to make someone better off without making someone else worse off.

Key Terms

shutdown price   economic efficiency
breakeven price   producer surplus

Quick-Check Quiz

Section 1: The Perfectly Competitive Firm in the Short Run

1. Which of the following is *not* part of the definition of a perfectly competitive market structure?
   a. many small firms
   b. standardized or identical product
   c. many individual brand names
   d. buyers and sellers with perfect information
   e. easy entry and exit

2. The demand curve of the individual firm in perfect competition is a
   a. vertical line at the market price.
   b. vertical line at the market quantity.
   c. downward-sloping line.
   d. horizontal line at the market price.
   e. horizontal line at the market quantity.

3. The individual firm in perfect competition is a
   a. price taker.
   b. price maker.
   c. price reviser.
   d. quantity taker.
   e. cost maker.

4. Firms maximize profits by producing the output quantity where
   a. $P = MR$.
   b. $MR = AVC$.
   c. $MC = AVC$.
   d. $MR = MC$.
   e. $P = AFC$.

5. In the short run, a perfectly competitive firm's shutdown price is just equal to the
   a. minimum point on the average-fixed-cost curve.
   b. minimum point on the average-variable-cost curve.
   c. minimum point on the average-total-cost curve.
   d. maximum point on the average-variable-cost curve.
   e. maximum point on the marginal-cost curve.

6. In the long run, a perfectly competitive firm's shutdown price is just equal to the
   a. minimum point on the average-fixed-cost curve.
   b. minimum point on the average-variable-cost curve.
   c. minimum point on the average-total-cost curve.
   d. maximum point on the average-variable-cost curve.
   e. maximum point on the marginal-cost curve.

7. A perfectly competitive firm's breakeven price is just equal to the
   a. minimum point on the average-fixed-cost curve.
   b. minimum point on the average-variable-cost curve.
   c. minimum point on the average-total-cost curve.
   d. maximum point on the average-variable-cost curve.
   e. maximum point on the marginal-cost curve.

8. In the short run, a perfectly competitive firm's supply curve is that portion of the marginal-cost curve above the minimum point on the
   a. total-variable-cost curve.
   b. total-cost curve.
   c. average-fixed-cost curve.
   d. average-variable-cost curve.
   e. average-total-cost curve.

9. In the long run, a perfectly competitive firm's supply curve is that portion of the marginal-cost curve above the minimum point on the
   a. total-variable-cost curve.
   b. total-cost curve.
   c. average-fixed-cost curve.
   d. average-variable-cost curve.
   e. average-total-cost curve.

Section 2: The Long Run

1. In a perfectly competitive industry, in the long run, entry and exit stop only when
   a. barriers to entry and exit are sufficiently high.
   b. individual firms receive economic profits.
   c. individual firms take economic losses.
   d. individual firms earn a normal profit.
   e. all firms have shut down.

2. The difference between the price firms would have been willing to accept for their products and the price they actually receive is called
   a. consumer surplus.
   b. producer surplus.
   c. consumer excess.
   d. producer excess.
   e. accounting profit.

3. Which of the following is *not* one of the requirements for economic efficiency?
   a. productive efficiency
   b. allocative efficiency
   c. firms producing output at the level at which *ATC* is lowest
   d. firms producing output at the level where $P = MC$
   e. All of the above are requirements for economic efficiency.

Practice Questions and Problems

Section 1: The Perfectly Competitive Firm in the Short Run

1. List the four characteristics of the perfectly competitive market structure.

   _____

   _____

   _____

   _____

2. The individual firm in perfect competition is a price _____ (maker, taker), and its demand curve is a(n) _____ line at the _____ .

3. The equation that determines the profit-maximizing output level is _____ .

4. The firm's short-run shutdown price is the _____ point of the _____ curve.

5. The firm's long-run shutdown price is the _____ point of the _____ curve.

6. The firm's breakeven price is the _____ point of the _____ curve.

7. The table below shows some of the cost curves for Joe's Gourmet Burger Stand that you calculated in Chapter 8 on the costs of doing business. Let's assume that burger stands are a perfectly competitive industry. (Actually, they're probably monopolistically competitive, but we won't worry about that now.)

Burgers	TC	TR	MR	AFC	AVC	ATC	MC
0	$ 5.50	$_____					
1	9.00	_____	$_____	$5.50	$3.50	$9.00	$3.50
2	10.00	_____	_____	2.75	2.25	5.00	1.00
3	10.50	_____	_____	1.83	1.67	3.50	.50
4	11.50	_____	_____	1.38	1.50	2.88	1.00
5	13.00	_____	_____	1.10	1.50	2.60	1.50
6	15.00	_____	_____	.92	1.58	2.50	2.00
7	17.50	_____	_____	.79	1.71	2.50	2.50
8	20.50	_____	_____	.69	1.88	2.56	3.00
9	24.00	_____	_____	.61	2.06	2.67	3.50
10	28.00	_____	_____	.55	2.25	2.80	4.00

a. In the short-run, Joe's shutdown price is _____ .

b. In the long run, Joe's breakeven price is _____ .

c. Let's say that the market price for burgers is \$3. Fill in the total-revenue and marginal-revenue columns in the table, and plot marginal cost and marginal revenue in the graph below.

Marginal Revenue and Marginal Cost

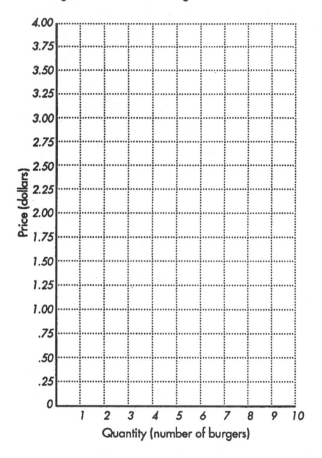

d. The number of burgers that maximizes Joe's profit is _____ .

e. Assuming Joe produces 8 burgers, his profit is _____ .

8. Using the table on page 237, let's find Joe's short-run supply curve. For the prices listed below, find Joe's profit-maximizing output (number of burgers) and Joe's profit at each price. (*Hints*: Don't go through all the calculations you did in question 7—just use the $MR = MC$ rule. And be sure to look for shutdown situations.)

Market Price	Number of Burgers	Profit
\$3.50	_____	\$_____
3.00	_____	_____
2.50	_____	_____
2.00	_____	_____
1.50	_____	_____
1.00	_____	_____

9. Changes in production costs can affect Joe's breakeven and shutdown prices and his supply curve. The table below shows what would happen to Joe's production costs if the cost of the meat for each hamburger increased by $.50: the *AVC, ATC,* and *MC* curves all increase by $.50 at each level of output.

Burgers	TC	AFC	AVC	ATC	MC
0	$ 5.50				
1	9.50	$5.50	$4.00	$9.50	$4.00
2	11.00	2.75	2.75	5.50	1.50
3	12.00	1.83	2.17	4.00	1.00
4	13.50	1.38	2.00	3.38	1.50
5	15.50	1.10	2.00	3.10	2.00
6	18.00	.92	2.08	3.00	2.50
7	21.00	.79	2.21	3.00	3.00
8	24.50	.69	2.38	3.06	3.50
9	28.50	.61	2.56	3.17	4.00
10	33.00	.55	2.75	3.30	4.50

The graph below already contains Joe's original cost curves. Plot Joe's new average-cost curves and marginal-cost curve from the table. Then, use the table and graph to answer the questions below.

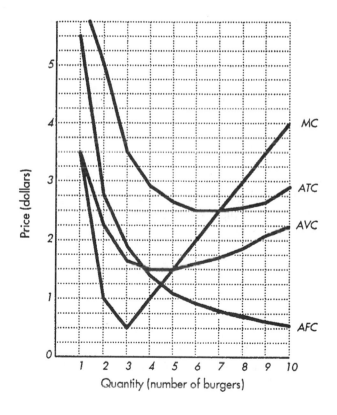

a. Joe's breakeven price now is _____ .

b. Joe's shutdown price now is _____ .

c. Explain why Joe's breakeven and shutdown prices increased compared to those in question 7.

_____

_____

_____

_____

d. The table below shows Joe's supply curve based on his original costs (what you figured out for question 8 above). Fill in the column labeled "New Number of Burgers" using the *MR* = *MC* rule and watching for shutdown situation.

Market Price	Old Number of Burgers	New Number of Burgers
$3.50	9	_____
3.00	8	_____
2.50	7	_____
2.00	6	_____
1.50	5	_____
1.00	0	_____

e. Joe's supply curve has _____ (increased, decreased).

f. Explain why the change in marginal costs caused Joe's supply curve to change.

_____

_____

_____

g. Suppose that the cost of hamburger meat had *decreased* by $.50 instead of increased. What would happen to Joe's supply curve? Explain your answer.

_____

_____

_____

10. You just saw in question 9 that changes in Joe's production costs can affect Joe's breakeven and shutdown prices and his supply curve. The table on the following page shows what would happen to Joe's *original* production costs (see the table on page 237) if the total fixed cost increased from $5.50 to $9: the *AFC* and *ATC* curves increase, but the *MC* and *AVC* curves are the same as before.

Burgers	TC	AFC	AVC	ATC	MC
0	$ 9.00				
1	12.50	$9.00	$3.50	$12.50	$3.50
2	13.50	4.50	2.25	6.75	1.00
3	14.00	3.00	1.67	4.67	.50
4	15.00	2.25	1.50	3.75	1.00
5	16.50	1.80	1.50	3.30	1.50
6	18.50	1.50	1.58	3.08	2.00
7	21.00	1.29	1.71	3.00	2.50
8	24.00	1.12	1.88	3.00	3.00
9	27.50	1.00	2.06	3.06	3.50
10	31.50	.90	2.25	3.15	4.00

Once again, the graph below contains Joe's original cost curves. Plot Joe's curves from the table, and then use the table and graph to answer the questions that follow.

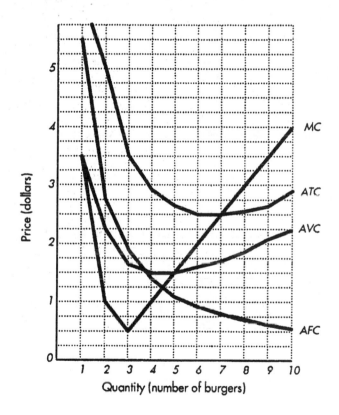

a. Joe's breakeven price now is _____ .

b. Joe's shutdown price now is _____ .

c. Explain why Joe's breakeven price increased compared to that in question 7.

_____

_____

_____

_____

d. Explain why Joe's shutdown price is the same as in question 7, even though Joe's fixed costs increased.

_____

_____

_____

e. Again, the table below shows Joe's supply curve based on his original costs. Fill in the column labeled "New Number of Burgers" using the $MR = MC$ rule and watching for shutdown situations.

Market Price	Old Number of Burgers	New Number of Burgers
$3.50	9	_____
3.00	8	_____
2.50	7	_____
2.00	6	_____
1.50	5	_____
1.00	0	_____

f. Explain why the change in fixed costs does not change Joe's supply curve.

_____

_____

_____

g. Would an increase in fixed costs affect Joe's decision about staying in the burger market in the long run? Explain your answer.

_____

_____

_____

Section 2: The Long Run

1. In the long run, new firms will enter a market if existing firms are earning _____ .

2. In the long run, existing firms will leave a market if they are taking _____ .

3. The number of firms in a market stays constant only if firms are receiving a(n) _____ .

4. To achieve _____ efficiency, firms must produce goods at the lowest possible cost.

5. To achieve _____ efficiency, firms must produce the goods consumers most want.

6. Allocative efficiency requires that _____ equals _____ .

7. Economic efficiency requires both _____ and _____ efficiency.

8. The graph below shows the cost curves for a typical firm in a perfectly competitive market.

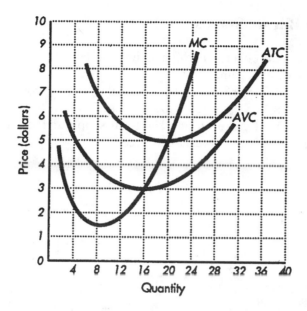

a. The long-run equilibrium price is _____ , and the long-run equilibrium quantity is

_____ .

b. Explain why that quantity is productively efficient.

_____

_____

_____

_____

c. Explain why that quantity is allocatively efficient.

_____

_____

_____

_____

d. Explain why that quantity is economically efficient.

_____

_____

_____

_____

Thinking About and Applying Perfect Competition

I. Effects of Entry on Burger Stands

Section 2 in this chapter looks at the effects on profits of the entry and exit of firms. To examine these ideas, let's look at the burger stand industry again.

We start out with Joe's Gourmet Burger Stand and the rest of the perfectly competitive burger stand industry in long-run equilibrium, and see how they react to changes. Graph a below shows the current market equilibrium, determined by demand curve D_1 and short-run supply curve SRS_1, which determine Joe's demand curve and *MR* curve at $2.50, Joe's breakeven price.

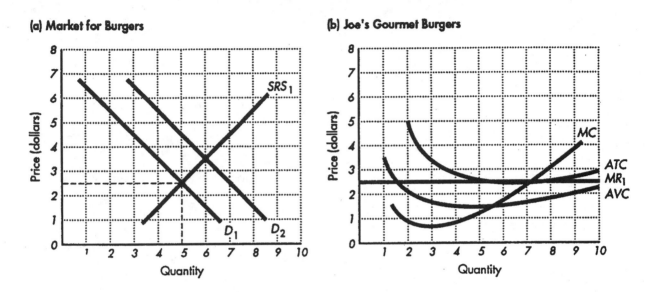

1. Suppose that a new scientific study shows that eating burgers is much better for your health than eating oat bran or other "healthy" foods. The demand for burgers jumps overnight to D_2, raising the price to $3.50.

   a. How is Joe going to respond to the higher price in the short-run?

   _____

   _____

   b. Will he do anything different in the long run?

   _____

   _____

   _____

   _____

2. In the short run, Joe can enjoy his economic profits. Explain why he won't keep earning economic profits in the long run.

_____

_____

_____

_____

3. As new firms enter the market and start selling more burgers, the short-run market supply curve will shift to the right. Assuming this is a constant-cost industry, draw in the long-run supply curve (*LRS*) on graph a on the previous page, and sketch in what the new short-run market supply curve (*SRS₂*) must look like after long-run equilibrium has been restored.

4. Why would the price have to go up in the short run to restore market equilibrium and then return to $2.50 in the long run?

_____

_____

_____

_____

II. Prices, Profits, and Market Changes

On page A4 of its April 28, 1993, edition, the *Wall Street Journal* reported that Mobil Oil's profit was up for the first quarter of 1993, giving the following reasons:

> Mobil benefitted from natural-gas prices that rose 35%. . . . Mobil . . . said earnings in its chemical business fell because of depressed prices brought about by surplus capacity in that industry.

1. Suppose that the changes in the prices of natural gas and chemicals were caused by shifts in demand. If natural gas and chemicals are sold in perfectly competitive markets, sketch new demand curves (*D₂*) on the graphs that follow that could produce the price changes described in the article.

(a) Market for Natural Gas

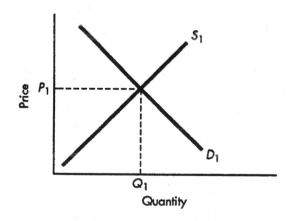

(b) Market for Chemicals

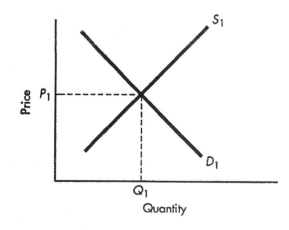

2. Suppose that the changes in the prices of natural gas and chemicals were caused by shifts in supply. If natural gas and chemicals are sold in perfectly competitive markets, sketch new supply curves on the graphs below that could produce the price changes described in the article.

(a) Market for Natural Gas

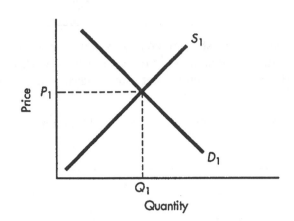

(b) Market for Chemicals

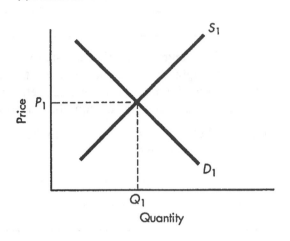

3. On the basis of the information above, the number of new natural gas wells drilled should

_____ (increase, decrease) in the long run.

4. On the basis of the information above, the number of sellers of industrial chemicals should

_____ (increase, decrease) in the long run.

Chapter 10 (*Economics* Chapter 24)   Homework Problems

Name _____

1. Describe a perfectly competitive market structure in terms of number of firms, ease of entry and exit, and product differentiation.

2. Draw the short-run cost and revenue curves for a firm making an economic profit in a perfectly competitive industry. Show the firm's short-run supply curve.

3. Why might a firm continue to produce at a loss in the short run instead of shutting down?

4. a. If $P >$ _____ , a perfectly competitive firm will make an economic profit in the short run.

   b. If $P =$ _____ , a perfectly competitive firm will make zero economic profit, or a normal profit.

   c. If _____ $\leq P <$ _____ , a perfectly competitive firm will continue to produce at a loss in the short run.

   d. If $P <$ _____ , a perfectly competitive firm will shut down in the short run.

5. Josie's Thingamajigs, a perfectly competitive firm, has fixed costs of $100,000. It receives a price of $90 for each unit of output it produces. Its current output is 2,000 units, where its average variable costs are at their minimum (which is $50). What advice would you give Josie in the short run? Circle as many as apply. (*Hint:* Draw a picture.)

    a. Increase output.

    b. Increase price.

    c. Decrease price.

    d. Decrease output.

    e. Do not change output.

    f. Shut down.

    g. Leave the industry.

    h. Call home.

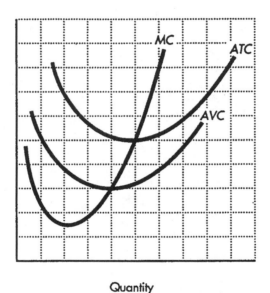

Quantity

What would your advice be in the long run?

If your instructor assigns these problems, write your answers above, then tear out this page and hand it in.

Answers

Quick-Check Quiz

Section 1: The Perfectly Competitive Firm in the Short Run

1. c; 2. d; 3. a; 4. d; 5. b; 6. c; 7. c; 8. d; 9. e
If you missed any of these questions, you should go back and review Section 1 in Chapter 10 (*Economics*, Chapter 24).

Section 2: The Long Run

1. d; 2. b; 3. e
If you missed any of these questions, you should go back and review Section 2 in Chapter 10 (*Economics*, Chapter 24).

Practice Questions and Problems

Section 1: The Perfectly Competitive Firm in the Short Run

1. many firms
   identical or standardized product
   easy entry and exit
   perfect information
2. taker; horizontal; market price
3. $MR = MC$
4. minimum; average-variable-cost
5. minimum; average-total-cost
6. minimum; average-total-cost
7. a. $1.50 (When the market price is at or above the short-run shutdown price, it is worth producing burgers. The shutdown price is the lowest value on the *AVC* curve. The table shows that value as $1.50.)
   b. $2.50 (At the breakeven price, it is just barely worthwhile to remain in the burger stand business rather than do something else. The breakeven price is the lowest value on the *ATC* curve. The table shows that value as $2.50.)
   c.

Burgers	TC	TR	MR	AFC	AVC	ATC	MC
0	$ 5.50	$ 0					
1	9.00	3.00	$3.00	$5.50	$3.50	$9.00	$3.50
2	10.00	6.00	3.00	2.75	2.25	5.00	1.00
3	10.50	9.00	3.00	1.83	1.67	3.50	.50
4	11.50	12.00	3.00	1.38	1.50	2.88	1.00
5	13.00	15.00	3.00	1.10	1.50	2.60	1.50
6	15.00	18.00	3.00	.92	1.58	2.50	2.00
7	17.50	21.00	3.00	.79	1.71	2.50	2.50
8	20.50	24.00	3.00	.69	1.88	2.56	3.00
9	24.00	27.00	3.00	.61	2.06	2.67	3.50
10	28.00	30.00	3.00	.55	2.25	2.80	4.00

TR is the $3 price times the number of units produced.

MR is just the market price ($3). In perfect competition, Joe always can sell another burger at the market price.

Marginal Revenue and Marginal Cost

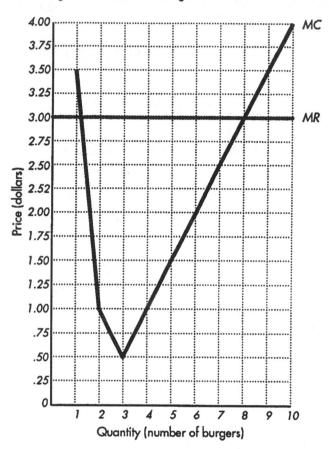

d. 8 (This is the quantity where $MR = MC$.)

e. $3.50 (Total revenue minus total cost. If you got $3.52 for your profit, you didn't do anything wrong. You figured the profit per burger [$P - ATC$] and then multiplied that times the number of burgers. Your answer is a little different because the *ATC* for 8 burgers is not exactly $2.56—it's actually $2.5625.)

Market Price	Number of Burgers	Profit
$3.50	9	$ 7.50
3.00	8	3.50
2.50	7	0
2.00	6	–3.00
1.50	5	–5.50
1.00	0	–5.50

Let's look at how to solve problems like these, starting with a relatively easy one: a market price of $3.50. This price is Joe's *MR,* and he wants to make all the burgers that have an *MC* less than or equal to *MR*. Starting with 1 burger, look down the table. *MC* does not get bigger than *MR* until you get to the tenth burger. All the burgers up through 9 are worth making to Joe. If he makes 9 burgers when the price is $3.50, his *TR* is $31.50 (9 × $3.50). His *TC* is only $24, so he earns a profit of $31.50 – $24 = $7.50. If you are having problems at this point, look back through Section 3 of the previous chapter and Section 1 of this chapter, and then try again. If it still doesn't make sense, ask your instructor for help.

At a market price of $3, we start running into complications. The *MC* of the first burger is $3.50, which is more than our *MR* of $3. Should we stop there? No. At that small output level, *MC* still is falling. We want to find the output level where *MR* = *MC* and *MC* is rising.

When the market price drops to $2, Joe starts losing money. Should he shut down? Not yet. He is still covering his variable costs (*P* is more than *AVC*), so he is losing less money producing than he would be if he shut down.

When the market price drops further to $1.50, Joe is on the borderline of shutting down: $1.50 is his shutdown price. Whether he shuts down or keeps producing, he loses the same amount of money.

When the price is down to $1, Joe has had it: he has shut down because he can no longer cover his variable costs. He has no revenue coming in, but he still has $5.50 in costs. Remember from the chapter on costs that the $5.50 is Joe's fixed cost. No matter how low the price goes, Joe never has to lose more than his fixed costs because he can shut down. If you had Joe making 4 burgers when the price was $1, you did a good job following the *MR* = *MC* rule, but Joe is losing more money than he has to. Whenever profits are negative, check to see whether you can cut your losses by shutting down rather than by following the *MR* = *MC* rule.

9.

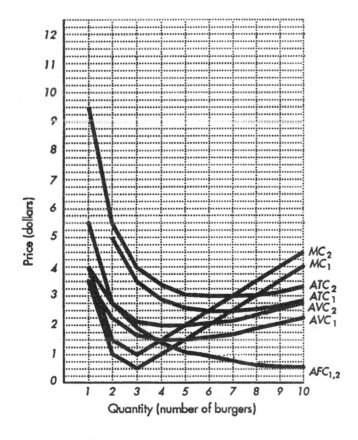

a. $3 (The breakeven price is the lowest value on the *ATC* curve. If the market price is $3, Joe will make just a normal profit.)

b. $2 (The shutdown price is the lowest value on the *AVC* curve. If the market price is below $2, Joe is better off shutting down, with a loss equal to his fixed costs.)

c. Joe's *ATC* increased by $.50 because the price of hamburger meat increased, so Joe must get a price that is $.50 higher now in order to break even. Because hamburger meat is part of Joe's variable costs, the shutdown price also has increased by $.50.

d.

Market Price	Old Number of Burgers	New Number of Burgers
$3.50	9	8
3.00	8	7
2.50	7	6
2.00	6	5
1.50	5	0
1.00	0	0

The method for answering this question is the same we used for question 8 above—only the values of the marginal cost have changed. Let's just look at a couple of prices here.

When the market price is $3.50, only the first 8 hamburgers are worth producing. The marginal cost of the ninth hamburger has increased to $4. Joe would give up $.50 profit by making a hamburger that adds $4 to his costs and only $3.50 to his revenues.

When the market price is $1.50, producing 4 units (the quantity where $MR = MC$) would leave Joe with a loss of about $7.50; Joe can cut his losses to $5.50 (his fixed cost) if he shuts down and produces zero units.

e. decreased (At each possible market price, the quantity Joe will supply is smaller than before.)

f. In deciding how many burgers to produce, Joe looked at his marginal revenue (the market price) and his marginal costs, and basically produced all the burgers whose marginal cost was less than or equal to their marginal revenue. Because Joe's marginal costs have increased, there are now *fewer* burgers whose marginal cost is low enough to be worth making.

g. Joe's supply will *increase* if his costs decrease. When costs decrease, there are *more* burgers whose marginal cost is low enough to be worth making.

10.

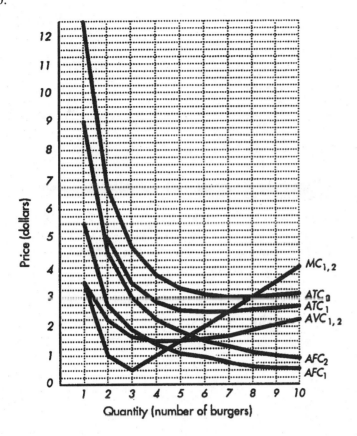

a. $3 (The breakeven price is the lowest value on the *ATC* curve.)
b. $1.50 (The shutdown price is the lowest value on the *AVC* curve.)
c. Joe's *ATC* increased because his fixed costs increased. Average fixed cost (*AFC*) is part of average total costs (*ATC*).
d. Joe's shutdown price is determined by his average-variable-cost (*AVC*) curve. The increase in fixed costs doesn't change Joe's variable costs, so it doesn't change Joe's shutdown price.
e.

Market Price	Old Number of Burgers	New Number of Burgers
$3.50	9	9
3.00	8	8
2.50	7	7
2.00	6	6
1.50	5	5
1.00	0	0

f. Joe's supply curve is the same, whether his fixed costs are $5.50 or $9. Joe's marginal cost isn't affected by his fixed costs, so the amount he will supply at various market prices is not affected by fixed costs.
g. The change in fixed costs *does* affect Joe's breakeven price. Before the change in fixed costs, Joe would be willing to keep on making burgers in the long run as long as the market price was at least $2.50 per burger. Now, with the higher fixed costs, Joe needs a market price of at least $3, or he will exit the burger market in the long run.

Section 2: The Long Run

1. economic profits
2. economic losses
3. normal profit
4. productive
5. allocative
6. price; marginal cost
7. productive; allocative
8. a. $5; 20 (Long-run equilibrium requires that $P = ATC$, so the firm is just breaking even. Profit maximization requires that $MR = MC$. Because $P = MR$ all the time in perfect competition, for long-run equilibrium you must have $P = MR = MC = ATC$. $MC = ATC$ at $5 and 20 units of output. When P is $5, the firm is both maximizing its profit and breaking even.)
   b. Twenty units is productively efficient because that is the lowest-cost output—ATC is at its low point.
   c. Twenty units is allocatively efficient because consumers pay a price equal to marginal cost.
   d. Because 20 units is both productively efficient and allocatively efficient, it must also be economically efficient.

Thinking About and Applying Perfect Competition

I. *Effects of Entry on Burger Stands*

1. a. Joe can increase his output from 7 burgers to 9 burgers. At the higher price, it is profitable for him to make more burgers in his current burger stand.
   b. He probably will not do anything different in the long run. Even though he could expand his burger stand, if Joe is good in business, he already is using the lowest-cost combination of inputs and producing at the low point on his long-run average-cost curve. A larger burger stand might lead to diseconomies of scale.
2. Economic profits in the industry will attract new sellers into the market, increasing the supply of burgers. The increased supply will drive the market price down, reducing Joe's economic profits.

II. *Prices, Profits, and Market Changes*

1.

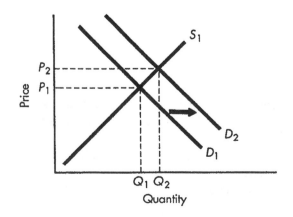

(a) Market for Natural Gas

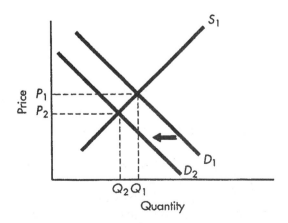

(b) Market for Chemicals

Your new demand curve for natural gas should be to the right of the old demand curve, showing an increase in demand and a higher price. Your new demand curve for chemicals should be to the left of the old demand curve, showing a decrease in demand and a lower price.

2.

(a) Market for Natural Gas

(b) Market for Chemicals

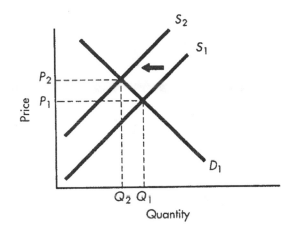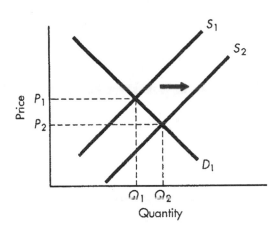

Your new supply curve for natural gas should be to the left of the old supply curve, showing a decrease in supply and an increase in price. Your new supply curve for chemicals should be to the right of the old supply curve, showing an increase in supply and a lower price.

3. increase (The profits generated by higher prices should encourage firms to drill more wells, *ceteris paribus.*)

4. decrease (The low prices and negative profits in the chemical industry should encourage firms to leave the market in the long run.)

MONOPOLY

FUNDAMENTAL QUESTIONS

1. What is monopoly?

    Monopoly is the market structure at the other extreme from perfect competition. Instead of many firms, there is only one supplier of a product for which there are no close substitutes. The U.S. Postal Service is a **monopolist** in the market for letter mail; your electricity, water, natural gas, and cable TV also probably are provided by monopolists.

2. How is a monopoly created?

    For a monopoly to be able to stay a monopoly, there usually has to be something that serves as a **barrier to entry**—something that keeps potential competitors out of the monopolist's market. Three types of barriers exist: natural barriers, such as economies of scale; actions taken by firms that create barriers, such as ownership of an essential resource; and actions taken by governments that create barriers, such as patents and licenses.

3. What does the demand curve for a monopoly firm look like, and why?

    Because the monopolist is the only producer of a good or service, the monopolist's demand curve is the entire industry demand curve. Like market demand curves in general, the monopolist's demand curve is downward sloping: the monopolist must lower prices to increase sales. And the monopolist's marginal-revenue curve lies below the demand curve. Price and marginal revenue are not the same for a **monopoly firm.**

4. Why would someone want to have a monopoly in some business or activity?

    In some ways, monopolies are like the perfectly competitive firms we looked at in the last chapter: they can earn normal profits, make economic profits, or take economic losses. Just having a monopoly on a process to make ordinary rocks at a cost of $5 million a pound does not mean that you will get rich. In perfect competition, economic profits are only temporary because new entrants soon eliminate them. If you are fortunate enough to have a profitable monopoly, barriers to entry let you keep making profits for a long time.

5. Under what conditions would a monopolist charge different customers different prices for the same product?

    The simple answer is that a monopolist uses price discrimination whenever it adds to the monopolist's profits. There are some conditions that are necessary for price discrimination to be profitable for a monopolist: the firm cannot be a price taker; the firm must be able to separate

257

buyers according to their price elasticities; and the firm must be able to prevent resale of the product.

Price discrimination does not work for many products. Although buyers usually have different elasticities, frequently they either cannot be separated or cannot be kept separate. Suppose that your local grocery store knows that some buyers really like Crest toothpaste and are willing to pay a high price to get that brand but that other buyers will only choose Crest when it is on sale. Can the grocery store put out some tubes of Crest priced at $3 for buyers who really like Crest and another batch of tubes of Crest priced at $1 for the people who don't care that much? Obviously not—everybody would take the $1 tubes. The store might place discount coupons for Crest in the newspaper. This strategy price-discriminates by separating those people who have the time and want to clip the coupons from those who do not.

It is easier for electric companies and telephone companies to discriminate among different groups of buyers. They can just look and see whether it's a large business, a small business, or a family using the electricity or the telephone line, and set the price accordingly.

6. How do the predictions of the models of perfect competition and monopoly differ?

Unlike perfect competition, monopoly is inefficient. Moreover, it imposes costs on society by producing less output and selling it at a higher price.

Key Terms

monopoly
monopoly firm (monopolist)
barrier to entry
natural monopoly
local monopoly

regulated monopoly
monopoly power
dumping
predatory dumping
deadweight loss

potential competition
X-inefficiency
rent seeking

Quick-Check Quiz

Section 1: The Market Structure of Monopoly

1. Which of the following statements about monopoly is *false*?
   a. It is a market structure.
   b. A monopolist is the sole supplier of a product.
   c. The monopolist's product has no close substitutes.
   d. To remain a monopoly, there must be barriers to entry.
   e. Monopolists are price takers.

2. Which of the following is *not* a barrier to entry?
   a. large economies of scale
   b. ownership of an essential resource
   c. large profits
   d. patents
   e. government licenses

3. Monopoly power is
   a. a common way to provide electricity and gasoline in the United States.
   b. the ability to set prices.
   c. the ability to control the political process.
   d. a common way to avoid regulation.
   e. the same as regulation.

Section 2: The Demand Curve Facing a Monopoly Firm

1. The monopolist's demand curve is
   a. horizontal at the market price.
   b. vertical at the market price.
   c. horizontal at the market quantity.
   d. vertical at the market quantity.
   e. the same as the industry demand curve.

2. The monopolist's marginal-revenue curve
   a. is horizontal at the market price.
   b. is horizontal at half the market price.
   c. is identical to the monopolist's demand curve.
   d. lies below the demand curve.
   e. lies above the demand curve.

3. A monopolist can sell 20 units of output at a price of $50 per unit. To sell 21 units, the monopolist must cut the price of all units to $49. What is the monopolist's marginal revenue from the twenty-first unit sold?
   a. $29
   b. $50
   c. $49
   d. $1
   e. −$1

Section 3: Profit Maximization

1. A monopoly maximizes profit by producing at the level where
   a. $MR = MC$.
   b. $P = MC$.
   c. $P = MR$.
   d. $P = ATC$.
   e. $MC = ATC$.

2. A monopolist's price is the
   a. prevailing market price determined by demand and supply.
   b. value on the vertical axis where $MR = MC$.
   c. point on the demand curve corresponding to the quantity where $MR = MC$.
   d. point on the demand curve corresponding to the quantity where $P = MC$.
   e. point on the supply curve corresponding to the quantity where $MR = MC$.

3. In the long run, the monopolist's economic profits
    a. will be lost to new entrants.
    b. can continue.
    c. are inevitable.
    d. will lead to shutdown.
    e. will result in higher prices for the monopolist's inputs.

Section 4: Price Discrimination

1. Price discrimination is
    a. refusing to serve certain groups of people.
    b. providing different customers different products.
    c. charging different customers different prices for different products.
    d. providing different customers the same products.
    e. charging different customers different prices for the same products.

2. Which of the following is *not* a condition for successful price discrimination?
    a. The firm must be a monopolist.
    b. The firm must be able to separate customers according to price elasticity.
    c. The firm cannot be a price taker.
    d. The firm must be able to prevent resale of the product.
    e. All of the above are conditions for successful price discrimination.

3. Dumping is
    a. setting a higher price on goods sold domestically than on goods sold in foreign markets.
    b. setting a higher price on goods sold in foreign markets than on goods sold domestically.
    c. selling inferior-quality products in foreign markets for the same price as domestic goods.
    d. selling inferior-quality products in domestic markets for the same price as foreign goods.
    e. selling superior-quality products in foreign markets for the same price as domestic goods.

Section 5: Comparison of Perfect Competition and Monopoly

1. Compared with a perfectly competitive industry, a monopolist produces
    a. more output at a lower price.
    b. more output at a higher price.
    c. less output at a higher price.
    d. less output at a lower price.
    e. the same output at a higher price.

2. X-inefficiency is
    a. a reduction in consumer surplus without a corresponding increase in profit when a perfectly competitive firm is monopolized.
    b. the outcome of threatened entry by possible rival firms.
    c. the tendency of firms not faced with competition to become inefficient.
    d. the use of resources to transfer existing wealth without increasing production.
    e. charging higher prices in domestic markets than in foreign markets.

3. Deadweight loss is
   a. a reduction in consumer surplus without a corresponding increase in profit when a perfectly competitive firm is monopolized.
   b. the outcome of threatened entry by possible rival firms.
   c. the tendency of firms not faced with competition to become inefficient.
   d. the use of resources to transfer existing wealth without increasing production.
   e. charging higher prices in domestic markets than in foreign markets.

Practice Questions and Problems

Section 1: The Market Structure of Monopoly

1. A monopoly firm is the _____ supplier of a product for which there are _____ substitutes.

2. A monopoly remains that way because of _____ .

3. Barriers to entry are anything that _____ the ability of firms to enter a market in which existing firms are earning _____ .

4. Monopoly power is the ability to _____ .

5. A _____ monopoly is a firm that has a monopoly within a limited geographic area.

6. A _____ monopoly is a firm whose behavior is monitored and prescribed by a government entity.

7. A _____ monopoly is a monopoly that results from large economies of scale.

Section 2: The Demand Curve Facing a Monopoly Firm

1. The demand curve facing a monopoly is the same as the _____ demand curve.

2. As price declines, total revenue increases in the _____ portion of the demand curve, reaches a maximum at the _____ point, and declines in the _____ portion.

3. The table below gives the demand curve for a monopolist.

Price	Quantity	TR	MR
$6	0	$_____	
5	1	_____	$_____
4	2	_____	_____
3	3	_____	_____
2	4	_____	_____
1	5	_____	_____
0	6	_____	_____

(a) Total Revenue

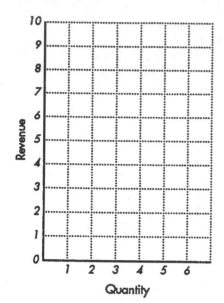

(b) Demand and Marginal Revenue

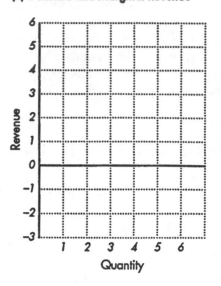

a. In the table, calculate the monopolist's total revenue (*TR*) and marginal revenue (*MR*). Then plot the total-revenue curve on graph a and the demand and marginal-revenue curves on graph b.

b. Over what price range is demand elastic?

_____

c. Over what price range is demand inelastic?

_____

d. At what price is demand unit-elastic?

_____

4. In monopoly, price is _____ (less than, more than, equal to) marginal revenue; in perfect competition, price is _____ (less than, more than, equal to) marginal revenue.

Section 3: Profit Maximization

1. A monopolist maximizes profit by choosing the output level where _____ equals _____ and then charging the corresponding price on the _____ at the quantity produced.

2. The table below lists the cost curves for our old friend Joe, along with a demand curve for burgers. Because new nutritional evidence has convinced most people that burgers are not healthy, Joe's is the only burger stand left in town; he now has a monopoly.

Burgers	TC	Price	TR	MR	AFC	AVC	ATC	MC
1	$ 9.00	$6.50	$____	$____	$5.50	$3.50	$9.00	$3.50
2	10.00	6.00	____	____	2.75	2.25	5.00	1.00
3	10.50	5.50	____	____	1.83	1.67	3.50	.50
4	11.50	5.00	____	____	1.38	1.50	2.88	1.00
5	13.00	4.50	____	____	1.10	1.50	2.60	1.50
6	15.00	4.00	____	____	.92	1.58	2.50	2.00
7	17.50	3.50	____	____	.79	1.71	2.50	2.50
8	20.50	3.00	____	____	.69	1.88	2.56	3.00
9	24.00	2.50	____	____	.61	2.06	2.67	3.50
10	28.00	2.00	____	____	.55	2.25	2.80	4.00

a. In the table, calculate Joe's *TR* and *MR*.

b. To maximize his profits, Joe should make _____ burgers and charge _____ per burger.

c. At this quantity and price, Joe's profit is _____ .

d. On the graph below, plot Joe's demand, *MR, MC,* and *ATC* curves. Then mark Joe's profit-maximizing quantity and price.

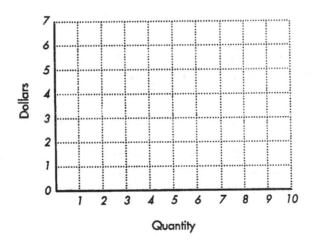

e. In this market, the efficient quantity is _____ burgers.

f. At a price of _____ , Joe would get a fair rate of return.

g. Shade in the deadweight loss on the graph.

Section 4: Price Discrimination

1. _____ is charging different customers different _____ for the same product.

2. Dumping is setting a _____ (higher, lower) price on goods sold domestically than on goods sold in foreign markets.

3. Predatory dumping is dumping to drive competitors out of the _____ .

Section 5: Comparison of Perfect Competition and Monopoly

1. Compared with a perfectly competitive industry with the same costs, a monopoly firm charges a _____ (higher, lower) price and produces a _____ (smaller, larger) quantity.

2. Compared with a perfectly competitive industry, a monopoly firm gets _____ (larger, smaller) profits and generates a _____ (larger, smaller) consumer surplus.

3. The deadweight loss from a monopoly is the difference between the reduction in _____ surplus and the increase in the firm's gain that is produced when a perfectly competitive industry is monopolized.

4. Monopolists can be forced to behave as if competition actually existed by the threat of _____ competition.

5. _____ is the tendency of a firm not faced with competition to become inefficient.

6. _____ is the use of resources simply to transfer wealth from one group to another without increasing production or total wealth.

Thinking About and Applying Monopoly

I. Monopoly and Innovation: The Two Faces of Patents

Economists in general are not at all enthusiastic about monopolies, but patents can be an exception. As we see in more detail in later chapters, there are risks involved in innovation: you may work for years developing a new product that nobody wants. Patents, a temporary monopoly granted for seventeen years, provide an incentive for innovation.

1. Explain why patents provide an incentive for innovation.

_____

_____

2. Are there any negative effects of patents? If yes, what are they?

3. In order to get a patent, you must provide the U.S. Patent Office with detailed information on your innovation, information that is available to the public. Although no one can copy your innovation exactly, how does the public nature of patent information help reduce the monopoly effects of patents?

II. Revisiting Price Discrimination in Airline Fares

In the chapter on elasticity we introduced the idea of price discrimination; and in Chapter 6 of this Study Guide, we looked at price discrimination in airline fares. Airlines often impose restrictions on travelers who want to get their discounted fares. Typical restrictions might include:

Travel must begin on or after May 27 and be completed by September 15.
The nonrefundable tickets require 14-day advance purchase.
Travelers must stay at their destination over a Saturday night.

People taking a vacation usually can plan their trip far in advance and don't mind spending a weekend away. Business travelers, on the other hand, often have to travel without much advance notice and want to be back home on weekends.

Airlines aren't monopolies (in most markets, airlines are oligopolies), but we can use their price-cut policies to further analyze price discrimination.

1. On the basis of the restrictions they set and the effect of those restrictions on business and vacation travelers, airlines must think that _____ (business, vacation) travelers have a higher price elasticity of demand.

2. Use the requirements for price discrimination to explain why airlines put restrictions on their discount tickets.

3. The main customers for discounted tickets will be _____ (business, vacation) travelers.

4. Do airlines think the demand for airline tickets for vacation travel is elastic, inelastic, or unit-elastic? Explain your answer.

_____

_____

_____

Chapter 11 (*Economics* Chapter 25)   Homework Problems

Name _____

1. Name three types of barriers to entry.

2. What three conditions are necessary for price discrimination?

3. In the mid-1980s, as a result of an antitrust suit, AT&T's monopoly on long-distance phone service was broken. As new firms entered the industry, the price of long-distance calls _____ , and the quantity of long-distance calls _____ .

4. Why do manufacturers offer rebates and coupons on their merchandise? Why not just set a lower price in the first place?

5. In the last ten years, the Wichita State University Shocker baseball team has been to more College World Series than any other school in the country. For home games, current WSU students can get in for free. WSU faculty and staff members can get a discounted rate for tickets, but everyone else must pay the regular price.

   a. Why do the Shockers charge different prices to different groups of people?

   b. Based on the Shockers' pricing structure, which group has the highest elasticity of demand? Which group has the lowest elasticity of demand?

   c. How do you think the Shockers are able to segregate the different groups and prevent resale of the tickets?

If your instructor assigns these problems, write your answers above, then tear out this page and hand it in.

Answers

Quick-Check Quiz

Section 1: The Market Structure of Monopoly

1. e; 2. c; 3. b
If you missed any of these questions, you should go back and review Section 1 in Chapter 11 (*Economics,* Chapter 25).

Section 2: The Demand Curve Facing a Monopoly Firm

1. e; 2. d; 3. a
If you missed any of these questions, you should go back and review Section 2 in Chapter 11 (*Economics,* Chapter 25).

Section 3: Profit Maximization

1. a; 2. c; 3. b
If you missed any of these questions, you should go back and review Section 3 in Chapter 11 (*Economics,* Chapter 25).

Section 4: Price Discrimination

1. e; 2. a; 3. a
If you missed any of these questions, you should go back and review Section 4 in Chapter 11 (*Economics,* Chapter 25).

Section 5: Comparison of Perfect Competition and Monopoly

1. c; 2. c; 3. a
If you missed any of these questions, you should go back and review Section 5 in Chapter 11 (*Economics,* Chapter 25).

Practice Questions and Problems

Section 1: The Market Structure of Monopoly

1. only; no close
2. barriers to entry
3. impedes; economic profits
4. set prices
5. local
6. regulated
7. natural

Section 2: The Demand Curve Facing a Monopoly Firm

1. industry
2. elastic; unit-elastic; inelastic

3. a.

Price	Quantity	TR	MR
$6	0	$0	
5	1	5	$ 5
4	2	8	3
3	3	9	1
2	4	8	−1
1	5	5	−3
0	6	0	−5

(a) Total Revenue

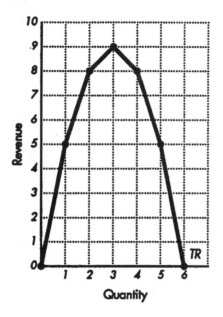

(b) Demand and Marginal Revenue

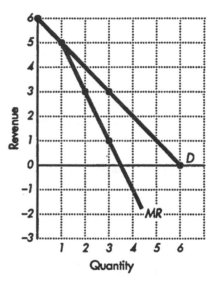

b. from $6 down to $3 (In this range, cutting price increases total revenue.)

c. from $0 up to $3 (In this range, cutting price decreases total revenue.)

d. $3 (Demand is unit-elastic in the middle of a demand curve. *Note:* If these ideas don't seem familiar, refer back to the chapter on elasticity.)

4. more than; equal to

Section 3: Profit Maximization

1. marginal revenue; marginal cost; demand curve
2. a.

Burgers	TC	Price	TR	MR	AFC	AVC	ATC	MC
1	$ 9.00	$6.50	$ 6.50	$ 6.50	$5.50	$3.50	$9.00	$3.50
2	10.00	6.00	12.00	5.50	2.75	2.25	5.00	1.00
3	10.50	5.50	16.50	4.50	1.83	1.67	3.50	.50
4	11.50	5.00	20.00	3.50	1.38	1.50	2.88	1.00
5	13.00	4.50	22.50	2.50	1.10	1.50	2.60	1.50
6	15.00	4.00	24.00	1.50	.92	1.58	2.50	2.00
7	17.50	3.50	24.50	.50	.79	1.71	2.50	2.50
8	20.50	3.00	24.00	−.50	.69	1.88	2.56	3.00
9	24.00	2.50	22.50	−1.50	.61	2.06	2.67	3.50
10	28.00	2.00	20.00	−2.50	.55	2.25	2.80	4.00

b. 5 (The fifth burger is the last one whose MR is greater than or equal to MC.); $4.50 (At this price, consumers want to buy the 5 burgers Joe wants to sell.)
c. $9.50 (Profit = TR − TC = $22.50 − $13 = $9.50)
d.

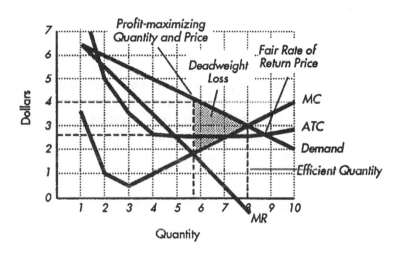

e. 8 (The efficient quantity is the quantity where price equals marginal cost.)
f. about $2.60 (Joe gets a fair rate of return—a normal profit—when the price is just enough to cover all of his costs; that is, when P = ATC. On the graph, it's where the demand curve crosses the ATC curve.)
g. See d above.

Section 4: Price Discrimination

1. Price discrimination; prices
2. higher
3. market

Section 5: Comparison of Perfect Competition and Monopoly

1. higher; smaller
2. larger; smaller
3. consumer
4. potential
5. X-inefficiency
6. Rent seeking

Thinking About and Applying Monopoly

I. *Monopoly and Innovation: The Two Faces of Patents*

1. If successful, the innovation will generate monopoly profits, at least for a while. The possibility of monopoly profits, over and above a normal profit, makes risk-taking worthwhile.
2. Yes. Like most monopolies, patent monopolies lead to higher prices. When the demand for a patented product is very inelastic, like the demand for life-saving drugs, the price can be driven very high.
3. Looking at other people's patents can help a company develop similar but not identical products, providing competition for the patented product. Many innovators prefer not to patent their innovations, reasoning that it is better not to give their competitors too much information.

II. *Price Discrimination in Airline Fares*

1. vacation (Vacation travelers don't mind the restrictions of 14-day advance purchase and a Saturday stayover, but many business travelers do.)
2. For price discrimination to be effective, three conditions are required: the firm cannot be a price taker, the firm must be able to separate customers according to price elasticity, and the firm must be able to prevent resale of the product. As oligopolists, airlines have some control over fares. The restrictions on advance purchase and Saturday stayover effectively separate vacation travelers from many business travelers. Finally, resale is discouraged both by putting individuals' names on the tickets and by making discount tickets nonrefundable.
3. vacation (If business travelers had a higher elasticity, airlines would have cut the price of their tickets.)
4. Elastic. Because airlines reduced the price for vacation travelers, they must think demand is elastic, that a price cut would increase revenues.

MONOPOLISTIC COMPETITION AND OLIGOPOLY

FUNDAMENTAL QUESTIONS

1. What is monopolistic competition?

   As its name suggests, monopolistic competition is a market structure with some of the characteristics of monopoly and some of the characteristics of perfect competition. Like perfect competition, there are a large number of firms, and entry into the market is easy. Because entry into the market is easy, monopolistically competitive firms earn a normal profit in the long run.

   The difference between monopolistic competition and perfect competition is in the type of product sold: a standardized product in perfect competition and a differentiated product in monopolistic competition. Each firm in monopolistic competition has a monopoly on its own versions or brands of the product: as in a monopoly, the firm's demand curve is downward sloping. Unlike a monopoly, however, in monopolistic competition many competitors make almost identical products.

   Because price does not equal marginal cost, monopolistically competitive firms are not economically efficient. This inefficiency is the price consumers pay for variety.

2. What behavior is most common in monopolistic competition?

   In monopolistic competition, the most common behavior is product differentiation, not price competition. Among the nonprice elements that differentiate products are quality, color, style, location, size, safety features, taste, and packaging.

3. What is oligopoly?

   Oligopoly is a market structure in which there are a few large firms and entry is difficult but not impossible. Oligopolies can produce identical products, like steel and cement, or differentiated products, like automobiles and colas. Oligopoly is different from other market structures because firms are interdependent: any action taken by one firm usually provokes a reaction by other firms. If General Motors cuts the prices of its cars, Ford and Chrysler (plus Toyota, Volkswagen, Honda, and the rest) will find some way to react.

4. In what form does rivalry occur in an oligopoly?

   In oligopolies, **strategic behavior** is the rule. When making their decisions, firms have to predict how their rivals will respond. The *kinked demand curve* is evidence that competitors match price decreases but ignore price increases. Even when a decision is not related to price, strategic behavior comes into play. For example, a **dominant strategy** produces better results whatever a competitor does.

5. Why does cooperation among rivals occur most often in oligopolies?

Cooperation is difficult among the large number of firms in perfectly competitive or monopolistically competitive markets: too many sellers have to be organized to make cooperation practical. Cooperation is an integral part of oligopoly because there are only a few interdependent firms. In a *price-leadership oligopoly,* a dominant firm decides on prices and price changes and other firms follow along. In a **cartel,** independent firms organize themselves and agree on prices and production limits.

Several other **facilitating practices** can be used to increase cooperation among firms, including **cost-plus/markup pricing** to ensure that firms with the same costs charge the same price, and **most-favored-customer (MFC)** policies, which discourage selective price cutting.

Key Terms

strategic behavior
game theory
dominant strategy
sequential game

cartel
facilitating practices
cost-plus/markup pricing
most-favored customer (MFC)

adverse selection
moral hazard

Quick-Check Quiz

Section 1: Monopolistic Competition

1. Monopolistic competition is a market structure in which firms produce a
   a. differentiated product, and entry is difficult but not impossible.
   b. standardized product, and entry is difficult but not impossible.
   c. standardized product, and entry is impossible.
   d. differentiated product, and entry is easy.
   e. standardized product, and entry is easy.

2. In the short run, a monopolistically competitive firm can receive
   a. only a normal profit.
   b. only a positive economic profit.
   c. only a negative economic profit.
   d. only a normal profit or a negative economic profit.
   e. a positive or negative economic profit, or a normal profit.

3. Compared to a perfectly competitive market structure, firms in a monopolistically competitive market structure in the long run produce
    a. less output at higher cost.
    b. more output at higher cost.
    c. less output at lower cost.
    d. more output at lower cost.
    e. either more or less output at higher cost.

4. In both perfect competition and monopolistic competition, firms
    a. produce differentiated products.
    b. produce standardized products.
    c. receive only a normal profit in the long run.
    d. engage in nonprice competition.
    e. always receive only a normal profit in the short run.

Section 2: Oligopoly and Interdependence

1. Which of the following is *not* a characteristic of oligopoly?
    a. Entry is difficult but not impossible.
    b. There are a few firms.
    c. Differentiated products may be produced.
    d. Firms make strategic decisions without considering their competitors.
    e. Standardized products may be produced.

2. Which of the following occurs only in an oligopoly?
    a. a downward-sloping market demand curve
    b. a downward-sloping demand curve for the individual firm
    c. interdependence and strategic behavior
    d. a differentiated product
    e. a standardized product

3. The shape of the demand curve for an oligopolist depends on
    a. the market marginal-revenue curve.
    b. how rival firms react to price changes.
    c. the amount of monopolistic competition in the market.
    d. whether price is more or less than marginal revenue.
    e. the prevalence of adverse selection.

4. A kinked demand curve occurs when
    a. other firms follow price cuts but not price increases.
    b. other firms follow price increases but not price cuts.
    c. price leadership is operating.
    d. economic profits exist for all firms in an oligopoly.
    e. economic profits exist for some but not all firms in an oligopoly.

5. The type of decision-making behavior that occurs when firm X's best choice depends on firm Y's actions, and firm Y's best choice depends on firm X's actions, is called
   a. nondeterministic behavior.
   b. tactical behavior.
   c. contestable behavior.
   d. strategic behavior.
   e. deterministic behavior.

Section 3: Summary of Market Structures and the Information Assumption

1. In which of the following market structures do firms produce the output level where $P = MC$?
   a. perfect competition
   b. monopolistic competition
   c. oligopoly
   d. monopoly
   e. Firms produce the output level where $P = MC$ in all of the above market structures.

2. In which of the following structures do firms receive no economic profits in the long run?
   a. only in perfect competition
   b. only in monopoly
   c. only in monopolistic competition
   d. in both perfect competition and monopolistic competition
   e. in both monopoly and monopolistic competition

Practice Questions and Problems

Section 1: Monopolistic Competition

1. Monopolistic competition is a market structure in which _____ firms are producing a(n) _____ product and entry is _____ .

2. Firms in monopolistic competition compete primarily through _____ (product differentiation, price).

3. Monopolistically competitive firms maximize their profits by producing the output level where _____ = _____ .

4. Compared with firms in perfectly competitive markets, monopolistically competitive firms charge _____ (higher, lower) prices and produce _____ (more, less) output.

5. The diagram below show the demand, marginal-revenue, and cost curves for Paul's Pizza, a monopolistically competitive firm.

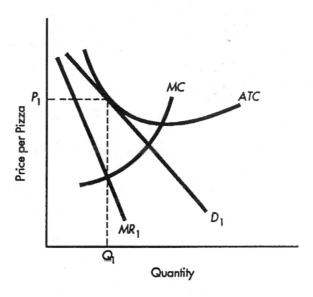

a. At the price and quantity marked, is Paul's Pizza maximizing its profits? Explain your answer.

_____

_____

_____

b. At the price and quantity marked, is Paul's Pizza earning a positive economic profit, a negative economic profit, or a normal profit? Explain your answer.

_____

_____

_____

6. Suppose Paul develops a new, super spicy pizza that many people start buying. Assuming that the super spicy pizza does not cost any more to make than Paul's other pizzas, sketch in new demand and marginal-revenue curves for Paul's Pizza that reflect the increased demand for the pizza, and shade in the rectangle that measures Paul's economic profits.

7. Why will Paul's economic profits probably last for only a little while?

_____

_____

_____

Section 2: Oligopoly and Interdependence

1. Oligopoly is a market structure in which _____ firms are producing a _____ product and entry is _____ .

2. Strategic behavior occurs in oligopolies because the firms in an oligopoly are _____ .

3. The shape of the demand curve and marginal-revenue curve for an oligopolist depends on how _____ react to changes in _____ and _____ .

4. _____ describes oligopolistic behavior as a series of strategic moves and countermoves.

5. A strategy that produces better results no matter what strategy an opposing firm follows is a(n) _____ strategy.

6. A(n) _____ game occurs when a firm can wait and see what its rival does before deciding on its own strategy.

7. An organization of independent firms whose purpose is to control and limit production and increase prices and profits is a(n) _____ .

8. Briefly describe how a price-leadership oligopoly operates.

_____

_____

_____

_____

9. Briefly explain how cost-plus/markup pricing and most-favored-customer agreements facilitate cooperation among oligopolists.

_____

_____

_____

_____

10. Joe's and Moe's are two competing gas stations in town. Both are considering adding a video game parlor to their stations. The payoff matrix below shows the expected daily profits for each gas station:

Joe's Station

		Adds Video Games		Doesn't Add Video Games	
Moe's Station	**Adds Video Games**	Joe's	$200	Joe's	$100
		Moe's	$500	Moe's	$300
	Doesn't Add Video Games	Joe's	$250	Joe's	$180
		Moe's	$350	Moe's	$400

a. Does Joe have a dominant strategy? If yes, what is it?

_____

_____

b. Does Moe have a dominant strategy? If yes, what is it?

_____

_____

c. If you were Joe, would you add video games, not add video games, or wait to see what Moe does? Explain your answer.

_____

_____

d. If you were Moe, would you add video games, not add video games, or wait to see what Joe does? Explain your answer.

_____

_____

Section 3: Summary of Market Structures and the Information Assumption

1. Summarize the characteristics of the four market structures you've been studying by filling in the table below.

Characteristic	Perfect Competition	Monopoly	Monopolistic Competition	Oligopoly
Number of firms	_____	_____	_____	_____
Type of product	_____	_____	_____	_____
Entry conditions	_____	_____	_____	_____
Demand curve for firm	_____	_____	_____	_____
Price and marginal cost	_____	_____	_____	_____
Long-run profit	_____	_____	_____	_____

2. A(n) _____ occurs when people alter their behavior from what was anticipated when a transaction was made.

3. _____ and _____ are ways that firms protect themselves from adverse selection.

4. _____ occurs when low-quality consumers or producers force higher-quality consumers or producers out of the market.

5. _____ , _____ , and _____ are ways firms can provide information to consumers.

Thinking About and Applying Monopolistic Competition and Oligopoly

I. Is Advertising Profitable in Monopolistic Competition?

Paul's Pizza is thinking about using advertising to differentiate its pizza from all the other pizzas in town. An advertising agency has developed two possible campaigns: a small-scale campaign that will add $5 per hour to Paul's costs and a larger campaign that will add $10 per hour to Paul's costs. The agency also estimated the increases in demand it expects Paul's Pizza to get from each campaign.

1. The table on the following page shows Paul's current demand and costs.

   a. Paul's current profit-maximizing quantity is _____ pizza(s).

   b. His current profit-maximizing price is _____ .

   c. At this quantity and price, Paul's economic profit is _____ .

Paul's Pizza: Current Demand and Costs

Quantity Sold/Hour	ATC	MC	P	MR
1	$26.50	$12.50	$12.00	$12.00
2	16.25	6.00	11.00	10.00
3	11.50	2.00	10.00	8.00
4	9.25	2.50	9.00	6.00
5	8.00	3.00	8.00	4.00
6	7.25	3.50	7.00	2.00
7	6.79	4.00	6.00	0
8	6.50	4.50	5.00	−2.00

2. The table below shows the agency's estimates of Paul's demand and costs assuming the smaller campaign.

   a. Paul's profit-maximizing quantity here is _____ pizzas.

   b. His profit maximizing price is _____ .

   c. At this quantity and price, Paul's economic profit would be _____ .

Paul's Pizza: With Smaller Advertising Campaign

Quantity Sold/Hour	ATC	MC	P	MR
1	$31.50	$12.50	$15.00	$15.00
2	18.75	6.00	13.75	12.50
3	13.17	2.00	12.50	10.00
4	10.50	2.50	11.25	7.50
5	9.00	3.00	10.00	5.00
6	8.08	3.50	8.75	2.50
7	7.50	4.00	7.50	0
8	7.13	4.50	6.25	2.50

3. The table below shows the agency's estimates of Paul's demand and costs assuming the larger campaign.

    a. Paul's profit-maximizing quantity here is _____ pizzas.

    b. His profit-maximizing price is _____ .

    c. At this quantity and price, Paul's economic profit would be _____ .

Paul's Pizza: With Larger Advertising Campaign				
Quantity Sold/Hour	*ATC*	*MC*	*P*	*MR*
1	$36.50	$12.50	$15.60	$15.60
2	21.25	6.00	14.30	13.00
3	14.83	2.00	13.00	10.40
4	11.75	2.50	11.70	7.80
5	10.00	3.00	10.40	5.20
6	8.92	3.50	9.10	2.60
7	8.21	4.00	7.80	0
8	7.75	4.50	6.50	−2.60

4. If you were Paul, which campaign would you choose? Explain your answer.

_____

_____

_____

_____

II. Cartel Cheating

The key difference between oligopoly and other market structures is that oligopolists are interdependent: the decisions of one affect others. In many situations, interdependence creates conflicting incentives both to cooperate with others and to "cheat" on one's cooperation.

You can see how this happens in oligopolies by looking at the choices faced by a member of a cartel such as OPEC. Let's make you the oil minister of Scheherazade, a hypothetical small member of OPEC. You are responsible for managing your country's oil output and price, and your objective is to maximize your country's total revenues from oil (your marginal cost of producing more oil is so low that you don't have to pay any attention to costs).

Last week, the OPEC countries met and agreed to charge $25 per barrel for oil. Scheherazade was given an output quota of 300,000 barrels per day. The graph below shows your current position and possible options. D_1 is the demand curve for your oil if the rest of OPEC ignores any price changes you make, and D_2 is your demand curve if the rest of OPEC matches any price changes. Like the kinked demand curve model, the other members of OPEC will ignore any price increases you make but will match any price cuts they know about. Use this information to answer the questions on the following page.

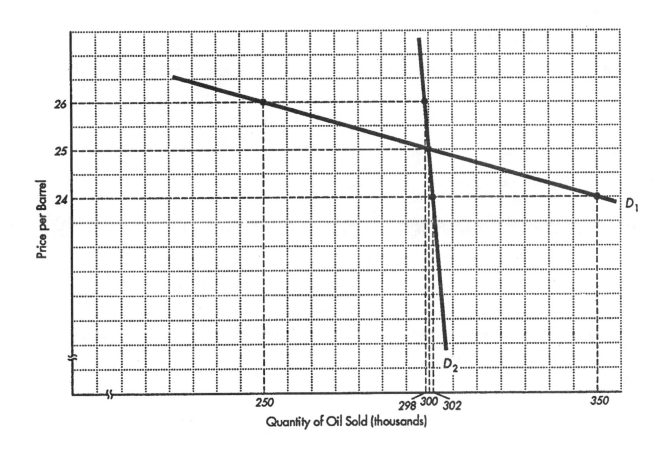

1. At $25 per barrel, Scheherazade takes in _____ from selling 300,000 barrels.

2. If you could get the rest of OPEC to go along with raising its price to $26 per barrel, Scheherazade would take in _____ .

3. Unfortunately, the rest of OPEC thinks that $25 is the best price and will not go along with a higher price. If only Scheherazade raises its price to $26, it will take in _____ .

4. Because raising your price individually will not increase your revenues, you can try cutting the price to $24. If the rest of OPEC matches your price cut, Scheherazade will take in _____ .

5. Late one night, the buyer for Euro-Oil, a large oil refiner, knocks quietly on your door. She offers to buy 350,000 barrels of oil a day from Scheherazade if you cut the price to $24 and keep the price cut a secret. Would this deal be profitable for Scheherazade? Explain your answer.

_____

_____

_____

_____

III. Luxury Root Beer

The *Wall Street Journal* featured a small firm called Thomas Kemper Soda Co. in its May 25, 1993, edition (page B2):

> Thousands of small-business owners would love nothing more than to tap the upscale market where margins are big and mass marketers are scarce. . . . Entrepreneur Laura Bracken is proving that in the austere 1990s, it is possible to peddle even root beer as a luxury. . . . Sales should hit about $2 million this year, double last year's revenue.
>
> The secret is aggressive marketing, good timing, and a distinctive product. That combination enables Thomas Kemper Soda to charge a whopping $5 a six-pack for its soda.

Unlike other root beers, Thomas Kemper Soda Co. root beer is brewed in small batches, not mixed from syrup; is packaged in bottles and kegs, not cans; and is distributed primarily through bars.

Use what you've learned about monopolistic competition to explain how Thomas Kemper Soda Co. can succeed at selling a product that costs buyers more than twice as much as that of most of its competitors.

_____

_____

_____

Chapter 12 (*Economics* Chapter 26)   Homework Problems

Name _____

1. Describe monopolistic competition in terms of number of firms, product differentiation, and ease of entry and exit.

2. Describe oligopoly in terms of number of firms, product differentiation, and ease of entry and exit.

3. Under which market structure(s) do we find allocative efficiency?

4. Which market structure(s) could earn positive economic profits in the long run?

5. Before 1981, most life insurance companies did not include a blood test as part of the physical examination required before an applicant became eligible to buy life insurance. What happened in the 1980s that induced insurance companies to require blood tests?

If your instructor assigns these problems, write your answers above, then tear out this page and hand it in.

Answers

Quick-Check Quiz

Section 1: Monopolistic Competition

1. d; 2. e; 3. a; 4. c
If you missed any of these questions, you should go back and review Section 1 in Chapter 12 (*Economics*, Chapter 26).

Section 2: Oligopoly and Interdependence

1. d; 2. c; 3. b; 4. a; 5. d
If you missed any of these questions, you should go back and review Section 2 in Chapter 12 (*Economics*, Chapter 26).

Section 3: Summary of Market Structures and the Information Assumption

1. a; 2. d
If you missed either of these questions, you should go back and review Section 3 in Chapter 12 (*Economics*, Chapter 26).

Practice Questions and Problems

Section 1: Monopolistic Competition

1. many; differentiated; easy
2. product differentiation
3. *MR; MC*
4. higher; less
5. a. Yes. $MR = MC$ at the quantity marked.
   b. a normal profit ($P = ATC$)
6.

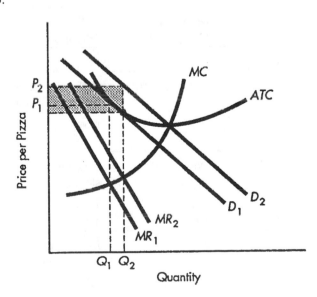

7. Other pizza makers will emulate Paul's innovation, shifting the demand for Paul's pizzas downward.

Section 2: Oligopoly and Interdependence

1. few; differentiated or standardized; difficult but not impossible
2. interdependent
3. competitors; price; product
4. Game theory
5. dominant
6. sequential
7. cartel
8. One firm determines the price, and all other firms follow along and match any price changes.
9. Cost-plus/markup pricing leads to the same or very similar pricing behavior among rival firms. Firms with the same production costs figure their prices by adding the same profit margin to their costs, so that their prices come out the same without any need for collusion.

   Most-favored-customer agreements discourage price cutting by requiring a firm to cut its price to the price of all firms with most-favored-customer agreements rather than use selective price cuts to attract new customers from other firms.

10. a. Yes. Joe has a dominant strategy: add video games. If Moe adds video games, Joe is better off if he adds video games ($200 compared to $100); if Moe doesn't add video games, Joe is still better off if he adds video games ($250 compared to $180).

    b. No. Moe doesn't have a dominant strategy. If Joe adds video games, Moe is better off to add them too ($500 compared to $350), but if Joe doesn't add video games, Moe is better off ($400 compared to $300) not adding video games.

    c. Because Joe has a dominant strategy in adding video games, he should go ahead and act.

    d. Moe doesn't have a dominant strategy, so his decision is more complex than Joe's. Waiting to see what Joe does would be a reasonable decision, although Moe also could justify going ahead and adding video games now because he expects that Joe will choose to add video games (adding games is Joe's best choice).

Section 3: Summary of Market Structures and the Information Assumption

1.

Characteristic	Perfect Competition	Monopoly	Monopolistic Competition	Oligopoly
Number of firms	Many	One	Many	Few
Type of product	Undifferentiated	One	Differentiated	Differentiated or undifferentiated
Entry conditions	Easy	Difficult or impossible	Easy	Difficult
Demand curve for firm	Horizontal (perfectly elastic)	Downward sloping	Downward sloping	Downward sloping
Price and marginal cost	$MC = P$	$MC < P$	$MC < P$	$MC < P$
Long-run profit	Zero	Yes	Zero	Dependent on whether entry occurs

2. Moral hazard
3. Downpayments; deductibles
4. Adverse selection
5. Brand names; quarantees; sunk costs

Thinking About and Applying Monopolistic Competition and Oligopoly

I. Is Advertising Profitable in Monopolistic Competition?

1. a. 5 (The first 5 pizzas have $MR > MC$. The sixth pizza's MR is $2, less than its MC of $3.50, so it is not worth making and selling.)
   b. $8 (This is the price at which consumers will buy 5 pizzas.)
   c. zero ($P = ATC$)
2. a. 5 (The first 5 pizzas have $MR > MC$. The sixth pizza's MR is $2.50, less than its MC of $3.50, so it is not worth making and selling.)
   b. $10 (This is the price at which consumers will buy 5 pizzas.)
   c. $5 (profit per pizza = $10 [$P$] – $9 [$ATC$] = $1; $1 profit per pizza × 5 pizzas = $5)
3. a. 5 (The first 5 pizzas have $MR > MC$. The sixth pizza's MR is $2.60, less than its MC of $3.50, so it is not worth making and selling.)
   b. $10.40 (This is the price at which consumers will buy 5 pizzas.)
   c. $2 (profit per pizza = $10.40 [$P$] – $10 [$ATC$] = $.40; $.40 profit per pizza × 5 pizzas = $2)
4. The smaller advertising campaign gives Paul $5 economic profit, compared with the normal profit he currently is earning. The larger advertising campaign gives Paul only $2 economic profit; compared with the smaller campaign, it adds more to Paul's costs than it generates in increased demand and revenue, so it is not worth the money. The law of diminishing returns applies to advertising campaigns, too: the first few dollars spent on advertising frequently have more impact on demand than additional dollars have.

II. Cartel Cheating

1. $7,500,000 ($25 × 300,000)
2. $7,748,000 ($26 × 298,000)
3. $6,500,000 ($26 × 250,000)
4. $7,248,000 ($24 × 302,000)
5. Yes. Scheherazade will take in $8,400,000 ($24 × 350,000), so it will be quite profitable. What makes it profitable is keeping it secret so that the rest of OPEC does not match your price. Secret cheating on cartel agreements is usually profitable for any member of the cartel as long as the other members of the cartel do not find out about the cheating and match the price cut immediately.

III. Luxury Root Beer

Kemper is using product differentiation to succeed. Its root beer is made and packaged differently and is sold through different channels.

THE NEW ECONOMY

FUNDAMENTAL QUESTIONS

1. What is the difference between the New Economy and the Old Economy?

Our economy has always changed over time because of changes in technology. In the last years of the 1900s and the early years of the 2000s, rapid improvements in information processing and communication technology (personal computers, the Internet, the World Wide Web, etc.) have not only created many new businesses but also forced many existing companies to change the way they do business. Many people see these changes as so fundamental that they use the phrase "the New Economy" to refer to those businesses and markets that have adapted to the new information processing and communication technologies. The phrase "the Old Economy" is used either to refer to the pre-1990 economy or to those present-day businesses which have not yet taken advantage of the new technologies.

2. What are networks and what are the economics of networks?

A network is a group of people, businesses, or other organizations that are connected to each other in some way. People with telephones are a network: they can talk back and forth among themselves. People who have electricity in their homes are a network; so are people hooked up to a city's water system. Users of a particular computer program or operating system also make up a network.

Networks have some unique economic characteristics. First, networks involve standards, an agreed-on set of characteristics that lets all parts of the network mesh together. For example, the telephone that you bought last week has to be made to the standards of the telephone system, or you won't be able to use it. Different networks can use different standards; in the United States, most electric appliances are designed to the standard of 110 volts at a frequency of 60 hertz, while many other parts of the world use 220 volts and 50 hertz. An electric razor made to U.S. standards doesn't work in most of the rest of the world.

Networks also have **positive feedback** effects. The value of a network to members goes up as the number of people in the network goes up. Think about it for a moment: would you pay more to have a telephone that let you talk to 100 people, or a telephone that let you talk to 100,000 people? Adding more people to a network makes the network more valuable and attracts even more people to the network. The value of a network actually increases much faster than the size of the network.

3. What do epidemics have to do with markets?

Both epidemics and markets can have a **tipping point.** Many diseases can persist for a long time in a population, causing only a few people to get sick. Epidemics happen when something changes and a large enough number of people (the tipping point) gets sick so that the disease spreads rapidly among the population, making nearly everybody sick.

Markets can tip in the same way, leading to everyone's buying the same product or brand. In the late 1800s, many firms went into the telephone business, trying to build networks of users of their telephones. In almost all cases, most of these firms went out of business, leaving only one phone company in the market in each city. Think about how competition between phone companies would work: would a potential customer rather sign up with a firm that had 1,000 other customers or a firm that had 5,000 other customers? The firm that got big fast would have a more valuable network, and thereafter would attract most of the new customers. Eventually, customers of the smaller network would shift over to the bigger network, so they could talk to more people. The market would tip to whichever phone company got big first.

Key Terms

basic research
applied research
development

positive feedback or positive
  network externalities
standards war
closed system

open system
tipping point
personalized selling

Quick-Check Quiz

Section 1: A New Economics?

1. Technological change in which of the following industries distinguishes the New Economy from the Old Economy?
   a. electricity
   b. railroads
   c. information processing
   d. radio
   e. television

2. Basic research is intended to
   a. have no useful outcome.
   b. have a practical payoff.
   c. turn research discoveries into practical applications.
   d. create new knowledge.
   e. use technology to create a more polite society.

3. Development (as in R&D) is intended to
   a. have no useful outcome.
   b. have a practical payoff.
   c. turn research discoveries into practical applications.
   d. create new knowledge.
   e. use technology to create a more polite society.

4. Applied research is intended to
   a. have no useful outcome.
   b. have a practical payoff.
   c. turn research discoveries into practical applications.
   d. create new knowledge.
   e. use technology to create a more polite society.

5. Technological change is *not* likely to have which of the following effects?
   a. Increase the range of economies of scale.
   b. Decrease the range of economies of scale.
   c. Not affect the range of economies of scale.
   d. Shift the average total cost curve upward.
   e. Shift the average total cost curve downward.

6. A patent gives its owner exclusive ownership of a patented process or product for how long?
   a. 1 year
   b. 5 years
   c. 10 years
   d. 17 years
   e. forever

Section 2: Networks

1. What characteristic makes the economics of networks unusual?
   a. negative feedback
   b. positive feedback
   c. positive influence
   d. negative influence
   e. negative expectations

2. Which factor increases the value of membership in a network?
   a. raising the price of access to the network
   b. lowering the price of access to the network
   c. increasing the number of members of the network
   d. decreasing the number of members of the network
   e. government regulation of the network

3. When consumer VCRs were first marketed, there were two different, incompatible types of videotapes: Betamax and VHS. The market battle between Betamax and VHS is an example of
   a. a bilateral monopoly.
   b. a standards war.
   c. negative network externalities.
   d. duplicate monopolies.
   e. perfect competition.

4. If a network doubles its number of members, the value of the network to each user will
   a. stay the same.
   b. double.
   c. be almost four times as high.
   d. be cut in half.
   e. be about one-fourth as high.

Section 3: Epidemics and Market Tipping

1. Which of the following combinations describes a market that is likely to tip?
   a. positive feedback and buyers who desire a variety of product options
   b. negative feedback and buyers who desire a variety of product options
   c. positive feedback only, because variety doesn't matter
   d. positive feedback and buyers who don't care about variety
   e. negative feedback and buyers who don't care about variety

2. Many websites give away information for free. What is the economic explanation for this?
   a. Government subsidizes websites.
   b. People who own websites never took any economics classes.
   c. People who own websites care more about the public than about making money.
   d. The marginal cost is zero.
   e. The average cost is zero.

Practice Questions and Problems

Section 1: A New Economics?

1. In the 1980s, the top stock market leaders were _____ (oil companies, retailers, high-tech firms); in the 1990s, the top stock market leaders were _____ (oil companies, retailers, high-tech firms)

2. What does technological change do to the average-cost curve? _____

3. What legal document gives a person or firm the exclusive right to a product or process?
   _____

4. What size firm is most likely to be first to innovate, _____ (small, large), and what size firm is most likely to lag behind in innovation? _____ (small, large)

Section 2: Networks

1. The key characteristics of the economics of networks is the existence of _____ feedback that makes the value of a network to an individual member _____ (go up, go down, stay the same) as the number of members goes up.

2. Small networks are _____ (more, less) valuable to members than large networks are.

3. As a network grows, the graph of the demand for membership shifts _____ .

4. Network standards that are controlled by a single firm that keeps its system private are called _____ systems; network standards that are available to any firm are called _____ systems.

5. When two or more technologies are competing in the market to determine which one will be adopted by consumers, there is a _____ .

Section 3: Epidemics and Market Tipping

1. Markets are said to _____ when sales of a particular product suddenly start to increase.

2. In network markets, _____ makes markets likely to tip, with only one network product's remaining on the market. On the other hand, a demand for _____ can prevent even a network market from tipping.

3. Personalized selling is an example of _____ . Explain why personalized selling is more common in the New Economy than in the Old Economy.

_____

_____

_____

Thinking About and Applying the New Economy

I. Metcalf's Law

Metcalf's Law (named after Bob Metcalf, the inventor of Ethernet) says, "The value of a network goes up with the square of the number of users." This is just a slightly simplified version of the formula in the chapter (value = $n^2 - n$). Use Metcalf's Law to calculate the value of the networks in the table below, then plot the relationship between the number of users and the value of the network.

Number of Users	Value of Network
(n)	(n^2)
10	100
20	_____
30	_____
40	_____

Mathematically, this is an example of an _____ relationship.

II. Telephone Networks

Alexander Graham Bell invented the telephone in the 1870s. In the 1890s, after Bell's patents expired, several competing telephone companies were started in many cities in the United States. At that time, telephone companies had to spend large amounts of money to run wires from their central switching stations to each individual customer to connect that customer to the telephone network. Once the wires were installed, the cost of providing a telephone call to the customer was very low.

By the 1910s, in most U.S. cities there was only one telephone company serving the entire city; any competing telephone companies had gone out of business. Use what you have learned about the economics of networks to explain why it makes economic sense for there to be only one telephone company in any city.

_____

_____

_____

_____

Chapter 27 (*Economics* Chapter 27)   Homework Problems

Name _____

1. Technological change in what industry makes the New Economy different from the Old Economy?

2. What factor makes the economics of networks different?

3. What factor is common to epidemics and network markets?

4. List three factors that can make large firms less likely to innovate than small firms.

5. The market for personal computer word processors has tipped to Microsoft Word; Word sells many more copies today than all other word processors combined. There are many different programs available for creating materials for the Internet; that market doesn't show any signs of tipping. What factor cited in the text do Internet programmers probably want that word processor users don't care much about?

If your instructor assigns these problems, write your answers above, then tear out this page and hand it in.

Answers

Quick-Check Quiz

Section 1: A New Economics?

1. c; 2. d; 3. c; 4. b; 5. d; 6. d
If you missed any of these questions, you should go back and review Section 1 in Chapter 13 (*Economics,* Chapter 27).

Section 2: Networks

1. b; 2. c; 3. b; 4. c
If you missed any of these questions, you should go back and review Section 2 in Chapter 13 (*Economics,* Chapter 27).

Section 3: Epidemics and Market Tipping

1. d; 2. d
If you missed any of these questions, you should go back and review Section 3 in Chapter 13 (*Economics,* Chapter 27).

Practice Questions and Problems

Section 1: A New Economics?

1. retailers; high-tech firms
2. It shifts it downward.
3. patent
4. small; large

Section 2: Networks

1. positive; go up
2. less
3. outward
4. closed; open
5. standards war

Section 3: Epidemics and Market Tipping

1. tip
2. positive feedback; variety
3. price discrimination; The New Economy makes it much easier to collect information about individuals' tastes and willingness to pay.

Thinking About and Applying the New Economy

I. Metcalf's Law

Number of Users	Value of Network
(n)	(n^2)
10	100
20	400
30	900
40	1,600

exponential

II. Telephone Networks

Telephone systems are networks that are subject to positive feedback. A person thinking about getting a telephone connection for the first time would get more value from signing up with a larger telephone network than a smaller one. Larger networks thus grow larger; smaller networks fall further and further behind in the value they can offer customers, and eventually disappear.

GOVERNMENT POLICY TOWARD BUSINESS

FUNDAMENTAL QUESTIONS

1. What is antitrust policy?

   Antitrust policy is a set of government laws and policies intended to prevent acts by business that reduce, or could reduce, competition. The basic antitrust policy of the United States is contained in the Sherman Act of 1890, along with the Clayton Antitrust Act and the Federal Trade Commission Act, both passed in 1914.

   Two interpretations of antitrust policy have been applied in the past. The "rule of reason" interpretation held that being a monopoly or attempting to be a monopoly was not in itself illegal; to be illegal an action had to be unreasonable in a competitive sense, and anticompetitive effects had to be demonstrated. According to the "per se rule," activities that were potentially monopolizing tactics were illegal, whether or not anticompetitive effects could be demonstrated. Although the courts define the standard to be applied in antitrust cases, the administration in office appoints the judges and defines the degree to which antitrust policy will be enforced by allocating money to the Antitrust Division of the Department of Justice and the Federal Trade Commission.

2. What is the difference between economic regulation and social regulation?

   Economic regulation refers to government control over price and output decisions in a specific industry; **social regulation** refers to government control over other types of business decisions—for example, setting health and safety standards for products, and establishing performance and environmental procedures.

3. Why does the government intervene in business activity?

   There are several theories economists and others use to explain government decisions to intervene in business activity. Among them are the **public interest theory,** which says that government acts to promote the well-being of the general public, and the **capture theory,** which says that government acts to promote the well-being only of special-interest groups.

Key Terms

Herfindahl index	antitrust policy	per se rule
concentration	rule of reason	economic regulation

social regulation   rent seeking   adverse selection
privatization   public interest theory   moral hazard
contracting out   capture theory

Quick-Check Quiz

Section 1: Antitrust Policy

1. The Herfindahl index measures
    a. the success of the per se rule.
    b. concentration in a market.
    c. the profitability of firms in unregulated markets.
    d. the profitability of firms in regulated markets.
    e. the need for social regulation of industry.

2. Under the rule of reason,
    a. actions that could be anticompetitive are intrinsically illegal.
    b. only those actions that always have an anticompetitive effect are illegal.
    c. only those actions that are procompetitive are illegal.
    d. only those decisions made by regulatory agencies are automatically legal.
    e. to be illegal an action must be unreasonable in a competitive sense, and its anticompetitive effects must be demonstrated.

3. Under the per se rule,
    a. actions that could be anticompetitive are intrinsically illegal.
    b. only those actions that always have an anticompetitive effect are illegal.
    c. only those actions that are procompetitive are illegal.
    d. only those decisions made by regulatory agencies are automatically legal.
    e. to be illegal an action must be unreasonable in a competitive sense, and its anticompetitive effects must be demonstrated.

4. In terms of limiting certain types of business activities through antitrust laws, the United States
    a. is more restrictive than most other countries.
    b. is less restrictive than other countries.
    c. has procedures that are more restrictive than industrial European countries but less restrictive than industrial Asian countries.
    d. has procedures that are less restrictive than industrial European countries but more restrictive than industrial Asian countries.
    e. uses the same antitrust laws as the rest of the world.

Section 2: Regulation

1. *Economic regulation* refers to the
   a. ownership of all stock in a corporation by the national government.
   b. ownership of a controlling interest in a corporation by either national or state government.
   c. prescription of price and output for a specific industry.
   d. control of government by special-interest groups.
   e. prescription of health, safety, performance, and environmental standards that apply across several industries.

2. *Social regulation* refers to the
   a. ownership of all stock in a corporation by the national government.
   b. ownership of a controlling interest in a corporation by either national or state government.
   c. prescription of price and output for a specific industry.
   d. control of government by special-interest groups.
   e. prescription of health, safety, performance, and environmental standards that apply across several industries.

3. Economic regulation of transportation began
   a. because the industries were all natural monopolies.
   b. because large fixed costs limited entry.
   c. as part of the penalty for antitrust violations.
   d. because of the international nature of these industries.
   e. because antitrust laws were not in effect yet.

4. Since the 1970s,
   a. the transportation industry has been more tightly regulated by the government.
   b. the transportation industry has been taken over by the government and run by government agencies.
   c. the transportation industry has been largely deregulated.
   d. the transportation industry has become obsolete due to improvements in communications.
   e. regulation over the industry has shifted from individual states to the national government.

5. Which of the following statements is *not* true?
   a. The WTO specifies the level of tariffs its members will impose for trade among themselves.
   b. The intent of the WTO is to lower tariffs and increase trade.
   c. Under the MAI, nations would treat multinational corporations the same way they treat their own corporations.
   d. The WTO arose in response to the growth of multinational corporations.
   e. In most European nations, the traditional solution to the problems associated with natural monopolies was nationalization as opposed to regulation.

Section 3: Government and Business

1. In the public interest theory of government, government is viewed as acting primarily
    a. to promote the personal interests of government bureaucrats.
    b. out of concern for the well-being of the general public.
    c. to provide benefits for special-interest groups.
    d. to promote the personal financial interests of elected officials.
    e. to maximize the number of votes received by incumbents in future elections.

2. In the capture theory of government, government is viewed as acting primarily
    a. to promote the personal interests of government bureaucrats.
    b. out of concern for the well-being of the general public.
    c. to provide benefits for special-interest groups.
    d. to promote the personal financial interests of elected officials.
    e. to maximize the number of votes received by incumbents in future elections.

3. When a situation allows someone to change their behavior after making a transaction or or contract, what kind of information problem exists?
    a. adverse selection
    b. externality
    c. moral hazard
    d. distortion
    e. *per se* violation

4. When the misvaluing of unobservable qualities drives higher-quality products out of the market, what kind of information problem exists?
    a. adverse selection
    b. externality
    c. moral hazard
    d. distortion
    e. *per se* violation

Practice Questions and Problems

Section 1: Antitrust Policy

1. The two main approaches the U.S. government uses to intervene in business activities are

    _____ and _____ .

2. Calculate the Herfindahl index for both of the following three-firm markets:

    a. Firm A has a market share of 80 percent. Firm B has a market share of 10 percent. Firm C has a market share of 10 percent. This industry's Herfindahl index is _____ .

    b. Firm A has a market share of 35 percent. Firm B has a market share of 35 percent. Firm C has a market share of 30 percent. This industry's Herfindahl index is _____ .

3. According to the Justice Department's criterion, both of the markets in question 2 are _____ (highly competitive, moderately competitive, highly concentrated).

4. Antitrust policy is designed to control the growth of _____ and to encourage _____ .

5. List the three major antitrust laws in the United States and the dates they were passed.

_____

_____

_____

6. When judging the anticompetitive effects of a merger between businesses, the government relies primarily on the _____ .

7. Individuals and businesses who have been hurt by antitrust violations can sue for _____ damages.

Section 2: Regulation

1. The prescription of price and output for a specific industry is called _____ regulation; the prescribing of health, safety, performance, and environmental standards that apply across industries is called _____ regulation.

2. In the 1970s and early 1980s, the transportation and communications industries in the United States were _____ .

3. _____ is the term used to describe transferring a publicly owned enterprise to private ownership. _____ is the term used to describe using private firms to perform certain government functions.

Section 3: Government and Business

1. The *public interest theory* assumes that government intervenes in business activity to benefit _____ .

2. The *capture theory* assumes that government intervenes in business activity to benefit _____ .

3. Three types of market inefficiencies that can lead to government intervention are _____ , _____ , and _____ .

4. Insurance companies frequently write life insurance policies that don't pay off if the person insured commits suicide shortly after taking out the life insurance policy. What is the name of the information problem they are trying to prevent? _____

5. Six months ago you and your spouse bought a Mazda Miata, a wonderful two-seat convertible sports car. You enjoy the car very much, but you just found out that you and your spouse are expecting a

baby, and you need a bigger car. Even though you took very good care of your Miata, no one will pay you more than 75% of what you paid for the car, even though the car is practically new. You are a victim of what kind of information problem? _____

Thinking About and Applying Government Policy Toward Business

I. College Cartels

In the early 1990s, the Justice Department charged a group of prestigious universities in the United States with violations of the antitrust laws involving exchanging information on financial-aid packages to be offered to potential students. In many cases, the information exchange resulted in students' receiving financial aid offers from these universities that were identical in terms of the cost that the students' families would have to pay at each university.

1. The universities' behavior was a form of price fixing. Is price fixing handled under the per se rule or the rule of reason in U.S. antitrust law?

    _____

2. Why would universities engage in this kind of price fixing?

    _____

    _____

    _____

3. Suppose you're a student who thinks you've been overcharged by a university. How can you recover the money you lost?

    _____

    _____

    _____

Chapter 14 (*Economics* Chapter 28)   Homework Problems

Name _____

1. The public interest theory states that government acts to promote the well-being of _____ ,
    while the capture theory says that government acts to promote the well-being of _____ .

2. The antitrust policy of the United States is contained primarily in three acts. Name them.

3. Calculate the Herfindahl index for this six-firm market:

    Firm A has a market share of 60 percent. Firm B has a market share of 10 percent. Firm C has a market
    share of 8 percent. Firm D has a market share of 15 percent. Firm E has a market share of 6 percent. Firm
    F has a market share of 1 percent.

    How would the Justice Department characterize this industry?

4. From a recent article in the *Wall Street Journal*:

    Senate Majority Leader Robert Dole (R., Kan.) has revised his takings bill to require federal compensation
    to landowners whose property loses value because of regulation. . . . Unlike the House measure, whose
    scope is limited to regulations governing wetlands, endangered species, and water use on public lands, the
    Senate proposal would apply to all regulations.

    Does the House measure refer to economic regulations or social regulations?

5. From the July 3, 1995, edition of the *Wall Street Journal* (page A3):

> Microsoft Corp. is making contingency plans to cope with any Justice Department move to separate the company's proposed on-line computer service [MSN] from its Windows 95 operating system. . . . Complaints from competitors helped convince the Justice Department to investigate whether MSN's links to Windows 95 would give the company illegal advantages in the market for on-line services. To force Microsoft to remove the MSN software, the agency would have to convince a court that the service could quickly attain dominance against established competitors. . . . Microsoft executives argue vehemently MSN would increase competition, not diminish it.

Microsoft had set an August 24, 1995, release date for Windows 95. The Justice Department had an incentive to act quickly since the agency may have a more difficult time winning an injunction to remove MSN software once Windows 95 has been distributed. On the basis of the information in the article, which standard is being applied, the rule of reason or the per se rule?

If your instructor assigns these problems, write your answers above, then tear out this page and hand it in.

Answers

Quick-Check Quiz

Section 1: Antitrust Policy

1. b; 2. e; 3. a; 4. a
If you missed any of these questions, you should go back and review Section 1 in Chapter 14 (*Economics,* Chapter 28).

Section 2: Regulation

1. c; 2. e; 3. b; 4. c; 5. a
If you missed any of these questions, you should go back and review Section 2 in Chapter 14 (*Economics,* Chapter 28).

Section 3: Government and Business

1. b; 2. c; 3. c; 4. a
If you missed any of these questions, you should go back and review Section 3 in Chapter 14 (*Economics,* Chapter 28).

Practice Questions and Problems

Section 1: Antitrust Policy

1. antitrust policy; regulation
2. a. 6,600 ($80^2 + 10^2 + 10^2 = 6,400 + 100 + 100 = 6,600$)
   b. 3,350 ($35^2 + 35^2 + 30^2 = 1,225 + 1,225 + 900 = 3,350$)
3. highly concentrated
4. monopoly; competition
5. Sherman Act, 1890
   Clayton Antitrust Act, 1914
   Federal Trade Commission Act, 1914
6. Herfindahl index
7. triple

Section 2: Regulation

1. economic; social
2. deregulated
3. *Privatization; Contracting out*

Section 3: Government and Business

1. the general public
2. special interests
3. externalities; public goods; imperfect information

4. moral hazard
5. adverse selection

Thinking About and Applying Government Policy Toward Business

I. *College Cartels*

1. per se rule (Price fixing is always illegal; you don't have to demonstrate any unreasonable results.)
2. Even though universities are not profit-making businesses, they still can benefit from price fixing. By avoiding "bidding wars" for the very top students, the schools have more money to spend on other things, including more financial aid for other students.
3. You can file a personal antitrust suit as a private party against the university; you don't have to rely on the Justice Department. If you win your suit, you will collect triple damages—that is, you will get back three times the amount you were overcharged.

Sample Test I
Chapters 9–14
(*Economics* Chapters 23–28)

1. If a firm is producing at an output level for which marginal revenue is below marginal cost, then the firm
   a. faces total revenue that is greater than total cost.
   b. could increase profits by increasing output.
   c. could increase profits by decreasing output.
   d. is maximizing profit.
   e. should produce zero units of output.

2. Assume that marginal revenue equals rising marginal cost at 200 units of output. At this output level, a profit-maximizing firm's total fixed cost is $600 and its total variable cost is $400. If the price of the product is $4 per unit, the firm should produce
   a. 250 units.
   b. 200 units.
   c. zero units.
   d. 400 units.
   e. Not able to be determined from the information given.

3. Assume that marginal revenue equals rising marginal cost at 200 units of output. At this output level, a profit-maximizing firm's total fixed cost is $600 and its total variable cost is $400. If the price of the product is $4 per unit, and the firm produces at the profit-maximizing output level, the firm will earn an economic profit equal to
   a. $1,000.
   b. $800.
   c. −$200.
   d. zero.
   e. Not able to be determined from the information given.

Use the following figure to answer questions 4 and 5.

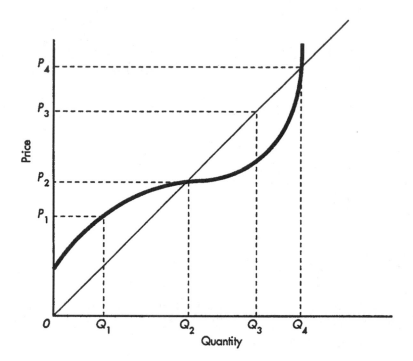

4. What is the profit-maximizing output level?
   a. Q_1
   b. Q_2
   c. Q_3
   d. Q_4
   e. 0

5. What type of market structure is depicted?
   a. monopoly
   b. oligopoly
   c. monopolistic competition
   d. perfect competition
   e. impossible to determine from the information given

6. If there is no qualitative or quantitative difference between a brand-name box of cornflakes and a generic box of cornflakes, but consumers perceive a difference in the products, then these products are said to be
   a. differentiated.
   b. homogeneous.
   c. standardized.
   d. perfectly competitive.
   e. monopolistic.

7. Which of the following is characteristic of a perfectly competitive industry?
   a. government regulation
   b. inability of firms to enter the industry
   c. reliance on advertising
   d. product differentiation
   e. a large number of firms

8. Which of the following indicates that the firm is a price taker?
   a. The firm must advertise to sell more of its product.
   b. The firm is such a small part of the industry that its actions cannot influence the price.
   c. The government sets the price.
   d. The firm determines the market price.
   e. The firm sells a differentiated product.

9. The ranking of market structures from least market power to most market power is
   a. monopoly, oligopoly, monopolistic competition, perfect competition.
   b. perfect competition, monopolistic competition, oligopoly, monopoly.
   c. monopoly, monopolistic competition, oligopoly, perfect competition.
   d. perfect competition, oligopoly, monopoly, monopolistic competition.
   e. All four structures have the same amount of market power.

Use the following figure to answer questions 10–12.

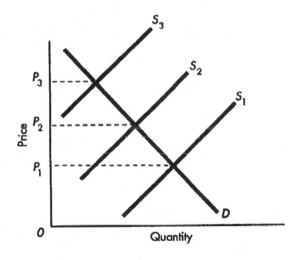
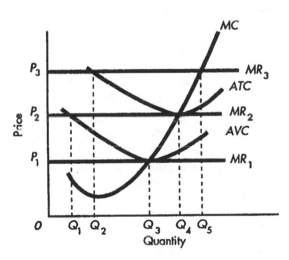

10. If the price facing the firm is P_2, then the firm
    a. should produce Q_5.
    b. earns an economic loss.
    c. earns an economic profit.
    d. should produce Q_3.
    e. should produce Q_4.

11. If the price facing the firm is P_3, the firm's total cost
    a. is greater than its total revenue.
    b. is less than its total revenue.
    c. is maximized.
    d. is minimized.
    e. exceeds total revenue by the greatest amount.

12. If the price facing the firm is P_3, what would we expect to occur over time?
    a. The market supply curve would shift to S_1.
    b. Firms would leave the market.
    c. The market supply curve would shift to S_2.
    d. Firms would earn economic losses.
    e. Below-normal profits would be earned.

13. A perfectly competitive firm is producing at the profit-maximizing output level and finds that its *AVC* is $6.50, its *ATC* is $6.67, and that it faces a market price of $6.49. Which of the following is true?
    a. The firm is earning a profit.
    b. The firm should absorb the $.18 loss and continue operating where $P = MC$.
    c. The firm should shut down because it will lose less than if it continues to produce.
    d. The firm should increase its production level to decrease costs.
    e. None of the above is true.

14. The perfectly competitive firm's short-run supply curve is the portion of its _____ that _____.
    a. *MC* curve; lies above minimum *ATC*
    b. *MC* curve; is positively sloped
    c. *ATC* curve; is positively sloped
    d. *MC* curve; lies above minimum *AVC*
    e. *AVC* curve; is positively sloped

15. The demand curve faced by a monopolist is
    a. perfectly elastic.
    b. equal to its marginal revenue curve.
    c. the market demand curve.
    d. more elastic than the demand curve faced by a perfectly competitive firm.
    e. nonexistent.

16. If the price elasticities of demand for a good differ among customer categories, then a price-discriminating monopolist would choose to
    a. establish a higher price for those customer categories with the most elastic demand.
    b. establish a lower price for those customer categories with the most elastic demand.
    c. establish an arbitrary price for all customer categories.
    d. establish prices that maximize consumer surplus.
    e. do none of the above.

Use the following figure to answer questions 17 and 18.

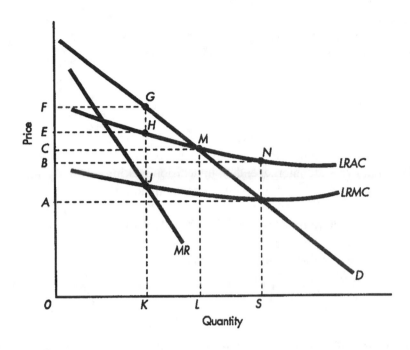

17. Assume that this natural monopoly is unregulated. What price and output combination will it choose to maximize profits?
    a. *OF; OK*
    b. *OC; OL*
    c. *OB; OS*
    d. *OF; OS*
    e. none of the above

18. Assume that this natural monopoly is regulated to a fair rate of return on investment. What price and output combination will result?
    a. *OB; OS*
    b. *OF; OK*
    c. *OC; OL*
    d. *OA; OS*
    e. none of the above

19. If a monopolistically competitive firm's advertising campaign is successful, then
    a. its demand will shift left and become more elastic.
    b. its demand will shift left and become more inelastic.
    c. its demand will shift right and become more elastic.
    d. its demand will shift right and become more inelastic.
    e. none of the above statements are correct.

20. Which of the following is a determinant of the shape of the demand curve facing an oligopolist?
    a. its marginal revenue curve
    b. its supply curve
    c. the way in which rival firms react to price changes
    d. the presence of externalities
    e. strategic deterrence

21. The number of firms in an oligopoly industry must be
    a. less than ten.
    b. large enough that firms cannot collude.
    c. large enough that firms cannot closely monitor each other.
    d. small enough that firms are interdependent in decision making.
    e. large enough that firms will see no reason to engage in nonprice competition.

22. An oligopoly market structure is *not* characterized by which of the following?
    a. the presence of differentiated products
    b. the presence of a few dominant firms with substantial entry barriers
    c. the interdependence of firms
    d. the presence of nondifferentiated products
    e. no barriers to entry

23. What effect or effects can new technology have on a firm's long-run average-cost curve?
    a. Lowers the entire curve.
    b. Reduces the range of economics of scale.
    c. Increases the range of economics of scale.
    d. Doesn't affect the range of economics of scale.
    e. All of the above are possible effects of new technology.

24. One explanation for government policy is that special interest groups dominate and are most often able to obtain legislation that benefits themselves at the expense of the rest of society. This is called the
    a. capture theory.
    b. theory of diminishing returns.
    c. median voter theory.
    d. public interest theory.
    e. socialist theory.

25. Following U.S. Justice Department guidelines, a Herfindahl index of 10,000 would indicate an industry that is considered _____ , whereas an index approaching zero would indicate an industry that is considered _____
    a. purely competitive; a monopoly.
    b. a monopoly; purely competitive.
    c. purely competitive; illegal.
    d. a duopoly; an oligopoly.
    e. diluted; concentrated

Answers to Sample Test I

1. c (Chapter 9, Section 2.b; *Economics* Chapter 23)
2. b (Chapter 9, Section 2.b; *Economics* Chapter 23)
3. c (Chapter 9, Section 2.b; *Economics* Chapter 23)
4. c (Chapter 9, Section 2.b; *Economics* Chapter 23)
5. d (Chapter 9, Section 3.c; *Economics* Chapter 23)
6. a (Chapter 9, Section 3.a; *Economics* Chapter 23)
7. e (Chapter 9, Section 3.b; *Economics* Chapter 23)
8. b (Chapter 9, Section 3.b; *Economics* Chapter 23)
9. b (Chapter 9, Section 3.c; *Economics* Chapter 23)
10. e (Chapter 10, Section 1.c; *Economics* Chapter 24)
11. b (Chapter 10, Section 1.c; *Economics* Chapter 24)
12. c (Chapter 10, Section 1.c; *Economics* Chapter 24)
13. c (Chapter 10, Section 1.e; *Economics* Chapter 24)

14. d (Chapter 10, Section 1.f; *Economics* Chapter 24)
15. c (Chapter 11, Section 2; *Economics* Chapter 25)
16. b (Chapter 11, Section 4.a; *Economics* Chapter 25)
17. a (Chapter 11, Section 5.e; *Economics* Chapter 25)
18. c (Chapter 11, Section 5.e; *Economics* Chapter 25)
19. d (Chapter 12, Section 1.c; *Economics* Chapter 26)
20. c (Chapter 12, Section 2.a; *Economics* Chapter 26)
21. d (Chapter 12, Section 2.a; *Economics* Chapter 26)
22. e (Chapter 12, Section 2.a; *Economics* Chapter 26)
23. e (Chapter 13, Section 1.a; *Economics* Chapter 27)
24. a (Chapter 14, Section 1.a; *Economics* Chapter 28)
25. b (Chapter 14, Section 1.e; *Economics* Chapter 28)

Sample Test II
Chapters 9–14
(*Economics* Chapters 23–28)

1. What could a firm do to decrease the price elasticity of demand for its product?
   a. Decrease the price of its product.
   b. Make a less differentiated product.
   c. Make a more differentiated product.
   d. Increase the number of substitutes for its product.
   e. None of the above.

Use the following table, which describes a perfectly competitive firm, to answer questions 2–4.

Quantity	Total Revenue ($)	Total Cost ($)
10	30	14
11	33	15
12	36	17
13	39	20
14	42	24
15	45	29

2. How many units of the product should the firm produce to maximize profit?
   a. 10
   b. 11
   c. 13
   d. 15
   e. Impossible to determine from the information given.

3. What is the average revenue for the firm?
   a. $2
   b. $3
   c. $4
   d. $5
   e. Impossible to determine from the information given.

4. How much profit will the firm make if it produces at the profit-maximizing output level?
   a. $16
   b. $18
   c. $14
   d. $20
   e. Impossible to determine from the information given.

5. Which of the following describes a total-revenue curve for a perfectly competitive firm?
   a. horizontal
   b. vertical
   c. the same as the firm's demand curve
   d. a positively sloped straight line through the origin
   e. a rectangular hyperbola

Use the following figure to answer questions 6–9.

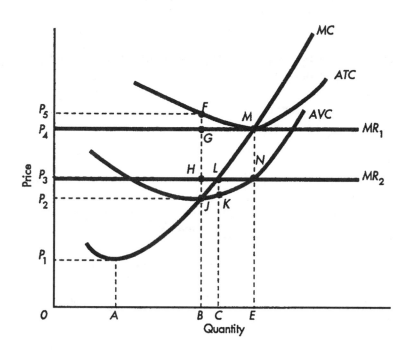

6. Given MR_1, what is the firm's profit-maximizing output level?
   a. $0A$
   b. $0B$
   c. $0C$
   d. $0E$
   e. none of the above

7. Given MR_2, what is the firm's profit-maximizing output level?
   a. $0A$
   b. $0B$
   c. $0C$
   d. $0E$
   e. The firm should not produce anything since $P < ATC$.

8. Given MR_2, at the profit-maximizing output level, what is the firm's total revenue?
   a. zero
   b. $0P_2JB$
   c. $0P_3HB$
   d. $0P_3LC$
   e. $0P_4ME$

9. What is the lowest price at which the firm would operate?
   a. P_1
   b. P_2
   c. P_3
   d. P_4
   e. 0

10. If, in the short run, P falls below ATC for a perfectly competitive firm, the firm
    a. earns an economic profit.
    b. should continue operating as long as price is at least as great as average fixed cost.
    c. should continue to operate as long as price is at least as great as average variable cost.
    d. should shut down because it is earning an economic loss.
    e. breaks even.

11. When a monopolist's demand curve is price elastic, then the marginal revenue curve is _____ and total revenue is _____ as quantity increases.
    a. positive; constant
    b. negative; decreasing
    c. positive; increasing
    d. zero; decreasing
    e. negative; increasing

Use the following figure to answer questions 12 and 13.

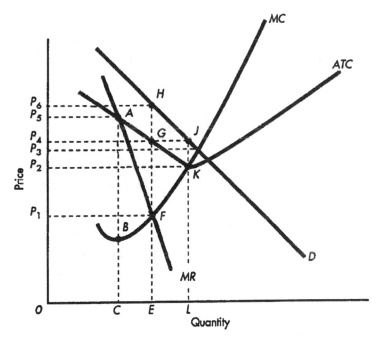

12. What are the profit-maximizing output level and price?
    a. P_1; OE
    b. P_6; OE
    c. P_4; OL
    d. P_5; OC
    e. P_6; OC

13. What is the maximum profit this monopolist can earn?
    a. OP_1FE
    b. P_1P_6HF
    c. P_4P_6HG
    d. OP_6HE
    e. P_2P_4JK

14. Which of the following is *not* possible for a monopolist in the short run?
    a. an economic profit
    b. breaking even
    c. an above-normal rate of return
    d. an economic loss
    e. All of the above are possible for a monopolist in the short run.

15. For a monopolistically competitive firm in the long run,
    a. $P = AFC$.
    b. $D = MR$.
    c. $P = MC$.
    d. $P = ATC$.
    e. $MC > MR$.

16. Assume that a monopolistically competitive firm is earning positive economic profits. In the long run, what will happen?
    a. Competition will cause the demand curve to become more elastic and shift right.
    b. Competition will cause the demand curve to become more inelastic and shift left.
    c. Competition will cause the demand curve to become more elastic and shift left.
    d. Competition will cause the demand curve to become more inelastic and shift right.
    e. All of the above are equally likely to happen.

Use the following figure to answer questions 17 and 18.

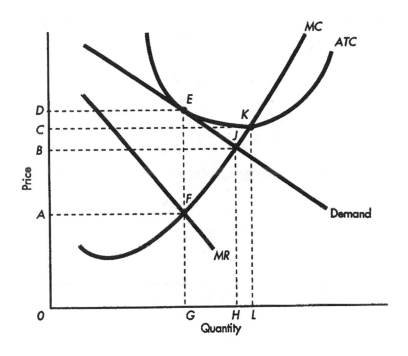

17. For this monopolistic competitor, the profit maximizing price and output level is
    a. *0A* and *0G*.
    b. *0B* and *0H*.
    c. *0C* and *0L*.
    d. *0D* and *0G*.
    e. *0A* and *0G*.

18. At the profit-maximizing output level, this monopolistic competitor is earning
    a. a positive economic profit.
    b. a negative economic profit.
    c. zero economic profits.
    d. an above-normal rate of return.
    e. windfall profits.

19. What would account for the instability of cartels?
    a. a small number of firms
    b. firms producing an undifferentiated product
    c. significant barriers to entry
    d. no legal constraints on collusion
    e. incentives for individual firms to break the agreement

Use the following figure to answer questions 20–22.

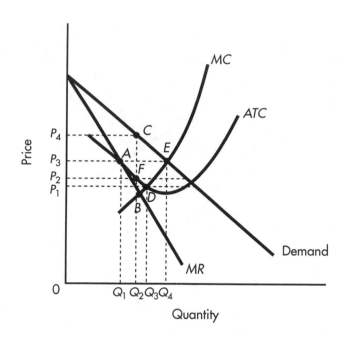

20. The firm in the figure above will maximize profits or minimize losses
    a. Q_3 and charging P_1.
    b. Q_2 and charging P_4.
    c. Q_2 and charging P_3.
    d. Q_2 and charging P_2.
    e. Q_1 and charging P_3.

21. The profit for the firm in the preceding figure is given by the area
    a. *BCE*.
    b. $0P_4CQ_2$.
    c. *CDE*.
    d. P_2P_4CE.
    e. P_1P_4CD.

22. In the preceding figure, a perfectly competitive firm would charge
    a. P_1 and produce Q_3.
    b. P_4 and produce Q_2.
    c. P_3 and produce Q_1.
    d. P_2 and produce Q_2.
    e. 0 and produce 0.

23. What gives you exclusive rights to manufacture a new innovative product for a limited number of years?
    a. copyright
    b. diseconomies of scale
    c. economics of scale
    d. sunk costs
    e. patent

24. The notion that government actions are undertaken to protect the best interests of society is called
    a. the self-interest theory of government.
    b. the capture theory of government.
    c. the public interest theory of government.
    d. the median voter theory.
    e. none of the above.

25. When the Supreme Court rules that it is the intent to abuse monopoly control, not monopoly control alone, that is illegal, it is following
    a. the per se rule.
    b. the contestable market rule.
    c. the cartel rule.
    d. the rule of reason.
    e. the rule of law.

Answers to Sample Test II

1. c (Chapter 9, Section 1.b; *Economics* Chapter 23)
2. c (Chapter 10, Section 1.c; *Economics* Chapter 24)
3. b (Chapter 10, Section 1.c; *Economics* Chapter 24)
4. d (Chapter 10, Section 1.c; *Economics* Chapter 24)
5. d (Chapter 10, Section 1.c; *Economics* Chapter 24)
6. d (Chapter 10, Section 1.c; *Economics* Chapter 24)
7. c (Chapter 10, Section 1.c; *Economics* Chapter 24)
8. d (Chapter 10, Section 1.c; *Economics* Chapter 24)
9. b (Chapter 10, Section 1.c; *Economics* Chapter 24)
10. c (Chapter 10, Section 1.d; *Economics* Chapter 24)
11. c (Chapter 11, Section 2.a; *Economics* Chapter 25)
12. b (Chapter 11, Section 3.b; *Economics* Chapter 25)
13. c (Chapter 11, Section 3.b; *Economics* Chapter 25)

14. c (Chapter 11, Section 3.c; *Economics* Chapter 25)
15. d (Chapter 12, Section 1.a; *Economics* Chapter 26)
16. c (Chapter 12, Section 1.a; *Economics* Chapter 26)
17. d (Chapter 12, Section 1.a; *Economics* Chapter 26)
18. c (Chapter 12, Section 1.a; *Economics* Chapter 26)
19. e (Chapter 12, Section 2.c; *Economics* Chapter 26)
20. b (Chapter 12, Section 1.b; *Economics* Chapter 26)
21. d (Chapter 12, Section 1.b; *Economics* Chapter 26)
22. a (Chapter 12, Section 1.b; *Economics* Chapter 26)
23. e (Chapter 13, Section 1.b; *Economics* Chapter 27)
24. c (Chapter 14, Section 1.a; *Economics* Chapter 28)
25. d (Chapter 14, Section 1.b; *Economics* Chapter 28)

Chapter 15
(*Economics* Chapter 29)

RESOURCE MARKETS

FUNDAMENTAL QUESTIONS

1. Who are the buyers and sellers of resources?

In any large shopping mall, almost anything you ever would want—candy, clothing, camping equipment, computer disks, maybe even a car—seems to be for sale. And if the mall does not have what you want, the grocery store does. But there is a vast constellation of products you never see for sale at the mall: things like railroad locomotives, factory buildings, aluminum ore, and farm- land. You can't go to the mall and hire a business manager, a baseball player, or a ballerina either.

Resources like these are not bought because they create utility for consumers. Nobody buys a ton of iron ore to enjoy looking at it; instead, the demand for resources like iron ore is derived from the value of the resources to businesses, in terms of producing other products that satisfy consumer wants. Economists classify resources into three groups: land, labor, and capital. These resources are sold by households to obtain income to buy the goods and services the households want.

2. How are resource prices determined?

Resource prices are set by the same kind of equilibrium process that we've studied for consumer markets: through the interactions of buyers and sellers. This equilibrium process determines the rate of payment for each resource and the quantity of that resource used. The payment received by a resource consists of two parts: the rate of pay needed to keep the resource in its current use, called **transfer earnings,** and any pay in excess of transfer earnings, called **economic rent.**

The rate of pay needed to keep a resource in its current use depends on opportunity costs—how much some *other* buyer is willing to pay for a particular resource. For example, a very talented basketball player is worth millions to a professional basketball team, but he will not quit playing basketball if his salary is cut. Most of his salary is economic rent (nobody else can play basketball the way he does).

3. How does a firm allocate its expenditures among the various resources?

A firm allocates its expenditures among resources in the same way that consumers allocate their incomes: so that the value per dollar is equal at the margin. Consumers get the most value from their incomes when the last dollar spent on all goods bought gives the same marginal utility. Firms are using resources efficiently when the last dollar spent gives the same marginal revenue product for all resources.

Key Terms

derived demand

economic rent

transfer earnings

marginal revenue product

  (*MRP*)

marginal factor cost (*MFC*)

monopsonist

Quick-Check Quiz

Section 1: Buyers and Sellers of Resources

1. The demand for resources is called a *derived demand* because it comes from
   a. the supply of resources.
   b. the marginal utility of owning a resource.
   c. what a resource can produce.
   d. consumers' needs for resources to use.
   e. how much a resource consumes.

2. Economists call the price paid for the use of land
   a. interest.
   b. proceeds.
   c. profits.
   d. rent.
   e. wages.

3. Economists call the price paid for the use of labor
   a. interest.
   b. proceeds.
   c. profits.
   d. rent.
   e. wages.

4. Economists call the price paid for the use of capital
   a. interest.
   b. proceeds.
   c. profits.
   d. rent.
   e. wages.

5. Residual claimants are
   a. entrepreneurs.
   b. bankers.
   c. workers.
   d. government employees.
   e. the unemployed.

6. Which of the following correctly identifies the buyers and sellers of resources?
   a. Firms and households buy resources; governments sell resources.
   b. Firms buy resources; households sell resources.
   c. Governments and households buy resources; firms sell resources.
   d. Households buy resources; firms sell resources.
   e. Governments buy resources; firms and households sell resources.

Section 2: The Market Demand for and Supply of Resources

1. Transfer earnings are
   a. labor earnings used to support nonworking family members.
   b. the part of total earnings needed to keep a resource in its current use.
   c. earnings shifted from one resource category to another.
   d. the same as economic rent.
   e. the excess residual income earned by entrepreneurs.

2. The payment needed to keep a resource in its current use depends mostly on the
   a. resource's opportunity cost.
   b. taxes paid by the resource's owner.
   c. taxes paid by the resource's user.
   d. resource's economic rent.
   e. derived demands for other resources.

3. Economic rent is the
   a. total price paid for renting an apartment.
   b. price paid for renting an apartment minus taxes and utilities.
   c. portion of earnings above transfer earnings.
   d. difference between transfer earnings and opportunity costs.
   e. payment to residual claimants.

4. Firms buy resources with the goal of
   a. maximizing output quantity.
   b. using all resources equally.
   c. maximizing profits.
   d. providing maximum utility to consumers.
   e. minimizing costs.

Section 3: How Firms Decide What Resources to Buy

1. The marginal revenue product (*MRP*) is the
   a. value of the additional output that an extra unit of a resource can produce.
   b. additional cost of an additional unit of a resource.
   c. additional cost of an additional unit of output.
   d. value of the additional revenue that an extra unit of output can produce.
   e. cost of the additional output that an extra unit of a resource can produce.

2. The marginal factor cost (*MFC*) is the
   a. value of the additional output that an extra unit of a resource can produce.
   b. additional cost of an additional unit of a resource.
   c. additional cost of an additional unit of output.
   d. value of the additional revenue that an extra unit of output can produce.
   e. value of the additional input used to make an extra unit of a resource.

3. A monopsonist is
   a. the only seller of a resource.
   b. the only seller of a product.
   c. the only buyer of a resource.
   d. a firm that maximizes *MRP*.
   e. a firm that minimizes *VMP*.

4. A firm's demand curve for a resource is the
   a. firm's *MC* curve.
   b. firm's *MFC* curve.
   c. resource's *MRP* curve.
   d. resource's *MFC* curve.
   e. resource's *MC* curve.

5. To maximize profits, a firm should hire resources up to the point where
   a. $MR = MRP$.
   b. $P = MC$.
   c. $MRP = MFC$.
   d. $MRP = MC$.
   e. $MR = MFC$.

Practice Questions and Problems

Section 1: Buyers and Sellers of Resources

1. In the table below, note the three types of resources and what each type's price is called.

Type	Price
_____	_____
_____	_____
_____	_____

2. The buyers of resources are _____ ; the sellers of resources are _____ .

3. The residual claimants are _____ .

Section 2: The Market Demand for and Supply of Resources

1. On a graph, the market demand curve for a resource looks _____ (the same as, different from) the demand curve for a consumer product.

2. What equation do you use to calculate the price elasticity of resource demand?

   _____

3. List the four factors that determine the elasticity of resource demand.

   _____

   _____

   _____

   _____

4. List the five factors that can shift the demand curve for a resource.

   _____

   _____

   _____

   _____

5. List the three factors that can shift the supply curve for a resource.

   _____

   _____

   _____

Section 3: How Firms Decide What Resources to Buy

1. The firm's demand curve for a resource is the resource's _____ curve.

2. To maximize profits, a firm should hire a resource up to the amount where _____ =

   _____ .

3. In perfectly competitive resource markets, resources are paid an amount _____ (equal to, more than, less than) the value of their marginal product.

4. In monopsonistic resource markets, resources are paid an amount _____ (equal to, more than, less than) the value of their marginal product.

5. A firm should allocate its budget on resources so that the last dollar spent yields the same _____ no matter which resource the dollar is spent on.

6. You have decided to make some extra money and gain some real-world experience by starting your own business. You have observed that there is a good market for handwoven doormats made of recycled rope. You can get old rope for free and can use your apartment as work space. Your only costs will be for hiring other students to work on making the mats. The table on the following page shows

how many mats you can make with different numbers of workers, how much you can sell the mats for, and how much you have to pay to attract workers.

a. Fill in all the blanks in the table. Then plot the *MRP* and *MFC* curves on the graph.

Number of Workers	Mats per Hour	*MPP*	Price per Mat	Total Revenue	*MR*	*MRP*	Wage per Hour	Total Labor Cost	*MFC*
1	8	____	$2.00	$____	$____	$____	$4.00	$____	$____
2	19	____	2.00	____	____	____	4.00	____	____
3	26	____	2.00	____	____	____	4.00	____	____
4	30	____	2.00	____	____	____	4.00	____	____
5	32	____	2.00	____	____	____	4.00	____	____
6	33	____	2.00	____	____	____	4.00	____	____

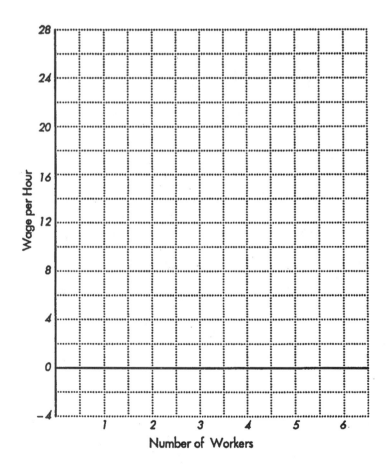

b. According to the table and graph, you would want to hire _____ workers.

c. In what kind of market structure are your doormats selling? Explain your answer.

d. In what kind of market structure are you hiring workers? Explain your answer.

7. When you started, many other students were willing to work for you. Most of those who tried weaving doormats hated the job, though, and now there are only six students in town who are willing to work for you. A few of them like the job enough to be willing to work for low wages, but you have to keep increasing your pay rate to attract more workers.

a. Refigure your labor costs and *MFC* in the table below. Then plot the *MRP* and *MFC* curves and the supply curve for your workers on the graph below. You have also managed to become a monopolist.

Number of Workers	Mats per Hour	MPP	Price per Mat	Total Revenue	MR	MRP	Wage per Hour	Total Labor Cost	MFC
1	8	8	$2.00	$16.00	$ 2.00	$16.00	$2.00	$_____	$_____
2	19	11	1.90	36.10	1.83	20.10	3.00	_____	_____
3	26	7	1.80	46.80	1.53	10.70	4.00	_____	_____
4	30	4	1.70	51.00	1.05	4.20	5.00	_____	_____
5	32	2	1.60	51.20	.10	.20	6.00	_____	_____
6	33	1	1.50	49.50	−1.70	−1.70	7.00	_____	_____

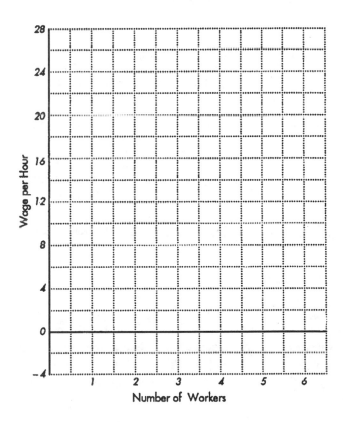

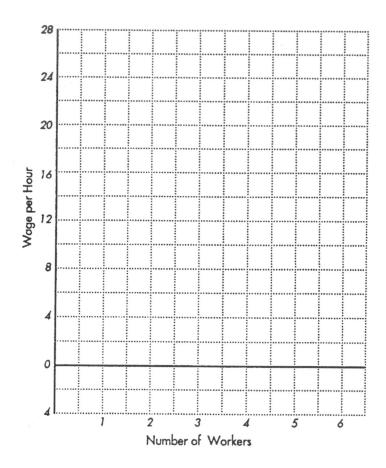

b. According to the table and graph, now you would want to hire _____ workers.

c. How can you tell from the table that you aren't hiring workers in a perfectly competitive market anymore?

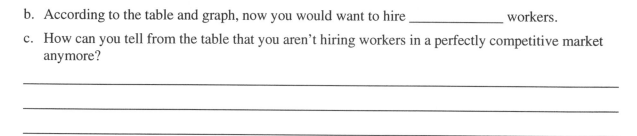

Thinking About and Applying Resource Markets

I. Cookies, Elves, and Economic Rent

If you've watched much television in the past few years, you've seen ads for a cookie company in which cute little cartoon elves make all the cookies. Let's take a look at elf economics.

In many ways, the elves in these commercials act like people; for example, they respond to incentives. Some elves really enjoy making cookies, so they would work for the cookie company for a low rate of pay. Other elves enjoy other things and only work for the cookie company at higher rates of pay. The table on the following page shows the supply curve for cookie-making elves.

Wage per Hour	Number of Elves Willing to Make Cookies
$1.00	1
2.00	2
3.00	3
4.00	4

1. If the wage rate for making cookies is less than $1, no elves are willing to make cookies; but a wage of $1 is enough to get one elf to be willing to make cookies.

   a. Because that $1 wage is just enough to attract that elf, what are the transfer earnings of that elf?

   _____

   b. At a wage of $1 per hour, does this elf get any economic rent? Explain your answer.

   _____

2. If the cookie company wants to hire two elves to make cookies, it has to raise the pay to $2. If the elf who already is working for $1 gets paid $2, his transfer earnings after the raise are _____ , and his economic rent is _____ .

3. At $2 per hour, a second elf is willing to work. When the wage rate is $2, the transfer earnings of this second elf are _____ , and his economic rent is _____ .

4. The cookie business is really booming, and the company needs to hire a third elf. It must pay a rate of _____ an hour to attract a third elf.

5. Assuming the wage rate is $3 per hour, note the transfer earnings and economic rent of each of the elves in the table below.

	Transfer Earnings	Economic Rent
First elf	_____	_____
Second elf	_____	_____
Third elf	_____	_____

6. Why don't all of the elves have the same transfer earnings?

   _____

II. Demand and Supply for Aerospace Engineers

Aerospace engineers design airplanes and spaceships. As in most engineering areas, becoming a specialist in aerospace engineering takes several years of study even if you already are an engineer, and even longer if you are just starting out in engineering. The time it takes to train new engineers makes the market for engineers behave differently from the market for many other occupations.

Let's say that the market for aerospace engineers is shown by MRP_1 and S_1 on the graph on the following page; salaries average $60,000 per year, and there are 40,000 aerospace engineers working. If the United States decides next year to start working on sending people to visit Mars and starts paying aerospace engineering firms to design spaceships for the trip, the MRP of aerospace engineers will increase to MRP_2.

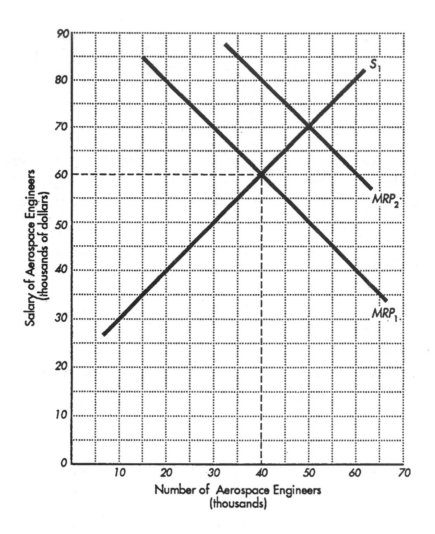

1. The supply curve (S_1) on the diagram shows the long-run supply of aerospace engineers, after people have had time to become aerospace engineers. On the graph, sketch in a supply curve for aerospace engineers that shows how the number of available aerospace engineers will respond to an overnight increase in salaries. (*Hint:* Can you change the number of engineers overnight when it takes several years of study to become an aerospace engineer?)

2. The "overnight" supply curve shows that the salary that current aerospace engineers will get shortly after *MRP* shifts to MRP_2 is _____.

3. Of the increase in salary, _____ is transfer earnings and _____ is economic rent.

4. After there has been enough time for new aerospace engineers to enter the market, salaries will end up at $70,000, with 50,000 engineers working. Will any of these engineers still be receiving economic rent? Explain your answer.

_____

_____

_____

_____

Chapter 15 (*Economics* Chapter 29)   Homework Problems

Name _____

1. The elasticity of resource demand is *smaller* the

    (higher/lower) the price elasticity of demand for the product the resource is used to produce.

    (larger/smaller) the resource's proportion of the total costs of producing a good.

    (greater/smaller) the number of substitutes for the resource.

    (longer/shorter) the time period.

    (You should circle four responses!)

    Would the *owners* of a resource prefer that the demand for their resource be elastic or inelastic?

2. There are five nonprice determinants for the demand for a resource. Write the five determinants and indicate how they would need to change for the demand for a resource to *decrease*.

3. Write the formulas for the marginal revenue product (*MRP*) and the marginal factor cost (*MFC*).

4. Manson's Muckraking Service currently employs 16 workers. At this level of employment, Manson's marginal revenue product is $12, his wage rate is $10, and his marginal factor cost is $11.

   a. Is Manson buying his labor in a perfectly competitive market?

       Yes   No   (*Circle one.*) How can you tell?

   b. Is Manson maximizing his profits at this level of employment?

       Yes   No   (*Circle one.*) If not, tell him what he should do, and why.

5. Although economists usually analyze product markets and resource markets separately, there are some important links between them. Suppose Jerry's Jumbo Jets makes (among other things) jet engines and parts. In a recent television interview, Jerry said U.S. defense budget reductions have depressed engine deliveries and spare parts sales. He also said his company would need to do some restructuring, including layoffs and plant closings, to improve its profit picture.

   a. Suppose the market for jet engines and spare parts (the product market in this example) was perfectly competitive. Defense budget reductions would _____ (increase, decrease) the demand for jet engines and spare parts, causing their prices to _____ (rise, fall).

   b. Use the definition of marginal revenue product (*MRP*) to explain why this change in the price of jet engines and spare parts would lead to a decrease in the number of workers hired (that is, to layoffs and plant closings).

If your instructor assigns these problems, write your answers above, then tear out this page and hand it in.

Answers

Quick-Check Quiz

Section 1: Buyers and Sellers of Resources

1. c; 2. d; 3. e; 4. a; 5. a; 6. b
If you missed any of these questions, you should go back and review Section 1 in Chapter 15 (*Economics, Chapter 29*).

Section 2: The Market Demand for and Supply of Resources

1. b; 2. a; 3. c; 4. c
If you missed any of these questions, you should go back and review Section 2 in Chapter 15 (*Economics, Chapter 29*).

Section 3: How Firms Decide What Resources to Buy

1. a; 2. b; 3. c; 4. c; 5. c
If you missed any of these questions, you should go back and review Section 3 in Chapter 15 (*Economics, Chapter 29*).

Practice Questions and Problems

Section 1: Buyers and Sellers of Resources

1.

Type	Price
land	rent
labor	wages
capital	interest

2. firms; households
3. entrepreneurs

Section 2: The Market Demand for and Supply of Resources

1. the same as
2. $e_r = \dfrac{\text{percentage change in quantity demanded of resource}}{\text{percentage change in price of resource}}$
3. price elasticity of the product
   proportion of total costs
   number of substitutes
   time period
4. prices of the product the resource is used to produce
   productivity of the resource
   number of buyers of the resource
   prices of related resources
   quantities of other resources

5. changes in tastes
   changes in number of suppliers
   changes in prices of other uses of the resource

Section 3: How Firms Decide What Resources to Buy

1. *MRP*
2. *MRP; MFC*
3. equal to
4. less than
5. marginal revenue product
6. a.

Number of Workers	Mats per Hour	MPP	Price per Mat	Total Revenue	MR	MRP	Wage per Hour	Total Labor Cost	MFC
1	8	8	$2.00	$16.00	$2.00	$16.00	$4.00	$ 4.00	$4.00
2	19	11	2.00	38.00	2.00	22.00	4.00	8.00	4.00
3	26	7	2.00	52.00	2.00	14.00	4.00	12.00	4.00
4	30	4	2.00	60.00	2.00	8.00	4.00	16.00	4.00
5	32	2	2.00	64.00	2.00	4.00	4.00	20.00	4.00
6	33	1	2.00	66.00	2.00	2.00	4.00	24.00	4.00

MPP = the change in output (mats per hour) from using another worker
Total revenue = mats per hour × price per mat
MR = change in total revenue divided by change in output, or *TR/MPP*
MRP = change in total revenue from using another worker
Total labor cost = number of workers × wage per hour
MFC = change in total labor cost from hiring one more worker
If you need help with these calculations, refer to Figures 4, 5, and 7 in the text.

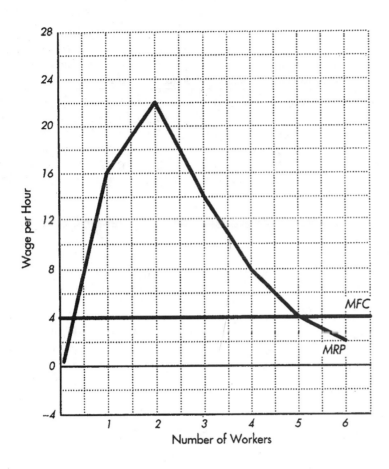

b. 5 (*MRP* = *MFC* for the fifth worker.)
c. Perfectly competitive. The output price (price per mat) is constant.
d. Perfectly competitive. The resource price (wage per hour) is constant.

7. a.

Number of Workers	Mats per Hour	MPP	Price per Mat	Total Revenue	MR	MRP	Wage per Hour	Total Labor Cost	MFC
1	8	8	$2.00	$16.00	$ 2.00	$16.00	$2.00	$ 2.00	$ 2.00
2	19	11	1.90	36.10	1.83	20.10	3.00	6.00	4.00
3	26	7	1.80	46.80	1.53	10.70	4.00	12.00	6.00
4	30	4	1.70	51.00	1.05	4.20	5.00	20.00	8.00
5	32	2	1.60	51.20	.10	.20	6.00	30.00	10.00
6	33	1	1.50	49.50	−1.70	−1.70	7.00	42.00	12.00

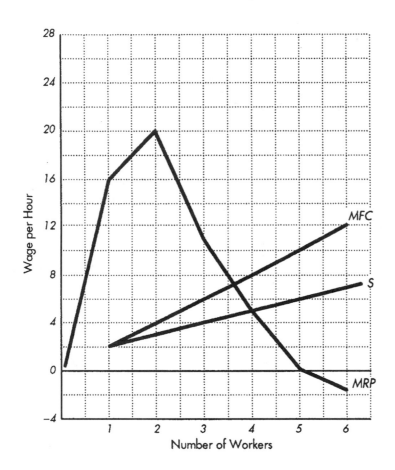

b. 3 (With the increasing *MFC*, only the first 3 workers now have an *MRP* that is more than their *MFC*.)

c. You have to increase wages to attract more workers, so you aren't facing a perfectly elastic supply curve for workers anymore.

Thinking About and Applying Resource Markets

I. Cookies, Elves, and Economic Rent

1. a. $1
   b. No. Transfer earnings are the amount needed to keep a resource in its current employment. Because the $1 wage is barely enough to make working worthwhile, all of the elf's wage is transfer earnings; there is no economic rent.
2. $1; $1 (Transfer earnings are determined by opportunity costs. Because the first elf was willing to work for $1, any payment over $1 is economic rent to that elf.)
3. $2; zero (The second elf's opportunity costs are not the same as the first elf's: the second will work only if the wage is $2 or more. At $2, the second elf gets no economic rent.)
4. $3
5.

	Transfer Earnings	Economic Rent
First elf	$1.00	$2.00
Second elf	2.00	1.00
Third elf	3.00	0

6. Their opportunity costs are different.

II. Demand and Supply for Aerospace Engineers

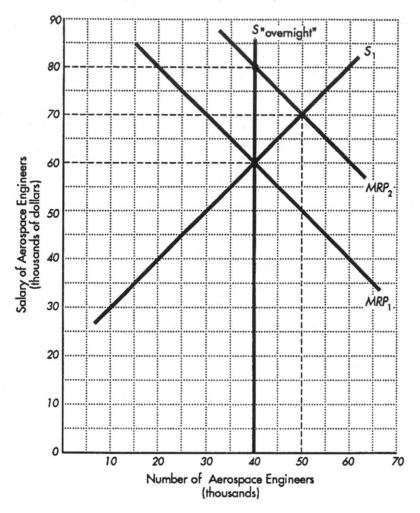

1. The "overnight" supply of aerospace engineers is perfectly inelastic (a vertical line) because the number of engineers cannot change at all in that short a time.
2. $80,000
3. zero; $20,000. (All of the increase is economic rent for the aerospace engineers currently in the market. They all were willing to work for $60,000, so any payment to them over $60,000 is all economic rent.)
4. Almost all of these engineers are receiving some economic rent; most of the additional 10,000 engineers would have been willing to become aerospace engineers for a salary between $60,000 and $70,000. Only those few engineers who would have chosen a different job if the salary was anything less than $70,000 receive no economic rent.

THE LABOR MARKET

FUNDAMENTAL QUESTIONS

1. Are people willing to work more for higher wages?

   Most people work to earn money to spend when they're not working. Even for people who really enjoy their jobs, the size of the paycheck affects how much they are willing to work. For individual workers, a higher wage rate has two effects: it encourages them to work more hours, but it also lets them enjoy more leisure time without lowering their standard of living. When wage rates get high enough, most people cut back the hours they work and take more leisure time, producing a **backward-bending labor supply curve.**

2. What are compensating wage differentials?

   The supply of and demand for different labor markets determine the wage and the number of people employed in those markets. If people and jobs were like wheat, there would be only one wage rate. But people and jobs differ, so wages are not all the same. **Compensating wage differentials** exist when differences in job characteristics result in wage differences. Economists are paid more than fast-food workers partly because much more education is required before one can become an economist.

3. Why might wages be higher for people with more human capital than for those with less human capital?

   Human capital is the skills and training acquired through education and on-the-job training. Human capital increases productivity, making workers more valuable to employers. Acquiring human capital has opportunity costs (time and money); therefore, it reduces the supply of labor for those jobs relative to the supply for jobs that do not require as much human capital.

4. What accounts for earnings disparities between males and females and between whites and nonwhites?

   A wide variety of factors affects the earnings of different groups of people. On average, people in some groups have more human capital than people in other groups; as we've seen, differences in human capital usually lead to differences in earnings. When a factor that is unrelated to marginal revenue product—for example, race, gender, or age—acquires a positive or negative value in the labor market, **discrimination** is occurring.

5. Are discrimination and freely functioning markets compatible?

In a freely functioning labor market, *discrimination* should not exist: there is a profit to be made in *not* discriminating. Of course, discrimination does exist. One source of labor market discrimination is employers' personal prejudice. Hiring people on the basis of personal prejudice adds to employers' costs and is not compatible with free markets. A second source, **statistical discrimination,** is a way of dealing with a lack of information: employers wrongly perceive that all members of a group have characteristics that make them less productive. Statistical discrimination can lead to **crowding** and **occupational segregation.**

Key Terms

backward-bending labor
   supply curve
labor force participation
compensating wage
   differentials

human capital
superstar effect
discrimination
statistical discrimination
crowding

occupational segregation
disparate treatment
disparate impact
comparable worth

Quick-Check Quiz

Section 1: The Supply of Labor

1. Which of these graphs shows a backward-bending supply curve for labor?

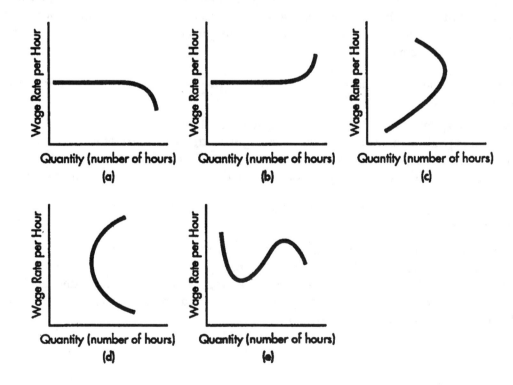

2. As wage rates increase in the economy, labor force participation
   a. is unaffected.
   b. increases.
   c. decreases at a steady rate.
   d. decreases at first and then increases.
   e. decreases slowly at first and then decreases more rapidly.

Section 2: Wage Differentials

1. Wage differences that make up for higher-risk or poor working conditions among different jobs are called
   a. human capital.
   b. disparate treatment.
   c. labor force participation differentials.
   d. compensating wage differentials.
   e. affirmative action plans.

2. Skills and training acquired through education and on-the-job training are called
   a. disparate treatment.
   b. labor force participation differentials.
   c. human capital.
   d. compensating wage differentials.
   e. affirmative action plans.

Section 3: Discrimination

1. When factors not related to workers' marginal productivity affect workers' value in the labor market,
   a. compensating wage differentials do not exist.
   b. discrimination is occurring.
   c. the labor supply curve does not bend backward.
   d. labor force participation is high.
   e. labor force participation is low.

2. Which of the following factors is *not* a reason why different groups receive different wages in the United States today?
   a. personal prejudice
   b. differences in education and training
   c. statistical discrimination
   d. unequal opportunities to acquire human capital
   e. All of the above are reasons why different groups receive different wages.

3. Statistical discrimination can occur when
   a. wages are based on individual workers' actual marginal productivity.
   b. employers base wage decisions on personal prejudice.
   c. employers with imperfect information about people's productivity rely on incorrect assumptions to set wages.
   d. occupational segregation causes labor market crowding.
   e. the immigration of unskilled people lowers the wages for all unskilled workers.

Section 4: Wage Differentials and Government Policies

1. Comparable worth is the idea that pay should be based on
   a. supply and demand for different types of labor.
   b. only the supply side of the labor market.
   c. the characteristics of the job.
   d. the degree of occupational segregation in a labor market.
   e. the percentage of jobs filled by minorities.

2. In legal terms, the disparate treatment standard judges employers on
   a. whether they personally are prejudiced against certain groups.
   b. whether their employment policies are intended to discriminate against certain groups.
   c. whether their employment policies affect different groups differently, regardless of the employers' intentions.
   d. the degree of occupational segregation within their firms.
   e. whether their affirmative action plans are written properly.

3. In legal terms, the disparate impact standard judges employers on
   a. whether they personally are prejudiced against certain groups.
   b. whether their employment policies are intended to discriminate against certain groups.
   c. whether their employment policies affect different groups differently, regardless of the employers' intentions.
   d. the degree of occupational segregation within their firms.
   e. whether their affirmative action plans are written properly.

Practice Questions and Problems

Section 1: The Supply of Labor

1. Sketch a backward-bending labor supply curve on the graph below.

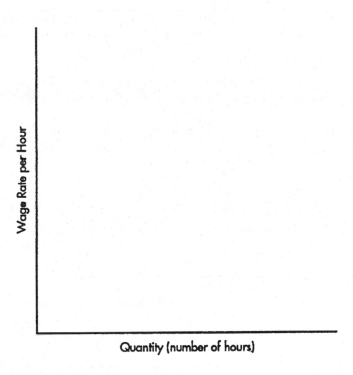

2. In the overall labor market, as wages increase, labor force _____ also increases.
3. In any labor market, the wage rate and number of jobs depend on the _____ and _____ curves for labor.

Section 2: Wage Differentials

1. Employers must pay _____ to get people to do unpleasant or dangerous jobs.
2. _____ is the skills and training acquired through education and on-the-job training.
3. Higher opportunity costs for acquiring the human capital needed for a job result in _____ (larger, smaller) numbers of people in that occupation, leading to wages that are _____ (higher, lower) than those for other jobs.

Section 3: Discrimination

1. Job market discrimination occurs when wages are based on anything besides workers' _____ .

2. Discrimination based on personal prejudice is usually _____ (costly, profitable) for a firm.

3. _____ discrimination can occur when employers use indicators of group performance that do not accurately reflect the productivity of individual workers.

4. The graph below shows the equilibrium wage rate and number of jobs in a labor market where half the supply of workers are male and half are female.

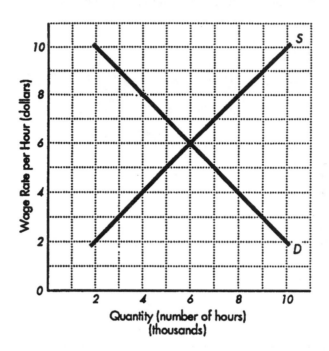

a. If employers' prejudices lead them to refuse to hire women, they will end up paying a wage rate of _____ per hour. (*Hint:* If women are not hired, they are not part of the supply as far as the employers in the market are concerned, so draw in the supply curve for men to find the wage.)

b. If you are a profit-maximizing employer, how can you take advantage of the other employers' prejudice?

_____

_____

_____

c. When women are excluded from some labor markets, they are forced into other labor markets; this is called _____ .

d. What effect does crowding have on women's wages?

_____

_____

_____

Section 4: Wage Differentials and Government Policies

1. Comparable worth uses _____ rather than demand and supply to determine wage rates.

2. Enforcement of civil rights laws regarding employment discrimination has led to two standards, or tests, of discrimination. The _____ standard, because it weighs the employer's intent, has little impact on the effects of past discrimination. Under the _____ standard, it is the effects of discrimination, not motivation, that matter.

Thinking About and Applying the Labor Market

I. Contests and CEO Pay

In many U.S. firms, the pay of the person running the company (the chief executive officer, or CEO) is a hundred times higher than the pay received by most company employees. It's hard to believe that these CEOs are so special that they have a marginal revenue product so much greater than the *MRP* of regular workers. Does this mean that there's no economic logic behind what companies pay CEOs?

Not necessarily. As the text points out, one way to look at CEO pay is that it's the "prize" for winning a contest among potential CEOs and that a high prize not only rewards the current CEO for his or her success but also acts as an incentive to other executives to work harder and more productively, in the hope that someday they will do well enough to "win" and become CEOs themselves.

Let's look at a different kind of contest to see how this idea works. Suppose someone in your town is sponsoring a road race for the ten best runners in town and has decided to offer $10,000 in prizes to the ten runners. The people organizing the race are looking at two different ways to award the $10,000 in prizes:

Method 1: Pay each runner $1,000 for participating in the race.
Method 2: Pay the winner $7,000, the second-place finisher $2,000, and the other eight runners $125 for participating.

1. Which method of awarding the prizes will result in all ten runners' working harder to train for the race? Explain your answer.

_____

_____

_____

2. Using your answer to question 1, explain why firms' high CEO salaries may be justified by high *MRP*s.

_____

_____

_____

II. Comparable Worth and High School Teachers

Labor markets in the United States frequently have resulted in wage patterns that seem discriminatory: minorities and women, on average, are paid substantially less than white males. One approach (known as *comparable worth*) to making wage patterns more equal is to disregard the market forces of demand and supply and to set wages for jobs on the basis of job characteristics. Using this approach, people who hold jobs that take place in the same sort of environment, that require the same level of responsibility, and that require the same amount of education should receive the same rate of pay.

The job market for high school teachers in most of the United States has worked this way for many years. In most high schools, teachers with the same education and years of experience are paid the same salary, regardless of the subject area they teach. This fits the comparable worth idea: the working conditions and demands on English teachers are the same as for math teachers. But ignoring demand and supply has some economic effects worth looking at.

1. Suppose U.S. high schools decide to improve the training of skilled workers by requiring students to take more math classes. The graphs below show the demand and supply (D_1 and S_1) for math teachers and English teachers before adding math classes, with both math and English teachers earning $30,000, and a new demand curve (D_2) for math teachers after adding more math classes. Mark on the graph the old and new equilibrium salary and number of math teachers.

(a) Market for Math Teachers

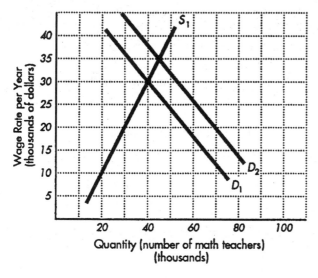

(b) Market for English Teachers

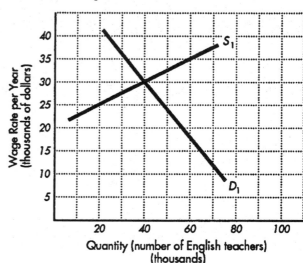

a. The market equilibrium salary for math teachers now is _____ .

b. Using the ideas in this chapter and the last, explain why the salary has to go up to attract new math teachers.

_____

_____

_____

_____

2. If the schools maintain equal salaries for all teachers, English teachers also will receive a salary of $35,000. Mark on graph b the quantity demanded and quantity supplied of English teachers when the salary is $35,000. Explain what will happen in the market for English teachers if their salaries are raised to $35,000.

_____

_____

_____

_____

3. One of the most useful characteristics of a market economy is that price changes signal changes in the relative scarcity of different products and resources, and encourage people to respond to those changes. Can you think of any ways that labor markets, by setting salaries through comparable worth, can do the same thing, without math teachers' receiving higher salaries than English teachers?

_____

_____

_____

_____

III. Discrimination and Minimum Wage Laws

Walter Williams, an economist and columnist, was quoted in the *Wall Street Journal* (September 22, 1987) as saying: "The brunt of the minimum wage law is borne by low-skilled workers . . . particularly black teenagers." In this chapter, we've found that discrimination in competitive labor markets usually is costly to employers, and that minimum wage laws can create a labor surplus in competitive labor markets. Use these two ideas to explain the logic behind Williams's comment. (*Hint:* Think about the effects of a surplus on the costs of discriminating.)

_____

_____

_____

Chapter 16 (*Economics* Chapter 30)   Homework Problems

Name _____

1. What are compensating wage differentials?

2. What do older workers usually have that entitles them to higher wages than younger workers?

3. Who benefits from minimum-wage laws? Who is hurt?

4. Name two sources of labor market discrimination.

5. The number of workers filling temporary or contract jobs, rather than regular full-time jobs is rising because using temporary and contract workers is less expensive than hiring regular workers. Let's explore some of the causes of these lower costs and their effects on employers' hiring decisions.

   Most full-time workers in the United States receive, in addition to their wages or salaries, substantial benefits—health insurance, pension plans, and so on. Many firms, however, do not pay these benefits to temporary and contract workers.

   Suppose magazine photographers are hired in a competitive market and receive a money wage of $20 per hour. Full-time photographers also receive benefits that cost their employers $5 per hour—a total of $25 per hour versus just $20 per hour.

   a. The *MFC* of a full-time photographer is _____ per hour.

   b. The *MFC* of a contract photographer is _____ per hour.

   c. If full-time and contract photographers are equally productive, we would expect magazines to hire _____ photographers.

   d. Explain why magazines might continue to hire some full-time photographers, even if contract photographers have a lower *MFC*. (*Hint:* Think about the variables that determine the number of workers hired.)

   _____

   _____

   _____

If your instructor assigns these problems, write your answers above, then tear out this page and hand it in.

Answers

Quick-Check Quiz

Section 1: The Supply of Labor

1. c; 2. b
If you missed either of these questions, you should go back and review Section 1 in Chapter 16 (*Economics*, Chapter 30).

Section 2: Wage Differentials

1. d; 2. c
If you missed either of these questions, you should go back and review Section 2 in Chapter 16 (*Economics*, Chapter 30).

Section 3: Discrimination

1. b; 2. e; 3. c
If you missed any of these questions, you should go back and review Section 1 in Chapter 16 (*Economics*, Chapter 30).

Section 4: Wage Differentials and Government Policies

1. c; 2. b; 3. c
If you missed any of these questions, you should go back and review Section 2 in Chapter 16 (*Economics*, Chapter 30).

Practice Questions and Problems

Section 1: The Supply of Labor

1.

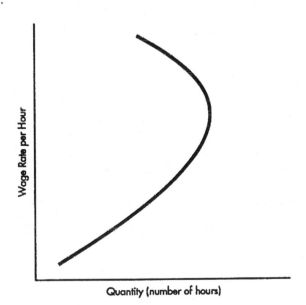

The bend backward comes at higher wage levels, where the income effect of wage increases becomes larger than the substitution effect. At lower wages, the labor supply curve looks like a regular supply curve, sloping upward to the right.

2. participation
3. demand; supply

Section 2: Wage Differentials

1. compensating wage differentials
2. Human capital
3. smaller; higher

Section 3: Discrimination

1. marginal revenue product
2. costly
3. Statistical
4. a. $8

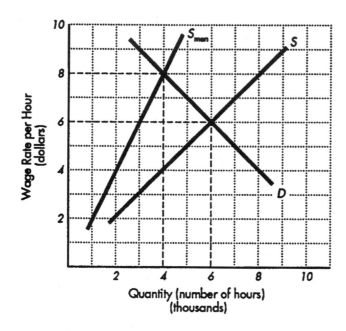

b. If other employers insist on hiring men at high wages, you can hire women at a lower wage, sell your product at a lower price, and earn substantial profits.
c. crowding
d. Wages in "crowded" labor markets are lower than otherwise because of the larger supply.

Section 4: Wage Differentials and Government Policies

1. job characteristics
2. disparate treatment; disparate impact

Thinking About and Applying the Labor Market

I. Contests and CEO Pay

1. Method 2 (Under method 1, a runner's performance doesn't affect his or her prize because every runner automatically gets $1,000. In contrast, method 2 provides a financial incentive for each runner to train hard for the race because his or her prize depends on doing better than the other runners.)

2. A high salary is more than a reward for a CEO's *MRP*; it also serves as an incentive for better performance by all the people in the company who want to be CEOs someday. The higher *MRP*s of *all* these people, not just the CEO, is what the CEO's salary is buying.

II. Comparable Worth and High School Teachers

1.

(a) Market for Math Teachers

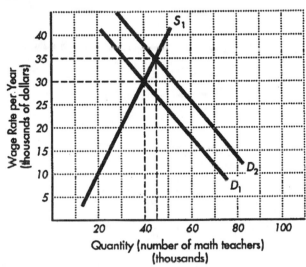

(b) Market for English Teachers

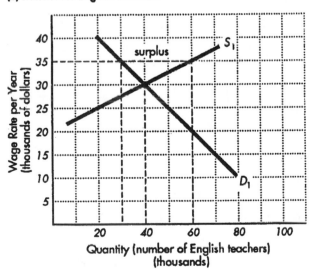

    a. $35,000

    b. The salary has to increase to pay the costs of acquiring the human capital needed to be a math teacher and to compete with other occupations for people with mathematical training and ability.

2. There will be a surplus in the market for English teachers as the salary increase attracts more people into that occupation; at the same time, schools may hire fewer English teachers at the higher salary.

3. There does not seem to be any way to do it. Either you keep salaries equal or you respond to changes. You can't do both.

III. *Discrimination and Minimum Wage Laws*

As we saw in this chapter, discriminatory hiring in competitive labor markets is usually costly to employers because it reduces supply and raises wages. When there is a surplus in the labor market, employers do not have to raise wages to attract new employees—there already is a pool of unemployed people looking for jobs. Employers can discriminate against some members of this pool (African American teenagers, for example) and still be able to get as many employees as they want to hire at the minimum wage.

THE CAPITAL MARKET

FUNDAMENTAL QUESTIONS

1. **What role does saving play in the economy?**

   In effect, **saving** is the way an economy can trade some current consumption for more future consumption. Saving permits accumulation of capital, which in turn increases production. The more capital—machines, factory buildings, trucks, computers, information libraries, and so on—a society's workers have, the more output the society can produce. The only way a society can accumulate more capital is to give up some current consumption: to save some of its output rather than consume all of it. The process of sacrificing current consumption to accumulate capital with which more output can be produced in the future is known as *roundabout production.*

2. **When is a dollar tomorrow better than a dollar today?**

   Never.

3. **What is capital?**

   Capital is the long-lasting equipment and buildings used in production. Examples of physical capital include the assembly lines used to produce automobiles, the trucks used by delivery companies, and the computers used by typists to type students' term papers.

4. **What is financial capital?**

   Financial capital is the funds used to buy physical capital. The sale of stock and the sale of bonds are the two ways that firms raise financial capital.

5. **How are the values of stocks and bonds determined?**

   Like other things in a market economy, the prices of stocks and bonds are determined in the financial capital market, on the basis of the demand and supply of financial capital.

6. **What is the relationship between the value of a stock and economic profit?**

   Stock prices reflect the present value of the economic profits a firm is expected to receive in the future.

Key Terms

saving

present value

future value

financial capital

annual return

dividend

capital gain

coupon

maturity date

face value

yield

Quick-Check Quiz

Section 1: Capital

1. The process of saving and accumulating capital in order to increase production and consumption in the future is called
   a. roundabout production.
   b. piecemeal production.
   c. delayed gratification of savings.
   d. the present value/future metaphor.
   e. current consumptionism.

2. To an economist, delaying consumption is called
   a. minimizing future value.
   b. maximizing present value.
   c. saving.
   d. capital.
   e. rounding production.

3. Present value is the
   a. value of savings forgone to acquire capital.
   b. value of capital forgone to acquire savings.
   c. difference between the rate of return and the rate of interest.
   d. equivalent value in the future of some amount received today.
   e. equivalent value today of some amount to be received in the future.

4. Future value is the
   a. value of savings forgone to acquire capital.
   b. value of capital forgone to acquire savings.
   c. difference between the rate of return and the rate of interest.
   d. equivalent value in the future of some amount received today.
   e. equivalent value today of some amount to be received in the future.

5. Which of the following statements about the demand and supply of capital is *false*?
   a. The demand for capital is represented by a downward-sloping curve.
   b. The supply of capital is represented by an upward-sloping curve.
   c. The demand for and supply of capital determine the price of capital.
   d. An increase in the price of capital lowers the rate of return on capital.
   e. The demand for capital shifts outward when interest rates rise.

6. When the rate of interest rises above the rate of return on capital, the demand for capital
   a. declines, the price of capital declines, and the rate of return on capital increases.
   b. declines, the price of capital increases, and the rate of return on capital increases.
   c. declines, the price of capital increases, and the rate of return on capital declines.
   d. declines, the price of capital declines, and the rate of return on capital declines.
   e. increases, the price of capital declines, and the rate of return on capital increases.

Section 2: Financial Capital

1. Financial capital is the money raised by
   a. selling a firm's output.
   b. selling a firm's inputs.
   c. taking out loans.
   d. selling shares of ownership.
   e. both taking out loans and selling shares of ownership.

2. The increase in the price of a share of stock is called the
   a. capital increment.
   b. capital gain.
   c. capital investment.
   d. dividend.
   e. coupon.

3. The payment a firm makes to its stockholders is called the
   a. capital increment.
   b. capital gain.
   c. capital investment.
   d. dividend.
   e. coupon.

4. The *Wall Street Journal* listing for the ZXW Corporation gives the closing price of the stock as $200 and the dividend as $4. What is the yield?
   a. 200
   b. 50
   c. 2.00
   d. 800
   e. 4.00

5. You own one share of stock in the ZXW Corporation. When you bought the stock, it sold for $125 per share; now it sells for $200 per share. Your capital gain is
   a. $75.
   b. $325.
   c. $62.50.
   d. $160.
   e. 75 percent.

6. A bond's *coupon* is
   a. the time when the payments end and the principal is paid back.
   b. the amount of principal that will be paid back when the bond matures.
   c. the annual rate of return on the bond if the bond were held to maturity.
   d. the fixed amount that the borrower agrees to pay the bondholder each year.
   e. none of the above.

7. A bond's *face value* is
   a. the time when the payments end and the principal is paid back.
   b. the amount of principal that will be paid back when the bond matures.
   c. the annual rate of return on the bond if the bond were held to maturity.
   d. the fixed amount that the borrower agrees to pay the bondholder each year.
   e. none of the above.

8. A bond's *maturity date* is
   a. the time when the payments end and the principal is paid back.
   b. the amount of principal that will be paid back when the bond matures.
   c. the annual rate of return on the bond if the bond were held to maturity.
   d. the fixed amount that the borrower agrees to pay the bondholder each year.
   e. none of the above.

9. A bond's *yield* is
   a. the time when the payments end and the principal is paid back.
   b. the amount of principal that will be paid back when the bond matures.
   c. the annual rate of return on the bond if the bond were held to maturity.
   d. the fixed amount that the borrower agrees to pay the bondholder each year.
   e. none of the above.

Practice Questions and Problems

Section 1: Capital

1. The process of saving and accumulating capital in order to increase production and consumption in the future is called _____ .

2. To an economist, saving is _____ .

3. Consumers and producers match their future plans with their current actions through

   _____ .

4. As the price of capital rises, the quantity of capital demanded _____ (rises, falls, stays the same) and the quantity of capital supplied _____ (rises, falls, stays the same).

5. When the interest rate rises, the present value of the marginal revenue product of capital

   _____ (rises, falls, stays the same), so the demand curve for capital shifts _____ (inward, outward).

6. When the interest rate falls, the present value of the marginal revenue product of capital

_____ (rises, falls, stays the same), so the demand curve for capital shifts _____

(inward, outward).

7. You're the owner of the Best Machine Shop. You've just seen a new computerized drill press that you're thinking about buying. The drill press costs $10,000, and you've calculated that buying it will add $1,000 per year (in present value terms) to the shop's revenues.

a. The rate of return on the drill press is _____ .

b. What additional piece of information do you need to decide whether the drill press is worth

buying? _____

c. The current interest rate is 9 percent. Should you buy the drill press? Explain your answer.

_____

_____

d. The interest rate just increased to 11 percent. Should you still buy the drill press? Explain your

answer.

_____

_____

e. Use your answers to c and d above to explain why the demand curve for capital shifts inward

when the interest rate rises.

_____

_____

_____

_____

f. Because the interest rate increased to 11 percent, machine shops have not bought as many com-

puterized drill presses as the manufacturer had expected. As a result, the price of drill presses just

dropped to $9,000. The rate of return on the drill press now is _____ . Is it worthwhile

for you to buy the drill press now? Explain your answer.

_____

_____

_____

_____

Section 2: Financial Capital

1. _____ capital is the money raised by a firm to buy _____ capital.

2. Financial capital consists of the shares of _____ the firm has sold and the _____

a firm has issued.

3. Stocks and bonds are bought and sold in the _____ market.

4. The return on a stock is the sum of the _____ and the _____ .

5. When the price of a bond increases, the yield _____ (increases, decreases).

6. There is a _____ (long, short)-term link between a firm's economic profit and the value of its stock but not a _____ (long, short)-term link.

Thinking About and Applying the Capital Market

I. Oil Wells and Interest Rates

Let's suppose you own a small oil well that produces one barrel of oil per day if you run the pump. If you don't run the pump, the oil stays in the ground and you can produce it later. Running the pump costs you $1 for every barrel you pump; you don't have any other costs to consider.

1. Your oil today sells for $21 per barrel. If the interest rate is 10 percent per year and you expect oil to sell for $24 per barrel next year, are you better off pumping and selling a barrel of oil today or leaving it in the ground for next year? Explain your answer.

   _____

   _____

   _____

2. If the interest rate is 10 percent, what is the minimum price next year that will convince you to wait until next year to sell your oil?

   _____

3. If the interest rate is 5 percent, what is the minimum price next year that will convince you to wait until next year to sell your oil?

   _____

II. Economic Profits and Stock Prices

In May 1998 the government charged Microsoft Corporation with violations of the antitrust laws. If the government wins its case, Microsoft's profits will be decreased in the future. Since the case is likely to take several years to come to a conclusion, what effect do you think the antitrust case will have on Microsoft's stock price today and why?

_____

_____

_____

_____

Chapter 17 (*Economics* Chapter 31)   Homework Problems

Name _____

1. What is the opportunity cost to consumers of saving?

2. What is the difference between capital and financial capital?

3. What is the present value of $10,000 you will receive in one year?

4. Why is $10,000 you will get next year not worth as much to you today as having $10,000 in your pocket today?

5. You are the proprietor of the A-1 Yo-Yo Company. Your production manager wants to buy a new yo-yo string–cutting machine that he estimates will add $500 to your profits next year, plus an additional $500 profit for each of the following three years. The machine costs $1,550 that must be paid today.

   a. Would buying the machine add to the present value of your profits if the interest rate was 10 percent? Why?

   b. Would buying the machine add to the present value of your profits if the interest rate was 12 percent? Why?

   c. Use the above results to explain why business investment spending is affected by interest rate.

If your instructor assigns these problems, write your answers above, then tear out this page and hand it in.

Answers

Quick-Check Quiz

Section 1. Capital

1. a; 2. c; 3. e; 4. d; 5. e; 6. a

If you missed any of these questions, you should go back and review Section 1 in Chapter 17 (*Economics, Chapter 31*).

Section 2: Financial Capital

1. e; 2. b; 3. d; 4. c; 5. a; 6. d; 7. b; 8. a; 9. c

If you missed any of these questions, you should go back and review Section 2 in Chapter 17 (*Economics, Chapter 31*).

Practice Questions and Problems

Section 1. Capital

1. roundabout production
2. delaying consumption
3. capital markets
4. falls; rises (The demand and supply curves for capital work like other demand and supply curves.)
5. falls; inward (When interest rates rise, present value always falls, making capital less valuable to firms. When capital is less valuable, firms do not demand as much.)
6. rises; outward (When interest rates fall, present value always rises, making capital more valuable to firms. When capital is more valuable, firms demand more than before.)
7. a. 10 percent (The rate of return is the income [$1,000] divided by the price of the asset [$10,000], stated as a percentage.)
   b. interest rate (Capital is worth buying if its rate of return is at least equal to the interest rate, the opportunity cost of capital.)
   c. Yes. The rate of return is more than the interest rate.
   d. No. Now the rate of return is less than the interest rate. You'd get a better return from just putting the money in the bank and collecting interest.
   e. When the interest rate went up, capital that used to be worth buying became unprofitable. Because less capital would be bought at the same price of capital, the demand curve must have shifted inward.
   f. 11.1 percent ($1,000/$9,000); yes. Now it is worthwhile again to buy the drill press because the rate of return at least equals the interest rate. These changes—the rate of interest rising and the price of capital falling because the demand for capital dropped—are the way capital markets reach equilibrium.

Section 2: Financial Capital

1. Financial; physical
2. stock; bonds
3. financial (or capital)
4. dividend; capital gain

5. decreases
6. long; short

Thinking About and Applying the Capital Market

I. *Oil Wells and Interest Rates*

1. You should leave it for next year. If you pump the oil now, you gain $20 now—the $21 price minus the $1 cost for pumping. If you save the $20 until next year at 10 percent interest, next year you will have $22 ($20 + $2 interest). If you wait until next year to produce the oil, you will have $23 next year ($24 price – $1 cost). $23 is more than $22.
2. $23. After you subtract your $1 cost, you would get $22 next year, the same as you would get by producing this year and saving the money for a year.
3. $22. After you subtract your $1 cost, you would get $21 next year, the same as you would get by producing this year and saving the money for a year.

II. *Economic Profits and Stock Prices*

Microsoft's stock price will decrease in the present if investors think the government is likely to win the case. The price will drop today, even though Microsoft's profits wouldn't be affected for several years, because the price of a stock is based on investors' expectations about future profits, not just current profits.

THE LAND MARKET: NATURAL RESOURCES AND ENVIRONMENTAL POLICY

FUNDAMENTAL QUESTIONS

1. **What is the difference between renewable and nonrenewable natural resources?**

   Natural resources are the nonproduced resources that are available on the planet Earth. Some natural resources, such as farm crops, can be reproduced. We can eat up this year's wheat harvest, knowing that farmers will plant more wheat that can be harvested next year.

   Other natural resources, such as minerals, can only be used once and can't be reproduced. If we use a million barrels of oil to produce the gasoline we burn up this year in our automobiles, that million barrels of oil is gone forever.

2. **What is the optimal rate of use of natural resources?**

   From the economist's perspective, the optimal rate of using natural resources balances the value of using them in the present with the value of using them in the future. For example, if you own some forest land, you could cut down all the trees and sell them this year, and replant the land with new seedlings. You would make a lot of money *this* year, but you wouldn't have any more trees to sell for a long time.

   If you cut down some of the trees this year, cut down some of the trees each year in the future, and replanted each year's cutting with new seedlings, you can keep on making money from selling trees forever. How many trees you should cut this year and how many you should save for future years depends on expected future prices and interest rates.

3. **Why might a market not result in the best use of the environment?**

   Economists agree that perfectly competitive markets are usually economically efficient: they produce the right amount of output and allocate the right amount of resources to alternative uses. **Market failure** is the failure of the market system to make economically efficient decisions. In the real world, markets sometimes fail to produce the economically efficient output or fail to allocate resources efficiently because of externalities, public goods, and other factors.

   Ideally, markets balance the **marginal social costs** and **marginal benefits (MB)** of a product. Market failure occurs when **social costs** do not equal social benefits. **Externalities** exist whenever **private costs** or benefits are different from social costs or benefits. If market decision makers pay attention only to equating private costs and benefits, then social costs and benefits will not be the same.

Public goods are goods for which the **principle of mutual exclusivity** does not hold. These goods are public in the sense that many people benefit from them, including those who don't pay for them. Since people don't have to pay for benefits they receive from public goods, the market demand curve does not include the value of all benefits gained from production and consumption of public goods. In turn, this leads to production of less than the efficient quantity of public goods by private markets.

4. Why does the government get involved in environmental issues?

Government gets involved in solving environmental problems because the private market system does not make efficient decisions when there are externalities. Government can resolve environmental problems through regulation, taxes and subsidies, or the assignment of private property rights.

5. Why are global warming problems so difficult to solve?

The lack of property rights is a major complication in global environmental problems. Nobody owns the air that blows from the United States into Canada. If U.S. power plant emissions cause acid rain in Canada, there is no market or government mechanism that allows the Canadians to restrict the behavior of U.S. firms, unless the Canadian government can convince the U.S. government to intervene. Solving global pollution problems requires governments to cooperate, sometimes in ways that aren't beneficial to their own interests.

Key Terms

nonrenewable (exhaustible)
  natural resources
renewable (nonexhaustible)
  natural resources
market failure
private costs

externality
social costs
private property right
marginal social costs
principle of mutual exclusivity
public good

free rider
emission standard
Coase theorem
emissions offset policy

Quick-Check Quiz

Section 1: Natural Resources

1. When a resource has a fixed supply, payments to the resource are
   a. pure interest.
   b. increased to their future value, depending on the interest rate.
   c. pure economic rent.
   d. pure transfer earnings.
   e. partial transfer earnings.

2. Natural resources that cannot be replaced or renewed are called
   a. scarce natural resources.
   b. nonexhaustible natural resources.
   c. unlimited natural resources.
   d. exhaustible natural resources.
   e. limited natural resources.

3. Natural resources that can be replaced or renewed are called
   a. scarce natural resources.
   b. nonexhaustible natural resources.
   c. unlimited natural resources.
   d. exhaustible natural resources.
   e. limited natural resources.

Section 2: Environmental Problems

1. Market failure occurs
   a. when governments levy taxes on business firms.
   b. when governments levy taxes on workers.
   c. when perfectly competitive markets do not achieve economic efficiency.
   d. whenever governments intervene in the decision-making processes of perfectly competitive markets.
   e. when markets produce an income distribution that is not equitable.

2. Externalities occur when
   a. someone outside a business makes decisions that affect the business.
   b. an activity creates costs or benefits that are borne by parties not directly involved in the activity.
   c. free-riding does not exist.
   d. taxes affect the amount of a good produced.
   e. private benefits equal social benefits.

3. When private costs are less than social costs,
   a. an externality exists.
   b. a market failure exists.
   c. a market is producing too much of a good.
   d. All of the above are true.
   e. Only a and c are true.

4. Public goods are goods
   a. to which the principle of mutual exclusivity does not apply.
   b. whose availability is not reduced by consumption.
   c. that have nothing to do with free-riding.
   d. for which all of the above are true.
   e. for which only a and b are true.

5. Which of the following is *not* a public good?
   a. national defense
   b. police protection
   c. broadcast television
   d. pizza
   e. All of the above are public goods.

Section 3: Public Policies

1. Which of the following is *not* one of the policies followed by the U.S. government in attempting to improve the environment?
   a. public ownership of polluting firms
   b. regulations
   c. taxes and subsidies
   d. assignment of private property rights
   e. emission standards

2. The Coase theorem says that problems created by lack of property rights can be resolved by those affected as long as
   a. someone—it doesn't matter who—is assigned the property right.
   b. the person causing an externality is assigned the property right.
   c. the person bearing the burden of an externality is assigned the property right.
   d. the government assigns the property right to a government agency.
   e. the parties to a problem assign the property right to the government.

3. In U.S. environmental policy, an emission standard is
   a. the minimum amount of clean air that can be emitted.
   b. the maximum allowable level of pollution from a specific source.
   c. the minimum allowable level of pollution from a wide area made up of many sources.
   d. a policy that enables a firm to trade off one type of emission for another as long as total emissions remain below some standard.
   e. a policy wherein pollution permits are issued and a market in the permits then develops.

4. In U.S. environmental policy, an emissions offset policy is
   a. the minimum amount of clean air that can be emitted.
   b. the maximum allowable level of pollution from a specific source.
   c. the minimum allowable level of pollution from a wide area made up of many sources.
   d. a policy that enables a firm to trade off one type of emission for another as long as total emissions remain below some standard.
   e. a policy wherein pollution permits are issued and a market in the permits then develops.

Practice Questions and Problems

Section 1: Natural Resources

1. When a resource has a fixed supply, the payment it receives is _____ .

2. Rent serves to _____ the fixed supply of a reosurce among competing uses.

3. Oil is a _____ (renewable, nonrenewable) natural resource because its supply _____ (can be replenished, is fixed).

4. Forests are a _____ (renewable, nonrenewable) natural resource because the supply of trees _____ (can be replenished, is fixed).

5. The price of nonrenewable resources usually increases over time at the same rate as the _____ .

6. Higher interest rates lead to _____ (faster, slower) use of renewable natural resources.

Section 2: Environmental Problems

1. Market failure is defined as the failure of a market system to achieve _____ efficiency.

2. Market failures can have two causes: _____ and _____ .

3. A(n) _____ occurs when a cost or benefit of an activity is borne by parties not directly involved in the activity.

4. When social costs are higher than private costs, the market produces _____ (too much, not enough) of the product.

5. Public goods are goods or services to which the principle of _____ does not apply.

6. You and your neighbors have decided to hire a private guard to patrol your neighborhood after dark to scare away burglars. Use your knowledge from this chapter to explain why your private guard is a public good, why problems with free-riding are likely to appear, and why police services usually are provided by governments rather than private groups.

_____

_____

_____

_____

Section 3: Public Policies

1. The optimal level of pollution is reached when the marginal _____ from a cleaner environment equal the marginal _____ of cleaning up the environment.

2. Give the name of the environmental policy that matches each description.

   a. Pollution permits are issued and a market in permits develops: _____

   b. A maximum allowable level of pollution from a specific source is set: _____

3. Let's make you the director of the Environmental Protection Agency (EPA). You have to decide how much pollution a particular water treatment plant should be allowed to produce. Right now, the plant produces 4 tons of pollutants per day. The plant is owned by the federal government, so any cleanup costs must be paid for through taxes. The costs and benefits of reducing pollution are shown on the next page.

Tons per Day	Marginal Benefits	Marginal Costs
3	$10 million	$ 1 million
2	5 million	4 million
1	2 million	16 million
0	1 million	100 million

a. Find the amount of pollution that gives consumers the most net gain (total gains from pollution reduction minus total costs of pollution reduction).

b. As director of the EPA, how do you explain to hostile environmentalists why you don't require the plant to clean up all of its pollution?

_____

_____

_____

_____

Thinking About and Applying the Land Market: Natural Resources and Environmental Policy

I. Hamburger Packaging and Pollution Policies

Trash disposal can create the same kinds of economic problems relating to externalities as other types of pollution. The graph below shows the demand and marginal costs of producing hamburgers (*MC*), not including the cost of disposing of the packaging, and the full cost of producing hamburgers (*MSC*), which includes the costs of disposal.

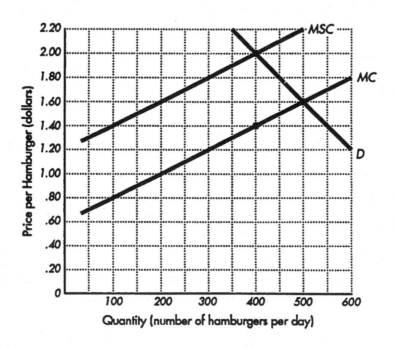

1. In a perfectly competitive market, _____ hamburgers will be sold every day at a price of

   _____ .

2. Taking into account the cost of disposing of the packaging, the optimal number of hamburgers sold is

   _____ , and the optimal price is _____ .

3. The marginal social cost of disposing of the hamburger packaging is _____ .

4. Suppose the government wants to limit the amount of trash from hamburger packaging.

   a. If it sets an emission standard limiting the number of packages the hamburger stand can throw away, what would be an economically efficient emission standard?

   _____

   b. Would setting this standard provide any incentives for the hamburger stand to develop different packaging techniques that reduce trash? Explain your answer.

   _____

   _____

   _____

   _____

5. Suppose instead that the government sets an effluent charge to internalize the costs of disposing of the packaging.

   a. How much is the optimal charge per package for the current packaging technique? _____

   b. If the effluent charge was based on the actual cost of disposing of the packaging, would the hamburger stand have any incentive to develop different packaging techniques that reduce trash? Explain your answer.

   _____

   _____

   _____

   _____

II. International Cooperation on Pollution Cleanup

Although across-border pollution problems can cause political problems, there have been instances where countries have cooperated in cleaning up pollution. One case was described recently in the *Wall Street Journal:*

> [Officials have] used a state law classifying lead slag as a hazardous waste to negotiate toxic-waste cleanups south of the border [in Mexico]. In the deal . . . a privately-owned Dallas lead recycler said it will pay $2.5 million . . . [for] improperly transporting lead waste from its Los Angeles smelter to Mexico.

Of the $2.5 million fine, $2 million was going to be spent to clean up the toxic waste, and $300,000 was going to a foundation that provides medical care for border-area residents. The Mexican government planned to use the lead recovered from the cleanup, valued at $100,000 to $200,000, to help pay the back wages to workers at the plant.

What characteristics of this agreement made it worthwhile for the United States and Mexico to cooperate in cleaning up the polluted site in Mexico? (*Hint*: Review the first few chapters in the text to refresh your memory on why people choose to engage in voluntary trade.)

_____

_____

_____

Chapter 18 (*Economics* Chapter 32)   Homework Problems

Name _____

1. What do economists mean by the phrase *market failure*?

2. List three reasons why market failure can occur.

3. a. What is an externality?

    b. Why does a market system produce more than the efficient quantity of a good that produces negative externalities?

4. Use the principle of mutual exclusivity to explain why national defense is a public good, but food isn't.

5. The U.S. government has decided to require that automobiles produce less pollution in the future. Two different policies for reducing pollution are under consideration:

  A. Require that automobile makers use a specific pollution-control technology on every new car.

  B. Charge automakers a tax based on how much pollution their new cars produce.

  Use the knowledge you have gained in this chapter to explain why economists would prefer policy B as the way to reduce pollution.

If your instructor assigns these problems, write your answers above, then tear out this page and hand it in.

Answers

Quick-Check Quiz

Section 1: Natural Resources

1. c; 2. d; 3. b
If you missed any of these questions, you should go back and review Section 1 in Chapter 18 (*Economics, Chapter 32*).

Section 2: Environmental Problems

1. c; 2. b; 3. d; 4. e; 5. d
If you missed any of these questions, you should go back and review Section 2 in Chapter 18 (*Economics, Chapter 32*).

Section 3: Public Policies

1. a; 2. a; 3. b; 4. e
If you missed any of these questions, you should go back and review Section 3 in Chapter 18 (*Economics, Chapter 32*).

Practice Questions and Problems

Section 1: Natural Resources

1. economic rent
2. allocate
3. nonrenewable; is fixed
4. renewable; can be replenished
5. interest
6. faster

Section 2: Environmental Problems

1. economic
2. externalities; public goods
3. externality
4. too much
5. mutual exclusivity
6. The guard is a public good because scaring away burglars benefits everyone in the neighborhood. If only some of your neighbors are willing to pay for the guard, everyone in the neighborhood will still gain. Because people benefit even if they don't pay, free-riding will be a problem. By levying taxes on everyone, governments get around free-rider problems: you don't have a choice about paying taxes.

Section 3: Public Policies

1. benefits; costs
2. a. emissions offset

   b. emission standard

3. a. 2 tons per day

   b. Removing the first ton of pollution (going from 4 tons to 3 tons) gives $10 million in benefits at a cost of only $1 million, for a net gain of $9 million. Removing the second ton of pollution (going from 3 tons to 2 tons) gives $5 million in benefits at a cost of $4 million, for a net gain of $1 million. Removing the third ton of pollution (going from 2 tons to 1 ton) gives only $2 million in benefits at a cost of $16 million, for a net loss of $14 million.

Thinking About and Applying the Land Market: Natural Resources and Environmental Policy

I. Hamburger Packaging and Pollution Policies

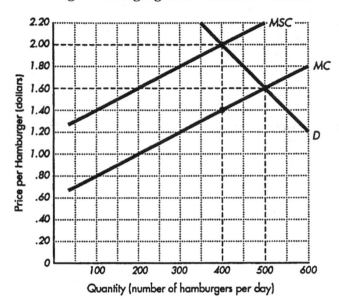

1. 500; $1.60 (In a perfectly competitive market, the equilibrium price and quantity are where the demand curve crosses the *MC* curve.)
2. 400; $2 (The optimal number of hamburgers is where the demand curve and the *MSC* curve cross.)
3. $.60 per hamburger (the difference between the *MSC* and *MC* curves at each quantity)
4. a. 400 packages per day (With this standard, the optimal number of hamburgers is produced.)
   b. No. Because the hamburger stand is limited to 400 packages per day and doesn't have to pay for the costs of disposing of the packaging, it has no incentive to find packaging materials that reduce disposal costs.
5. a. $.60 (the cost of disposing of the packaging)
   b. If the effluent charge is based on the actual cost of disposing of the packaging, the hamburger stand can save itself money by finding different techniques that reduce packaging costs. In general, using effluent charges creates more incentives for reducing pollution than does setting emission standards.

II. International Cooperation on Pollution Cleanup

Both sides benefit from the agreement. Mexico gets a cleaner environment plus some money from the recovered lead. The United States gets $300,000 to help provide medical care.

Sample Test I
Chapters 15–18
(*Economics* Chapters 29–32)

1. Which of the following statements best illustrates the relationship between the market for products and the market for resources?
   a. An increase in the price of compact disc players will decrease the demand for compact discs.
   b. An increase in the demand for tennis racquets will increase the demand for tennis balls.
   c. As income decrease, people demand relatively more ground beef.
   d. An increase in the demand for jet airplanes will increase the demand for aerospace workers.
   e. An increase in the price of movies will increase the demand for videocassette rentals.

2. The demand curve for labor shows a _____ relationship between the _____ and the quantity of labor demanded.
   a. positive; real wage
   b. negative; real wage
   c. positive; money wage
   d. negative; money wage
   e. constant; real wage

3. If the demand for a final product is very price-elastic, then
   a. the demand for a resource used to produce the product will be very price-inelastic.
   b. the demand for a resource used to produce the product will be very price-elastic.
   c. the demand for a resource used to produce the product will be unit-elastic.
   d. the demand for a resource used to produce the product will be positively sloped.
   e. the demand for a resource used to produce the product will increase.

4. Which of the following is generally true regarding resource supply?
   a. It is relatively elastic in the short run.
   b. It is relatively inelastic in the short run.
   c. It is unit-elastic in the short run.
   d. It is unit-elastic in the long run.
   e. It is infinitely elastic in the short run.

5. If Elizabeth is earning $50,000 as a management consultant but could earn no more than $20,000 doing anything else, her transfer earnings are _____ , while her economic rent is _____ .
   a. $20,000; $30,000
   b. $30,000; $20,000
   c. $20,000; $50,000
   d. $50,000; $30,000
   e. $50,000; $20,000

Consider the following table for questions 6 and 7.

Number of Workers	Output per Hour	Price of the Products ($)
0	0	4
1	6	4
2	11	4

6. The marginal revenue product of the
   a. fourth worker is $68.
   b. second worker is $6.
   c. first worker is $5.
   d. third worker is $4.
   e. fifth worker is $4.

7. If the prevailing wage rate is $9, how many workers should this firm hire?
   a. 1
   b. 2
   c. 3
   d. 4
   e. 5

8. If the marginal factor cost is more than the marginal revenue product, the firm
   a. is incurring a loss.
   b. is making a profit.
   c. could increase profits by hiring more of the resource.
   d. could increase profits by hiring less of the resource.
   e. is in equilibrium.

Use the following figure to answer questions 9–11.

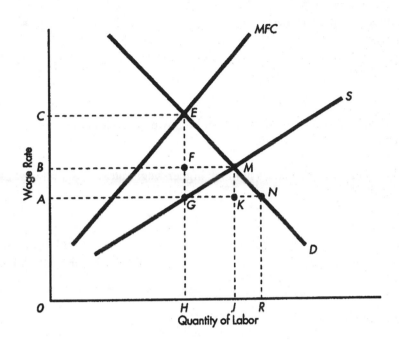

9. A monopsony will pay the wage rate _____ and hire _____ units of labor.
   a. *0A; 0H*
   b. *0B; 0J*
   c. *0C; 0H*
   d. *0B; 0H*
   e. *0A; 0R*

10. A competitive labor market will pay the wage _____ and hire _____ units of labor.
    a. *0A; 0H*
    b. *0B; 0J*
    c. *0C; 0H*
    d. *0B; 0H*
    e. *0A; 0R*

11. Assume that a union is formed to bargain with the monopsony. What is the maximum wage rate it could bargain for that would not cause any union members to lose their jobs?
    a. *0A*
    b. *0B*
    c. somewhere between *0A* and *0B*
    d. *0C*
    e. somewhere between *0B* and *0C*

12. If the *MRP/MPC* of workers is greater than the *MRP/MFC* of robots, to maximize profit and minimize cost, a firm should
    a. use more robots and more workers.
    b. use more robots.
    c. increase its price.
    d. use fewer robots and fewer workers.
    e. use more workers.

13. As the wage rate rises, the quantity of labor supplied by an individual generally
    a. decreases at first and then increases.
    b. decreases at a constant rate.
    c. increases at first and then decreases at much higher wage rates.
    d. remains constant.
    e. is perfectly inelastic.

14. It is often the case that firms do not pay individuals their particular *MRP*, but rather pay on the basis of the individual's job category. This inconsistency with labor market theory is likely the result of
    a. the desire of firms to provide equity for all.
    b. the exploitation of employees by big business.
    c. a law enacted in 1992.
    d. the inability of firms to measure individual *MRP*.
    e. the backward-bending supply of labor.

15. Discrimination, according to an economist, occurs when there exists a wage differential between two groups whose _____ is the same.
    a. gender
    b. marginal product
    c. marginal revenue product
    d. race
    e. religion

16. Which of the following is likely to increase the demand for union labor?
    a. an increase in the productivity of nonunion labor
    b. a decrease in the price of nonunion produced goods
    c. an increase in the demand for the output of union labor
    d. a decrease in the *MPP* of union labor
    e. none of the above

Use the following figure to answer question 17.

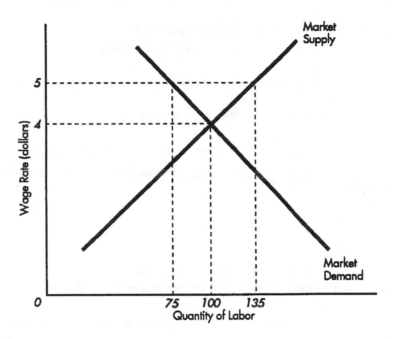

17. What is the consequence of the imposition of a minimum wage of $5?
    a. 135 workers will be employed at the minimum wage.
    b. 35 workers have lost jobs that they held at the equilibrium wage.
    c. 25 persons who did not choose to work at the equilibrium wage are available for work at the minimum wage but are not employed.
    d. 60 persons will be unemployed at the minimum wage.
    e. Everyone will be made better off.

18. Which of the following correctly uses the concept of present value?
    a. $1 received today has less value than $1 received in the future.
    b. The present value of $1 to be received in one year is more than $1 received today.
    c. Present value disregards risk and uncertainty.
    d. $1 to be received in one year has less value than $1 received today.
    e. None of the above.

19. A decrease in the interest rate
    a. shifts the demand curve for capital to the left, increasing the price and quality of capital.
    b. shifts the demand curve for capital to the right, increasing the price and quality of capital.
    c. shifts the demand curve for capital to the left, decreasing the price and quality of capital.
    d. shifts the demand curve for capital to the right, decreasing the price and quality of capital.
    e. has no effect on the capital market.

20. In what way is basic research distinguished from applied research in terms of technological change?
    a. Applied research is aimed at the creation of new knowledge and mostly occurs at academic institutions.
    b. Basic research always expects to have a practical payoff.
    c. Basic research is aimed at the creation of new knowledge and mostly occurs at academic institutions.
    d. Academic institutions, or universities, could not afford to engage in much basic research given today's budget constraints.
    e. Basic research is not related to technological advancement.

21. The long-run effect of the adoption of an innovation or technological change is
    a. a larger advertising budget.
    b. a reduction in costs.
    c. brighter employees.
    d. better employee benefits.
    e. improved hiring practices.

22. Which of the following would most likely result in a negative externality?
    a. Katie loses her money in the soda machine, becomes angry, and hurts her foot kicking the machine.
    b. Meiling's apartment is near the airport, and she is awakened early each morning by the sound of jets taking off.
    c. Marty pays to have her front yard professionally landscaped.
    d. Jim charges Mary $22 for economics tutoring, but she still fails the first exam.
    e. None of the above is correct.

Consider the following figure for questions 23–25.

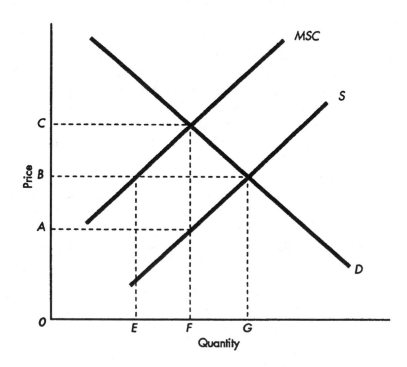

23. If this is a market in which production entails a negative externality, what would the market price and output be?
    a. *0B; 0E*
    b. *0C; 0F*
    c. *0A; 0F*
    d. *0B; 0G*
    e. *0A; 0E*

24. If this is a market in which production entails a negative externality, the socially optimal price and output are
    a. *0B* and *0E*.
    b. *0B* and *0F*.
    c. *0C* and *0F*.
    d. *0B* and *0G*.
    e. *0A* and *0E*.

25. If this is a market in which production entails a negative externality, a tax on producers equal to _____ will result in the socially optimal price and output.
    a. *0C – 0B*
    b. *0C – 0A*
    c. *0B – 0A*
    d. *0A*
    e. *0B*

Answers to Sample Test I

1. d (Chapter 14, Section 1.a; *Economics* Chapter 28)
2. b (Chapter 14, Section 2.a; *Economics* Chapter 28)
3. b (Chapter 14, Section 2.a; *Economics* Chapter 28)
4. b (Chapter 14, Section 2.b; *Economics* Chapter 28)
5. a (Chapter 14, Section 2.b; *Economics* Chapter 28)
6. e (Chapter 14, Section 3.a; *Economics* Chapter 28)
7. c (Chapter 14, Section 3.a; *Economics* Chapter 28)
8. d (Chapter 14, Section 3.b; *Economics* Chapter 28)
9. a (Chapter 14, Section 3.b; *Economics* Chapter 28)
10. b (Chapter 14, Section 3.b; *Economics* Chapter 28)
11. d (Chapter 15, Section 3.b; *Economics* Chapter 29)
12. e (Chapter 15, Section 3.c; *Economics* Chapter 29)
13. c (Chapter 15, Section 1.a; *Economics* Chapter 29)

14. d (Chapter 15, Section 3.d; *Economics* Chapter 29)
15. c (Chapter 16, Section 1.a; *Economics* Chapter 30)
16. c (Chapter 16, Section 3.c; *Economics* Chapter 30)
17. d (Chapter 16, Section 4.a; *Economics* Chapter 30)
18. d (Chapter 17, Section 1.b; *Economics* Chapter 31)
19. c (Chapter 17, Section 1.b; *Economics* Chapter 31)
20. c (Chapter 17, Section 2.a; *Economics* Chapter 31)
21. b (Chapter 17, Section 2.b; *Economics* Chapter 31)
22. b (Chapter 18, Section 2.b; *Economics* Chapter 32)
23. d (Chapter 18, Section 2.b; *Economics* Chapter 32)
24. c (Chapter 18, Section 2.b; *Economics* Chapter 32)
25. b (Chapter 18, Section 2.b; *Economics* Chapter 32)

Sample Test II
Chapters 15–18
(*Economics* Chapters 29–32)

1. The demand for labor indicates
   a. a direct relationship between the real wage and the quantity of labor available for employment.
   b. an inverse relationship between the real wage and the quantity of labor available for employment.
   c. an inverse relationship between the real wage and the quantity of labor employed.
   d. a direct relationship between the real wage and the quantity of labor employed.
   e. none of the above.

2. Assume that labor is the only variable input and that an additional input of labor increases total output from 63 to 71 units. If the product sells for $5 per unit in a perfectly competitive market, what is the marginal revenue product of this additional labor input?
   a. $63
   b. $315
   c. $8
   d. $40
   e. $71

3. In a perfectly competitive output market, which of the following is true?
   a. $MRP = P$
   b. $MRP = VMP$
   c. $MRP < VMP$
   d. $MRP > VMP$
   e. $MRP = MPP$

4. A firm's demand for labor is
   a. the supply curve for the resource.
   b. the marginal revenue product curve.
   c. the same as the economy's demand curve for labor.
   d. the same as the economy's supply curve for labor.
   e. positively shaped.

5. A firm would be motivated to hire an additional unit of a resource so long as
   a. $MRP > MFC$.
   b. $TR > TC$.
   c. $MRP < MFC$.
   d. $AR > ATC$.
   e. $MR > MC$.

6. Other things being equal, the marginal revenue product for labor hired by a firm with monopoly control in the output market is, in general,
   a. less than the marginal revenue product for labor hired by a firm with no monopoly control.
   b. more than the marginal revenue product for labor hired by a firm with no monopoly control.
   c. equal to the marginal revenue product for labor hired by a firm with no monopoly control.
   d. upward sloping.
   e. perfectly elastic.

7. An example of investment in human capital is
   a. the purchase of an industrial robot.
   b. the purchase of a computer to help tax attorneys.
   c. the purchase of higher education.
   d. unemployment compensation.
   e. paying a higher real wage.

8. The statement "You couldn't pay me enough to take that job" implies the basis for
   a. a backward-bending supply of labor curve.
   b. a backward-bending demand for labor curve.
   c. compensating wage differentials.
   d. conspicuous consumption.
   e. age-earnings profiles.

9. Comparable worth is the idea that pay should be
   a. determined on the basis of demand conditions.
   b. designed to eliminate shortages and surpluses in the labor market.
   c. determined on the basis of supply conditions.
   d. reflective of the attributes of the job.
   e. much higher than it currently is.

10. When comparing a firm operating in a monopsony to one operating in a perfectly competitive resource market, which of the following is true?
    a. The perfectly competitive firm faces an upward-sloping supply of labor curve.
    b. The perfectly competitive firm pays a wage rate that is lower than the factor's marginal cost.
    c. The monopsonist pays a lower wage than the perfectly competitive firm.
    d. The monopsonist pays a wage that is higher than the factor's marginal cost.
    e. The monopsonist faces a horizontal supply of labor curve.

11. An example of a monopsonist employer is
    a. United Mine Workers.
    b. Fraternal Order of Police.
    c. Phe Beta Kappa.
    d. Kmart.
    e. National Collegiate Athletic Association.

12. An example of a bilateral monopoly is
    a. retail clerks working in a mall department store.
    b. a contracted software engineer employed by McDonnel Douglas.
    c. a union comprising all workers in a one-company town.
    d. unskilled laborers working at a large construction firm.
    e. unskilled laborers working for a public utility.

Use the following figure to answer questions 13 and 14.

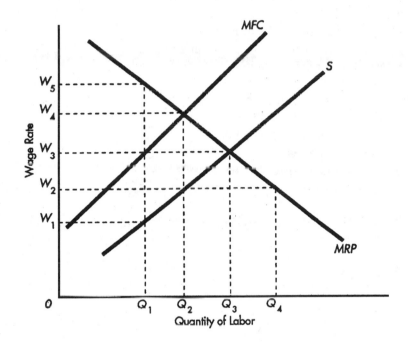

13. What wage and employment rates will result if this is a monopsonistic labor market?
    a. W_1 and Q_1
    b. W_2 and Q_3
    c. W_2 and Q_2
    d. W_5 and Q_1
    e. W_4 and Q_2

14. If a minimum wage is imposed on this monopsonistic labor market, which of the following statements is true?
    a. A minimum wage above W_5 will increase employment.
    b. A minimum wage below W_2 will increase employment.
    c. A minimum wage of W_4 will maximize employment.
    d. A minimum wage somewhere between W_2 and W_4 will increase employment.
    e. All of the above.

15. In general, the workers most negatively affected by an increase in minimum wage are
    a. government workers.
    b. skilled workers.
    c. those working in a monopsonistic market.
    d. union members.
    e. unskilled workers.

16. The opportunity cost of current consumption is a determinant of
    a. the percentage of income individuals allocate to savings.
    b. the risk of inflation.
    c. the occupation of the head of the household.
    d. the quantity of stocks and bonds firms are willing to issue.
    e. whether the government runs a deficit.

17. An increase in the interest rate would
    a. increase the present value of future earnings.
    b. decrease the present value of future earnings.
    c. lead to no change in the present value of future earnings.
    d. decrease the future value of current funds.
    e. have none of the above effects.

18. The present value of $8,000 to be received in one year if the interest rate on the best alternative use of the money is 6 percent is
    a. $7,547.17.
    b. $480.00.
    c. $7,520.00
    d. $6,742.19.
    e. $7,823.40.

19. A firm will choose to invest in a piece of equipment if
    a. the firm needs to decrease efficiency.
    b. the firm needs to downsize.
    c. the marginal revenue product is less than the interest rate.
    d. the expected rate of return is less than the cost of borrowing the funds for the expenditure.
    e. the expected rate of return is at least as great as the cost of borrowing the funds for the expenditure.

20. If the purchase price of capital decreases,
    a. the rate of return on capital decreases.
    b. the supply of capital decreases.
    c. the demand for capital increases.
    d. the rate of return on capital increases.
    e. none of the above effects occur.

21. Other things being equal, the difference between today's price and tomorrow's price for a nonrenewable resource will _____ as interest rates _____
    a. rise; rise.
    b. fall; rise.
    c. rise; fall.
    d. remain constant; rise.
    e. remain constant; fall.

22. Why may a firm not innovate?
    a. because rivals are innovating
    b. because employees do not want innovation
    c. because it is costly to innovate
    d. because innovation has little payoff
    e. because innovation makes no sense

23. The relationship between economic profit and stock value is
    a. nonexistent.
    b. inverse.
    c. direct and perfect each year.
    d. direct but only over a substantial period of time.
    e. inverse but only over a substantial period of time.

24. If once a good is produced, the cost of preventing consumption by others is extremely high, the good is characterized by
    a. positive externalities.
    b. negative externalities.
    c. nonexcludability.
    d. nonrivalry.
    e. rivalry.

25. The optimal level of pollution is
    a. zero.
    b. the quantity where total costs equal marginal benefits.
    c. the quantity where marginal social costs equal marginal social benefits.
    d. less than 10 percent.
    e. where the firm's costs are minimized.

Answers to Sample Test II

1. c (Chapter 14, Section 2.a; *Economics* Chapter 28)
2. d (Chapter 14, Section 3.b; *Economics* Chapter 28)
3. b (Chapter 14, Section 3.d; *Economics* Chapter 28)
4. b (Chapter 14, Section 3.d; *Economics* Chapter 28)
5. a (Chapter 14, Section 3.b; *Economics* Chapter 28)
6. a (Chapter 14, Section 3.d; *Economics* Chapter 28)
7. c (Chapter 15, Section 2.b; *Economics* Chapter 29)
8. c (Chapter 15, Section 2.a; *Economics* Chapter 29)
9. d (Chapter 16, Section 2.b; *Economics* Chapter 30)

10. c (Chapter 16, Section 3.a; *Economics* Chapter 30)
11. e (Chapter 16, Section 3.b; *Economics* Chapter 30)
12. c (Chapter 16, Section 3.b; *Economics* Chapter 30)
13. c (Chapter 16, Section 4.a; *Economics* Chapter 30)
14. d (Chapter 16, Section 4.a; *Economics* Chapter 30)
15. e (Chapter 16, Section 4.a; *Economics* Chapter 30)
16. a (Chapter 17, Section 1.a; *Economics* Chapter 31)
17. b (Chapter 17, Section 1.b; *Economics* Chapter 31)
18. a (Chapter 17, Section 1.b; *Economics* Chapter 31)

19. e (Chapter 17, Section 1.b; *Economics* Chapter 31)
20. d (Chapter 17, Section 1.b; *Economics* Chapter 31)
21. a (Chapter 17, Section 1.b; *Economics* Chapter 32)
22. c (Chapter 17, Section 2.c; *Economics* Chapter 31)

23. d (Chapter 17, Section 3.d; *Economics* Chapter 31)
24. c (Chapter 18, Section 2.c; *Economics* Chapter 32)
25. c (Chapter 18, Section 2.b; *Economics* Chapter 32)

AGING, SOCIAL SECURITY, AND HEALTH CARE

FUNDAMENTAL QUESTIONS

1. Why worry about social security?

   Pension plans serve several functions in the economy. They provide income for people after they retire, and they also provide an incentive for older workers to retire. Social security is a mandatory, government-run pension program. Benefits for today's retirees are paid from taxes collected from today's workers. Social security may have problems in the future as the baby boom generation starts to retire.

2. Why is health care heading the list of U.S. citizens' concerns?

   People in the United States already spend more than 14 percent of their income—$1 out of every $7—on health care, and the percentage is increasing steadily. Several factors are responsible: an aging population, the way the U.S. health-care system is set up, and new medical technologies.

   For most people in the United States, medical bills are paid primarily by private or public insurance programs. Because we pay little of our medical bills directly out of our own pockets, we don't pay much attention to prices—our demand is inelastic. Other countries using different payment systems have developed health-care systems that cost considerably less but that provide equal quality in terms of infant mortality and life expectancy.

Key Terms

Medicare
Medicaid
health maintenance organization (HMO)

preferred provider organization (PPO)
managed competition
managed care

Quick-Check Quiz

Section 1: Aging and Social Security

1. In 2000, the portion of the U.S. population age sixty-five or older was about
   a. 3.2 percent.
   b. 4.7 percent.
   c. 9.1 percent.
   d. 12.5 percent.
   e. 21.2 percent.

2. Taxes to pay for social security are levied on
   a. employees only.
   b. private employers only.
   c. government employers only.
   d. both employees and employers.
   e. neither employees nor employers; social security is paid for by a national sales tax.

3. Relative to the amount workers and their employers paid in social security taxes during working years, the average retired worker receives
   a. more than twice as much money back in social security benefits, even when accumulated interest is included.
   b. more than twice as much money back in social security benefits, not including accumulated interest.
   c. about the same amount of money back in social security benefits, when accumulated interest is included.
   d. only about half as much money back in social security benefits, not including accumulated interest.
   e. only about half as much money back in social security benefits, even when accumulated interest is included.

4. Proposed solutions to the social security problem do *not* include
   a. means testing.
   b. increasing benefit levels.
   c. increasing the eligibility age.
   d. privatization.
   e. both c and d.

Section 2: Health Economics

1. In the United States, the fastest-growing segment of national expenditures is for
   a. military spending.
   b. housing.
   c. health care.
   d. transportation.
   e. welfare payments.

2. Health-care costs are rising because
    a. hospital and nursing-home costs are increasing.
    b. physicians' fees are increasing.
    c. the population is aging.
    d. of all of the above factors.
    e. of only b and c.

3. Demand for health care is relatively inelastic because
    a. individual consumers don't pay the cost of medical care directly, so they don't respond much to price increases.
    b. people spend only a small portion of their income on health care.
    c. health care is considered by most people to be a luxury rather than a necessity.
    d. most health-care spending is for the rapidly growing number of babies in the United States.
    e. growing numbers of people in the United States do not have health insurance.

4. Medicare is
    a. a federal program that provides health care for the elderly and those with disabilities.
    b. a private charity that gives medical care to the poor.
    c. provided by doctors and nurses who are employees of the federal government.
    d. provided by doctors and nurses who are employees of state governments.
    e. a joint federal-state program that provides health care for those who otherwise couldn't afford it.

5. Medicaid is
    a. a federal program that provides health care for the elderly and those with disabilities.
    b. a private charity that gives medical care to the poor.
    c. provided by doctors and nurses who are employees of the federal government.
    d. provided by doctors and nurses who are employees of state governments.
    e. a joint federal-state program that provides health care for those who otherwise couldn't afford it.

6. The prospective payment system (PPS) is
    a. the use of a preassigned reimbursement rate by Medicare to reimburse hospitals and physicians.
    b. an organization that provides comprehensive medical care to a voluntarily enrolled consumer population in return for a fixed, prepaid amount of money.
    c. a group of physicians who contract to provide services at a price discount.
    d. a payment plan whereby workers pay for medical care after retirement while they are still working.
    e. a system for deciding which individuals will receive more medical care.

7. A health maintenance organization (HMO) is
    a. the use of a preassigned reimbursement rate by Medicare to reimburse hospitals and physicians.
    b. an organization that provides comprehensive medical care to a voluntarily enrolled consumer population in return for a fixed, prepaid amount of money.
    c. a group of physicians who contract to provide services at a price discount.
    d. a payment plan whereby workers pay for medical care after retirement while they are still working.
    e. a system for deciding which individuals will receive more medical care.

8. A preferred provider organization (PPO) is
   a. the use of a preassigned reimbursement rate by Medicare to reimburse hospitals and physicians.
   b. an organization that provides comprehensive medical care to a voluntarily enrolled consumer population in return for a fixed, prepaid amount of money.
   c. a group of physicians who contract to provide services at a price discount.
   d. a payment plan whereby workers pay for medical care after retirement while they are still working.
   e. a system for deciding which individuals will receive more medical care.

9. The concept of managed care
   a. refers to a situation where the patient receives medical care from a single firm that provides physicians, hospital care, and other medical treatment.
   b. includes HMOs.
   c. includes PPOs.
   d. is described by option a, and includes both HMOs and PPOs.
   e. is described by option a, and includes HMOs but not PPOs.

Practice Questions and Problems

Section 1: Aging and Social Security

1. The percentage of the population age sixty-five or older is expected to start increasing rapidly around the year _____, when the baby boom generation begins to reach age sixty-five.

2. The formal name of the social security program, abbreviated OASDI, is _____ .

3. Social security taxes in the United States are imposed on both _____ and _____ , and both groups are charged _____ (the same, different) amounts.

4. By the year 2030, the ratio of younger workers in the labor force to social security recipients is expected to be just _____ workers in the labor force for every social security recipient.

Section 2: Health Economics

1. Compared with other industrialized countries, the United States spends a _____ (smaller, about equal, larger) percentage of its output on health care.

2. Compared with other expenditures in the U.S. economy, spending on health care is growing _____ (slowly, at about the same rate, rapidly).

3. In the United States today, the demand for health care is usually _____ (elastic, inelastic, unit-elastic) because the individual consumer _____ (does, does not) pay much, if any, of the cost of health care.

4. Assume that you are covered by health insurance that pays all of your medical-care costs.

   a. Your doctor charges $30 for an office visit. If you're feeling a little bit sick and are trying to decide whether to see your doctor, how will the $30 cost of seeing your doctor affect your decision?

   _____

   _____

   b. If you decide to see your doctor and the doctor wants to do blood tests that cost $500, do you have any reason to tell her to skip the tests because you're not very sick anyway?

   _____

   _____

   c. Does the doctor have any reason not to do the tests?

   _____

   _____

   d. Suppose that instead of having regular health insurance, you and your doctor are part of an HMO. In an HMO, why does the doctor have a reason not to do the tests?

   _____

   _____

5. Explain why the laws of economics apply to health care.

   _____

   _____

   _____

Thinking About and Applying Aging, Social Security, and Health Care

I. Who Pays for Social Security?

According to current law, both workers and employers pay equal amounts in social security taxes: in 1995, both paid 7.65 percent of workers' wages in social security taxes. But who really pays these taxes? Let's look at the effects of social security taxes on labor markets and on an employer's decisions about employment.

Remember the company making handwoven doormats from recycled rope that you started back in the chapter on resource markets? Let's use those figures to analyze the effects of social security taxes. From the employer's point of view, the tax reduces the *MRP* of labor because the employer doesn't get to keep all the income workers produce. Some of that income goes to the government.

1. a. In the following table, calculate the amount of the social security tax (7.65 percent of *MFC*) and the *MRP* after the tax.

Number of Workers	Mats per Hour	*MPP*	Price per Mat	Total Revenue	*MR*	*MRP*	Wage per Hour	Total Labor Cost	*MFC* Before Tax	Tax (7.65% of *MFC*)	*MRP* After Tax
1	8	8	$2.00	$16	$2	$16	$4.00	$ 4.00	$4.00	_____	_____
2	19	11	2.00	38	2	22	4.00	8.00	4.00	_____	_____
3	26	7	2.00	52	2	14	4.00	12.00	4.00	_____	_____
4	30	4	2.00	60	2	8	4.00	16.00	4.00	_____	_____
5	32	2	2.00	64	2	4	4.00	20.00	4.00	_____	_____
6	33	1	2.00	66	2	2	4.00	24.00	4.00	_____	_____

b. Draw the *MRP* before the tax and after the tax on graph b.

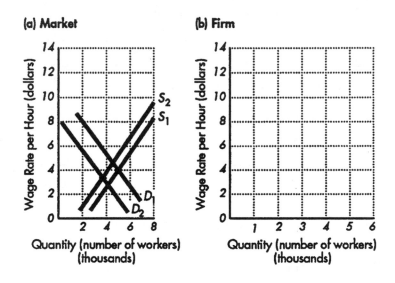

(a) Market   (b) Firm

c. Before the tax, _____ workers were hired. After the tax, _____ workers were hired.

2. The tax reduced the demand for labor, didn't it? Social security taxes also are levied on individual workers (7.65 percent of your pay), so the tax reduces the wages you get to spend. This reduction in wages reduces the supply of labor. Curves D_2 and S_2 on graph a show the effects of the decrease in the supply and demand for labor and the drop in equilibrium wage to $3.80 per hour.

a. In the following table, recalculate the tax and the *MRP* after tax.

Number of Workers	Mats per Hour	MPP	Price per Mat	Total Revenue	MR	MRP	Wage per Hour	Total Labor Cost	MFC Before Tax	Tax (7.65% of MFC)	MRP After Tax
1	8	8	$2.00	$16	$2	$16	$4.00	$ 4.00	$3.80	_____	_____
2	19	11	2.00	38	2	22	4.00	8.00	3.80	_____	_____
3	26	7	2.00	52	2	14	4.00	12.00	3.80	_____	_____
4	30	4	2.00	60	2	8	4.00	16.00	3.80	_____	_____
5	32	2	2.00	64	2	4	4.00	20.00	3.80	_____	_____
6	33	1	2.00	66	2	2	4.00	24.00	3.80	_____	_____

b. The number of workers hired after the tax is _____.

3. Before the tax, the wage rate was _____ per hour. After the tax, the wage rate a worker

actually gets to take home and spend is _____ per hour.

II. The Inelastic Demand for Health Care

As medical technology has developed and as doctors have raised their fees, the cost of providing health care has risen sharply. Part of the reason why cost increases have resulted in large price increases is that the demand for health care is inelastic. Because private or government health insurance pays for most health care, individual consumers don't respond much to price increases by reducing the amount of health care they demand.

The following graphs show the supply curves for health care for 1995 and for 2000. Health-care costs are expected to continue to rise, so the supply curve for 2000 is to the left of the supply curve for 1995.

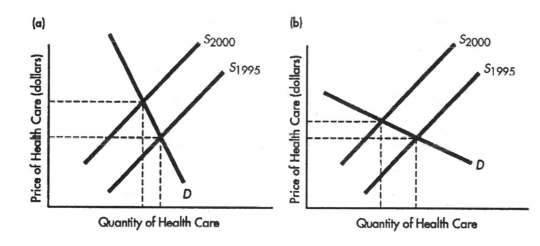

(a)

(b)

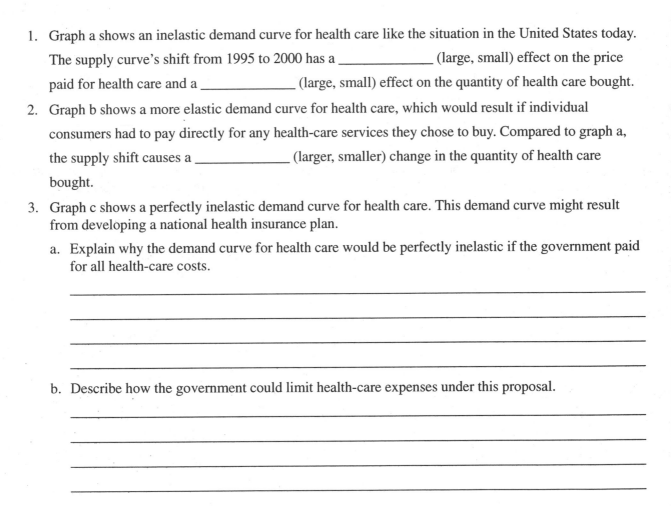

1. Graph a shows an inelastic demand curve for health care like the situation in the United States today. The supply curve's shift from 1995 to 2000 has a _____ (large, small) effect on the price paid for health care and a _____ (large, small) effect on the quantity of health care bought.

2. Graph b shows a more elastic demand curve for health care, which would result if individual consumers had to pay directly for any health-care services they chose to buy. Compared to graph a, the supply shift causes a _____ (larger, smaller) change in the quantity of health care bought.

3. Graph c shows a perfectly inelastic demand curve for health care. This demand curve might result from developing a national health insurance plan.

   a. Explain why the demand curve for health care would be perfectly inelastic if the government paid for all health-care costs.

   _____

   _____

   _____

   _____

   b. Describe how the government could limit health-care expenses under this proposal.

   _____

   _____

   _____

   _____

Chapter 19 (*Economics* Chapter 33)   Homework Problems

Name _____

1. List several factors that explain why the average age of the U.S. population is increasing.

2. Who pays for social security benefits received by the elderly: is it younger workers, or do the elderly just get back the money they themselves paid in to social security?

3. Many people argue that privatizing part or all of social security is an untested, "risky scheme." What other countries have already privatized their equivalent of our social security system?

4. Suppose you are part of a health insurance plan that pays 80 percent of your health-care costs; you have to pay the other 20 percent. Explain why this health insurance plan makes your demand for medical care more inelastic than it would be if you had to pay all the costs yourself.

5. Several people in Congress have talked about a "health-care savings plan" as a way to reduce the problems with health care in the United States. Under one version of this plan, people would receive tax benefits from putting up to $5,000 per year into a "health-care savings account." When they incur health-care expenses, the expenses would be paid out of this account. Any costs over $5,000 per year would be covered by a separate health insurance plan.

One element of the plan is the idea that if you didn't use all of the $5,000 you saved in a year, you could take out the money remaining and spend it for other things, without losing the tax benefits. Use your economic reasoning, and the information you have learned in this chapter, to explain why people would demand less health care under this plan than under a standard health insurance system.

If your instructor assigns these problems, write your answers above, then tear out this page and hand it in.

Answers

Quick-Check Quiz

Section 1: Aging and Social Security

1. d; 2. d; 3. a; 4. b

If you missed any of these questions, you should go back and review Section 1 in Chapter 19 (*Economics,* Chapter 33).

Section 2: Health Economics

1. c; 2. d; 3. a; 4. a; 5. e; 6. a; 7. b; 8. c; 9. d

If you missed any of these questions, you should go back and review Section 2 in Chapter 19 (*Economics,* Chapter 33).

Practice Questions and Problems

Section 1: Aging and Social Security

1. 2010
2. Old Age Survivors and Disability Insurance
3. workers; employers; the same
4. 2

Section 2: Health Economics

1. larger
2. rapidly
3. inelastic; does not
4. a. It won't. With health insurance, the office visit is free to you. Of course, it's not free to the insurance company.
    b. No. Again, the tests don't cost you anything directly.
    c. No. If the doctor owns the testing lab or is worried about malpractice suits, she has an incentive to order as many tests as possible.
    d. In an HMO, the doctor is paid a set amount to take care of you for the year. Spending money on tests costs the doctor money, so she has an incentive to avoid unnecessary tests or other expenses.
5. Health care is a scarce resource, which means that providing health care has opportunity costs. Like other products and services, health care has a downward-sloping demand curve and an upward-sloping supply curve.

Thinking About and Applying Aging, Social Security, and Health Care

I. *Who Pays for Social Security?*

1. a.

Number of Workers	Mats per Hour	MPP	Price per Mat	Total Revenue	MR	MRP	Wage per Hour	Total Labor Cost	MFC Before Tax	Tax (7.65% of MFC)	MRP After Tax
1	8	8	$2.00	$16	$2	$16	$4.00	$ 4.00	$4.00	$.31	$15.69
2	19	11	2.00	38	2	22	4.00	8.00	4.00	.31	21.69
3	26	7	2.00	52	2	14	4.00	12.00	4.00	.31	13.69
4	30	4	2.00	60	2	8	4.00	16.00	4.00	.31	7.69
5	32	2	2.00	64	2	4	4.00	20.00	4.00	.31	3.69
6	33	1	2.00	66	2	2	4.00	24.00	4.00	.31	1.69

b.

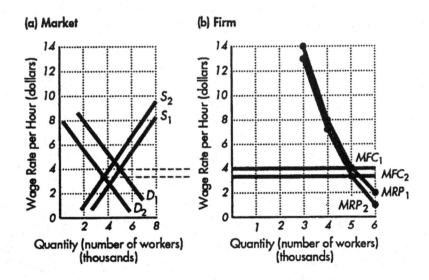

(a) Market

(b) Firm

c. 5; 4 (Refer back to the chapter on resource markets if you don't remember how to find the number of workers hired.)

2. a.

Number of Workers	Mats per Hour	MPP	Price per Mat	Total Revenue	MR	MRP	Wage per Hour	Total Labor Cost	MFC Before Tax	Tax (7.65% of MFC)	MRP After Tax
1	8	8	$2.00	$16	$2	$16	$4.00	$ 4.00	$3.80	$.29	$15.71
2	19	11	2.00	38	2	22	4.00	8.00	3.80	.29	21.71
3	26	7	2.00	52	2	14	4.00	12.00	3.80	.29	13.71
4	30	4	2.00	60	2	8	4.00	16.00	3.80	.29	7.71
5	32	2	2.00	64	2	4	4.00	20.00	3.80	.29	3.71
6	33	1	2.00	66	2	2	4.00	24.00	3.80	.29	1.71

b. 4

3. $4; $3.51 (The wage rate after the tax is $3.80 less 7.65 percent [$.29]: $3.80 − .29 = $3.51.)

II. *The Inelastic Demand for Health Care*

1. large; small
2. smaller; larger
3. a. Under a national health insurance plan, where all health-care costs are paid by the government, there is no incentive for individual consumers to reduce the amount of health care consumed when the price rises. The demand for health care is perfectly inelastic—completely insensitive to price.

   b. Restricting access to some kinds of health care (fewer coronary bypass operations, for example) or providing lower-quality care (requiring tonsil removals to be outpatient procedures, for example) are some of the possible ways to lower costs. Almost any way of lowering costs significantly would require providing less health care than people want.

INCOME DISTRIBUTION, POVERTY, AND GOVERNMENT POLICY

FUNDAMENTAL QUESTIONS

1. Are incomes distributed equally in the United States?

No. In a market system, income is derived from the ownership of resources: people with more resources, or with more highly valued resources, receive higher incomes. Doctors are more highly paid than ditch diggers; people who have accumulated lots of capital receive more interest than people without any savings. In the United States, the top 20 percent of the population earns over 44 percent of the total national income, and the bottom 20 percent of the population earns less than 5 percent of the national income.

A **Lorenz curve** shows the degree to which income is distributed equally (or unequally) within a society. If all incomes are the same, the Lorenz curve is a straight line; the more unequally distributed incomes are, the more bowed the Lorenz curve becomes. Lorenz curves provide an easy way to compare income distributions across countries or within the same country at different times.

2. How is poverty measured, and does poverty exist in the United States?

Poverty can be measured in two ways. Lorenz curves look at poverty in relative terms. What share of the national income do the poorest people get? Poverty also can be looked at in absolute terms: What per capita income is necessary to meet basic human needs? The official U.S. poverty statistics gathered by the federal government use an absolute standard to set the minimum income level that avoids poverty, based on the cost of a nutritionally adequate diet. Officially, income includes earnings and **cash transfers,** but not all **in-kind transfers** (for example, food stamps and Medicaid). Using this standard, over 14 percent of the U.S. population—over 36 million people—live in poverty.

3. Who are the poor?

The incidence of poverty is distributed unevenly across groups within the United States. Age is one factor here. Younger and older people make up most of the poverty group. The percentage of families headed by a female that are below the poverty line is much higher than that of families headed by a male; African American and Hispanic families have larger percentages below the poverty line than do white families.

Many people who are poor stay that way for only a little while; they find new jobs, for example, and move back above the poverty line. But there are large numbers of people for whom poverty is a normal condition. Of those people in poverty at any specific time, about half will still be in poverty in ten years.

4. What are the determinants of income?

For individuals, the major determinants of income are employment, place of residence, and education. The poor are primarily those without jobs, those who live either in the centers of large cities or in rural areas, and those without much education.

5. How does the government try to reduce poverty?

Changing the income distribution in society has been the main target of government policy to reduce poverty; since 1929, income inequality in the United States has decreased. **Progressive income taxes,** whereby richer people pay proportionally more of their income in taxes, reduce income inequality and generate revenue that can be used for transfer payments to the poor. These are the main transfer programs:

Social insurance (social security, unemployment insurance, Medicare)
Cash welfare (Aid to Families with Dependent Children, Supplemental Security Income)
In-kind transfers (Medicaid, food stamps, school lunch program, energy assistance)
Employment programs (jobs and job training, Head Start)

Transfer programs may have reduced the incentives to work and may have increased the number of poor people. Economists have long proposed a **negative income tax (NIT)** as a way to overcome the effects of welfare on incentives to work, but the idea has not been politically popular.

Key Terms

Lorenz curve	progressive income tax	Gini ratio
cash transfer	proportional tax	negative income tax (NIT)
in-kind transfers	regressive tax	

Quick-Check Quiz

Section 1: Income Distribution and Poverty

1. A graph that shows the degree to which income is distributed unequally within a society is called a(n)
   a. Lorenz curve.
   b. in-kind curve.
   c. poverty line.
   d. poverty ratio plot.
   e. absolute income standard.

Use the graph below to answer question 2.

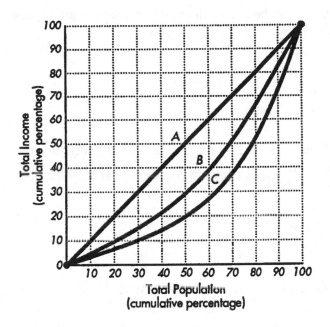

2. Which of the following statements about these Lorenz curves is correct?
   a. Line *A* shows the most unequally distributed income.
   b. Line *C* shows a more equal income distribution than line *B* does.
   c. Line *A* shows a perfectly equal distribution.
   d. All of the above are correct.
   e. Only a and b are correct.

3. Relative to developed nations, developing nations have
   a. the same income distribution.
   b. a more unequal income distribution.
   c. a more equal income distribution.
   d. an almost perfectly equal income distribution.
   e. an almost perfectly unequal income distribution.

4. The U.S. official statistics define poverty as a(n)
   a. relative measure, based on the income level of the poorest 15 percent of the population.
   b. absolute measure, based on the cost of a nutritionally adequate diet.
   c. absolute measure, based on the cost of housing.
   d. relative measure, based on the income level of the poorest 5 percent of the population.
   e. relative measure, based on the accumulated wealth of the poorest 10 percent of the population.

5. In determining whether a family has a standard of living above or below the poverty line, the official U.S. statistics include as income
   a. only money earned by family members.
   b. money earned by family members, plus cash transfers.
   c. money earned by family members, plus in-kind transfers.
   d. money earned by family members, plus cash and in-kind transfers.
   e. money earned by the head of the household, plus cash and in-kind transfers.

Section 2: The Poor

1. Of the people currently below the poverty line, what percentage are expected to still be below the poverty line in ten years?
   a. about 5 percent
   b. about 15 percent
   c. about 30 percent
   d. about 50 percent
   e. about 75 percent

2. Which of the groups below has a higher percentage of its members in poverty compared with the average for the United States?
   a. Hispanics
   b. African Americans
   c. households headed by people age sixty-five or older
   d. All of the above have a higher poverty percentage.
   e. Only b and c above have a higher poverty percentage.

3. Which of the following is *not* a determinant of income?
   a. unemployment
   b. age
   c. place of residence
   d. human capital
   e. All of the above are determinants of income.

Section 3: Government Antipoverty Policies

1. A progressive tax has a rate that
   a. declines as income increases, leading to the more equal distribution of income.
   b. declines as income increases, leading to the less equal distribution of income.
   c. increases as income increases, leading to the more equal distribution of income.
   d. increases as income increases, leading to the less equal distribution of income.
   e. stays the same as income increases, having no effect on income distribution.

2. A regressive tax has a rate that
   a. declines as income increases, leading to the more equal distribution of income.
   b. declines as income increases, leading to the less equal distribution of income.
   c. increases as income increases, leading to the more equal distribution of income.
   d. increases as income increases, leading to the less equal distribution of income.
   e. stays the same as income increases, having no effect on income distribution.

3. A proportional tax has a rate that
   a. declines as income increases, leading to the more equal distribution of income.
   b. declines as income increases, leading to the less equal distribution of income.
   c. increases as income increases, leading to the more equal distribution of income.
   d. increases as income increases, leading to the less equal distribution of income.
   e. stays the same as income increases, having no effect on income distribution.

4. When talking about income distribution, the term *equity* is frequently used to mean
   a. equal distribution of income.
   b. equal opportunities to earn income.
   c. equal transfer payments for all.
   d. all of the above.
   e. only a and b.

Practice Questions and Problems

Section 1: Income Distribution and Poverty

1. The _____ curve shows the amount of income inequality within a society.

2. The table below gives income distribution data for the United States and Mexico for the late 1980s. On the graph below, draw the Lorenz curves for the two countries. The country with the more equal income distribution is _____ .

	Lowest 20%	Second 20%	Third 20%	Fourth 20%	Highest 20%
Mexico	3	7	12	20	58
United States	5	12	18	25	40

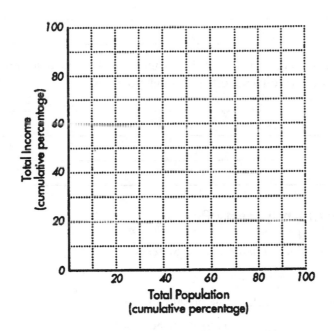

3. The poverty line for 1993 said that a family of four was in poverty if its income was less than
   a. $9,862.
   b. $10,609.
   c. $12,675.
   d. $14,764.
   e. $15,260.

4. The federal government's definition of income for calculating whether a family is below the poverty line includes market _____ , the _____ equivalent of some noncash transfers, and _____ transfers. It does not include all _____ transfers.

5. Poverty _____ (increases, decreases) when the economy enters a recession and _____ (increases, decreases) when the economy is growing strongly.

Section 2: The Poor

1. The poor are primarily those without _____ .

2. In terms of age, the highest incidence of poverty is for _____ . Older people are _____ (more, less) likely to be poor than middle-aged people.

3. List several determinants of income.

   _____

   _____

   _____

   _____

4. Looking at all the statistics in Section 2 of the chapter, which of the determinants of income seems to be the most important in avoiding poverty? Explain your answer.

   _____

   _____

   _____

   _____

Section 3: Government Antipoverty Policies

1. Since 1929, income distribution in the United States has _____ (become more equal, become less equal, stayed the same).

2. A progressive tax rate _____ as income increases.

3. A regressive tax rate _____ as income increases.

4. A proportional tax rate _____ as income increases.

5. List the four main types of programs to fight poverty in the United States.

_____

_____

_____

_____

6. The _____ ratio provides a measure of the dispersion of family income. A ratio of _____ means all families have the same income; a ratio of _____ would mean that one family receives all the income.

Thinking About and Applying Income Distribution, Poverty, and Government Policy

I. Welfare and Incentives to Work

A story in *New York Newsday* called "Problem of the Poor," stated:

> Liberal critics and welfare-rights groups point to [New York's] high poverty rate—60 percent above the national average—citing inadequate welfare benefits, a lack of public housing and other holes in the safety net. Yet New York has provided some of the most generous welfare benefits in the country, both in terms of the amount of benefits offered and the number of people covered. . . . The level of cash benefits in the basic welfare program is 50 percent above that of the median state in the United States.

The article also points out that about 16 percent of the people in New York City receive cash payments from public assistance programs, compared to less than 8 percent for the United States as a whole.

1. Use what you've learned in this chapter and previous chapters about the supply of labor to explain why generous welfare programs in New York City might increase the number of people living in poverty in New York.

_____

_____

_____

_____

2. Recent changes in some states' welfare programs use the idea of "workfare": welfare recipients are required to work to receive benefits. How does a workfare program change incentives? Do you think workfare is a good idea or a bad idea? Why?

_____

_____

_____

_____

II. The Negative Income Tax

Economists in the United States in general agree that a negative income tax plan, as described in Section 3.f in the chapter, would be a more efficient way to alleviate poverty than the current U.S. poverty programs. Refer to Sections 3.c and e on the effectiveness of current programs, and describe why economists prefer the negative income tax proposal to current programs.

_____

_____

_____

_____

Chapter 20 (*Economics* Chapter 34)   Homework Problems

Name _____

1. What are the major determinants of income?

2. In which two general locations are poor people most likely to live?

3. What do the terms cash transfers and in-kind transfers refer to, and what are two examples of each type of transfer?

4. Determine whether each tax below is progressive, proportional, or regressive. Assume the Poor family has an income of $10,000, and the Rich family has an income of $100,000.
    a. The Poor family pays $300 per year in sales tax, while the Rich family pays $2,000.

    b. The Poor family pays $800 per year in income tax, while the Rich family pays $12,000.

    c. The Poor family pays $765 per year in social security tax, while the Rich family pays $7,650.

5. One of the statistics cited in the chapter is that 25 percent of people with less than eight years of education are in poverty, while only 4 percent of people with one or more years of college are in poverty.

   a. Refer to the chapter on labor markets and explain in economic terms why people with more education receive higher incomes.

   b. A politician, reading the statistics cited in part a of this question, has suggested passing a law requiring everyone to stay in school until they complete at least one year of college. The politician claims that this law would reduce the poverty level to 4 percent. Use your economic reasoning, and experience in education, to evaluate this proposal.

If your instructor assigns these problems, write your answers above, then tear out this page and hand it in.

Answers

Quick-Check Quiz

Section 1: Income Distribution and Poverty

1. a; 2. c; 3. b; 4. b; 5. b
If you missed any of these questions, you should go back and review Section 1 in Chapter 20 (*Economics*, Chapter 34).

Section 2: The Poor

1. d; 2. d; 3. e
If you missed any of these questions, you should go back and review Section 2 in Chapter 20 (*Economics*, Chapter 34).

Section 3: Government Antipoverty Policies

1. c; 2. b; 3. e; 4. e
If you missed any of these questions, you should go back and review Section 3 in Chapter 20 (*Economics*, Chapter 34).

Practice Questions and Problems

Section 1: Income Distribution and Poverty

1. Lorenz
2. the United States

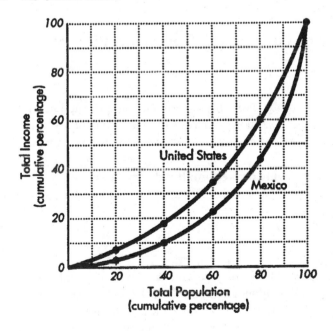

3. d

4. earnings; cash; cash; in-kind
5. increases; decreases

Section 2: The Poor

1. jobs
2. young people; more
3. employment
   wages
   age
   health
   gender
   place of residence
   education
4. Human capital, specifically education. Only 4 percent of those with one year or more of college fall below the poverty line, whereas 25 percent of the people with less than eight years of education are below the poverty line.

Section 3: Government Antipoverty Policies

1. become more equal
2. increases
3. decreases
4. stays the same
5. social insurance
   cash welfare
   in-kind transfers
   employment programs
6. Gini; 0; 1

Thinking About and Applying Distribution, Poverty, and Government Policy

I. Welfare and Incentives to Work

1. Welfare programs raise the opportunity cost of working. Not only do you have to give up leisure to work, but you also have to give up welfare benefits. The more generous the welfare benefits, the higher the opportunity costs of working. When those costs are too high to make working worthwhile, people are better off staying on welfare.
2. Workfare removes the choice of not working and staying on welfare. It reduces the opportunity cost of working by making nonworkers ineligible for welfare benefits. Whether you think it's a good idea or not depends on your values.

II. The Negative Income Tax

The economy would be more productive, and government spending would be lower, if people currently receiving welfare payments were working (where possible). Economists conclude that U.S. poverty programs create significant disincentives to working for people currently receiving welfare: the lost benefits from gaining additional income are very large. An NIT would provide cash support for poor people without creating such large disincentives for working.

Sample Test
Chapters 19–20
(*Economics* Chapters 33–34)

1. The baby boom generation will start turning 65 around the year 2012. This will cause major problems with which Federal government program?
   a. defense
   b. national parks
   c. social security
   d. education
   e. police

2. How is the social security system financed?
   a. an income tax
   b. an excise tax
   c. a payroll tax on employees
   d. a payroll tax on employers
   e. a payroll tax on both employees and employers

3. What percentage of the income of a worker receiving the minimum wage is taken out for social security taxes?
   a. Zero percent
   b. 1.5 percent
   c. 5 percent
   d. 6.2 percent
   e. 7.65 percent

4. Holding all else constant, social security benefits have the effect on retirement of
   a. decreased freedom for the elderly.
   b. delaying retirement.
   c. speeding up retirement.
   d. eliminating opportunity costs.
   e. all of the above.

5. The effect of Medicare and Medicaid, as well as medical insurance programs in general in which individual consumers don't directly pay the cost of medical care, has been to make the demand for health care
   a. more elastic.
   b. more inelastic.
   c. more price sensitive.
   d. more perfectly competitive.
   e. none of the above.

6. If we observe that the rate of return for medical education in cardiology is substantially higher than for other fields, then we can expect that
   a. more new physicians will choose to become general practitioners.
   b. the supply of cardiologists will decrease as a result.
   c. more new physicians will enter the field of cardiology.
   d. cardiology will no longer be an available choice.
   e. the demand for cardiologists will increase.

Consider the following figure for questions 7 and 8.

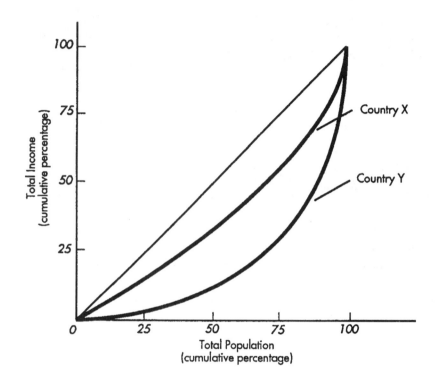

7. The poorest 25 percent of Country X's population receives _____ percentage of total income as the poorest 25 percent of Country Y's population.
   a. the same
   b. less
   c. half as high a
   d. twice as high a
   e. 25 percent as much

8. The richest 25 percent of Country Y's population receives
   a. the same total income as the richest 25 percent of Country X's population.
   b. 25 percent of Country Y's total income.
   c. 70 percent of Country Y's total income.
   d. less total income than the richest 25 percent of Country X's population.
   e. 40 percent of Country Y's total income.

9. Which kind of tax tends to increase income inequality?
    a. estate taxes
    b. regressive taxes
    c. proportional taxes
    d. progressive taxes
    e. income taxes

10. The major theoretical advantage of the negative income tax, according to economists, is that it
    a. is a major source of government revenue.
    b. will decrease the national deficit.
    c. preserves individuals' incentive to work.
    d. enjoys bipartisan support in Congress.
    e. has been widely successful in Europe.

11. All of the following are implications for a society of an aging population *except*
    a. increased total expenditures on health-care services.
    b. more retired persons.
    c. a smaller percentage of the population producing goods and services.
    d. a higher incidence of births.
    e. greater social security payments to the populace.

12. A curve showing the degree of income inequality within a society is the
    a. Lorenz curve.
    b. demand/supply curve.
    c. Gini coefficient.
    d. inequality proportion.
    e. line of income equality.

13. The richest 10 percent of the world's population receives about what percent of the world's income?
    a. 10 percent
    b. 20 percent
    c. 40 percent
    d. 60 percent
    e. 80 percent

14. OASDI is an abbreviation for the program commonly called
    a. social security.
    b. Medicaid.
    c. the negative income tax.
    d. Education Training Grants.
    e. Roth IRAs.

15. OASDI is an abbreviation whose initials stand for
    a. Old-Fashioned Spousal Discretionary Incomes.
    b. Old Age and Senior Discretionary Insurance.
    c. Older and Special Disabled Income.
    d. FICA.
    e. Old Age, Survivors, and Disability Insurance.

16. The supply curve for medical care will shift to the left if
    a. the cost of medical care is falling.
    b. resource prices are falling or if diseconomies of scale are being experienced.
    c. resource prices are rising or if economies of scale are being experienced.
    d. resource prices are falling or if economies of scale are being experienced.
    e. resource prices are rising or if diseconomies of scale are being experienced.

17. In the United States, the wealthiest one-half of 1 percent of households own approximately which percent of the nation's wealth?
    a. 30 percent
    b. 40 percent
    c. 50 percent
    d. 70 percent
    e. 90 percent

18. The market system works to ensure that resources
    a. are allocated in the fairest possible manner to members of society.
    b. go to those who desire them the most, even if they cannot pay for them.
    c. flow to their highest-valued uses.
    d. invariably end up going to their lowest-valued uses.
    e. are allocated by government fiat.

19. In a market system, incomes are distributed according to
    a. the principle of equality.
    b. the dictates of a central authority.
    c. whoever has the greatest needs.
    d. the ownership of resources.
    e. the strength of an individual's work ethic.

20. Poverty is a measure of the
    a. general health of a population.
    b. success or failure of an economy to provide for its citizens' needs.
    c. evenness of the income distribution.
    d. quality of life, as exemplified through standards of living.
    e. quality of life, as exemplified through cultural and sporting events.

21. Which of the following is *not* an in-kind transfer?
    a. food stamps
    b. medical services provided under Medicaid
    c. social security retirement benefits
    d. legal aid for the poor
    e. school lunch programs

22. Which of the following statements concerning poverty distribution is true?
    a. Poverty rates rise when per capita GDP increases.
    b. The poverty line is a fixed income level that's the same for all countries.
    c. The incidence of poverty in developing countries is smaller than in developed countries.
    d. Poverty rates increase with economic growth.
    e. Poverty rates rise during periods of economic stagnation.

23. Which of the following is the most important determinant of an individual's income?
    a. health status
    b. geographic location
    c. work status
    d. marital status
    e. family size

24. If the tax rate increases along with income, then that tax is a(n)
    a. in-kind transfer.
    b. proportional tax.
    c. cash transfer.
    d. regressive tax.
    e. progressive tax.

25. A family with an income of $10,000 pays $500 in tax, while a family with an income $100,000 pays $3,000 in tax. This tax is
    a. progressive.
    b. predictive.
    c. proportional.
    d. regressive.
    e. reversive.

Answers to Sample Test

1. c (Chapter 19, Section 1.a; *Economics* Chapter 33)
2. e (Chapter 19, Section 1.a; *Economics* Chapter 33)
3. d (Chapter 19, Section 1.a; *Economics* Chapter 33)
4. c (Chapter 19, Section 1.a; *Economics* Chapter 33)
5. b (Chapter 19, Section 2.a; *Economics* Chapter 33)
6. c (Chapter 19, Section 2.b; *Economics* Chapter 33)
7. d (Chapter 20, Section 1.a; *Economics* Chapter 34)
8. c (Chapter 20, Section 1.a; *Economics* Chapter 34)
9. b (Chapter 20, Section 3.a; *Economics* Chapter 34)
10. c (Chapter 20, Section 3.f; *Economics* Chapter 34)
11. d (Chapter 19, Preview; *Economics* Chapter 33)
12. a (Chapter 20, Section 1.a; *Economics* Chapter 34)
13. e (Chapter 20, Section 1.b; *Economics* Chapter 34)

14. a (Chapter 19, Section 1.a; *Economics* Chapter 33)
15. e (Chapter 19, Section 1.a; *Economics* Chapter 33)
16. e (Chapter 19, Section 2.b; *Economics* Chapter 33)
17. a (Chapter 20, Preview; *Economics* Chapter 34)
18. c (Chapter 20, Preview; *Economics* Chapter 34)
19. d (Chapter 20, Section 1.a; *Economics* Chapter 34)
20. d (Chapter 20, Section 1.b; *Economics* Chapter 34)
21. c (Chapter 20, Section 1.d; *Economics* Chapter 34)
22. e (Chapter 20, Section 1.e; *Economics* Chapter 34)
23. c (Chapter 20, Section 2.b; *Economics* Chapter 34)
24. e (Chapter 20, Section 3.a; *Economics* Chapter 34)
25. d (Chapter 20, Section 3.a; *Economics* Chapter 34)

WORLD TRADE EQUILIBRIUM

FUNDAMENTAL QUESTIONS

1. What are the prevailing patterns of trade between countries? What goods are traded?

   Trade occurs because specialization in production, based on **comparative advantage,** leads to increased output. Countries specialize in those products for which their opportunity costs are lower than costs in other nations; countries then trade what they produce beyond their own consumption and receive other countries' products in return.

   The bulk of world trade occurs within industrialized countries; trade between industrialized countries and developing countries accounts for most of the rest. Canada is the largest buyer of U.S. exports, and Japan is the largest source of U.S. imports. Petroleum, motor vehicles, and petroleum products are the goods that have the largest trading volume, although world trade occurs across a great variety of products.

2. What determines the goods a nation will export?

   A nation exports those goods for which it has a comparative advantage over other nations—that is, those goods for which its opportunity costs are lower than the opportunity costs of other nations. The **terms of trade**—how much of an exported good must be given up to obtain one unit of an imported good—are limited by the domestic opportunity costs of the trading countries.

3. How are the equilibrium price and the quantity of goods traded determined?

   As with most other markets, demand and supply determine the equilibrium price and quantity. For internationally traded goods, the **export supply curve** shows how much countries are willing to export at different world prices. The **import demand curve** shows how much countries are willing to import at different world prices. The international equilibrium price and quantity traded equal the point at which the export supply curve and the import demand curve intersect.

4. What are the sources of comparative advantage?

   There are two major sources of comparative advantage: productivity differences and factor abundance. Productivity differences come from differences in labor productivity and human capital, and from differences in technology. Factor abundance affects comparative advantage because countries have different resource endowments. The United States, with a large amount of high-quality farmland, has a comparative advantage in agriculture.

   Productivity differences and factor abundance explain most, but not all, trade patterns. Other sources of comparative advantage are human skills differences, product life cycles, and consumer preferences. Consumer preferences explain **intraindustry trade,** in which countries are both exporters and importers of a product. Some consumers prefer brands made in their own country; others prefer foreign brands.

Key Terms

absolute advantage
comparative advantage

terms of trade
export supply curve

import demand curve
intraindustry trade

Quick-Check Quiz

Section 1: An Overview of World Trade

1. The bulk of world trade occurs
   a. in the Eastern trading area.
   b. among developing countries.
   c. among industrial countries.
   d. between developing and industrial countries.
   e. between industrial countries and the Eastern trading area.

2. The United States imports the most from
   a. Canada.
   b. Germany.
   c. Japan.
   d. Mexico.
   e. Russia.

3. The United States exports the most to
   a. Canada.
   b. Germany.
   c. Japan.
   d. Mexico.
   e. Russia.

4. The most heavily traded good in the world is
   a. crude petroleum.
   b. airplanes.
   c. motor vehicles.
   d. televisions.
   e. wheat.

Section 2: An Example of International Trade Equilibrium

1. A nation has an absolute advantage in producing a good when
   a. it can produce a good more efficiently than can other nations.
   b. the opportunity cost of producing a good, in terms of the forgone output of other goods, is lower than that of other nations.
   c. it can produce a good less efficiently than can other nations.
   d. the opportunity cost of producing a good, in terms of the forgone output of other goods, is higher than that of other nations.
   e. the nation's export supply curve is below its import demand curve.

2. A nation has a comparative advantage in producing a good when
   a. it can produce a good for a lower input cost than can other nations.
   b. the opportunity cost of producing a good, in terms of the forgone output of other goods, is lower than that of other nations.
   c. it can produce a good for a higher input cost than can other nations.
   d. the opportunity cost of producing a good, in terms of the forgone output of other goods, is higher than that of other nations.
   e. the nation's export supply curve is below its import demand curve.

3. The terms of trade are the
   a. price of your country's currency in terms of another country's currency.
   b. price of another country's currency in terms of your country's currency.
   c. amount of an export good that must be given up to obtain one unit of an import good.
   d. amount of an import good that must be given up to obtain one unit of an export good.
   e. amount of imports divided by the amount of exports.

4. Limits on the terms of trade are determined by the
   a. difference between domestic and world prices.
   b. domestic opportunity costs of production within one country.
   c. opportunity costs in each country.
   d. ratio of the domestic price to the world price.
   e. ratio of the world price to the domestic price.

5. The export supply and import demand curves for a country measure the
   a. international surplus and shortage, respectively, at different world prices.
   b. international shortage and surplus, respectively, at different world prices.
   c. domestic surplus and shortage, respectively, at different world prices.
   d. domestic shortage and surplus, respectively, at different world prices.
   e. domestic surplus and shortage, respectively, at different exchange rates.

Section 3: Sources of Comparative Advantage

1. The productivity-differences explanation of comparative advantage stresses
   a. differences in labor productivity among countries.
   b. the advantage that comes to a country that is the first to develop and produce a product.
   c. the relative amounts of skilled and unskilled labor in a country.
   d. differences in the amounts of resources countries have.
   e. differences in tastes within a country.

2. The factor-abundance explanation of comparative advantage stresses
   a. differences in labor productivity among countries.
   b. the advantage that comes to a country that is the first to develop and produce a product.
   c. the relative amounts of skilled and unskilled labor in a country.
   d. differences in the amounts of resources countries have.
   e. differences in tastes within a country.

3. The human-skills explanation of comparative advantage stresses
   a. differences in labor productivity among countries.
   b. the advantage that comes to a country that is the first to develop and produce a product.
   c. the relative amounts of skilled and unskilled labor in a country.
   d. differences in the amounts of resources countries have.
   e. differences in tastes within a country.

4. The product-life-cycle explanation of comparative advantage stresses
   a. differences in labor productivity among countries.
   b. the advantage that comes to a country that is the first to develop and produce a product.
   c. the relative amounts of skilled and unskilled labor in a country.
   d. differences in the amounts of resources countries have.
   e. differences in tastes within a country.

5. The consumer-preferences explanation of comparative advantage stresses
   a. differences in labor productivity among countries.
   b. the advantage that comes to a country that is the first to develop and produce a product.
   c. the relative amounts of skilled and unskilled labor in a country.
   d. differences in the amounts of resources countries have.
   e. differences in tastes within a country.

Practice Questions and Problems

Section 1: An Overview of World Trade

1. The country that imports the most from the United States is _____ ; the country that exports the most to the United States is _____ .

2. World trade is _____ (distributed across many, dominated by only a few) products.

3. The product that accounts for the most world trade is _____ .

4. Use Table 1 in the text to answer the following questions.
   a. Trade just within industrial countries accounts for _____ percent of world trade.
   b. Trade just within the developing countries accounts for _____ percent of world trade.

Section 2: An Example of International Trade Equilibrium

1. _____ (Comparative, Absolute) advantage is based on the relative opportunity costs of producing goods in different countries.

2. _____ (Comparative, Absolute) advantage occurs when a country can produce a good more efficiently than can other nations.

3. The _____ are the amount of an export good that must be given up to obtain one unit of an import good.

4. The _____ (export supply, import demand) curve is derived from the domestic surplus at different world prices.

5. The _____ (export supply, import demand) curve is derived from the domestic shortage at different world prices.

6. The table below shows the number of hours of labor needed to produce a ton of mangos and a ton of papayas in Samoa and in Fiji.

	Samoa	Fiji
Mangos	2	6
Papayas	1	2

   a. The country that has an absolute advantage in producing mangos is _____ .

   b. The country that has an absolute advantage in producing papayas is _____ .

   c. The opportunity cost of 1 ton of papayas in Samoa is _____ .

   d. The opportunity cost of 1 ton of papayas in Fiji is _____ .

   e. The country that has a comparative advantage in papayas is _____ .

   f. The opportunity cost of 1 ton of mangos in Samoa is _____ .

   g. The opportunity cost of 1 ton of mangos in Fiji is _____ .

   h. The country that has a comparative advantage in mangos is _____ .

   i. The limits on the terms of trade are 1 ton of mangos for between _____ and _____ tons of papayas.

7. The graphs on the next page show the soybean markets in the United States and in France (we assume that no other country in the world is involved in trade in soybeans).

   a. Before doing an analysis, let's look at the soybean markets in the two countries. The price in the United States without trade is _____ per bushel; in France it is _____ per bushel. Because market prices reflect opportunity costs, the country that has a comparative advantage in soybean production and that should export soybeans is _____ .

   b. On graph c on the following page, draw in the import demand and export supply curves for the United States and France.

(a) United States

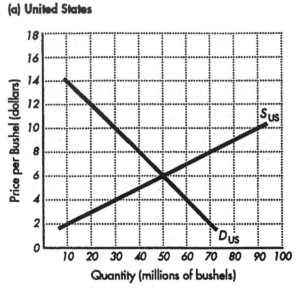

(b) France

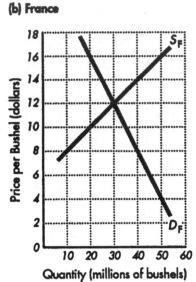

(c) World

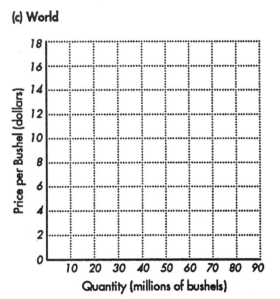

c. The equilibrium world price of soybeans is _____ per bushel. The quantity traded is _____ bushels.

d. The United States produced _____ bushels of soybeans and consumed _____ bushels. The United States is an _____ (exporter, importer) of soybeans.

e. France produced _____ bushels of soybeans and consumed _____ bushels. France is an _____ (exporter, importer) of soybeans.

f. In the problem above, what is the effect of trade on the price of soybeans in the United States? _____
    France? _____

Section 3: Sources of Comparative Advantage

1. Name the comparative-advantage theory that matches each explanation of comparative advantage listed below.

   a. Differences in labor productivity among countries: _____

   b. The advantage that comes to a country that is the first to develop and produce a product:

   _____

   c. The relative amounts of skilled and unskilled labor in a country: _____

   d. Differences in the amounts of resources countries have: _____

   e. Differences in tastes within a country: _____

2. The productivity-differences theory of comparative advantage is known as the _____ model.

3. The factor-abundance theory of comparative advantage is known as the _____ model.

4. Differences in consumer tastes within a country explain _____ , in which a country is both an exporter and an importer of a differentiated product.

Thinking About and Applying World Trade Equilibrium

I. World Trade Equilibrium

The graphs on the following page show the domestic markets for wheat in the United States, Canada, Argentina, and Russia.

1. Draw the import demand and export supply curves for the four countries; then sum the import demand and export supply curves for the four countries to draw the world import demand and export supply curves on graph e.

(a) United States

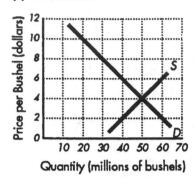

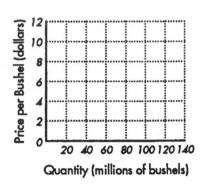

(b) Canada

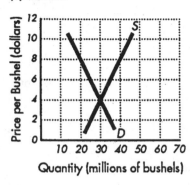

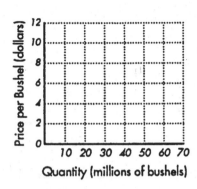

(e) World

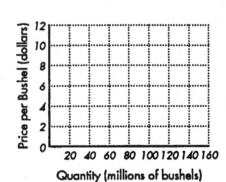

(c) Argentina

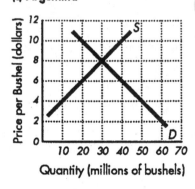

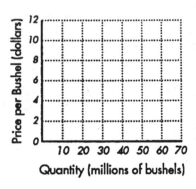

(d) Russia

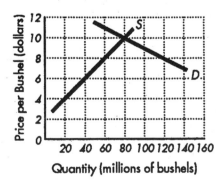

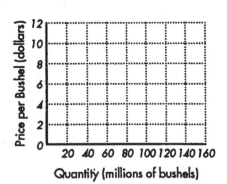

2. The equilibrium world price is _____ ; the quantity traded is _____ bushels.

3. The United States produced _____ bushels and consumed _____ bushels. The United States is a(n) _____ (exporter, importer, nontrader) of wheat.

4. Canada produced _____ bushels and consumed _____ bushels. Canada is a(n) _____ (exporter, importer, nontrader) of wheat.

5. Argentina produced _____ bushels and consumed _____ bushels. Argentina is a(n) _____ (exporter, importer, nontrader) of wheat.

6. Russia produced _____ bushels and consumed _____ bushels. Russia is a(n) _____ (exporter, importer, nontrader) of wheat.

II. Triangular Trade

Many people complain about the trade imbalance between the United States and Japan. Economists generally don't worry much about trade imbalances with specific countries; they believe that trade between any two countries need not balance as long as each country's trade with all countries taken together is roughly balanced. Let's look a little further at this idea.

The graphs on the following page show the domestic markets for bananas, oranges, and sugar in Guatemala, Honduras, and Costa Rica.

1. Draw the import demand and export supply curves for the three countries for each product; then sum the import demand and export supply curves for each product to draw the world import demand and export supply curves on the world graphs.

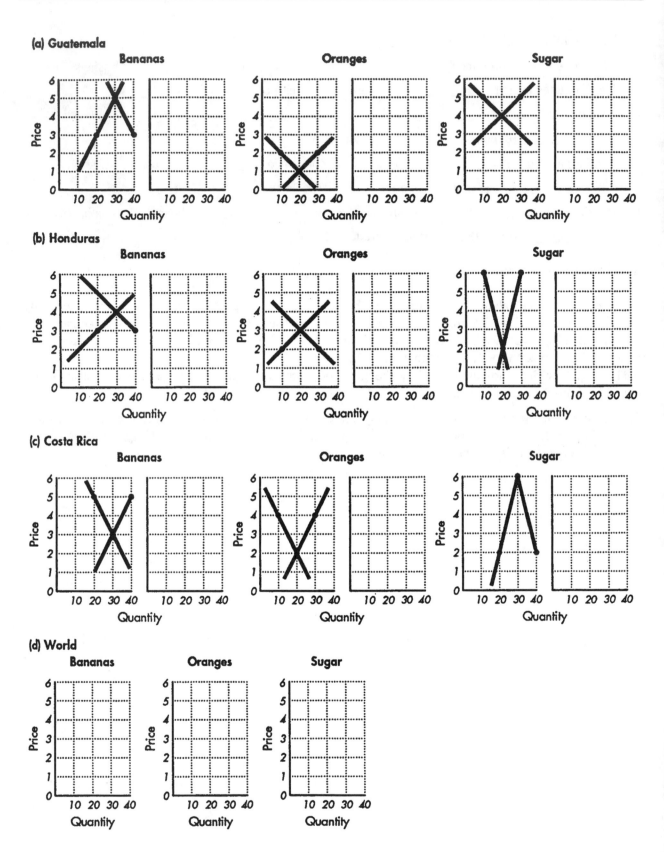

(a) Guatemala

Bananas   Oranges   Sugar

(b) Honduras

Bananas   Oranges   Sugar

(c) Costa Rica

Bananas   Oranges   Sugar

(d) World

Bananas   Oranges   Sugar

2. Find the equilibrium world price and quantity traded for each product, the amounts produced and consumed of each product in each country, and the status of each country as an importer, exporter, or nontrader.

	World Price	Quantity Traded
Bananas	$_____	_____
Oranges	_____	_____
Sugar	_____	_____

	Amount Produced	Amount Consumed	Status
Guatemala			
Bananas	_____	_____	_____
Oranges	_____	_____	_____
Sugar	_____	_____	_____
Honduras			
Bananas	_____	_____	_____
Oranges	_____	_____	_____
Sugar	_____	_____	_____
Costa Rica			
Bananas	_____	_____	_____
Oranges	_____	_____	_____
Sugar	_____	_____	_____

3. On the diagram below, put in the amounts of dollars flowing between each pair of countries, and which product and how much of it flows between each pair of countries.

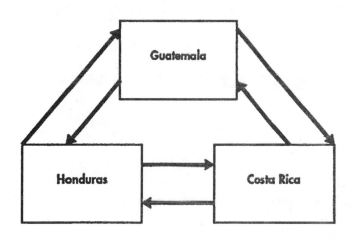

Chapter 21 (*Economics* Chapter 35)   Homework Problems

Name _____

1. Compare and contrast the concepts of absolute advantage and comparative advantage. Which is the determining factor in ascertaining what products a country should produce?

2. If Japan exports television sets to the United States, this results in a(n) _____ (increase, decrease) in the price of television sets in the United States and a(n) _____ (increase, decrease) in the price of television sets in Japan. If the United States exports beef to Japan, this results in a(n) _____ (increase, decrease) in the price of beef in the United States and a(n) _____ (increase, decrease) in the price of beef in Japan.

3. In the past, many developing countries were anxious to adopt the high-technology production techniques used by the industrial countries. Knowing the sources of comparative advantage, can you see how adopting high-technology production techniques may work against developing countries?

4. How does the theory of comparative advantage explain the fact that the United States exports cars to Germany and also imports cars from Germany?

5. A recent edition of the *Wall Street Journal* reported that Chile has pushed ahead of the United States as the world's largest producer of copper. The article notes:

> Chile has great advantages: Its new mines tap such high grade ore and are so huge and cost efficient that they would be very profitable even if copper prices slumped to 61 cents a pound, as they did from 1984 until 1986. Some, but not all U.S. mines could survive. Most in Africa, Australia, Canada and the former Soviet Union wouldn't stand a chance . . .
>
> [A] combination of better ore and looser environmental regulations elsewhere has all but dried up exploration in the U.S. . . . "It's not that we're more lenient here," says Gustavo Lagos, director of the mining center at the Universidad Catolica de Chile. "There are no people in Atacama and no scenery to destroy."

a. According to the article, does Chile have an absolute advantage in copper production? A comparative advantage? Defend your answers.

b. Which theory of the sources of comparative advantage applies here?

If your instructor assigns these problems, write your answers above, then tear out this page and hand it in.

Answers

Quick-Check Quiz

Section 1: An Overview of World Trade

1. c; 2. a; 3. a; 4. c

If you missed any of these questions, you should go back and review Section 1 in Chapter 21 (*Economics,* Chapter 35).

Section 2: An Example of International Trade Equilibrium

1. a; 2. b; 3. c; 4. c; 5. c

If you missed any of these questions, you should go back and review Section 2 in Chapter 21 (*Economics,* Chapter 35).

Section 3: Sources of Comparative Advantage

1. a; 2. d; 3. c; 4. b, 5. e

If you missed any of these questions, you should go back and review Section 3 in Chapter 21 (*Economics,* Chapter 35).

Practice Questions and Problems

Section 1: An Overview of World Trade

1. Canada; Canada
2. distributed across many
3. motor vehicles
4. a. 47
   b. 15

Section 2: An Example of International Trade Equilibrium

1. Comparative
2. Absolute
3. terms of trade
4. export supply
5. import demand
6. a. Samoa (Mangos cost only 2 hours of labor in Samoa; they cost 6 hours of labor in Fiji.)
   b. Samoa (Papayas cost only 1 hour of labor in Samoa; they cost 2 hours of labor in Fiji.)
   c. $\frac{1}{2}$ ton of mangos (Mangos take twice as much labor time as papayas in Samoa, so you can produce half as many mangos in the same amount of time.)
   d. $\frac{1}{3}$ ton of mangos (Mangos take three times as much labor time as papayas in Fiji, so you can produce one-third as many mangos in the same amount of time.)
   e. Fiji (Fiji has the lower opportunity cost: it has to give up only $\frac{1}{3}$ ton of mangos to get a ton of papayas, whereas Samoa has to give up $\frac{1}{2}$ ton.)
   f. 2 tons of papayas (Papayas take half as much labor time as mangos in Samoa, so you can produce twice as many papayas in the same amount of time.)

g. 3 tons of papayas (Papayas take one-third as much labor time as mangos in Fiji, so you can produce three times as many papayas in the same amount of time.)

h. Samoa (Samoa has the lower opportunity cost: it has to give up only 2 tons of papayas to get a ton of mangos, whereas Fiji has to give up 3 tons.)

i. 2; 3

7. a. $6; $12; United States

b.

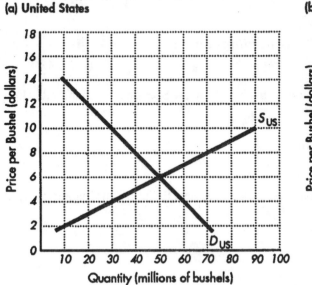

(a) United States

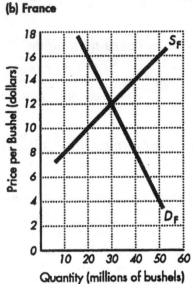

(b) France

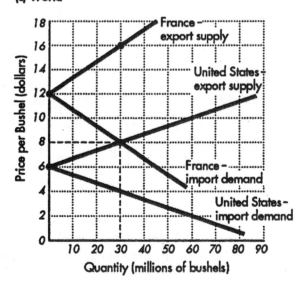

(c) World

c. $8; 30 million

d. 70 million; 40 million; exporter

e. 10 million; 40 million; importer

f. The price went up from $6 to $8; the price went down from $12 to $8.

Section 3: Sources of Comparative Advantage

1. a. productivity differences
   b. product life cycle
   c. human skills
   d. factor abundance
   e. consumer preferences
2. Ricardian
3. Heckscher-Ohlin
4. intraindustry trade

Thinking About and Applying World Trade Equilibrium

I.   World Trade Equilibrium

1. See the solution on page 446.
   The domestic prices before trade vary between $4 (United States and Canada) and $10 (Russia). Russia will begin demanding imports if the world price is below $10; if the price goes below $8, Argentina also will demand imports. The United States and Canada will begin supplying exports if the world price goes above $4; if the price goes above $8, Argentina also will supply exports. Graph e shows the amounts these countries will supply (export) and demand (import) at various prices.
2. $8; 60 million
3. 70 million; 30 million; exporter
4. 40 million; 20 million; exporter
5. 30 million; 30 million; nontrader
6. 60 million; 120 million; importer

II. Triangular Trade

1. See the solution on page 447.

(a) United States

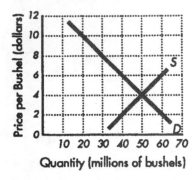

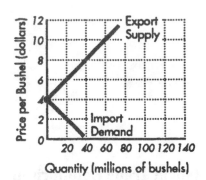

(b) Canada

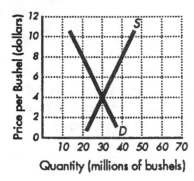

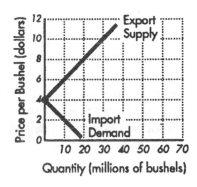

(e) World

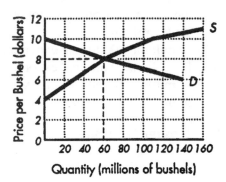

(c) Argentina

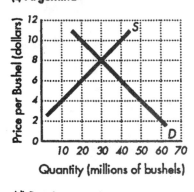

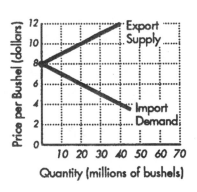

(d) Russia

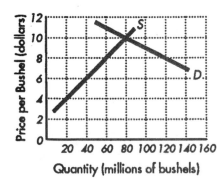

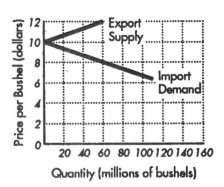

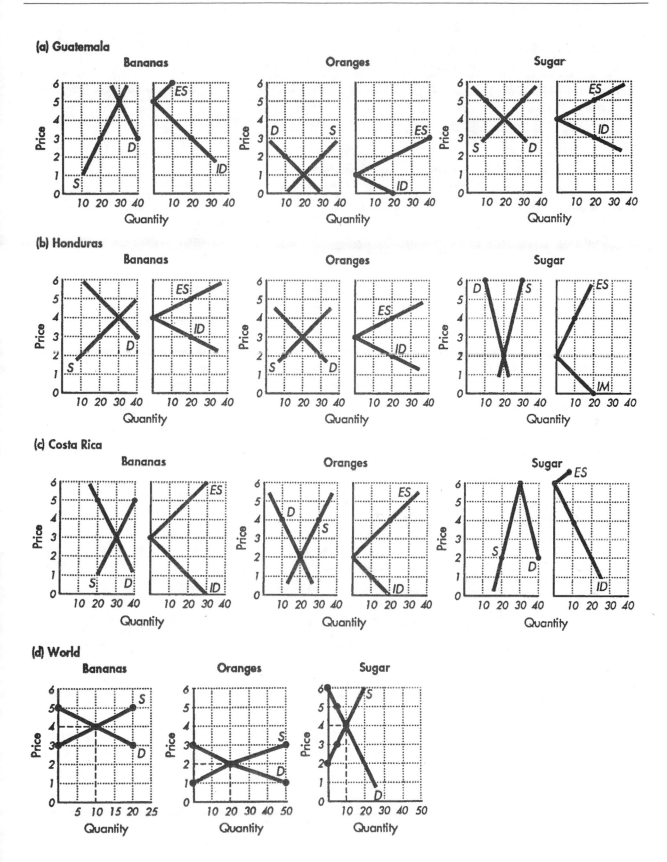

(a) Guatemala

Bananas   Oranges   Sugar

(b) Honduras

Bananas   Oranges   Sugar

(c) Costa Rica

Bananas   Oranges   Sugar

(d) World

Bananas   Oranges   Sugar

2.

	World Price	Quantity Traded
Bananas	$4	20
Oranges	2	20
Sugar	4	10

	Amount Produced	Amount Consumed	Status
Guatemala			
Bananas	25	35	Importer
Oranges	30	10	Exporter
Sugar	20	20	Nontrader
Honduras			
Bananas	30	30	Nontrader
Oranges	10	30	Importer
Sugar	25	15	Exporter
Costa Rica			
Bananas	35	25	Exporter
Oranges	20	20	Nontrader
Sugar	25	35	Importer

3.

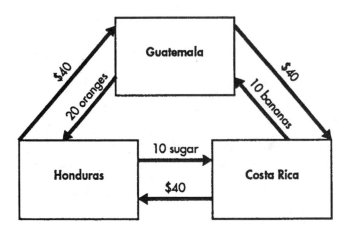

INTERNATIONAL TRADE RESTRICTIONS

FUNDAMENTAL QUESTIONS

1. Why do countries restrict international trade?

Most countries follow some sort of **commercial policy** to influence the direction and volume of international trade. Despite the costs to domestic consumers, countries frequently try to protect domestic producers by restricting international trade. Lobbying for trade restrictions is an example of the rent-seeking activities discussed in the chapter on government and public choice.

To help hide the special-interest nature of most trade restrictions, several arguments commonly are used. These include saving domestic jobs, creating fair trade, raising revenue through tariffs, protecting key defense industries, allowing new industries to become competitive, and giving **increasing-returns-to-scale industries** an advantage over foreign competitors. Although a few of these arguments have some validity, most have little or no merit.

2. How do countries restrict the entry of foreign goods and promote the export of domestic goods?

Several tactics are used for these purposes. **Tariffs,** or taxes on products imported into the United States, protect domestic industries by raising the price of foreign goods. Quotas restrict the amount or value of a foreign product that may be imported; **quantity quotas** limit the amount of a good that may be imported, and **value quotas** limit the monetary value of a good that may be imported. **Subsidies,** payments made by the government to domestic firms, both encourage exports and make domestic products cheaper to foreign buyers. In addition, a wide variety of other tactics, among them health and safety standards, are used to restrict imports.

3. What sorts of agreements do countries enter into to reduce barriers to international trade?

Groups of countries can establish **free trade areas,** where member countries have no trade barriers among themselves, or **customs unions,** where member countries not only abolish trade restrictions among themselves but also set common trade barriers on nonmembers. The United States, Mexico, and Canada established a free trade area in 1994. The best-known customs union is the European Economic Community (EEC), composed of most of the countries in Western Europe. Because they do not include all countries, free trade areas can result in both **trade diversion,** which reduces efficiency, and **trade creation,** which allows a country to obtain goods at lower cost.

Key Terms

commercial policy

strategic trade policy

increasing-returns-to-scale
  industry

tariff

quantity quota

value quota

subsidies

free trade area

customs union

trade diversion

trade creation

Quick-Check Quiz

Section 1: Arguments for Protection

1. The basic objective of commercial policy is to
   a. promote free and unrestricted international trade.
   b. protect domestic consumers from dangerous, low-quality imports.
   c. protect domestic producers from foreign competition.
   d. protect foreign producers from domestic consumers.
   e. promote the efficient use of scarce resources.

2. Using trade restrictions to save domestic jobs
   a. usually costs consumers much more than the job saved is worth.
   b. usually just redistributes jobs from other industries to the protected industry.
   c. may provoke other countries to restrict U.S. exports.
   d. does all of the above.
   e. does only b and c above.

3. Some arguments for trade restrictions have economic validity. Which of the following arguments has *no* economic validity?
   a. the infant industry argument
   b. the national defense argument
   c. the government revenue creation from tariffs argument
   d. the creation of domestic jobs argument
   e. All of the above have some economic validity.

4. The objective of strategic trade policy is to
   a. protect those industries needed for national defense.
   b. provide domestic decreasing-cost industries an advantage over foreign competitors.
   c. develop economic alliances with other countries.
   d. carefully develop free trade areas to counteract customs unions.
   e. increase government revenues through tariffs.

Section 2: Tools of Policy

1. A tariff is a
   a. tax on imports or exports.
   b. government-imposed limit on the amount of a good that can be imported.
   c. government-imposed limit on the value of a good that can be imported.
   d. payment by government to domestic producers.
   e. payment by government to foreign producers.

2. A subsidy is a
   a. tax on imports or exports.
   b. government-imposed limit on the amount of a good that can be imported.
   c. government-imposed limit on the value of a good that can be imported.
   d. payment by government to domestic producers.
   e. payment by government to foreign producers.

3. A quantity quota is a
   a. tax on imports or exports.
   b. government-imposed limit on the amount of a good that can be imported.
   c. government-imposed limit on the value of a good that can be imported.
   d. payment by government to domestic producers.
   e. payment by government to foreign producers.

4. A value quota is a
   a. tax on imports or exports.
   b. government-imposed limit on the amount of a good that may be imported.
   c. government-imposed limit on the value of a good that may be imported.
   d. payment by government to domestic producers.
   e. payment by government to foreign producers.

5. Which of the following are *not* used to restrict trade?
   a. health and safety standards
   b. government procurement regulations requiring domestic purchasing
   c. subsidies
   d. cultural and institutional practices
   e. All of the above are used to restrict trade.

Section 3: Preferential Trade Agreements

1. An organization of nations whose members have no trade barriers among themselves but are free to fashion their own trade policies toward nonmembers is a
   a. customs union.
   b. trade group.
   c. international cartel.
   d. free trade area.
   e. international economic alliance.

2. An organization of nations whose members have no trade barriers among themselves but impose common trade barriers on nonmembers is a
   a. customs union.
   b. trade group.
   c. international cartel.
   d. free trade area.
   e. international economic alliance.

3. Trade diversion occurs when a preferential trade agreement
   a. allows a country to buy imports from a nonmember country at a lower price than that charged by member countries.
   b. reduces economic efficiency by shifting production to a higher-cost producer.
   c. allows a country to obtain goods at a lower cost than is available at home.
   d. reduces trade flows between nonmember countries.
   e. increases economic efficiency by shifting production to a higher-cost producer.

4. Trade creation occurs when a preferential trade agreement
   a. allows a country to buy imports from a nonmember country at a lower price than that charged by member countries.
   b. reduces economic efficiency by shifting production to a higher-cost producer.
   c. allows a country to obtain goods at a lower cost than is available at home.
   d. reduces trade flows between nonmember countries.
   e. increases economic efficiency by shifting production to a higher-cost producer.

Practice Questions and Problems

Section 1: Arguments for Protection

1. The main reason governments restrict foreign trade is to protect _____ producers from _____ competition.

2. Governments can generate revenues by restricting trade through _____ ; this is a common tactic in _____ (industrial, developing) countries.

3. The argument that new industries should receive temporary protection is known as the _____ argument.

4. Strategic trade policy aims at identifying industries with _____ and giving them an advantage over their foreign competitors.

5. Using trade restrictions to protect domestic jobs usually costs consumers _____ (more, less) money than the jobs are worth to the workers holding them.

6. Trade restrictions usually _____ (create more, redistribute) domestic jobs within the economy.

Section 2: Tools of Policy

1. Tariffs are _____ on imports or exports. In the United States, tariffs on _____ (imports, exports) are illegal under the Constitution.

2. Quotas can be used to set limits on the _____ or _____ of a good allowed to be imported into a country.

3. List three trade barriers to trade besides tariffs and quotas.

_____

_____

_____

4. The graph below shows the U.S. market for tangerines. The world price for tangerines is $10 per bushel. On the graph, mark the quantity demanded and quantity supplied by U.S. sellers when the price is $10.

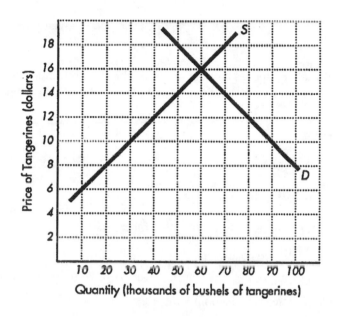

a. If the United States does not restrict imports of tangerines, it will import _____ tangerines at the price of _____ .

b. Suppose the United States imposes a $4 per bushel tariff on imported tangerines. On the graph above, mark the quantity demanded and the quantity supplied by U.S. sellers when the price is $14. The United States would import _____ tangerines at a price of _____ .

c. With the $4 tariff, _____ tangerines will be produced in the United States, and U.S. growers will receive _____ per bushel.

5. The graph below shows the U.S. market for tangerines again. The world price for tangerines is again $10 per bushel.

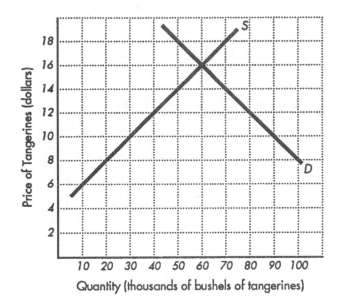

a. Suppose the United States imposes a quota of 40,000 bushels on imported tangerines. On the graph, mark the price at which the United States will import 40,000 tangerines. The price is

_____ .

b. With a quota of 40,000, _____ tangerines will be produced in the United States. U.S. tangerine growers will receive _____ for each bushel sold.

Section 3: Preferential Trade Agreements

1. A(n) _____ is a group of nations whose members have no trade barriers among themselves but impose common trade barriers on nonmembers.

2. A(n) _____ is a group of nations whose members have no trade barriers among themselves but have their own trade policies toward nonmembers.

3. The European Union (formerly known as the European Economic Community) is a(n) _____ . List the six original member countries and the six that joined later.

Original Members	Later Members
_____	_____
_____	_____
_____	_____
_____	_____
_____	_____
_____	_____

Thinking About and Applying International Trade Restrictions

I. Rent Seeking in the Automobile Industry

Table 1 in the text shows the costs to consumers and the gains to producers from trade restrictions on various imports into the United States.

1. Look through Table 1. Can you find any industry for which the benefits of trade restrictions (producer gains) are larger than the costs (total consumer losses)?

   _____

2. Let's take a look at some of the reasons why trade restrictions cause net losses to the United States. Look back at problem 5 on page 454, the problem with an import quota on tangerines. Before the quota was imposed, foreign tangerine growers received _____ for the tangerines they sold in the United States. After the quota, foreign tangerine growers received _____ for the tangerines they sold in the United States. Do you think U.S. producers got to keep all the extra money U.S. consumers spent for tangerines after the quota was imposed? Explain your answer.

   _____

   _____

   _____

   _____

3. a. Look back to Table 1 in your text again, and find the consumer losses and producer gains from trade restraints on automobiles. Consumer losses are _____ . Producer gains are

   _____ .

   b. In a good year, auto sales in the United States are around 10 million. U.S. consumers are paying _____ extra per car, and U.S. automakers are receiving _____ extra per car, as a result of trade restraints.

4. The most significant restriction on auto imports into the United States has been the voluntary export restraint agreement between the United States and Japan, whereby the Japanese agreed to set a quota on exports of automobiles to the United States and each Japanese automaker was given a specific number of cars that could be exported. Explain why the export quotas help prevent competition among Japanese automakers.

   _____

   _____

   _____

   _____

5. Use the ideas you learned in the chapter on government and public choice to explain why the U.S. government would encourage restrictions on importing Japanese autos, even though the restrictions cost U.S. car buyers large amounts of money. (*Hint:* Look at the title of this problem.)

_____

_____

_____

_____

II. Tax Effects of Import Restrictions

According to *Newsweek:*

> Lower-income families are hit hardest by trade restrictions, because they spend a far greater share of their earnings at the store. In 1989, for example, households earning more than $50,000 laid out 3.3 percent of their disposable incomes on clothing, but households in the $20,000-to-$30,000 bracket spent 4.6 percent— and families earning $10,000 to $15,000 spent 5.4 percent. The quotas and tariffs that force import prices up to protect U.S. apparel jobs don't matter much in Beverly Hills, but they put a big dent in pocketbooks in Watts. (July 12, 1993, p. 45)

Let's look more closely at the effects of tariffs and quotas on apparel on different income groups. Assuming that 20 percent of the price of clothing is due to tariffs and quotas, calculate the dollar cost of tariffs and quotas on families making the incomes given below. Then calculate the percentage of its income each family pays due to tariffs and quotas.

1. Family income = $50,000

   Cost: _____

   Percentage of income: _____

2. Family income = $25,000

   Cost: _____

   Percentage of income: _____

3. Family income = $10,000

   Cost: _____

   Percentage of income: _____

4. Tariffs and quotas on clothing are equivalent to a _____ (progressive, proportional, regressive) tax.

Chapter 22 (*Economics* Chapter 36)   Homework Problems

Name _____

1. Government policy aimed at influencing international trade flows is called _____ .

2. Generally speaking, protection from foreign competition benefits _____ at the expense of

    _____ .

3. List five barriers to international trade.

4. The North American Free Trade Agreement (NAFTA) created a free trade area within the United States, Canada, and Mexico. Who benefits and who is hurt by this agreement?

5. Table 1 in the text shows that consumer losses (in the form of higher prices and fewer goods and services) far outweigh producer gains when domestic industries are protected from foreign competition. Clearly, U.S. consumers would be better off if the United States unilaterally eliminated barriers to trade. Instead, U.S. policy has been to negotiate trade treaties. Why doesn't the United States unilaterally eliminate trade restrictions instead of bothering with trade treaties? (*Hint:* Remember what you learned about rent seeking and public choice theory in Chapter 5.)

If your instructor assigns these problems, write your answers above, then tear out this page and hand it in.

Answers

Quick-Check Quiz

Section 1: Arguments for Protection

1. c; 2. d; 3. d; 4. b
If you missed any of these questions, you should go back and review Section 1 in Chapter 22 (*Economics,* Chapter 36).

Section 2: Tools of Policy

1. a; 2. d; 3. b; 4. c; 5. e
If you missed any of these questions, you should go back and review Section 2 in Chapter 22 (*Economics,* Chapter 36).

Section 3: Preferential Trade Agreements

1. d; 2. a; 3. b; 4. c
If you missed any of these questions, you should go back and review Section 3 in Chapter 22 (*Economics,* Chapter 36).

Practice Questions and Problems

Section 1: Arguments for Protection

1. domestic; foreign
2. tariffs; developing
3. infant industry
4. decreasing costs
5. more
6. redistribute

Section 2: Tools of Policy

1. taxes; exports
2. quantity; value
3. subsidies
   government procurement regulations requiring domestic purchasing
   health and safety standards
   cultural or institutional barriers

4.

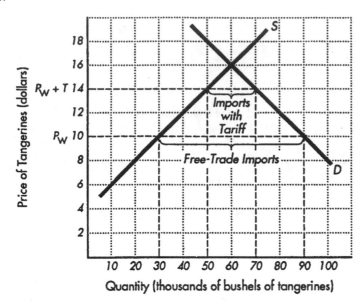

a. 60,000; $10 (At a world price of $10, the United States demands 90,000 bushels but produces only 30,000 bushels. The difference [90,000 – 30,000] is how much the United States will import.)

b. 20,000; $14 (The tariff raises the price of tangerines in the United States to $14 [the $10 world price + the $4 tariff]. At this price, U.S. consumers demand 70,000 tangerines, and U.S. producers supply 50,000, leaving 20,000 to be imported.)

c. 50,000; $14

5.

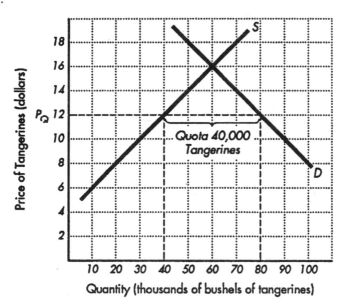

a. $12 (The quota limits imports to 40,000. From the U.S. supply and demand curves, the price where the difference between U.S. demand and U.S. supply is 40,000 is at $12 per bushel: U.S. consumers buy 80,000 bushels, and U.S. producers supply 40,000 bushels.)

b. 40,000; $12

Section 3: Preferential Trade Agreements

1. customs union
2. free trade area
3. customs union

Original Members	Later Members
France	United Kingdom
West Germany	Ireland
Italy	Denmark
Belgium	Greece
Netherlands	Spain
Luxembourg	Portugal

Thinking About and Applying International Trade Restrictions

I. Rent Seeking in the Automobile Industry

1. no (Except for peanuts, where the gains are estimated to equal the losses, the losses to consumers are larger than the gains to producers.)
2. $10; $12; no; some of the extra money U.S. consumers paid went to foreign sellers of tangerines, who received a higher price.
3. a. $5,800,000,000; $2,600,000,000
   b. $580; $260
4. Cartels try to raise prices by cutting back output. From the point of view of an individual firm in a cartel, cutting price to expand sales is usually profitable; such cheating contributes to the eventual collapse of most cartels. By using the Japanese government to enforce limits on output, Japanese car-makers were able to raise prices without worrying about any cheating their competitors might do.
5. Trade restraints are an example of rent-seeking behavior. Import quotas on automobiles transfer wealth from consumers (a relatively small amount from many car buyers) to automakers and auto workers (a relatively large amount to each one). The cost to car buyers is hidden in the price of the automobile and so does not provoke consumer resentment against politicians who vote for restraints. The automakers and auto workers, of course, know who is responsible for their added wealth and reward cooperative politicians with campaign contributions and votes.

II. Tax Effects of Import Restrictions

1. $330 (3.3 percent of $50,000 = $1,650 spent on clothing; 20 percent of $1,650 = $330); 0.66 percent ($330/$50,000 = .0066 = 0.66 percent)
2. $165 (4.6 percent of $25,000 = $1,150 spent on clothing; 20 percent of $1,150 = $230); 0.92 percent ($230/$25,000 = .0092 = 0.92 percent)
3. $108 (5.4 percent of $10,000 = $540 spent on clothing; 20 percent of $540 = $108); 1.08 percent ($108/$10,000 = .0108 = 1.08 percent)
4. regressive (The percentage of income paid in the "tax" is highest for low-income families and then decreases for higher-income families.)

EXCHANGE-RATE SYSTEMS AND PRACTICES

FUNDAMENTAL QUESTIONS

1. How does a commodity standard fix exchange rates between countries?

    A commodity standard exists when exchange rates are based on the values of different currencies in terms of some commodity. The **gold standard,** in general use between 1880 and 1914, fixed the value of countries' currencies in terms of how much currency was needed to buy an ounce of gold. Fixing the value of currencies in terms of gold also fixes the relative value of all currencies to one another. For example, if the value of an ounce of gold is 20 U.S. dollars and its value is also 200 Mexican pesos, then a U.S. dollar has the same value as 10 Mexican pesos. As long as countries fix the value of their currencies in terms of some commodity, the relative values of those currencies stay the same.

2. What kinds of exchange-rate arrangements exist today?

    The gold standard ended with World War I. Since then, many exchange-rate systems have been tried. At the present time, nations use a variety of exchange-rate arrangements, including fixed exchange rates, freely floating exchange rates, and **managed floating exchange rates.**

3. How is equilibrium determined in the foreign-exchange market?

    Equilibrium is determined in foreign-exchange markets the same way it's determined in other markets: by the intersection of supply and demand curves. The demand for a currency, such as the U.S dollar, comes from the desire of people in other countries to buy things in the United States; the supply of U.S. currency to the foreign-exchange market comes from U.S. residents' desire to buy things from foreign countries.

4. How do fixed and floating exchange rates differ in their adjustment to shifts in supply and demand for currencies?

    With floating exchange rates, the foreign-exchange market adjusts automatically to shifts in supply and demand, the same way perfectly competitive markets for products adjust. With fixed exchange rates, a government can try to maintain the fixed rate through intervention in the foreign-exchange market, although this is unlikely to work unless the shifts in supply and demand are temporary. A **fundamental disequilibrium** usually requires a currency devaluation.

5. What are the advantages and disadvantages of fixed and floating exchange rates?

   Fixed exchange rates require that a nation match its macroeconomic policies to those of the country or countries to which its currency is pegged; this limits a country's ability to set its own policies. Floating exchange rates allow countries to follow their own macroeconomic policies.

6. What determines the kind of exchange-rate system a country adopts?

   Countries in general can choose what kind of exchange-rate system they want to use. The choice seems to depend on four characteristics: the size of the country (in terms of economic output), the nature of the **economy** (how large a fraction of the GNP is devoted to international trade), the country's experience with inflation, and trade diversification.

Key Terms

gold standard	foreign exchange market	appreciate
gold exchange standard	intervention	depreciate
reserve currency	devaluation	fundamental disequilibrium
International Monetary Fund	equilibrium exchange rates	speculators
(IMF)	managed floating exchange	open economy
World Bank	rates	multiple exchange rates

Quick-Check Quiz

Section 1: Past and Current Exchange-Rate Arrangements

1. Which of the following describes a gold standard?
   a. a currency that is used to settle international debts and is held by governments to use in foreign exchange market interventions
   b. an exchange-rate system in which each nation fixes the value of its currency in terms of gold but buys and sells the U.S. dollar rather than gold to maintain fixed exchange rates
   c. the buying or selling of currencies by a government or central bank to achieve a specified exchange rate
   d. the exchange rates that are established in the absence of government foreign exchange market intervention
   e. a system whereby national currencies are fixed in terms of their value in gold, thus creating fixed exchange rates between currencies

2. Which of the following describes a gold exchange standard?
   a. a currency that is used to settle international debts and is held by governments to use in foreign exchange market interventions
   b. an exchange-rate system in which each nation fixes the value of its currency in terms of gold but buys and sells the U.S. dollar rather than gold to maintain fixed exchange rates
   c. the buying or selling of currencies by a government or central bank to achieve a specified exchange rate
   d. the exchange rates that are established in the absence of government foreign exchange market intervention
   e. a system whereby national currencies are fixed in terms of their value in gold, thus creating fixed exchange rates between currencies

3. Which of the following describes a reserve currency?
   a. a currency that is used to settle international debts and is held by governments to use in foreign exchange market interventions
   b. an exchange-rate system in which each nation fixes the value of its currency in terms of gold but buys and sells the U.S. dollar rather than gold to maintain fixed exchange rates
   c. the buying or selling of currencies by a government or central bank to achieve a specified exchange rate
   d. the exchange rates that are established in the absence of government foreign exchange market intervention
   e. a system whereby national currencies are fixed in terms of their value in gold, thus creating fixed exchange rates between currencies

4. Which of the following describes foreign exchange market intervention?
   a. a currency that is used to settle international debts and is held by governments to use in foreign exchange market interventions
   b. an exchange-rate system in which each nation fixes the value of its currency in terms of gold but buys and sells the U.S. dollar rather than gold to maintain fixed exchange rates
   c. the buying or selling of currencies by a government or central bank to achieve a specified exchange rate
   d. the exchange rates that are established in the absence of government foreign exchange market intervention
   e. a system whereby national currencies are fixed in terms of their value in gold, thus creating fixed exchange rates between currencies

5. Which of the following describes equilibrium exchange rates?
   a. a currency that is used to settle international debts and is held by governments to use in foreign exchange market interventions
   b. an exchange-rate system in which each nation fixes the value of its currency in terms of gold but buys and sells the U.S. dollar rather than gold to maintain fixed exchange rates
   c. the buying or selling of currencies by a government or central bank to achieve a specified exchange rate
   d. the exchange rates that are established in the absence of government foreign exchange market intervention
   e. a system whereby national currencies are fixed in terms of their value in gold, thus creating fixed exchange rates between currencies

6. The Bretton Woods system
   a. created the International Monetary Fund and the World Bank.
   b. set a gold exchange standard.
   c. used the U.S. dollar as a reserve currency.
   d. tried to maintain exchange rates through foreign exchange market intervention.
   e. was and did all of the above.

Section 2: Fixed or Floating Exchange Rates

1. Currency appreciation is
   a. a decrease in the value of a currency under floating exchange rates.
   b. an increase in the value of a currency under floating exchange rates.
   c. a decrease in the value of a currency under fixed exchange rates.
   d. an increase in the value of a currency under fixed exchange rates.
   e. resetting the pegged value of a currency.

2. Currency depreciation is
   a. a decrease in the value of a currency under floating exchange rates.
   b. an increase in the value of a currency under floating exchange rates.
   c. a decrease in the value of a currency under fixed exchange rates.
   d. an increase in the value of a currency under fixed exchange rates.
   e. resetting the pegged value of a currency.

3. Which of the following statements about fixed and floating exchange rates is *false*?
   a. Fixed exchange rates put pressure on a nation to manage its macroeconomic policy in concert with other nations.
   b. Floating exchange rates put pressure on a nation to manage its macroeconomic policy in concert with other nations.
   c. Speculators are more likely to be a problem under fixed exchange rates than under floating exchange rates.
   d. Fixed exchange rates can force a devaluation in the event of fundamental disequilibrium.
   e. Floating exchange rates adjust automatically to changes in demand and supply.

Section 3: The Choice of an Exchange-Rate System

1. Economically, an open economy is one in which
   a. no trade with other countries take place.
   b. there are no trade restraints.
   c. a large fraction of the country's GDP is devoted to internationally traded goods.
   d. exchange rates are freely floating, with no government intervention in foreign-exchange markets.
   e. other nations may freely invest.

2. Which of the following circumstances would make it likely that a country would choose a fixed exchange rate?
   a. The country is large, in terms of GDP.
   b. The country has an open economy.
   c. The country's inflation experience has diverged from its trading partner's.
   d. The country has a very diversified trading pattern.
   e. Both b and d would make it likely that a country would choose a fixed exchange rate.

3. Multiple exchange rates
    a. are impossible.
    b. eventually lead to fixed exchange rates.
    c. eventually lead to a gold standard.
    d. have the same effects as taxes and subsidies.
    e. are easier to administer than a single exchange rate.

Practice Questions and Problems

Section 1: Past and Current Exchange-Rate Arrangements

1. From about 1880 to 1914, most currencies were fixed in value in terms of _____ .

2. The Bretton Woods agreement of 1944 set up two international financial institutions that are still active today. Name the two institutions that match the descriptions below.

    a. Supervises exchange-rate arrangements and lends money to member countries experiencing problems meeting their external financial obligations: _____

    b. Makes loans and provides technical expertise to developing countries: _____

3. A(n) _____ is a deliberate decrease in the official value of a currency.

4. Today, the major industrial countries determine the value of their currencies through _____ .

5. The _____ was introduced in 1999 as the eventual replacement for the currencies of several European countries.

6. Under a gold standard, if gold is worth $35 per ounce in the United States and 175 francs per ounce in France, _____ franc(s) will exchange for $1.

7. Under a gold standard, if gold is worth $20 per ounce in the United States and 10 marks per ounce in Germany, _____ mark(s) will exchange for $1.

Section 2: Fixed or Floating Exchange Rates

1. The U.S. demand for German marks comes from the desire of _____ (U.S., German) citizens for _____ (U.S., German) goods.

2. The U.S. supply of German marks comes from the desire of _____ (U.S., German) citizens for _____ (U.S., German) goods.

3. If U.S. citizens decide that they want to buy more Mercedes-Benz automobiles from Germany, the U.S. _____ (demand for, supply of) marks will _____ (increase, decrease).

4. If German citizens decide they want to buy fewer IBM computers from the United States, the U.S. _____ (demand for, supply of) marks will _____ (increase, decrease).

5. The two graphs below show the current U.S. demand for and supply of German marks. The exchange rate between marks and dollars floats freely.

(a)

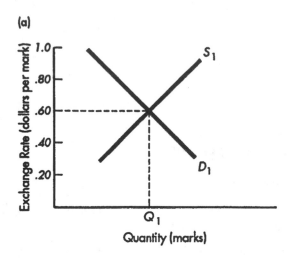

(b)

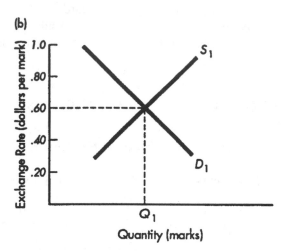

a. The current exchange rate in dollars per mark is _____ .

b. The current exchange rate in marks per dollar is _____ .

c. On graph a, sketch in a new demand or supply curve (whichever is appropriate) that shows the effects of a decrease in the purchase of German BMW automobiles by U.S. residents.

d. With the change in demand, the dollar _____ (appreciates, depreciates) relative to the mark, and the mark _____ (appreciates, depreciates) relative to the dollar.

e. On graph b, sketch in a new demand or supply curve (whichever is appropriate) that shows the effects of a decrease in the purchase of Boeing airplanes (made in the United States) by German airlines.

f. With the change in supply, the dollar _____ (appreciates, depreciates) relative to the mark, and the mark _____ (appreciates, depreciates) relative to the dollar.

Section 3: The Choice of an Exchange-Rate System

1. Countries with fixed exchange rates are likely to be _____ (large, small), to be (more open, less open), to trade with _____ (many countries, mostly one country), and to have a _____ (similar, different) inflation history compared with their trading partners.

2. Some countries use _____ exchange rates to provide subsidies for activities they favor and taxes for activities they do not.

3. Section 3.b in the text, on multiple exchange rates, cites Venezuela as a country that was using multiple exchange rates in 1985. Use the exchange rates listed there to find the costs in Venezuelan bolivars (Bs) of the transactions below.

   a. $10,000 interest payment on debt owed by a Venezuelan company to Citibank in New York:

   _____

   b. $10,000 purchase of drilling supplies by the Venezuelan national oil company: _____

   c. $10,000 purchase of personal computers by the Venezuelan education agency: _____

   d. $10,000 purchase of a Chevrolet by a Venezuelan citizen: _____

Thinking About and Applying Exchange-Rate Systems and Practices

Floating Exchange Rates?

The headline in the *Wall Street Journal* on April 28, 1993, read "U.S. Slows Yen's Rise, Easing Japanese Tension" (page C1). The exchange rate between the dollar and the yen had dropped from 125 yen per dollar in early January 1993 to below 110 yen per dollar in April 1993. (Since then, it has dropped even further, to around 85 yen per dollar in mid-1995.) The article said:

> Marking the Clinton administration's first intervention in the foreign-exchange markets, the Federal Reserve Bank of New York repeatedly sold yen for dollars after the U.S. currency hit a postwar low of 109.25 yen. By late yesterday afternoon in New York, the dollar had risen about 1% against the yen.

1. Explain why the headline is correct when it talks about the yen's "rise" between January and April.

   _____

   _____

   _____

2. Use demand and supply analysis to explain the effect that the Federal Reserve's selling yen for dollars would have on the exchange rate between dollars and yen.

   _____

   _____

   _____

3. How can economists say that both the United States and Japan have adopted floating exchange rates, when the Federal Reserve acts to control exchange rates?

   _____

   _____

   _____

Chapter 23 (*Economics* Chapter 37)   Homework Problems

Name _____

1. Under the gold standard, what determined the exchange rate between two countries' currencies?

2. How are the exchange rates between the dollar and other major currencies determined today?

3. What four characteristics are important in a country's choice of what type of exchange-rate system to use?

4. If the United States and its major trading partners went back on the gold standard, how would they have to change their macroeconomic policymaking?

5. Suppose the exchange rate between the U.S. dollar and the British pound is floating. What effect will each of the following have on the demand or supply of dollars, and what will happen to the price of a dollar in pounds (the exchange rate)?

   a. British Airways decides to buy 200 new Boeing 777 airliners.

   b. British Land Rovers become much more popular in the United States.

   c. The U.S. stock market booms, attracting large numbers of British investors.

   d. The Federal Reserve lowers interest rates in the United States, making British bonds more attractive to U.S. investors.

If your instructor assigns these problems, write your answers above, then tear out this page and hand it in.

Answers

Quick-Check Quiz

Section 1: Past and Current Exchange-Rate Arrangements

1. e; 2. b; 3. a; 4. c; 5. d; 6. e
If you missed any of these questions, you should go back and review Section 1 in Chapter 23 (*Economics,* Chapter 37).

Section 2: Fixed or Floating Exchange Rates

1. b; 2. a; 3. b
If you missed any of these questions, you should go back and review Section 2 in Chapter 23 (*Economics,* Chapter 37).

Section 3: The Choice of an Exchange-Rate System

1. c; 2. b; 3. d
If you missed any of these questions, you should go back and review Section 3 in Chapter 23 (*Economics,* Chapter 37).

Practice Questions and Problems

Section 1: Past and Current Exchange-Rate Arrangements

1. gold
2. a. International Monetary Fund (IMF)
   b. World Bank
3. devaluation
4. managed floating exchange rates
5. euro
6. 5 (It takes five times as many francs as dollars to buy an ounce of gold [175 francs per ounce/$35 per ounce], so $1 would be equivalent to five times as many francs.)
7. 0.5 mark (It takes half as many marks as dollars to buy an ounce of gold [10 marks per ounce/$20 per ounce], so $1 would be equivalent to half as many marks.)

Section 2: Fixed or Floating Exchange Rates

1. U.S.; German
2. German; U.S.
3. demand for; increase (The Mercedes-Benz factory in Germany wants to be paid in its own currency [marks]. U.S. buyers of German products have to buy marks with dollars. Because we want to buy more marks than before, the demand for marks will increase.)
4. supply of; decrease (IBM in the United States wants to be paid in its own currency [dollars]. German buyers of U.S. products have to sell marks to get dollars. Because they want to sell fewer marks than before, the supply of marks will decrease.)

5.

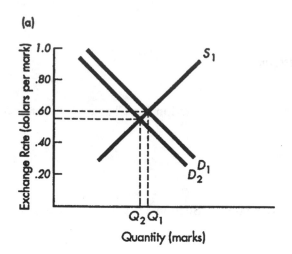

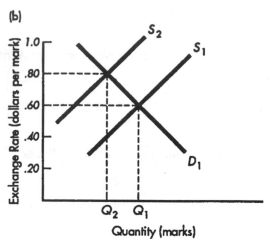

a. 0.60 dollar per mark (It takes $.60 to buy 1 mark, in dollars per mark. You can read this value from the intersection of demand and supply on the graphs.)

b. 1.67 marks per dollar (The exchange rate in marks per dollar is the inverse of the exchange rate in dollars per mark: 1/0.60 = 1.67. Exchange rates can be expressed either way.)

c. U.S. buyers of German products are the demanders of marks (they need to buy marks to pay Germans), so the demand curve will shift. If we buy fewer BMWs, the demand for marks will decrease, as shown on graph a. The size of the shift on the graph does not matter.

d. appreciates; depreciates (It takes fewer dollars now to buy a mark than it did before [0.55 dollar per mark instead of 0.60], so that dollar is more valuable relative to the mark. And it now takes 1.82 marks to buy a dollar [1/0.55]. It takes more marks now to buy a dollar than before, so the mark is less valuable relative to the dollar.)

e. German buyers of U.S. products are the sellers of marks (they need to sell marks to get dollars to pay Americans), so the supply curve will shift. If they buy fewer Boeing planes, the supply of marks will decrease, as shown on graph b. The size of the shift on the graph does not matter.

f. depreciates; appreciates (It takes more dollars now to buy a mark than it did before [0.80 dollar per mark instead of 0.60], so the dollar is less valuable relative to the mark. And it now takes only 1.25 marks to buy a dollar [1/0.80]. It takes fewer marks now to buy a dollar than before, so the mark is more valuable relative to the dollar.)

Section 3: The Choice of an Exchange-Rate System

1. small; more open; mostly one country; similar
2. multiple
3. a. Bs43,000 (The exchange rate for interest payments on foreign debt was Bs4.30 per dollar, so buying $10,000 cost Bs43,000 [$10,000 times 4.30].)
   b. Bs60,000 (The exchange rate for the national petroleum company was Bs6.00 per dollar, so buying $10,000 cost Bs60,000 [$10,000 times 6.00].)
   c. Bs75,000 (The exchange rate for government agencies was Bs7.50 per dollar, so buying $10,000 cost Bs75,000 [$10,000 times 7.50].)
   d. Bs144,000 (The exchange rate for other transactions was the free market rate of Bs14.40 per dollar, so buying $10,000 cost Bs144,000 [$10,000 times 14.40].)

Thinking About and Applying Exchange-Rate Systems and Practices

Floating Exchange Rates?

1. The yen "rose" (appreciated) during that time because the number of yen needed to buy a dollar decreased, making the yen more valuable relative to the dollar. A U.S. product that cost $1 would have cost a Japanese buyer 125 yen in January but only about 110 yen in April.
2. Looking at the markets for dollars and yen, selling yen and buying dollars would have increased the supply of yen, lowering the price of yen; it also would have increased the demand for dollars, raising the price of dollars.
3. At any moment, the Federal Reserve (or other central bank) can affect exchange rates to a limited extent. What limits the Fed's actions in this case is its limited supply of yen to sell. Most of the time, the exchange rate is determined by market demand and supply.

1. What determines which goods a country will specialize in?
    a. Its opportunity costs of production are equal to those of other countries.
    b. Its opportunity costs of production are higher than those of other countries.
    c. Its degree of subsidization is greater than that of other countries.
    d. Its opportunity costs of production are lower than those of other countries.
    e. Its product quality is higher than that of other countries.

Refer to the following table to answer questions 2–6. The data indicate that both Japan and Taiwan produce camcorders and clothing; Japan can make 20 camcorders or 4 units of clothing in a day, and Taiwan can make 10 camcorders or 10 units of clothing in a day.

	Camcorders	Clothing
Japan	20	4
Taiwan	10	10

2. Japan has an absolute advantage in producing
    a. camcorders.
    b. clothing.
    c. both camcorders and clothing.
    d. neither camcorders nor clothing.
    e. clothing and an absolute disadvantage in producing camcorders.

3. Japan has a comparative advantage in producing
    a. camcorders.
    b. clothing.
    c. both camcorders and clothing.
    d. neither camcorders nor clothing.
    e. clothing and an absolute disadvantage in producing camcorders.

4. What is the opportunity cost of one camcorder in Japan?
    a. 4 units of clothing
    b. 10 units of clothing
    c. $\frac{1}{5}$ unit of clothing
    d. 1 unit of clothing
    e. $\frac{1}{2}$ unit of clothing

5. What is the opportunity cost of one unit of clothing in Japan?
   a. 20 camcorders
   b. 10 camcorders
   c. 1 camcorder
   d. $\frac{1}{5}$ camcorder
   e. $\frac{1}{20}$ camcorder

6. What are the limits on the terms of trade for one unit of clothing?
   a. between 4 camcorders and 20 camcorders
   b. between 1 camcorder and 10 camcorders
   c. between 1 camcorder and 20 camcorders
   d. between 1 camcorder and 2 camcorders
   e. between $\frac{1}{5}$ camcorder and 1 camcorder

7. What happens when the world price is below the domestic "no-trade" equilibrium price?
   a. The domestic shortage can be eliminated by rationing.
   b. The domestic surplus can be consumed at home.
   c. The domestic shortage can be eliminated by foreign imports.
   d. The quantity demanded is equal to that supplied by the world.
   e. The domestic shortage can be eliminated by foreign imports.

8. Most empirical studies indicate that restrictions on international trade
   a. cause a net increase in jobs in the domestic economy.
   b. promote both exports and imports.
   c. promote imports and restrict exports.
   d. restrict both imports and exports.
   e. harm consumers.

9. In general, protecting domestic producers from foreign competition benefits
   a. both domestic producers and foreign producers.
   b. all groups in the domestic economy.
   c. both domestic producers and domestic consumers.
   d. domestic producers at the expense of domestic consumers.
   e. foreign producers and domestic consumers.

10. The consequences of protection in the affected industry are generally known to be
    a. lower prices for the product, lower profits for owners, and lower wages for workers.
    b. higher prices for the output, lower profits for owners, and lower wages for workers.
    c. higher prices for the product, lower profits for owners, and higher wages for workers.
    d. lower prices for the product, higher profits for owners, and higher wages for workers.
    e. higher prices for the product, higher profits for owners, and higher wages for workers.

11. All of the following are basic principles of the GATT *except* the statement that
    a. barriers to trade should apply equally across all countries.
    b. quotas should be eliminated.
    c. disagreements should be settled through consultation.
    d. developing nations with underutilized comparative advantages should be favored using selectivity.
    e. once tariffs have been lowered, they cannot be increased without compensation to trading partners.

Consider the following figure for questions 12–16.

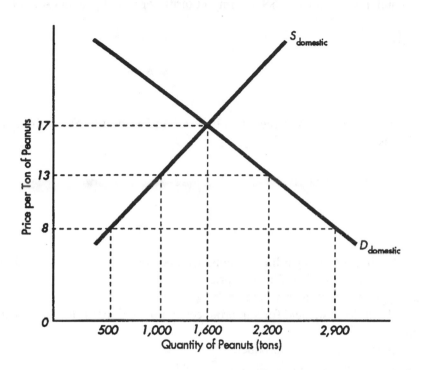

12. Without international trade, the domestic price and equilibrium quantity of peanuts are
    a. $8 per ton and 1,000 tons.
    b. $13 per ton and 1,600 tons.
    c. $8 per ton and 2,900 tons.
    d. $17 per ton and 1,600 tons.
    e. $13 per ton and 2,200 tons.

13. Suppose that the world equilibrium price is $8 per ton and free trade prevails. Then
    a. this country will export 500 tons of peanuts.
    b. there will be a shortage of peanuts, driving prices up.
    c. this country will import 2,400 tons of peanuts.
    d. domestic producers will produce 1,600 tons of peanuts.
    e. consumers will demand no peanuts at a price of $8.

14. Suppose that the world equilibrium price is $8 per ton, and this country imposes a $5 per ton tariff on peanut imports. Then
    a. the equilibrium price must rise to $17.
    b. the price to domestic consumers and producers will be $13.
    c. imports of peanuts will increase by 1,000 tons.
    d. a surplus of 500 tons will be created.
    e. a shortage of 500 tons will be created.

15. Suppose that this country wanted to completely eliminate all imports of peanuts. Given these demand and supply data and a world price of $8, the import tariff per ton of peanuts should be
   a. $3.
   b. $8.
   c. $9.
   d. $5.
   e. $7.

16. The total tariff revenue to the government that imposes a $5 import tariff per ton of peanuts with a world price of $8 is
   a. $1,200.
   b. $6,000.
   c. $5,000.
   d. $2,200.
   e. $2,900.

17. Which of the following is true regarding a comparison between import quotas with import tariffs?
   a. A tariff raises the worldwide equilibrium price.
   b. A quota raises government tax revenue.
   c. With a quota, both domestic and foreign producers enjoy a higher price for products sold in the domestic market.
   d. Quotas benefit consumers of the product.
   e. Quotas increase the quantity of the good available to consumers.

18. Suppose that the price of an ounce of gold is 10 dinars in Bahrain and $400 in the United States. Then the
   a. Bahraini dinar is worth 40 times the value of a U.S. dollar.
   b. Bahraini dinar is worth one-fortieth the value of a U.S. dollar.
   c. U.S. dollar is worth 40 times the value of a Bahraini dinar.
   d. U.S. economy must be 40 times larger than that of Bahrain.
   e. Bahrain economy must be 40 times larger than that of the United States.

19. Suppose that the official gold value of the Portuguese escudo changes from 300 escudos per ounce to 200 escudos per ounce. We can then say that
   a. the Portuguese escudo has been devalued.
   b. the Portuguese escudo has appreciated in value.
   c. gold is now more expensive to purchase in Portugal.
   d. the Portuguese economy is expected to experience rapid inflation.
   e. the Portuguese escudo has depreciated in value because of free market fluctuations.

Consider the following figure for questions 20 and 21.

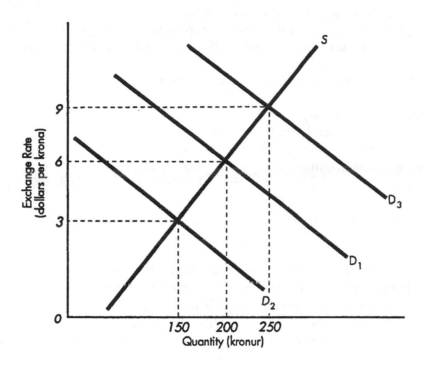

20. Suppose that U.S. residents significantly increase their demand for imported Icelandic sweaters. The greater U.S. demand will
    a. increase the demand for Icelandic kronur from D_1 to D_3 and increase the exchange rate to $9.
    b. decrease the demand for Icelandic kronur from D_1 to D_2 and increase the exchange rate to $6.
    c. increase the demand for Icelandic kronur from D_1 to D_3 and decrease the kronur price to $6.
    d. decrease the demand for Icelandic kronur from D_1 to D_2 and decrease the kronur price to $6.
    e. not affect the foreign exchange market for Icelandic kronur.

21. The demand curves shown for Icelandic kronur are based on _____ , and the supply curve shown for Icelandic kronur is based on _____ .
    a. economists' preferences for dollars; economists' preferences for dollars
    b. the supply of Icelandic kronur; the supply of Icelandic products
    c. U.S. demand for Icelandic goods; Icelandic demand for U.S. products
    d. Icelandic demand for U.S. products; U.S. demand for Icelandic products
    e. the supply of U.S. dollars in Iceland; the supply of Icelandic kronur in the United States

22. The Bretton Woods System of exchange rates was established
    a. to solidify support for the then-existing gold standard.
    b. to peg the worldwide price of silver to the price of gold.
    c. in Europe before World War II to develop flexible exchange rates.
    d. in the United States in 1944 to develop a gold exchange standard.
    e. by a mechanism that made gold the reserve currency of the system.

23. The International Monetary Fund was created to achieve each of the following purposes *except*
    a. to supervise exchange-rate practices of member countries.
    b. to help finance economic development in poor countries.
    c. to encourage the free convertibility of member countries' currency.
    d. to lend money to countries that are having difficulty meeting their international payments obligations.
    e. to collect and disburse each country's annual membership fee or quota.

24. The World Bank was created to
    a. help finance economic development in poor countries.
    b. supervise exchange-rate practices of member countries.
    c. encourage the free convertibility of member countries' currency.
    d. lend money to countries that are having difficulty meeting their international payments obligations.
    e. collect and disburse each country's annual membership fee or quota.

25. In international finance, the term *appreciate* refers to
    a. a decrease in the value of a currency under floating exchange rates.
    b. a decrease in the value of a currency under fixed exchange rates.
    c. an increase in the value of a currency under floating exchange rates.
    d. an increase in the value of a currency under fixed exchange rates.
    e. foreign policy consequences of an accommodative fiscal policy by which one country helps another.

Answers to Sample Test

1. d (Chapter 21, Preview; *Economics* Chapter 35)
2. a (Chapter 21, Section 2.a; *Economics* Chapter 35)
3. a (Chapter 21, Section 2.a; *Economics* Chapter 35)
4. c (Chapter 21, Section 2.a; *Economics* Chapter 35)
5. b (Chapter 21, Section 2.a; *Economics* Chapter 35)
6. b (Chapter 21, Section 2.b; *Economics* Chapter 35)
7. c (Chapter 21, Section 2.b; *Economics* Chapter 35)
8. e (Chapter 22, Section 1.a; *Economics* Chapter 36)
9. d (Chapter 22, Section 1.a; *Economics* Chapter 36)
10. e (Chapter 22, Section 1.a; *Economics* Chapter 36)
11. d (Chapter 22, Section 2.a; *Economics* Chapter 36)
12. d (Chapter 22, Section 2.a; *Economics* Chapter 36)
13. c (Chapter 22, Section 2.a; *Economics* Chapter 36)
14. b (Chapter 22, Section 2.a; *Economics* Chapter 36)
15. c (Chapter 22, Section 2.a; *Economics* Chapter 36)
16. b (Chapter 22, Section 2.a; *Economics* Chapter 36)
17. c (Chapter 22, Section 2.b; *Economics* Chapter 36)
18. a (Chapter 23, Section 1.a; *Economics* Chapter 37)
19. b (Chapter 23, Section 1.d; *Economics* Chapter 37)
20. a (Chapter 23, Section 2.a; *Economics* Chapter 37)
21. c (Chapter 23, Section 2.a; *Economics* Chapter 37)
22. d (Chapter 23, Section 1.b; *Economics* Chapter 37)
23. b (Chapter 23, Section 1.c; *Economics* Chapter 37)
24. a (Chapter 23, Section 1.c; *Economics* Chapter 37)
25. c (Chapter 23, Section 2.b; *Economics* Chapter 37)